DEVOTIONS
for
MORNING
&
EVENING
with
OSWALD
CHAMBERS

DEVOTIONS
→ · FOR
MORNING
→ · AND
EVENING
→ · WITH
OSWALD
CHAMBERS

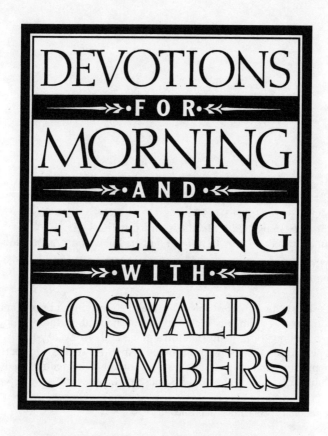

DEVOTIONS ·FOR· MORNING ·AND· EVENING ·WITH· OSWALD CHAMBERS

The Complete Daily Devotions of
My Utmost for His Highest
And
Daily Thoughts for Disciples

INSPIRATIONAL PRESS

NEW YORK

First Inspirational Press edition published in 1994.

Inspirational Press
A division of BBS Publishing Corporation
386 Park Avenue South
New York, NY 10016

Inspirational Press is a registered trademark of BBS Publishing Corporation.

Published by arrangement with Discovery House Publishers.

Library of Congress Catalog Card Number: 94-77196

ISBN: 0-88486-102-3

Designed by Hannah Lerner

Printed in the United States of America.

KEY TO REFERENCES

The letters at the end of the evening extracts refer to titles of works by Oswald Chambers from which the extracts have been taken. Figures indicate page numbers.

AHW	As He Walked (Our Brilliant Heritage volume)
AUG	Approved Unto God
BE	Biblical Ethics
BFB	Baffled to Fight Better
BP	Biblical Psychology
BSG	Bringing Sons unto Glory
CHI	Conformed to His Image
DDG	The Discipline of Divine Guidance (Christian Discipline volume 1)
DF	The Dedication of Following (The Love of God volume)
DL	The Discipline of Loneliness (Christian Discipline volume 2)
DP	The Discipline of Peril (Christian Discipline volume 1)
DPA	The Discipline of Patience (Christian Discipline volume 2)
DPR	The Discipline of Prayer (Christian Discipline volume 2)
DS	The Discipline of Suffering (Christian Discipline volume 1)
GH	Grow up into Him (Our Brilliant Heritage volume)
GW	God's Workmanship
HG	The Highest Good
HGM	He Shall Glorify Me
IWP	If Thou Wilt Be Perfect
IYA	If Ye Shall Ask . . .
LG	The Love of God
MC	The Making of a Christian (The Love of God volume)
MFL	The Moral Foundations of Life
MIC	The Message of Invincible Consolation (The Love of God volume)
MU	The Ministry of the Unnoticed (The Love of God volume)
NKW	Not Knowing Whither

NP   Now is it Possible? (The Love of God volume)
OBH   Our Brilliant Heritage
OPG   Our Portrait in Genesis
PH   The Place of Help
PR   The Psychology of Redemption
PS   The Philosophy of Sin
PSB   The Pilgrims' Song Book (The Highest Good volume)
SA   Shadow of an Agony
SHH   Shade of His Hand
SHL   The Servant as His Lord
SSM   Studies in the Sermon on the Mount
SSY   So Send I You
TGR   Thy Great Redemption (The Highest Good volume)
WG   Workmen of God

JANUARY

LET US KEEP TO THE POINT

My eager desire and hope being that I may never feel ashamed,
but that now as ever I may do honour to Christ in my own per-
son by fearless courage. (Phil. 1:20, MOFFAT)

My Utmost for His Highest. "My eager desire and hope being that I may never feel ashamed." We shall all feel very much ashamed if we do not yield to Jesus on the point He has asked us to yield to Him. Paul says—"My determination is to be my utmost for His Highest." To get there is a question of will, not of debate nor of reasoning, but a surrender of will, an absolute and irrevocable surrender on that point. An over-weening consideration for ourselves is the thing that keeps us from that decision, though we put it that we are considering others. When we consider what it will cost others if we obey the call of Jesus, we tell God He does not know what our obedience will mean. Keep to the point; He does know. Shut out every other consideration and keep yourself before God for this one thing only—My Utmost for His Highest. I am determined to be absolutely and entirely for Him and for Him alone.

My Undeterredness for His Holiness. "Whether that means life or death, no matter!" (v. 21). Paul is determined that nothing shall deter him from doing exactly what God wants. God's order has to work up to a crisis in our lives because we will not heed the gentler way. He brings us to the place where He asks us to be our utmost for Him, and we begin to debate; then He produces a providential crisis where we have to decide—for or against, and from that point the "Great Divide" begins.

If the crisis has come to you on any line, surrender your will to Him absolutely and irrevocably.

And when they came down from the mountain . . . (Mark 9:9)

We are not built for mountains and dawns and artistic affinities: they are for moments of inspiration, that is all. We are built for the valley, for the ordinary stuff of life, and this is where we have to prove our mettle. A false Christianity takes us up on the mount and we want to stay there. But what about the devil-possessed world? Oh, let it go to hell! We are having a great time up here.

The intellectualist or dreamer who by his dreams or isolation is not made fitter to deal with actual life, proves that his dreams are mere hysterical drivel. If his dreams only succeed in making him hold aloof from his fellow-men, a visionary who deals only with things belonging to the mountain-top, he is self-indulgent to a degree. No man has any right to be a spectator of his fellow-men; he ceases to be in touch with reality.

It is a great thing to be on the mount with God, and the mountains are meant for inspiration and meditation; but a man is taken there only in order that he may go down afterwards among the devil-possessed and lift them up . . .

If we cannot live in the demon-possessed valley, with the hold of God on us, lifting up those who are down by the power of the thing that is in us, our Christianity is only an abstraction.

SA 88, 91

WILL YOU GO OUT WITHOUT KNOWING

He went out, not knowing whither he went. (Heb. 11:8)

Have you been "out" in this way? If so, there is no logical statement possible when anyone asks you what you are doing. One of the difficulties in Christian work is this question—"What do you expect to do?" You do not know what you are going to do; the only thing you know is that God knows what He is doing. Continually revise your attitude towards God and see if it is a going out of everything, trusting in God entirely. It is this attitude that keeps you in perpetual wonder—you do not know what God is going to do next. Each morning you wake it is to be a "going out," building in confidence on God. "Take no thought for your life, . . . nor yet for your body"—take no thought for the things for which you did take thought before you "went out."

Have you been asking God what He is going to do? He will never tell you. God does not tell you what He is going to do; He reveals to you Who He is. Do you believe in a miracle-working God, and will you go out in surrender to Him until you are not surprised an atom at anything He does?

Suppose God is the God you know Him to be when you are nearest to Him—what an impertinence worry is! Let the attitude of the life be a continual "going out" in dependence upon God, and your life will have an ineffable charm about it which is a satisfaction to Jesus. You have to learn to go out of convictions, out of creeds, out of experiences, until so far as your faith is concerned, there is nothing between yourself and God.

> *When thou vowest a vow unto God, defer not to pay it: for he hath no pleasure in fools: pay that which thou vowest. (Ecclesiastes 5:4)*

At New Year time we hear much of vowing. Solomon's advice is—'Don't vow: because if you make a vow, even in ordinary matters, and do not fulfil it, you are the worse for it.' To make a promise may simply be a way of shirking responsibility. Never pile up promises before men, and certainly not before God. It is better to run the risk of being considered indecisive, better to be uncertain and not promise, than to promise and not fulfil. 'Better is it that thou shouldest not vow, than that thou shouldest vow and not pay.' Ecclesiastes 5:5

Modern ethical teaching bases everything on the power of the will, but we need to recognize also the perils of the will. The man who has achieved a moral victory by the sheer force of his will is less likely to want to become a Christian than the man who has come to the moral frontier of his own need. It is the obstinate man who makes vows, and by the very fulfillment of his vow he may increase his inability to see things from Jesus Christ's standpoint. When a man is stirred, either by joy or sorrow, or by the seasons of the year, he is apt to make vows which are beyond the possibility of human power to keep.

Jesus Christ bases the entrance to His Kingdom not on a man's vowing and making decisions, but on the realization of his inability to decide. Decisions for Christ fail because the bedrock of Christianity is ignored. It is not our vows before God that tell, but coming to God exactly as we are, in all our weakness, and being held and kept by Him. Make no vows at this New Year time, but look to God and bank on the Reality of Jesus Christ.

GW 132

5

CLOUDS AND DARKNESS

Clouds and darkness are round about Him. (Ps. 97:2)

A man who has not been born of the Spirit of God will tell you that the teachings of Jesus are simple. But when you are baptized with the Holy Ghost, you find "clouds and darkness are round about Him." When we come into close contact with the teachings of Jesus Christ we have our first insight into this aspect of things. The only possibility of understanding the teaching of Jesus is by the light of the Spirit of God on the inside. If we have never had the experience of taking our commonplace religious shoes off our commonplace religious feet, and getting rid of all the undue familiarity with which we approach God, it is questionable whether we have ever stood in His presence. The people who are flippant and familiar are those who have never yet been introduced to Jesus Christ. After the amazing delight and liberty of realizing what Jesus Christ *does*, comes the impenetrable darkness of realizing Who He *is*.

Jesus said: "The words that I speak unto you," not the words I have spoken, "they are spirit, and they are life." The Bible has been so many words to us—clouds and darkness—then all of a sudden the words become spirit and life because Jesus re-speaks them to us in a particular condition. That is the way God speaks to us, not by visions and dreams, but by words. When a man gets to God it is by the most simple way of words.

I was not disobedient to the heavenly vision. (Acts 26:19)

Life is not as idle ore,
But iron dug from central gloom,
. . . .
And batter'd by the shocks of doom
To shape and use.

Thank God for the sight of all you have never yet been. The vision is not an ecstasy or a dream, but a perfect understanding of what God wants, it is the Divine light making manifest the calling of God. You may call the vision an emotion or a desire, but it is something that absorbs you. Learn to thank God for making known His demands. You have had the vision, but you are not there yet by any means. You have seen what God wants you to be but what you are not yet. Are you prepared to have this 'iron dug from central gloom' battered into 'shape and use'? 'Battering' conveys the idea of a black-smith putting good metal into right useful shape. The batterings of God come in commonplace days and commonplace ways, God is using the anvil to bring us into the shape of the vision. The length of time it takes God to do it depends upon us. If we prefer to loll on the mount of transfiguration, to live on the memory of the vision, we are of no use to live with the ordinary stuff of which human life is made up. We have not to live always in ecstasy and conscious contemplation of God, but to live in reliance on what we saw in the vision when we are in the midst of actualities. It is when we are going through the valley to prove whether we will be the 'choice' ones, that most of us turn tail; we are not prepared for the blows which must come if we are going to be turned into the shape of the vision.

SSY 26

WHY CANNOT I FOLLOW THEE NOW?

Peter said unto Him, Lord, why cannot I follow Thee now?
(John 13:37)

There are times when you cannot understand why you cannot do what you want to do. When God brings the blank space, see that you do not fill it in, but wait. The blank space may come in order to teach you what sanctification means, or it may come after sanctification to teach you what service means. Never run before God's guidance. If there is the slightest doubt, then He is not guiding. Whenever there is doubt—*don't.*

In the beginning you may see clearly what God's will is— the severance of a friendship, the breaking off of a business relationship, something you feel distinctly before God is His will for you to do, never do it on the impulse of that feeling. If you do, you will end in making difficulties that will take years of time to put right. Wait for God's time to bring it round and He will do it without any heartbreak or disappointment. When it is a question of the providential will of God, wait for God to move.

Peter did not wait on God; he forecast in his mind where the test would come, and the test came where he did not expect it. "I will lay down my life for Thy sake." Peter's declaration was honest but ignorant. "Jesus answered him. . . The cock shall not crow, till thou hast denied Me thrice." This was said with a deeper knowledge of Peter than Peter had of himself. He could not follow Jesus because he did not know himself, of what he was capable. Natural devotion may be all very well to attract us to Jesus, to make us feel His fascination, but it will never make us disciples. Natural devotion will always deny Jesus somewhere or other.

A new commandment I give unto you, that ye love one another;
as I have loved you, that ye also love one another. (John 13:34)

There is no subject more intimately interesting to modern people than man's relationship to man; but men get impatient when they are told that the first requirement is that they should love God first and foremost. 'The first of all the commandments is . . . thou shalt love the Lord thy God with all thy heart, and with all thy soul, and with all thy mind, and with all thy strength: this is the first commandment.' In every crisis in our lives, is God first in our love? in every perplexity of conflicting duties, is He first in our leading? 'And the second is like, namely, this, Thou shalt love thy neighbour as thyself.' Remember the standard, '*as I have loved you*'. I wonder where the best of us are according to that standard? How many of us have turned away over and over again in disgust at men, and when we get alone with the Lord Jesus He speaks no word, but the memory of Him is quite sufficient to bring the rebuke—'as I have loved you'. It takes severe training to think habitually along the lines Jesus Christ has laid down, although we act on them impulsively at times.

How many of us are letting Jesus Christ take us into His school of thinking? The saint who is thoughtful is like a man fasting in the midst of universal intoxication. Men of the world hate a thoughtful saint. They can ridicule a living saint who does not think, but a thinking saint—I mean of course, one who lives rightly as well—is the annoyance, because the thinking saint has formed the Mind of Christ and re-echoes it. Let us from this time forth determine to bring into captivity every thought to the obedience of Christ.

BE 124

THE AFTERWARDS
OF THE LIFE OF POWER

Whither I go, thou canst not follow Me now; but thou shalt follow Me afterwards. (John 13:36)

"And when He had spoken this, He saith unto him, Follow Me." Three years before, Jesus had said—"Follow Me," and Peter had followed easily, the fascination of Jesus was upon him, he did not need the Holy Spirit to help him to do it. Then he came to the place where he denied Jesus, and his heart broke. Then he received the Holy Spirit, and now Jesus says again—"Follow Me." There is no figure in front now saving the Lord Jesus Christ. The first "Follow Me" had nothing mystical in it, it was an external following; now it is a following in internal martyrdom (cf. John 21:18).

Between these times Peter had denied Jesus with oaths and curses, he had come to the end of himself and all his self-sufficiency, there was not one strand of himself he would ever rely upon again, and in his destitution he was in a fit condition to receive an impartation from the risen Lord. "He breathed on them, and saith unto them, Receive ye the Holy Ghost." No matter what changes God has wrought in you, never rely upon them, build only on a Person, the Lord Jesus Christ, and on the Spirit He gives.

All our vows and resolutions end in denial because we have no power to carry them out. When we have come to the end of ourselves, not in imagination but really, we are able to receive the Holy Spirit. *"Receive ye the Holy Ghost"*—the idea is that of invasion. There is only one lodestar in the life now, the Lord Jesus Christ.

Ye be witnesses unto yourselves, that ye are the children of them which killed the prophets. (Matthew 23:31)

In the spiritual life we do not go from good to better, and from better to best; because there is only One to Whom we go, and that One is The Best, viz., God Himself. There can be no such thing as God's second best. We can perversely put ourselves out of God's order into His permissive will, but that is a different matter. In seeking the Best we soon find that our enemy is our good things, not our bad. The things that keep us back from God's best are not sin and imperfection, but the things that are right and good and noble from the natural standpoint. To discern that the natural virtues antagonize surrender to God is to bring our soul at once into the centre of our greatest battlefield. Very few of us debate with the sordid and the wrong, but we do debate with the good; and the higher up we go in the scale of the natural virtues, the more intense is the opposition to Jesus Christ, which is in inverse ratio to what one would naturally imagine.

NKW 47

WORSHIP

And he pitched his tent having Bethel on the west and Ai on the east: and there he builded an altar. (Gen. 12:8)

Worship is giving God the best that He has given you. Be careful what you do with the best you have. Whenever you get a blessing from God, give it back to Him as a love gift. Take time to meditate before God and offer the blessing back to Him in a deliberate act of worship. If you hoard a thing for yourself, it will turn into spiritual dry rot, as the manna did when it was hoarded. God will never let you hold a spiritual thing for yourself, it has to be given back to Him that He may make it a blessing to others.

Bethel is the symbol of communion with God; Ai is the symbol of the world. Abraham pitched his tent between the two. The measure of the worth of our public activity for God is the private profound communion we have with Him. Rush is wrong every time, there is always plenty of time to worship God. Quiet days with God may be a snare. We have to pitch our tents where we shall always have quiet times with God, however noisy our times with the world may be. There are not three stages in spiritual life—worship, waiting and work. Some of us go in jumps like spiritual frogs, we jump from worship to waiting, and from waiting to work. God's idea is that the three should go together. They were always together in the life of Our Lord. He was unhasting and unresting. It is a discipline, we cannot get into it all at once.

And he went down with them . . . and was subject unto them.
(Luke 2:51)

An extraordinary exhibition of submissiveness! and 'the disciple is not above his master'. Think of it: thirty years at home with brothers and sisters who did not believe in him! We fix on the three years which were extraordinary in Our Lord's life and forget altogether the earlier years at home, thirty years of absolute submission. Perhaps something of the same kind is happening to you, and you say—'I don't know why I should have to submit to this.' Are you any better than Jesus Christ? 'As He is, so are we in this world.' The explanation of it all is our Lord's prayer—'that they may be one, even as We are one'. If God is putting you through a spell of submission, and you seem to be losing your individuality and everything else, it is because Jesus is making you one with Him.

MU 48

INTIMATE WITH JESUS

Have I been so long with you, and yet hast thou not known Me?
(John 14:9)

These words are not spoken as a rebuke, nor even with surprise; Jesus is leading Philip on. The last One with whom we get intimate is Jesus. Before Pentecost the disciples knew Jesus as the One Who gave them power to conquer demons and to bring about a revival (see Luke 10:18-20). It was a wonderful intimacy, but there was a much closer intimacy to come—"I have called you friends." Friendship is rare on earth. It means identity in thought and heart and spirit. The whole discipline of life is to enable us to enter into this closest relationship with Jesus Christ. We receive His blessings and know His word, but do we know Him?

Jesus said, "It is expedient for you that I go away"—in that relationship, so that He might lead them on. It is a joy to Jesus when a disciple takes time to step more intimately with Him. Fruit bearing is always mentioned as the manifestation of an intimate union with Jesus Christ (John 15:1-4).

When once we get intimate with Jesus we are never lonely, we never need sympathy, we can pour out all the time without being pathetic. The saint who is intimate with Jesus will never leave impressions of himself, but only the impression that Jesus is having unhindered way, because the last abyss of his nature has been satisfied by Jesus. The only impression left by such a life is that of the strong calm sanity that Our Lord gives to those who are intimate with Him.

Abraham said, Behold now I have taken it upon me to speak unto the Lord . . . (Genesis 18:27)

Intercessory prayer is part of the sovereign purpose of God. If there were no saints praying for us, our lives would be infinitely balder than they are, consequently the responsibility of those who never intercede and who are withholding blessing from our lives is truly appalling. The subject of intercessory prayer is weakened by the neglect of the idea with which we ought to start. We take for granted that prayer is preparation for work, whereas prayer is *the* work, and we scarcely believe what the Bible reveals, viz. that through intercessory prayer God creates on the ground of the Redemption; it is His chosen way of working. We lean to our own understanding, or we bank on service and do away with prayer, and consequently by succeeding in the external we fail in the eternal, because in the eternal we succeed only by prevailing prayer . . .

Jesus Christ carries on intercession for us in heaven; the Holy Ghost carries on intercession for all men.

DPR 59, 60

DOES MY SACRIFICE LIVE?

And Abraham built an altar. . . and bound Isaac his son.
(Gen. 22:9)

This incident is a picture of the blunder we make in thinking that the final thing God wants of us is the sacrifice of death. What God wants is the sacrifice *through* death which enables us to do what Jesus did, viz., sacrifice our lives. Not—I am willing to go to death with Thee, but—I am willing to be identified with Thy death so that I may sacrifice my life to God. We seem to think that God wants us to give up things! God purified Abraham from this blunder, and the same discipline goes on in our lives. God nowhere tells us to give up things for the sake of giving them up. He tells us to give them up for the sake of the only thing worth having—viz., life with Himself. It is a question of loosening the bands that hinder the life, and immediately those bands are loosened by identification with the death of Jesus, we enter into a relationship with God whereby we can sacrifice our lives to Him.

It is of no value to God to give Him your life for death. He wants you to be a *"living* sacrifice," to let Him have all your powers that have been saved and sanctified through Jesus. This is the thing that is acceptable to God.

Ye shall ask what ye will. (John 15:7)

A great many people do not pray because they do not feel any sense of need. The sign that the Holy Ghost is in us is that we realize, not that we are full, but that we are empty, there is a sense of absolute need. We come across people who try us, circumstances that are difficult, conditions that are perplexing, and all these things awaken a dumb sense of need, which is a sign that the Holy Ghost is there. If we are ever free from the sense of need, it is not because the Holy Ghost has satisfied us, but because we have been satisfied with as much as we have. 'A man's reach should exceed his grasp.' A sense of need is one of the greatest benedictions because it keeps our life rightly related to Jesus Christ . . .

When we learn to pray in the Holy Ghost, we find there are some things for which we cannot pray, there is a sense of restraint. Never push and say, 'I know it is God's will and I am going to stick to it.' Beware, remember what is recorded of the children of Israel: 'He gave them their request; but sent leanness into their soul' (Psalm 106:15). Let the Spirit of God teach you what He is driving at and learn not to grieve Him. If we are abiding in Jesus Christ we shall ask what He wants us to ask, whether we are conscious of doing so or not.

IYA 60

INTERCESSORY INTROSPECTION

And I pray God your whole spirit and soul and body be preserved blameless. (1 Thess. 5:23)

"Your whole spirit. . ." The great mystical work of the Holy Spirit is in the dim regions of our personality which we cannot get at. Read the 139th Psalm; the Psalmist implies—"Thou art the God of the early mornings, the God of the late at nights, the God of the mountain peaks, and the God of the sea; but, my God, my soul has further horizons than the early mornings, deeper darkness than the nights of earth, higher peaks than any mountain peaks, greater depths than any sea in nature—Thou Who art the God of all these, be my God. I cannot reach to the heights or to the depths; there are motives I cannot trace, dreams I cannot get at—my God, search me out."

Do we believe that God can garrison the imagination far beyond where we can go? *"The blood of Jesus Christ cleanseth us from all sin"*—if that means in conscious experience only, may God have mercy on us. The man who has been made obtuse by sin will say he is not conscious of sin. Cleansing from sin is to the very heights and depths of our spirit if we will keep in the light as God is in the light, and the very Spirit that fed the life of Jesus Christ will feed the life of our spirits. It is only when we are garrisoned by God with the stupendous sanctity of the Holy Spirit, that spirit, soul and body are preserved in unspotted integrity, undeserving of censure in God's sight, until Jesus comes.

We do not allow our minds to dwell as they should on these great massive truths of God.

. . . believeth all things. (1 Corinthians 13:7)

It is a great thing to be a believer, but easy to misunderstand what the New Testament means by it. It is not that we believe Jesus Christ can *do* things, or that we believe in a plan of salvation; it is that we believe *Him*; whatever happens we will hang on to the fact that He is true. If we say, 'I am going to believe He will put things right', we shall lose our confidence when we see things go wrong. We are in danger of putting the cart before the horse and saying a man must believe certain things before he can be a Christian; whereas his beliefs are the result of his being a Christian, not the cause. Our Lord's word 'believe' does not refer to an intellectual act, but to a moral act; with our Lord to believe means to commit. 'Commit yourself to Me', and it takes a man all he is worth to believe in Jesus Christ.

The Great Life is to believe that Jesus Christ is not a fraud. The biggest fear a man has is never fear for himself, but fear that his Hero won't get through; that He won't be able to explain things satisfactorily; for instance, why there should be war and disease. The problems of life get hold of a man and make it difficult for him to know whether in the face of these things he really is confident in Jesus Christ. The attitude of a believer must be, 'Things do look black, but I believe Him; and when the whole thing is told I am confident my belief will be justified and God will be revealed as a God of love and justice.' It does not mean that we won't have problems, but it does mean that our problems will never come in between us and our faith in Him. 'Lord, I don't understand this, but I am certain that there will be an explanation, and in the meantime I put it on one side.' Our faith is in a Person Who is not deceived in anything He says or in the way He looks at things. Christianity is personal, passionate devotion to Jesus Christ as God manifest in the flesh.

AUG 114

THE OPENED SIGHT

To open their eyes . . . that they may receive . . . (Acts 26:18)

This verse is the grandest condensation of the propaganda of a disciple of Jesus Christ in the whole of the New Testament.

The first sovereign work of grace is summed up in the words—"that they may receive remission of sins." When a man fails in personal Christian experience, it is nearly always because he has never *received* anything. The only sign that a man is saved is that he has received something from Jesus Christ. Our part as workers for God is to open men's eyes that they may turn themselves from darkness to light; but that is not salvation, that is conversion—the effort of a roused human being. I do not think it is too sweeping to say that the majority of nominal Christians are of this order; their eyes are opened, but they have received nothing. Conversion is not regeneration. This is one of the neglected factors in our preaching to-day. When a man is born again, he knows that it is because he has received something as a gift from Almighty God and not because of his own decision. People register their vows, and sign their pledges, and determine to go through, but none of this is salvation. Salvation means that we are brought to the place where we are able to receive something from God on the authority of Jesus Christ, viz., remission of sins.

Then there follows the second mighty work of grace—"and inheritance among them which are sanctified." In sanctification the regenerated soul deliberately gives up his right to himself to Jesus Christ, and identifies himself entirely with God's interest in other men.

*That ye may be blameless and harmless, the sons of God, with-
out rebuke, in the midst of a crooked and perverse generation,
among whom ye shine as lights in the world. (Philippians 2:15)*

Is it possible to be blameless in our social life? The apostle Paul
says it is, and if we were asked whether we believed God could
make us blameless, we would all say 'Yes'. Well, has He done
it? If God has not sanctified us and made us blameless, there is
only one reason why He has not—we do not want Him to. 'This
is the will of God, even your sanctification.' We have not to
urge God to do it, it is His will; is it our will? Sanctification is
the work of the supernatural power of God . . .

Beware of praising Jesus Christ whilst all the time you cunningly refuse to let the Spirit of God work His salvation efficaciously in your life. Remember, the battle is in the will; whenever we say 'I can't', or whenever we are indifferent, it means
'I won't'. It is better to let Jesus Christ uncover the obstinacy.
If there is one point where we say 'I won't' then we shall never
know His salvation. From the moment that God uncovers a
point of obstinacy in us and we refuse to let Him deal with it,
we begin to be sceptical, to sneer and watch for defects in the
lives of others. But when once we yield to Him entirely. He
makes us blameless in our personal life, in our practical life,
and in our profound life. It is not done by piety, it is wrought
in us by the sovereign grace of God, and we have not the slightest desire to trust in ourselves in any degree, but in Him alone.

NP 141, 143

WHAT MY OBEDIENCE TO GOD
COSTS OTHER PEOPLE

They laid hold upon one Simon . . . and on him they laid the cross. (Luke 23:26).

If we obey God it is going to cost other people more than it costs us, and that is where the sting comes in. If we are in love with our Lord, obedience does not cost us anything, it is a delight, but it costs those who do not love Him a good deal. If we obey God it will mean that other people's plans are upset, and they will gibe us with it—"You call this Christianity?" We can prevent the suffering; but if we are going to obey God, we must not prevent it, we must let the cost be paid.

Our human pride entrenches itself on this point, and we say—I will never accept anything from anyone. We shall have to, or disobey God. We have no right to expect to be in any other relation than our Lord Himself was in (see Luke 8:2-3).

Stagnation in spiritual life comes when we say we will bear the whole thing ourselves. We cannot. We are so involved in the universal purposes of God that immediately we obey God, others are affected. Are we going to remain loyal in our obedience to God and go through the humiliation of refusing to be independent, or are we going to take the other line and say—I will not cost other people suffering? We can disobey God if we choose, and it will bring immediate relief to the situation, but we shall be a grief to our Lord. Whereas if we obey God, He will look after those who have been pressed into the consequences of our obedience. We have simply to obey and to leave all consequences with Him.

Beware of the inclination to dictate to God as to what you will allow to happen if you obey Him.

Ye are they which have continued with me in my temptations.
(Luke 22:28)

We are apt to imagine that our Lord was only tempted once and that then His temptations were over. His temptations went on from the first moment of His conscious life to the last, because His holiness was not the holiness of Almighty God, but the holiness of man, which can only progress by means of the things that go against it (see Hebrews 2:18, 4:15). Are we going with Jesus in His temptations? It is true that He is with us in our temptations, but are we with Him in His? Many of us cease to go with Jesus from the moment we have an experience of what He can do. Like Peter, we have all had moments when Jesus has had to say to us, 'What, could ye not watch with me one hour?'

The temptations of our Lord in the days of His flesh are the kind of temptations He is subjected to in the temple of our body. Watch when God shifts your circumstances and see whether you are going with Jesus or siding with the world, the flesh and the devil. We wear His badge, but are we going with Him? 'Upon this many of his disciples went back and walked no more with him.'

The temptation may be to do some big startling thing in order to prove that we really are the children of God. Satan said to Jesus, 'If thou be the Son of God, cast thyself down from hence,' and to us he says, 'If you are saved and sanctified and true to God, everyone you know should be saved too.' If that were true, Jesus Christ is wrong in His revelation of God. If by our salvation and right relationship to God, we can be the means of turning our world upside down, what has Jesus Christ been doing all these years? The temptation is to claim that God does something that will prove who we are and what He has done for us. It is a temptation of the devil, and can only be detected as a temptation by the Spirit of God.

NP 152

HAVE YOU EVER BEEN
ALONE WITH GOD?

When they were alone He expounded all things to His disciples.
(Mark 4:34)

Our Solitude with Him. Jesus does not take us alone and expound things to us all the time; He expounds things to us as we can understand them. Other lives are parables. God is making us spell out our own souls. It is slow work, so slow that it takes God all time and eternity to make a man and woman after His own purpose. The only way we can be of use to God is to let Him take us through the crooks and crannies of our own characters. It is astounding how ignorant we are about ourselves! We do not know envy when we see it, or laziness, or pride. Jesus reveals to us all that this body has been harbouring before His grace began to work. How many of us have learned to look in with courage?

We have to get rid of the idea that we understand ourselves; it is the last conceit to go. The only One Who understands us is God. The greatest curse in spiritual life is conceit. If we have ever had a glimpse of what we are like in the sight of God, we shall never say—"Oh, I am so unworthy," because we shall know we are, beyond the possibility of stating it. As long as we are not quite sure that we are unworthy, God will keep narrowing us in until He gets us alone. Wherever there is any element of pride or of conceit, Jesus cannot expound a thing. He will take us through the disappointment of a wounded pride of intellect, through disappointment of heart. He will reveal inordinate affections—things over which we never thought He would have to get us alone. We listen to many things in classes, but they are not an exposition to us yet. They will be when God gets us alone over them.

Likewise the Spirit also helpeth our infirmities. (Romans 8:26)

To ask how we are to get our prayers answered is a different point of view from the New Testament. According to the New Testament, prayer is God's answer to our poverty, not a power we exercise to obtain an answer. We have the idea that prayer is only an exercise of our spiritual life. 'Pray without ceasing.' We read that the disciples said to our Lord, 'Lord, teach us to pray.' The disciples were good men and well-versed in Jewish praying, yet when they came in contact with Jesus Christ, instead of realizing they could pray well, they came to the conclusion they did not know how to pray at all, and our Lord instructed them in the initial stages of prayer. Most of us can probably remember a time when we were religious, before we were born again of the Spirit of God, when we could pray fairly well; but after we were born again we became conscious of what Paul mentions here, our utter infirmity—'I do not know how to pray.' We become conscious not only of the power God has given us by His Spirit, but of our own utter infirmity. We hinder our life of devotion when we lose the distinction in thinking between these two. Reliance on the Holy Spirit for prayer is what Paul is bringing out in this verse. It is an unrealized point, we state it glibly enough, but Paul touches the thing we need to remember, he uncovers the truth of our infirmity. The whole source of our strength is receiving, recognizing and relying on the Holy Spirit.

IYA 100

HAVE YOU EVER BEEN
ALONE WITH GOD?

When He was alone the twelve. . . asked of Him. . . (Mark 4:10)

His Solitude with Us. When God gets us alone by affliction, heartbreak, or temptation, by disappointment, sickness, or by thwarted affection, by a broken friendship, or by a new friend-ship—when He gets us absolutely alone, and we are dumb-founded, and cannot ask one question, then He begins to expound. Watch Jesus Christ's training of the twelve. It was the disciples, not the crowd outside, who were perplexed. They constantly asked Him questions, and He constantly expounded things to them; but they only understood after they had received the Holy Spirit (see John 14:26).

If you are going on with God, the only thing that is clear to you, and the only thing God intends to be clear, is the way He deals with your own soul. Your brother's sorrows and perplexities are an absolute confusion to you. We imagine we understand where the other person is, until God gives us a dose of the plague of our own hearts. There are whole tracts of stubbornness and ignorance to be revealed by the Holy Spirit in each one of us, and it can only be done when Jesus gets us alone. Are we alone with Him now, or are we taken up with little fussy notions, fussy comradeships in God's service, fussy ideas about our bodies? Jesus can expound nothing until we get through all the noisy questions of the head and are alone with Him.

Except ye be converted, and become as little children . . .
(Matthew 18:3)

I have continually to convert the natural life into submission to the Spirit of God in me and not say—I will never do anything natural again; that is fanatical. When by the providence of God my body is brought into new conditions, I have to see that my natural life is converted to the dictates of the Spirit of God in me. Because it has been done once is not proof that it will be done again, 'Except ye be converted, and become as little children . . .' is true for all the days of the saintly life, we have continually to turn to God. The attitude of continuous conversion is the only right attitude towards the natural life, and it is the one thing we object to. Either we say the natural is wrong and try to kill it, or else we say that the natural is all there is, and that everything natural and impulsive is right. Neither attitude is right. The hindrance in spiritual life is that we will not be continuously converted, there are 'wadges' of obstinacy where our pride spits at the throne of God and says—'I shan't; I am going to be boss.' We cannot remain boss by the sheer power of will; sooner or later our wills must yield allegiance to some force greater than their own, either God or the devil.

NKW 51

CALLED OF GOD

Whom shall I send, and who will go for us? Then said I, Here am I; send me. (Isa. 6:8)

God did not address the call to Isaiah; Isaiah overheard God saying "Who will go for us?" The call of God is not for the special few, it is for everyone. Whether or not I hear God's call depends upon the state of my ears; and what I hear depends upon my disposition. "Many are called but few are chosen," that is, few prove themselves the chosen ones. The chosen ones are those who have come into a relationship with God through Jesus Christ whereby their disposition has been altered and their ears unstopped, and they hear the still small voice questioning all the time, "Who will go for us?" It is not a question of God singling out a man and saying "Now, *you* go." God did not lay a strong compulsion on Isaiah; Isaiah was in the presence of God and he overheard the call, and realized that there was nothing else for him but to say, in conscious freedom, "Here am I, send me." Get out of your mind the idea of expecting God to come with compulsions and pleadings. When our Lord called His disciples there was no irresistible compulsion from outside. The quiet passionate insistence of His "Follow Me" was spoken to men with every power wide awake. If we let the Spirit of God bring us face to face with God, we too shall hear something akin to what Isaiah heard, the still small voice of God; and in perfect freedom will say, "Here am I; send me."

For God giveth to a man that is good in his sight wisdom, and knowledge, and joy; but to the sinner he giveth travail, to gather and to heap up, that he may give to him that is good before God. This also is vanity and vexation of spirit. (Ecclesiastes 2:26)

There is a difference between God's order and God's permissive will. We say that God will see us through if we trust Him— 'I prayed for my boy, and he was spared in answer to my prayer.' Does that mean that the man who was killed was not prayed for, or that prayers for him were not answered? It is wrong to say that in the one case the man was delivered by prayer but not in the other. It is a misunderstanding of what Jesus Christ reveals. Prayer alters a man on the inside, alters his mind and his attitude to things. The point of praying is not that we get things from God, but that we learn by prayer to detect the difference between God's order and God's permissive will. God's order is—no pain, no sickness, no devil, no war, no sin: His permissive will is all these things. What a man needs to do is to get hold of God's order in the kingdom on the inside, and then he will begin to see how to handle the riddle of the universe on the outside.

The problem of the man who deals with practical things is not the problem of the universe, but the problem within his own breast. When I can see where the beast in me will end and where the wise man in me will end; when I have discovered that the only thing that will last is a personal relationship to God; then it will be time for me to solve the problems round about me. When once a man begins to know 'the plague of his own heart', it knocks the metaphysics out of him. It is in the actual circumstances of my life that I have to find out whether the wisdom of worshipping God can steer me.

SHH 19

DO YOU WALK IN WHITE?

Buried with Him . . . that . . . even so we also should walk in newness of life. (Rom. 6:4)

No one enters into the experience of entire sanctification without going through a "white funeral"—the burial of the old life. If there has never been this crisis of death, sanctification is nothing more than a vision. There must be a "white funeral," a death that has only one resurrection—a resurrection into the life of Jesus Christ. Nothing can upset such a life, it is one with God for one purpose, to be a witness to Him.

Have you come to your last days really? You have come to them often in sentiment, but have you come to them *really*? You cannot go to your funeral in excitement, or die in excitement. Death means you stop being. Do you agree with God that you stop being the striving, earnest kind of Christian you have been? We skirt the cemetery and all the time refuse to go to death. It is not striving to go to death, it is dying—"baptized into His death."

Have you had your "white funeral," or are you sacredly playing the fool with your soul? Is there a place in your life marked as the last day, a place to which the memory goes back with a chastened and extraordinarily grateful remembrance—"Yes, it was then, at that 'white funeral,' that I made an agreement with God."

"This is the will of God, even your sanctification." When you realize what the *will* of God is, you will enter into sanctification as naturally as can be. Are you willing to go through that "white funeral" now? Do you agree with Him that this is your last day on earth? The moment of agreement depends upon you.

Whatsoever ye shall ask in my name . . . (John 16:23)

Never make the blunder of trying to forecast the way God is going to answer your prayer. When God made a tremendous promise to Abraham, he thought out the best way of helping God fulfil His promise and did the wisest thing he knew according to flesh and blood common-sense reasoning. But for thirteen years God never spoke to him until every possibility of his relying on his own intelligent understanding was at an end. Then God came to him and said, 'I am God Almighty'— El Shaddai—'walk before me, and be thou perfect.' Over and over again God has to teach us how to stand and endure, watching actively and wondering. It is always a wonder when God answers prayer. We hear people say, 'We must not say it is wonderful that God answers prayer'; but it is wonderful. It is so wonderful that a great many people believe it impossible. Listen!—'Whatsoever ye shall ask in my name, that will I do.' Isn't that wonderful? It is so wonderful that I do not suppose more than half of us really believe it. 'Every one that asketh receiveth.' Isn't that wonderful? It is so wonderful that many of us have never even asked God to give us the Holy Spirit because we don't believe He will. 'If two of you shall agree on earth as touching anything that they shall ask, it shall be done for them of my father which is in heaven.' Isn't that wonderful? It is tremendously wonderful. 'The effectual fervent prayer of a righteous man availeth much.' Isn't that wonderful?

IYA 39

THE VOICE OF THE NATURE OF GOD

I heard the voice of the Lord saying, Whom shall I send?
(Isa. 6:8)

When we speak of the call of God, we are apt to forget the most important feature, viz., the nature of the One Who calls. There is the call of the sea, the call of the mountains, the call of the great ice barriers, but these calls are only heard by the few. The call is the expression of the nature from which it comes, and we can only record the call if the same nature is in us. The call of God is the expression of God's nature, not of our nature. There are strands of the call of God providentially at work for us which we recognize and no one else does. It is the threading of God's voice to us in some particular matter, and it is no use consulting anyone else about it. We have to keep that profound relationship between our souls and God.

The call of God is not the echo of my nature; my affinities and personal temperament are not considered. As long as I consider my personal temperament and think about what I am fitted for, I shall never hear the call of God. But when I am brought into relationship with God, I am in the condition Isaiah was in. Isaiah's soul was so attuned to God by the tremendous crisis he had gone through that he recorded the call of God to his amazed soul. The majority of us have no ear for anything but ourselves, we cannot hear a thing God says. To be brought into the zone of the call of God is to be profoundly altered.

He knew what was in man. (John 2:25)

There is a sentimental notion that makes us make ourselves out worse than we think we are, because we have a lurking suspicion that if we make ourselves out amazingly bad, someone will say. 'Oh no, you are not as bad as that'; but Jesus says we are worse. Our Lord never trusted any man, 'for he knew what was in man'; but He was not a cynic for He had the profoundest confidence in what He could do for every man, consequently He was never in a moral or intellectual panic, as we are, because we will put our confidence in man and in the things that Jesus put no confidence in. Paul says, 'Don't glory in men; don't say, I am of Paul, or I am of Apollos, and don't think of yourself more highly than you ought to think, but think according to the measure of faith, that is, according to what the grace of God has done in you.' Never trust (in the fundamental meaning of the word) any other saving Jesus Christ. That will mean you will never be unkind to anybody on the face of the earth, whether it be a degraded criminal or an upright moral man, because you have learned that the only thing to depend on in a man is what God has done in him. When you come to work for Jesus Christ, always ask yourself, 'Do I believe Jesus Christ can do anything for that case?' Am I as confident in His power as He is in His own? If you deal with people without any faith in Jesus Christ it will crush the very life out of you. If we believe in Jesus Christ, we can face every problem the world holds.

                                                        HG 66

THE VOCATION OF THE NATURAL LIFE

But when it pleased God . . . to reveal His Son in me . . .
(Gal. 1:15-16)

The call of God is not a call to any particular service; my interpretation of it may be because contact with the nature of God has made me realize what I would like to do for Him. The call of God is essentially expressive of His nature; service is the outcome of what is fitted to my nature. The vocation of the natural life is stated by the apostle Paul—"When it pleased God to reveal His Son in me that I might *preach* Him" (i.e., *sacramentally express*) "among the Gentiles."

Service is the overflow of superabounding devotion; but, profoundly speaking, there is no call to that, it is my own little actual bit and is the echo of my identification with the nature of God. Service is the natural part of my life. God gets me into a relationship with Himself whereby I understand His call, then I do things out of sheer love for Him on my own account. To serve God is the deliberate love-gift of a nature that has heard the call of God. Service is expressive of that which is fitted to my nature: God's call is expressive of His nature; consequently when I receive His nature and hear His call, the voice of the Divine nature sounds in both and the two work together. The Son of God reveals Himself in me, and I serve Him in the ordinary ways of life out of devotion to Him.

Ye did not choose me, but I chose you. (John 15:16)

There is so much talk about our decision for Christ, our determination to be Christians, our decision for this and for that.
When we come to the New Testament we find that the other
aspect, God's choosing of us, is the one that is brought out the
oftenest. 'Ye did not choose me, but I chose you . . . ' We are
not taken up into conscious agreement with God's purpose,
we are taken up into His purpose without any consciousness
on our part at all; we have no conception of what God is aiming at, and it gets more and more vague as we go on. At the
beginning of our Christian life we have our own particular
notions as to what God's purpose is—we are meant to go here,
or there; or, God has called us to do this or that piece of work.
We go and do the thing and still we find the big compelling of
God remains. The majority of the work we do is so much scaffolding to further the purpose of the big compelling of God.
'He took unto him the twelve.' He takes us all the time; there
is more than we have got at, something we have not seen.

PH 177

The call of God embarrasses us because of two things—it presents us with sealed orders, and urges us to a vast venture.
When God calls us He does not tell us along the line of our
natural senses what to expect; God's call is a command that
asks us, that means there is always a possibility of refusal on
our part. Faith never knows where it is being led, it knows and
loves the One Who is leading. It is a life of *faith*, not of intelligence and reason, but a life of knowing Who is making me 'go'.

NKW 12

IT IS THE LORD!

Thomas answered and said unto Him, My Lord and my God.
(John 20:28)

"Give Me to drink." How many of us are set upon Jesus Christ slaking our thirst when we ought to be satisfying Him? We should be pouring out now, spending to the last limit, not drawing on Him to satisfy us. "Ye shall be witnesses unto Me"— that means a life of unsullied, uncompromising and unbridled devotion to the Lord Jesus, a satisfaction to Him wherever He places us.

Beware of anything that competes with loyalty to Jesus Christ. The greatest competitor of devotion to Jesus is service for Him. It is easier to serve than to be drunk to the dregs. The one aim of the call of God is the satisfaction of God, not a call to do something for Him. We are not sent to battle for God, but to be used by God in His battlings. Are we being more devoted to service than to Jesus Christ?

And Peter answered and said to Jesus, Master, it is good for us to be here; and let us make three tabernacles; one for thee, and one for Moses, and one for Elias. (Mark 9:5)

When God gives us a time of exaltation it is always exceptional. It has its meaning in our life with God, but we must beware lest spiritual selfishness wants to make it the only time. The sphere of exaltation is not meant to teach us anything. We are apt to think that everything that happens to us is to be turned into useful teaching; it is to be turned into something better than teaching, viz. into character. We shall find that the spheres God brings us into are not meant to teach us something but to *make* us something. There is a great danger in asking, 'What is the use of it?' There is no *use* in it at all. If you want a life of usefulness, don't be a Christian after our Lord's stamp; you will be much more useful if you are not. The cry for the standard of usefulness knocks the spiritual Christian right out, he dare not touch it if he is going to remain true to his Master. Take the life of our Lord: for three years all He did was to walk about saying things and healing sick people—a useless life, judged from every standard of success and of enterprise. If our Lord and His disciples had lived in our day, they would have been put down as a most unuseful crowd. In spiritual matters we can never calculate on the line of—'What is the use of it?' 'What is the use of being at a Bible Training College? of learning Psychology and Ethics? *Do* something.' Great danger lies along that line 'The mountain-top experiences are rare moments, but they are meant for something in the purposes of God. It was not until Peter came to write his Epistles that he realized the full purpose of his having been on the Mount of Transfiguration.

MU 52

VISION AND DARKNESS

An horror of great darkness fell upon him. (Gen. 15:12)

Whenever God gives a vision to a saint, He puts him, as it were, in the shadow of His hand, and the saint's duty is to be still and listen. There is a darkness which comes from excess of light, and then is the time to listen. Genesis 16 is an illustration of listening to good advice when it is dark instead of waiting for God to send the light. When God gives a vision and darkness follows, wait. God will make you in accordance with the vision He has given if you will wait His time. Never try and help God fulfil His word. Abraham went through thirteen years of silence, but in those years all self-sufficiency was destroyed; there was no possibility left of relying on common-sense ways. Those years of silence were a time of discipline, not of displeasure. Never pump up joy and confidence, but stay upon God (cf. Isa. 50:10, 11).

Have I any confidence in the flesh? Or have I got beyond all confidence in myself and in men and women of God; in books and prayers and ecstasies; and is my confidence placed now in God Himself, not in His blessings? "I am the Almighty God"— El-Shaddai, the Father-Mother God. The one thing for which we are all being disciplined is to know that God is real. As soon as God becomes real, other people become shadows. Nothing that other saints do or say can ever perturb the one who is built on God.

They shall run and not be weary. (Isaiah 40:31)

Whenever there is the experience of fag or weariness or degradation, you may be certain you have done one of two things —either you have disregarded a law of nature, or you have deliberately got out of touch with God. There is no such thing as weariness in God's work. If you are in tune with the joy of God, the more you spend out in God's service, the more the recuperation goes on, and when once the warning note of weariness is given, it is a sign that something has gone wrong. If only we would heed the warning, we would find it is God's wonderfully gentle way of saying—'Not that way; that must be left alone; this must be given up.' Spiritual fatigue comes from the unconscious frittering away of God's time. When you feel weary or are exhausted, don't ask for hot milk, but get back to God. The secret of weariness and nervous disease in the natural world is the lack of a dominating interest, and the same is true in spiritual life. Much of what is called Christian work is veneered spiritual disease; it is Christian activity that counts— dominating life from God, and every moment is filled with an energy that is not our own, a super-abounding life that nothing can stand before.

NKW 37

ARE YOU FRESH FOR EVERYTHING?

Except a man be born again, he cannot see the kingdom of God.
(John 3:3)

Sometimes we are fresh for a prayer meeting but not fresh for cleaning boots!

Being born again of the Spirit is an unmistakable work of God, as mysterious as the wind, as surprising as God Himself. We do not know where it begins, it is hidden away in the depths of our personal life. Being born again from above is a perennial, perpetual and eternal beginning; a freshness all the time in thinking and in talking and in living, the continual surprise of the life of God. Staleness is an indication of something out of joint with God—"I must do this thing or it will never be done." That is the first sign of staleness. Are we freshly born this minute or are we stale, raking in our minds for something to do? Freshness does not come from obedience but from the Holy Spirit; obedience keeps us in the light as God is in the light.

Guard jealously your relationship to God. Jesus prayed "that they may be one, even as we are one"—nothing between. Keep all the life perennially open to Jesus Christ, don't pretend with Him. Are you drawing your life from any other source than God Himself? If you are depending upon anything but Him, you will never know when He is gone.

Being born of the Spirit means much more than we generally take it to mean. It gives us a new vision and keeps us absolutely fresh for everything by the perennial supply of the life of God.

*Ye call me Master and Lord; and ye say well; for so I am. If I
then, your Lord and Master, have washed your feet, ye also ought
to wash one another's feet. (John 13:13–14)*

We have to recognize that we are one half mechanical and one
half mysterious; to live in either domain and ignore the other
is to be a fool or a fanatic. The great supernatural work of God's
grace is in the incalculable part of our nature; we have to work
out in the mechanical realm what God works in the mysterious realm. People accept creeds, but they will not accept the
holy standards of Jesus Christ's teaching. To build on the fundamental work of God's grace and ignore the fact that we have
to work it out in a mechanical life produces humbugs, those
who make a divorce between the mysterious life and the practical life. In John 13 the mysterious and the mechanical are
closely welded together.

   You can't wash anybody's feet mysteriously; it is a purely
mechanical, matter-of-fact job; you can't do it by giving him
devotional books or by praying for him; you can only wash
anybody's feet by doing something mechanical. Our Lord did
not tell the disciples *how* they were to do it: He simply says—
'Do it.' He is not questioning whether or not they can do it; He
is saying that they must do what the mastery of His ruling
shows them they should do.

BE 56

RECALL WHAT GOD REMEMBERS

I remember . . . the kindness of thy youth. (Jer. 2:2)

Am I as spontaneously kind to God as I used to be, or am I only expecting God to be kind to me? Am I full of the little things that cheer His heart over me, or am I whimpering because things are going hardly with me? There is no joy in the soul that has forgotten what God prizes. It is a great thing to think that Jesus Christ has need of me—"Give Me to drink." How much kindness have I shown Him this past week? Have I been kind to His reputation in my life?

God is saying to His people—You are not in love with Me now, but I remember the time when you were —"I remember. . . the love of thine espousals." Am I as full of the extravagance of love to Jesus Christ as I was in the beginning, when I went out of my way to prove my devotion to Him? Does He find me recalling the time when I did not care for anything but Himself? Am I there now, or have I become wise over loving Him? Am I so in love with Him that I take no account of where I go? or am I watching for the respect due to me; weighing how much service I ought to give?

If, as I recall what God remembers about me, I find He is not what He used to be to me, let it produce shame and humiliation, because that shame will bring the godly sorrow that works repentance.

And we know that to them that love God . . . (Romans 8:28)

Do you remember how Paul never wearied of saying, 'Don't you know that your body is the temple of the Holy Ghost'? Recall what Jesus Christ said about the historic temple which is the symbol of the body; He ruthlessly turned out those that sold and bought in the temple, and said, 'It is written, my house shall be called the house of prayer; but ye have made it a den of thieves.' Let us apply that to ourselves. We have to remember that our conscious life, though only a tiny bit of our personality, is to be regarded by us as a shrine of the Holy Ghost. The Holy Ghost will look after the unconscious part we do not know, we must see we guard the conscious part, for which we are responsible, as a shrine of the Holy Ghost. If we recognize this as we should, we shall be careful to keep our body undefiled for Him.

IYA 104

WHAT AM I LOOKING AT?

Look unto Me, and be ye saved. (Isa. 45:22)

Do we expect God to come to us with His blessings and save us? He says—*Look unto Me*, and *be* saved. The great difficulty spiritually is to concentrate on God, and it is His blessings that make it difficult. Troubles nearly always make us look to God; His blessings are apt to make us look elsewhere. The teaching of the Sermon on the Mount is, in effect—Narrow all your interests until the attitude of mind and heart and body is concentration on Jesus Christ. "Look unto Me."

Many of us have a mental conception of what a Christian should be, and the lives of the saints become a hindrance to our concentration on God. There is no salvation in this way, it is not simple enough. "Look unto Me" and—not "you will be saved," but "you *are* saved." The very thing we look for, we shall find if we will concentrate on Him. We get preoccupied and sulky with God, while all the time He is saying—"Look up and be saved." The difficulties and trials—the casting about in our minds as to what we shall do this summer, or tomorrow, all vanish when we look to God.

Rouse yourself up and look to God. Build your hope on Him. No matter if there are a hundred and one things that press, resolutely exclude them all and look to Him. "Look unto Me," and salvation *is*, the moment you look.

Consecrate yourselves this day to the Lord. (Exodus 32:29)

We are never told to consecrate our gifts to God, but we are told to dedicate ourselves.

The joy of anything, from a blade of grass upwards, is to fulfill its created purpose. ' . . . that we should be to the praise of His glory' (Ephesians 1:12). We are not here to win souls, to do good to others, that is the natural outcome, but it is not our aim, and this is where so many of us cease to be followers. We will follow God as long as He makes us a blessing to others, but when He does not we will not follow. Suppose Our Lord had measured His life by whether or not He was a blessing to others! Why, He was a 'stone of stumbling' to thousands, actually to His own neighbours, to His own nation, because through Him they blasphemed the Holy Ghost, and in His own country 'He did not many mighty works there because of their unbelief (Matthew 13:58). If Our Lord had measured His life by its actual results. He would have been full of misery.

MU 63

TRANSFORMED BY INSIGHT

We all with open face, beholding as in a glass the glory of the Lord, are changed into the same image. (2 Cor. 3:18)

The outstanding characteristic of a Christian is this unveiled frankness before God so that the life becomes a mirror for other lives. By being filled with the Spirit we are transformed, and by beholding we become mirrors. You always know when a man has been beholding the glory of the Lord; you feel in your inner spirit that he is the mirror of the Lord's own character. Beware of anything which would sully that mirror in you; it is nearly always a good thing, the good that is not the best.

The golden rule for your life and mine is this concentrated keeping of the life open towards God. Let everything else—work, clothes, food, everything on earth—go by the board, saving that one thing. The rush of other things always tends to obscure this concentration on God. We have to maintain ourselves in the place of beholding, keeping the life absolutely spiritual all through. Let other things come and go as they may, let other people criticize as they will, but never allow anything to obscure the life that is hid with Christ in God. Never be hurried out of the relationship of abiding in Him. It is the one thing that is apt to fluctuate but it ought not to. The severest discipline of a Christian's life is to learn how to keep "beholding as in a glass the glory of the Lord."

In the day of prosperity be joyful, but in the day of adversity consider: God also hath set the one over against the other, to the end that man should find nothing after him. (Ecclesiastes 7:14)

The test of elemental honesty is the way a man behaves himself in grief and in joy. The natural elemental man expresses his joy or sorrow straight off. Today in our schools boys are taught stoicism; it produces an admirable type of lad externally, but not so admirable internally. When we are rightly related to God we must let things have their way with us and not pretend things are not as they are. It is difficult not to simulate sorrow or gladness, but to remain natural and steadfastly true to God as things come. Don't deal only with the section that is sad or with the section that is joyful, deal with them together. When we accept God's purpose for us in Christ Jesus, we know that 'all things work together for good'.

Stoicism has the effect of making a man hysterical and sentimental, it produces a denseness spiritually. When you are joyful, *be* joyful; when you are sad, *be* sad. If God has given you a sweet cup, don't make it bitter; and if He has given you a bitter cup, don't try and make it sweet; take things as they come. One of the last lessons we learn is not to be an amateur providence—'I shall not allow that person to suffer.' Suffering, and the inevitable result of suffering, is the only way some of us can learn, and if we are shielded God will ultimately take the one who interferes by the scruff of the neck and remove him. The fingers that caress a child may also hurt its flesh; it is the power of love that makes them hurt.

SHH 95

THE OVERMASTERING DIRECTION

I have appeared unto thee for this purpose. (Acts 26:16)

The vision Paul had on the road to Damascus was no passing emotion, but a vision that had very clear and emphatic directions for him, and he says, "I was not disobedient to the heavenly vision." Our Lord said, in effect, to Paul—Your whole life is to be overmastered by Me; you are to have no end, no aim, and no purpose but Mine. *"I have chosen him."*

When we are born again we all have visions, if we are spiritual at all, of what Jesus wants us to be, and the great thing is to learn not to be disobedient to the vision, not to say that it cannot be attained. It is not sufficient to know that God has redeemed the world, and to know that the Holy Spirit can make all that Jesus did effectual in me; I must have the basis of a personal relationship to Him. Paul was not given a message or a doctrine to proclaim, he was brought into a vivid, personal, overmastering relationship to Jesus Christ. Verse 16 is immensely commanding—"to make thee a minister and a witness." There is nothing there apart from the personal relationship. Paul was devoted to a Person not to a cause. He was absolutely Jesus Christ's, he saw nothing else, he lived for nothing else. "For I determined not to know anything among you, save Jesus Christ, and Him crucified."

He that findeth his life shall lose it; and he that loseth his life for
my sake shall find it. (Matthew 10:39)

We have to recognize that our personal life is meant for Jesus Christ. The modern jargon is for self-realization—'I must save my life': Jesus Christ says, 'whosoever shall lose his life for my sake shall find it.' The cross is the deliberate recognition of what our personal self is for, viz., to be given to Jesus, and we take up that cross daily and prove we are no longer our own. Whenever the call is given for abandon to Jesus Christ, people say it is offensive and out of taste. The counterfeit of abandon is that misleading phrase 'Christian service'. I will spend myself for God, I will do anything and everything but the one thing He asks me to do, viz., give up my right to myself to Him. 'But surely Christian service is a right thing?' Immediately we begin to say that, we are off the track. It is the right *Person*, the Lord Jesus Christ, not the right thing: don't stop short of the Lord Himself—'*for my sake*'. The great dominating recognition is that my personal self belongs to Jesus. When I receive the Holy Spirit, I receive not a possible oneness with Jesus Christ, but a real intense oneness with Him. The point is, will I surrender my individual life entirely to Him? It will mean giving up not only bad things, but things which are right and good (cf. Matthew 5:29–30). If you have to calculate what you are willing to give up for Jesus Christ, never say that you love Him. Jesus Christ asks us to give up the best we have got to Him, our right to ourselves.

SHL 85–6

LEAVE ROOM FOR GOD

But when it pleased God . . . (Gal. 1:15)

As workers for God we have to learn to make room for God—to give God "elbow room." We calculate and estimate, and say that this and that will happen, and we forget to make room for God to come in as He chooses. Would we be surprised if God came into our meeting or into our preaching in a way we had never looked for Him to come? Do not look for God to come in any particular way, but *look for Him*. That is the way to make room for Him. Expect Him to come, but do not expect Him only in a certain way. However much we may know God, the great lesson to learn is that at any minute He may break in. We are apt to overlook this element of surprise, yet God never works in any other way. All of a sudden God meets the life—"When it was the good pleasure of God. . ."

Keep your life so constant in its contact with God that His surprising power may break out on the right hand and on the left. Always be in a state of expectancy, and see that you leave room for God to come in as He likes.

. . . till Christ be formed in you. (Galatians 4:19)

Beware of refining away the radical aspect of our Lord's teaching by saying that God puts something in to counteract the wrong disposition—that is a compromise. Jesus never teaches us to curb and suppress the wrong disposition; He gives us a totally new disposition, He alters the mainspring of action. Our Lord's teaching can be interpreted only by the new Spirit which He puts in; it can never be taken as a series of rules and regulations.

A man cannot imitate the disposition of Jesus Christ; it is either there, or it is not. When the Son of God is formed in me, He is formed in my human nature, and I have to put on the new man in accordance with His life and obey Him; then His disposition will work out all the time. We make character out of our disposition. Character is what we make, disposition is what we are born with; and when we are born again we are given a new disposition. A man must make his own character, but he cannot make his disposition; that is a gift. Our natural disposition is gifted to us by heredity; by regeneration God gives us the disposition of His Son.

SSM 29

LOOK AGAIN AND CONSECRATE

If God so clothe the grass of the field. . . shall He not much more clothe you? (Matt. 6:30)

A simple statement of Jesus is always a puzzle to us if we are not simple. How are we going to be simple with the simplicity of Jesus? By receiving His Spirit, recognizing and relying on Him, obeying Him as He brings the word of God, and life will become amazingly simple. "Consider," says Jesus, "how much more your Father Who clothes the grass of the field will clothe you, if you keep your relationship right with Him." Every time we have gone back in spiritual communion it has been because we have impertinently known better than Jesus Christ. We have allowed the cares of the world to come in, and have forgotten the "much more" of our Heavenly Father.

"Behold the fowls of the air"—their main aim is to obey the principle of life that is in them and God looks after them. Jesus says that if you are rightly related to Him and obey His Spirit that is in you, God will look after your "feathers."

"Consider the lilies of the field"—they grow where they are put. Many of us refuse to grow where we are put, consequently we take root nowhere. Jesus says that if we obey the life God has given us, He will look after all the other things. Has Jesus Christ told us a lie? If we are not experiencing the "much more," it is because we are not obeying the life God has given us, we are taken up with confusing considerations. How much time have we taken up worrying God with questions when we should have been absolutely free to concentrate on His work? Consecration means the continual separating of myself to one particular thing. We cannot consecrate once and for all. Am I continually separating myself to consider God every day of my life?

Keep yourselves in the love of God. (Jude 21)

When God saves and sanctifies a man his personality is raised to its highest pitch of freedom, he is free now to sin if he wants to; before, he is not free, sin is impelling and urging him; when he is delivered from sin he is free not to sin, or free to sin if he chooses. The doctrine of sinless perfection and consequent freedom from temptation runs on the line that because I am sanctified, I cannot now do wrong. If that is so, you cease to be a man. If God puts us in such a condition that we could not disobey, our obedience would be of no value to Him. But blessed be His Name, when by His redemption the love of God is shed abroad in our hearts. He gives us something to do to manifest it. Just as human nature is put to the test in the actual circumstances of life, so the love of God in us is put to the test. 'Keep yourselves in the love of God,' says Jude, that is keep your soul open not only to the fact that God loves you, but that He is *in* you, in you sufficiently to manifest His perfect love in every condition in which you can find yourself as you rely on Him.

CHI 89

LOOK AGAIN AND THINK

Take no thought for your life. (Matt. 6:25)

A warning which needs to be reiterated is that the cares of this world, the deceitfulness of riches, and the lust of other things entering in, will choke all that God puts in. We are never free from the recurring tides of this encroachment. If it does not come on the line of clothes and food, it will come on the line of money or lack of money; of friends or lack of friends; or on the line of difficult circumstances. It is one steady encroachment all the time, and unless we allow the Spirit of God to raise up the standard against it, these things will come in like a flood. "Take no thought for your life." "Be careful about one thing only," says our Lord—"your relationship to Me." Common sense shouts loud and says—"That is absurd, I *must* consider how I am going to live, I *must* consider what I am going to eat and drink." Jesus says you must not. Beware of allowing the thought that this statement is made by One Who does not understand our particular circumstances. Jesus Christ knows our circumstances better than we do, and He says we must not think about these things so as to make them the one concern of our life. Whenever there is competition, be sure that you put your relationship to God first.

"Sufficient unto the day is the evil thereof." How much evil has begun to threaten you to-day? What kind of mean little imps have been looking in and saying—Now what are you going to do next month—this summer? "Be anxious for nothing," Jesus says. Look again and think. Keep your mind on the "much more" of your heavenly Father.

Not everyone that saith unto me, Lord, Lord, shall enter into the kingdom of heaven but he that doeth the will of my Father which is in heaven. (Matthew 7:21)

Human nature is fond of labels, but a label may be the counterfeit of confession. It is so easy to be branded with labels, much easier in certain stages to wear a ribbon or a badge than to confess. Jesus never used the word *testify*; He used a much more searching word—*confess*. 'Whosoever therefore shall confess me before men . . .' The test of goodness is confession by doing the will of God. 'If you do not confess me before men.' says Jesus, 'neither will your heavenly Father confess you.' Immediately we confess, we must have a badge, if we do not put one on, other people will. Our Lord is warning that it is possible to wear the label without having the goods; possible for a man to wear the badge of being His disciple when he is not. Labels are all right, but if we mistake the label for the goods we get confused. If the disciple is to discern between the man with the label and the man with the goods, he must have the spirit of discernment, viz., the Holy Spirit. We start out with the honest belief that the label and the goods must go together, they should do, but Jesus warns that sometimes they get severed, and we find cases where God honours His work although those who preach it are not living a right life. In judging the preacher, He says, judge him by his fruit.

SSM 105

BUT IT IS HARDLY CREDIBLE THAT ONE COULD SO PERSECUTE JESUS!

Saul, Saul, why persecutest thou Me? (Acts 26:14)

Am I set on my own way for God? We are never free from this snare until we are brought into the experience of the baptism of the Holy Ghost and fire. Obstinacy and self-will will always stab Jesus Christ. It may hurt no one else, but it wounds His Spirit. Whenever we are obstinate and self-willed and set upon our own ambitions, we are hurting Jesus. Every time we stand on our rights and insist that this is what we intend to do, we are persecuting Jesus. Whenever we stand on our dignity we systematically vex and grieve His Spirit; and when the knowledge comes home that it is Jesus Whom we have been persecuting all the time, it is the most crushing revelation there could be.

Is the word of God tremendously keen to me as I hand it on to you, or does my life give the lie to the things I profess to teach? I may teach sanctification and yet exhibit the spirit of Satan, the spirit that persecutes Jesus Christ. The Spirit of Jesus is conscious of one thing only—a perfect oneness with the Father, and He says, "Learn of Me, for I am meek and lowly in heart." All I do ought to be founded on a perfect oneness with Him, not on a self-willed determination to be godly. This will mean that I can be easily put upon, easily over-reached, easily ignored; but if I submit to it for His sake, I prevent Jesus Christ being persecuted.

For if ye live after the flesh, ye shall die: but if ye through the Spirit do mortify the deeds of the body, ye shall live. (Romans 8:13)

Sensuality is not sin, it is the way my body works in connection with external circumstances whereby I begin to satisfy myself. Sensuality will work in a man who is delivered from sin by Jesus Christ as well as in a man who is not. I do not care what your experience may be as a Christian, you may be trapped by sensuality at any time. Paul says, 'Mortify the deeds of the body'; mortify means to destroy by neglect. One of the first big moral lessons a man has to learn is that he cannot destroy *sin* by neglect, sin has to be handled by the Redemption of Jesus Christ, it cannot be handled by me. Heredity is a bigger problem than I can cope with; but if I will receive the gift of the Holy Spirit on the basis of Christ's Redemption, He enables me to work out that Redemption in my experience. With regard to sensuality, that is my business; I have to mortify it, and if I don't, it will never be mortified. If I take any part of my natural life and use it to satisfy myself, that is sensuality. A Christian has to learn that his body is not his own. 'What? know ye not that your body is the temple of the Holy Ghost . . . and ye are not your own?' Watch that you learn to mortify.

SA 70

BUT IT IS HARDLY CREDIBLE THAT ONE COULD BE SO POSITIVELY IGNORANT!

Who art Thou, Lord? (Acts 26:15)

"The Lord spake thus to me with a strong hand." There is no escape when Our Lord speaks, He always comes with an arrestment of the understanding. Has the voice of God come to you directly? If it has, you cannot mistake the intimate insistence with which it has spoken to you in the language you know best, not through your ears, but through your circumstances.

God has to destroy our determined confidence in our own convictions. "I know this is what I should do"—and suddenly the voice of God speaks in a way that overwhelms us by revealing the depths of our ignorance. We have shown our ignorance of Him in the very way we determined to serve Him. We serve Jesus in a spirit that is not His, we hurt Him by our advocacy for Him, we push His claims in the spirit of the devil. Our words sound all right, but our spirit is that of an enemy. "He rebuked them, and said, Ye know not what manner of spirit ye are of." The spirit of our Lord in an advocate of His is described in I Corinthians 13.

Have I been persecuting Jesus by a zealous determination to serve Him in my own way? If I feel I have done my duty and yet have hurt Him in doing it, I may be sure it was not my duty, because it has not fostered the meek and quiet spirit, but the spirit of self-satisfaction. We imagine that whatever is unpleasant is our duty! Is that anything like the spirit of our Lord—"I *delight* to do Thy will, O My God."

Except a man be born again, he cannot see the kingdom of God.
(John 3:3)

New birth is not the working of a natural law. The introduction of anything into this world is cataclysmic: before a tree can grow it must be planted; before a human being can evolve he must be born—a distinct and emphatic crisis. Every child born into the world involves a cataclysm to someone, the mother has practically to go through death. The same thing is true spiritually. Being 'born from above' is not a simple easy process; we cannot glide into the Kingdom of God. Common sense reasoning says we ought to be able to merge into the life of God, but according to the Bible, and in actual experience, that is not the order. The basis of things is not rational, it is tragic, and what Jesus Christ came to do was to put human life on the basis of Redemption whereby any man can receive the heredity of the Son of God and be lifted into the domain where He lives.

The historic Jesus represents the personal union of God and man. He lived on the human plane for thirty-three years and during that time He presented what God's normal Man was like. When we are regenerated we enter into the Kingdom of God, we begin to grow, and the goal is certain—' . . . we know that, when he shall appear, *we shall be like him*: for we shall see him as he is.' But before I can begin to see what Jesus Christ stands for I have to enter into another domain—'Except a man be born again, he cannot enter into the kingdom of God.' I enter into the life of God by its entering into me, that is, I deliberately undertake to become the home of the life of the Son of God, 'Bethlehem'. I do not draw my life from myself, I draw it from the One who is the Source of life.

BE 45

THE DILEMMA OF OBEDIENCE

And Samuel feared to shew Eli the vision. (1 Sam. 3:15)

God never speaks to us in startling ways, but in ways that are easy to misunderstand, and we say, "I wonder if that is God's voice?" Isaiah said that the Lord spake to him "with a strong hand," that is, by the pressure of circumstances. Nothing touches our lives but it is God Himself speaking. Do we discern His hand or only mere occurrence?

Get into the habit of saying, "Speak, Lord," and life will become a romance. Every time circumstances press, say, "Speak, Lord"; make time to listen. Chastening is more than a means of discipline, it is meant to get me to the place of saying, "Speak, Lord." Recall the time when God did speak to you. Have you forgotten what He said? Was it Luke 11:13, or was it 1 Thess. 5:23? As we listen, our ear gets acute, and, like Jesus, we shall hear God all the time.

Shall I tell my "Eli" what God has shown to me? That is where the dilemma of obedience comes in. We disobey God by becoming amateur providences—I must shield "Eli," the best people we know. God did not tell Samuel to tell Eli; he had to decide that for himself. God's call to you may hurt your "Eli," but if you try to prevent the suffering in another life, it will prove an obstruction between your soul and God. It is at your own peril that you prevent the cutting off of the right hand or the plucking out of the eye.

Never ask the advice of another about anything God makes you decide before Him. If you ask advice, you will nearly always side with Satan. "Immediately I conferred not with flesh and blood."

. . . and not one of them said that aught of the things which he possessed was his own; but they had all things common. Acts 4:32
. . . and let us consider one another to provoke unto love and good works; not forsaking the assembling of ourselves together . . . (Hebrews 10:24–5)

These two passages serve to indicate the main characteristic of Christianity, viz., the 'together' aspect; false religions inculcate an isolated holy life. Try and develop a holy life in private, and you find it cannot be done. Individuals can only live the true life when they are dependent on one another. After the Resurrection our Lord would not allow Mary to hold a spiritual experience for herself, she must get into contact with the disciples and convey a message to them—'Touch me not . . . but go unto my brethren, and say to them, I ascend unto my Father and your Father, and my God and your God.' After Peter's denial the isolation of misery would inevitably have seized on him and made him want to retire in the mood of 'I can never forgive myself', had not our Lord forestalled this by giving him something positive to do—'and when thou art converted, strengthen thy brethren'. Immediately you try to develop holiness alone and fix your eyes on your own whiteness, you lose the whole meaning of Christianity. The Holy Spirit makes a man fix his eyes on his Lord and on intense activity for others. In the early Middle Ages people had the idea that Christianity meant living a holy life apart from the world and its sociability, apart from its work and citizenship. That type of holiness is foreign to the New Testament; it cannot be reconciled with the records of the life of Jesus. The people of His day called Him 'the friend of publicans and sinners' because He spent so much time with them.

BE 29

DO YOU SEE YOUR CALLING?

Separated unto the Gospel. (Rom. 1:1)

Our calling is not primarily to be holy men and women, but to be proclaimers of the Gospel of God. The one thing that is all important is that the Gospel of God should be realized as the abiding Reality. Reality is not human goodness, nor holiness, nor heaven, nor hell; but Redemption; and the need to perceive this is the most vital need of the Christian worker to-day. As workers we have to get used to the revelation that Redemption is the only Reality. Personal holiness is an effect, not a cause, and if we place our faith in human goodness, in the effect of Redemption, we shall go under when the test comes.

Paul did not say he separated himself, but—"when it pleased God who separated me. . . ." Paul had not a hypersensitive interest in his own character. As long as our eyes are upon our own personal whiteness we shall never get near the reality of Redemption. Workers break down because their desire is for their own whiteness, and not for God. "Don't ask me to come into contact with the rugged reality of Redemption on behalf of the filth of human life as it is; what I want is anything God can do for me to make me more desirable in my own eyes." To talk in that way is a sign that the reality of the Gospel of God has not begun to touch me; there is no reckless abandon to God. God cannot deliver me while my interest is merely in my own character. Paul is unconscious of himself, he is recklessly abandoned, separated by God for one purpose—to proclaim the Gospel of God (cf. Rom 9:3).

Go ye therefore and make disciples. (Matthew 28:19)

The call to discipleship comes as mysteriously as being born from above; once a man hears it, it profoundly alters everything. It is like the call of the sea, the call of the mountains, not everyone hears these calls, only those who have the nature of the sea or the mountains—and then only if they pay attention to the call. To hear the call of God or the call to discipleship necessitates education in understanding and discernment. Never be afraid of the thing that is vague, the biggest things in life are vague as far as expression goes, but they are realities.

'Go ye therefore, and make disciples of all the nations'—not 'Go out and save souls', but 'Go and *make disciples*'. It is comparatively easy to proclaim salvation from sin, but Jesus comes and says, 'What about you—if *you* would be My disciple, deny yourself, take up that cross daily, and follow Me.' It has nothing to do with *eternal salvation*, it has everything to do with our temporal value to God, and most of us do not care anything about our temporal worth to God, all we are concerned about is being saved from hell and put right for heaven. There is something infinitely grander than that, and Jesus Christ gives us a marvellous chance of giving up our right to ourselves to Him in order that we might become the devoted *bondslaves* of the One who saves us so supernaturally.

HGM 142

FEBRUARY

THE CALL OF GOD

For Christ sent me not to baptize, but to preach the gospel.
(1 Cor. 1:17)

Paul states here that the call of God is to preach the gospel; but remember what Paul means by "the gospel," viz., the reality of Redemption in our Lord Jesus Christ. We are apt to make sanctification the end-all of our preaching. Paul alludes to personal experience by way of illustration, never as the end of the matter. We are nowhere commissioned to preach salvation or sanctification; we are commissioned to lift up Jesus Christ (John 12:32). It is a travesty to say that Jesus Christ travailed in Redemption to make *me* a saint. Jesus Christ travailed in Redemption to redeem the whole world, and place it unimpaired and rehabilitated before the throne of God. The fact that Redemption can be experienced by us is an illustration of the power of the reality of Redemption, but that is not the end of Redemption. If God were human, how sick to the heart and weary He would be of the constant requests we make for our salvation, for our sanctification. We tax His energies from morning till night for things for ourselves—something for *me* to be delivered from! When we touch the bedrock of the reality of the Gospel of God, we shall never bother God any further with little personal plaints.

The one passion of Paul's life was to proclaim the Gospel of God. He welcomed heart-breaks, disillusionments, tribulation, for one reason only, because these things kept him in unmoved devotion to the Gospel of God.

> *And he said unto them, Let us go over unto the other side of the*
> *lake; and they launched forth. (Luke 8:22)*

'If you obey Jesus you will have a life of joy and delight.' Well, it is not true. Jesus said to the disciples—'Let us go to the other side of the lake', and they were plunged into the biggest storm they had ever known. You say, 'If I had not obeyed Jesus I should not have got into this complication.' Exactly. The problems in our walk with God are to be accounted for along this line, and the temptation is to say, 'God could never have told me to go there, if He had done so this would not have happened.' We discover then whether we are going to trust God's integrity or listen to our own expressed scepticism. Scepticism of the tongue is only transitional; real scepticism is wrung out from the man who knows he did not get where he is on his own account—'I was not seeking my own, I came deliberately because I believe Jesus told me to, and now there is the darkness and the deep and the desolation.'

HGM 90

Darkness is not synonymous with sin; if there is darkness spiritually it is much more likely to be the shade of God's hand than darkness on account of sin; it may be the threshold of a new revelation coming through a big break in personal experience. Before the dawn there is desolation; but wait, the dawn will merge into glorious day—' . . . the light of dawn, that shineth more and more unto the perfect day'. If you are experiencing the darkness of desolation on individual lines, go through with it, and you will find yourself face to face with Jesus Christ as never before. 'I am come that they might have life'—life in which there is no death—'and that they might have it more abundantly.'

HGM 57

THE CONSTRAINT OF THE CALL

Woe is unto me, if I preach not the gospel! (1 Cor. 9:16)

Beware of stopping your ears to the call of God. Everyone who is saved is called to testify to the fact; but that is not the call to preach, it is merely an illustration in preaching. Paul is referring to the pangs produced in him by the constraint to preach the Gospel. Never apply what Paul says in this connection to souls coming in contact with God for salvation. There is nothing easier than getting saved because it is God's sovereign work—Come unto Me and I will save you. Our Lord never lays down the conditions of discipleship as the conditions of salvation. We are condemned to salvation through the Cross of Jesus Christ. Discipleship has an option with it—"If any man. . ."

Paul's words have to do with being made a servant of Jesus Christ, and our permission is never asked as to what we will do or where we will go. God makes us broken bread and poured-out wine to please Himself. To be "separated unto the gospel" means to hear the call of God; and when a man begins to overhear that call, then begins agony that is worthy of the name. Every ambition is nipped in the bud, every desire of life quenched, every outlook completely extinguished and blotted out, saving one thing only—"*separated unto the gospel.*" Woe be to the soul who tries to put his foot in any other direction when once that call has come to him. This College exists for you, and you—to see whether God has a man or woman here who cares about proclaiming His Gospel; to see whether God grips you. And beware of competitors when God does grip you.

Arm ye yourselves also with the same mind. (1 Peter 4:1)

Some people have on an armour of innocence, like Tennyson's knight whose 'strength was as the strength of ten because his heart was pure'; others have on an armour of love. Paul says, 'Put on the whole armour of God.' Don't rely on anything less than that, clothe yourself with your relationship to God, maintain it. If you do not arm yourself with the armour of God, you are open to interferences in your hidden personal life from supernatural powers which you cannot control; but buckle on the armour, bring yourself into real living contact with God, and you are garrisoned not only in the conscious realm but in the depths of your personality beneath the conscious realm. 'Praying always,' says Paul. Every time we pray our horizon is altered, our attitude to things is altered, not sometimes but every time, and the amazing thing is that we don't pray more. Prayer is a complete emancipation, it keeps us on the spiritual plane. When you are at one with another mind there is a telepathic influence all the time, and when born from above the communion is between God and yourself; 'Keep that going,' says Peter. 'Arm ye yourselves also with the same mind.'

Are you neglecting prayer? No matter what else is neglected, switch back at once, if you don't you will be a dangerous influence to the people round about you. Watch the snare of self-pity—'Why should I go through this?' Be careful, you are a danger spot. I feel as if Jesus Christ were staggered with surprise at some of us, amazed at the things we say to Him, astonished at our attitude to Him, at the sulks we get into, because we have forgotten to arm ourselves with the same mind.

PH 214

THE RECOGNIZED BAN
OF RELATIONSHIP

We are made as the filth of the world. (1 Cor. 4:9-13)

These words are not an exaggeration. The reason they are not true of us who call ourselves ministers of the gospel is not that Paul forgot the exact truth in using them, but that we have too many discreet affinities to allow ourselves to be made refuse. "Filling up that which is behind of the afflictions of Christ" is not an evidence of sanctification, but of being "separated unto the gospel."

"Think it not strange concerning the fiery trial which is to try you," says Peter. If we do think it strange concerning the things we meet with, it is because we are craven-hearted. We have discreet affinities that keep us out of the mire—I won't stoop, I won't bend. You do not need to, you can be saved by the skin of your teeth if you like; you can refuse to let God count you as one separated unto the gospel. Or you may say— "I do not care if I am treated as the offscouring of the earth as long as the Gospel is proclaimed." A servant of Jesus Christ is one who is willing to go to martyrdom for the reality of the gospel of God. When a merely moral man or woman comes in contact with baseness and immorality and treachery, the recoil is so desperately offensive to human goodness that the heart shuts up in despair. The marvel of the Redemptive Reality of God is that the worst and the vilest can never get to the bottom of His love. Paul did not say that God separated him to show what a wonderful man He could make of him, but *"to reveal His Son in me."*

> *Therefore all things whatsoever ye would that men should do to you, do ye even so to them. (Matthew 7:12)*

Our Lord's use of this maxim is positive, not negative. *Do* to others whatsoever ye would that they should do to you—a very different thing from not doing to others what you do not want them to do to you. What would we like other people to do to us? 'Well,' says Jesus, 'do that to them; don't wait for them to do it to you.' The Holy Ghost will kindle your imagination to picture many things you would like others to do to you, and that is His way of telling you what to do to them—'I would like people to give me credit for the generous motives I have.' Well, give them credit for having generous motives. 'I would like people never to pass harsh judgments on me.' Well, don't pass harsh judgments on them. 'I would like other people to pray for me.' Well, pray for them. The measure of our growth in grace is our attitude towards other people. 'Thou shalt love thy neighbour as thyself,' says Jesus. Satan comes in as an angel of light and says, 'But you must not think about yourself.' The Holy Spirit will make you think about yourself, because that is His way of educating you so that you may be able to deal with others. He makes you picture what you would like other people to do to you, and then He says, 'Now go and do those things to them.' This verse is our Lord's standard for practical ethical conduct.

SSM 90

THE OVERMASTERING MAJESTY
OF PERSONAL POWER

For the love of Christ constraineth us. (2 Cor. 5:14)

Paul says he is overruled, overmastered, held as in a vice, by the love of Christ. Very few of us know what it means to be held in a grip by the love of God; we are held by the constraint of our experience only. The one thing that held Paul until there was nothing else on his horizon, was the love of God. "The love of Christ constraineth us"—when you hear that note in a man or woman, you can never mistake it. You know that the Spirit of God is getting unhindered way in that life.

When we are born again of the Spirit of God, the note of testimony is on what God has done for us, and rightly so. But the baptism of the Holy Ghost obliterates that for ever, and we begin to realize what Jesus meant when He said—"Ye shall be witnesses unto Me." Not witnesses to what Jesus can do—that is an elementary witness—but *"witnesses unto me."* We will take everything that happens as happening to Him, whether it be praise or blame, persecution or commendation. No one can stand like that for Jesus Christ who is not constrained by the majesty of His personal power. It is the only thing that matters, and the strange thing is that it is the last thing realized by the Christian worker. Paul says he is gripped by the love of God, that is why he acts as he does. Men may call him mad or sober, but he does not care; there is only one thing he is living for, and that is to persuade men of the judgment seat of God, and of the love of Christ. This abandon to the love of Christ is the one thing that bears fruit in the life, and it will always leave the impression of the holiness and of the power of God, never of our personal holiness.

Then was Jesus led up of the Spirit into the wilderness to be tempted of the devil. (Matthew 4:1)

For thirty years Jesus had remained unknown, then He was baptized and had a wonderful manifestation of the Father's approval, and the next thing we read is that He is 'led up of the Spirit into the wilderness to be tempted of the devil'. The same thing puzzles us in our own spiritual experience; we have been born from above, or have had the wonderful experience of the baptism of the Holy Ghost—surely we are fit now to do something for God; and God deliberately puts us on the shelf, amongst the dust and the cobwebs, in an utterly unaccountable way.

The agony Jesus went through in the Temptation was surely because He had the vision of the long way and saw the suffering it would entail on men through all the ages if He took His Father's way. He knew it in a way we cannot conceive. His sensitiveness is beyond anything we can imagine. If He had not been true to His Father's way, His own home would not have been upset. His own nation would not have blasphemed the Holy Ghost. The way to approach Gethsemane is to try to understand the Temptation.

When we obey Jesus Christ it is never a question of what it costs us—it does not cost us anything, it is a delight—but of what it costs those whom we love, and there is always the danger of yielding to the temptation of the 'short cut'. Am I prepared to let my obedience to God cost other people something? Jesus deliberately took the long trail, and He says 'the disciple is not above his Master'. 'Because thou hast kept the word of my patience . . . ' We want to hurry things up by revivals. Over and over again we take the devil's advice and say, 'It must be done quickly— the need is the call; men must be saved.' An understanding of the inwardness of our Lord's temptation will throw light on the progress of Christian history as well as on personal experience.

PH 100

ARE YOU READY TO BE OFFERED?

Yea, and if I be offered upon the sacrifice and service of your faith,
I joy and rejoice with you all. (Phil. 2:17)

Are you willing to be offered for the work of the faithful—to pour out your life blood as a libation on the sacrifice of the faith of others? Or do you say—"I am not going to be offered up just yet, I do not want God to choose my work. I want to choose the scenery of my own sacrifice; I want to have the right kind of people watching and saying, 'Well done.'"

It is one thing to go on the lonely way with dignified heroism, but quite another thing if the line mapped out for you by God means being a door-mat under other people's feet. Suppose God wants to teach you to say, "I know how to be abased" —are you ready to be offered up like that? Are you ready to be not so much as a drop in a bucket—to be so hopelessly insignificant that you are never thought of again in connection with the life you served? Are you willing to spend and be spent; not seeking to be ministered unto, but to minister? Some saints cannot do menial work and remain saints because it is beneath their dignity.

And God is able to make all grace abound toward you!
(2 Corinthians 9:8)

Our Lord emptied Himself and had nothing all the days of His earthly life, consequently He was free for God to lavish His gifts through Him to others. Think of the rushes with which we come in front of our Heavenly Father; whenever we see an occasion we rush in and say, 'I can do this, you need not trouble God.' I wonder if we are learning determinedly to possess nothing? It is possessing things that makes us so conceited— 'Oh yes, I can give prayer for you; I can give this and that for you.' We have to get to the place about which Jesus talked to the rich young ruler where we are so absolutely empty and poor that we have nothing, and God knows we have nothing, then He can do through us what He likes. Would that we would quickly get rid of all we have, give it away till there is nothing left, then there is a chance for God to pour through in rivers for other people.

IWP 79

ARE YOU READY TO BE OFFERED?

I am already being poured out as a drink offering.
(2 Tim. 4:6, R.V. MARG.)

"I am ready to be offered." It is a transaction of will, not of sentiment. *Tell* God you are ready to be offered; then let the consequences be what they may, there is no strand of complaint now, no matter what God chooses. God puts you through the crisis in private, no one person can help another. Externally the life may be the same; the difference is in will. Go through the crisis in will, then when it comes externally there will be no thought of the cost. If you do not transact in will with God along this line, you will end in awakening sympathy for yourself.

"Bind the sacrifice with cords, even unto the horns of the altar." The altar means fire—burning and purification and insulation for one purpose only, the destruction of every affinity that God has not started and of every attachment that is not an attachment in God. You do not destroy it, God does; you bind the sacrifice to the horns of the altar; and see that you do not give way to self-pity when the fire begins. After this way of fire, there is nothing that oppresses or depresses. When the crisis arises, you realize that things cannot touch you as they used to do. What is your way of fire?

Tell God you are ready to be offered, and God will prove Himself to be all you ever dreamed He would be.

Hear ye then the parable of the sower . . . (Matthew 13:18)

It is the plough that prepares the ground for sowing the seed. The hard way through the field is the same soil as the good ground, but it is of no use for growing corn because it has never been ploughed. Apply that to your own soul and to the souls of men. There are lives that are absolutely stupid towards God, they are simply a way for the traffic of their own concerns. We are responsible for the kind of ground we are. No man on earth has any right to be a highroad; every man has the chance of allowing the plough to run through his life. Sorrow or bereavement or conviction of sin, anything that upsets the even, hard way of the life and produces concern, will act as the plough. A man's concern about his eternal welfare witnesses that the plough has begun to go through his self-complacency. The words of our Lord, 'Think not that I came to cast peace on the earth: I came not to cast peace, but a sword', are a description of what happens when the Gospel is preached—upset, conviction, concern and confusion.

SHL 112

THE DISCIPLINE OF DEJECTION

But we trusted . . . and beside all this, to-day is the third day . . .
(Luke 24:21)

Every fact that the disciples stated was right; but the inferences they drew from those facts were wrong. Anything that savours of dejection spiritually is always wrong. If depression and oppression visit me, I am to blame; God is not, nor is anyone else. Dejection springs from one of two sources—I have either satisfied a lust or I have not. Lust means—I must have it at once. Spiritual lust makes me demand an answer from God, instead of seeking God Who gives the answer. What have I been trusting God would do? And to-day—the immediate present—is the third day, and He has not done it; therefore I imagine I am justified in being dejected and in blaming God. Whenever the insistence is on the point that God answers prayer, we are off the track. The meaning of prayer is that we get hold of God, not of the answer. It is impossible to be well physically and to be dejected. Dejection is a sign of sickness, and the same thing is true spiritually. Dejection spiritually is wrong, and we are always to blame for it.

We look for visions from heaven, for earthquakes and thunders of God's power (the fact that we are dejected proves that we do), and we never dream that all the time God is in the commonplace things and people around us. If we will do the duty that lies nearest, we shall see Him. One of the most amazing revelations of God comes when we learn that it is in the commonplace things that the Deity of Jesus Christ is realized.

All these evil things come from within, and defile the man.
(Mark 7:23)

Solomon was the wisest and the wealthiest of kings, yet he says that 'the plague of his own heart' knocked him out (see 1 Kings 8:38). This is the first lesson every one of us has to learn. To begin with we are not prepared to accept Jesus Christ's diagnosis of the human heart, we prefer to trust our own ignorant innocence. Jesus Christ says, 'Out of the heart proceed fornication, adultery, murder, lasciviousness, thieving, lying,' etc. (Mark 7:21–23). No man has ever believed that. We have not the remotest conception that what Jesus says about the human heart is true until we come up against something further on in our lives. We are apt to be indignant and say—'I don't believe those things are in my heart', and we refuse the diagnosis of the only Master there is of the human heart. We need never know the plague of our own heart and the terrible possibilities in human life if we will hand ourselves over to Jesus Christ; but if we stand on our own right and wisdom at any second an eruption may occur in our personal lives, and we may discover to our unutterable horror that we can be murderers, etc. This is one of the most ghastly and humiliating and devastating truths in the whole of human experience . . .

Education cannot deal with the plague of the heart, all our vows cannot touch it; the only Being Who can deal with it is God through a personal relationship to Him, by receiving His Spirit after accepting the diagnosis of Jesus Christ.

SHH 104, 105

INSTANTANEOUS AND INSISTENT SANCTIFICATION

And the very God of peace sanctify you wholly.
(1 Thess. 5:23-24)

When we pray to be sanctified, are we prepared to face the standard of these verses? We take the term sanctification much too lightly. Are we prepared for what sanctification will cost? It will cost an intense narrowing of all our interests on earth, and an immense broadening of all our interests in God. Sanctification means intense concentration on God's point of view. It means every power of body, soul and spirit chained and kept for God's purpose only. Are we prepared for God to do in us all that He separated us for? And then after His work is done in us, are we prepared to separate ourselves to God even as Jesus did? "For their sakes I sanctify Myself." The reason some of us have not entered into the experience of sanctification is that we have not realized the meaning of sanctification from God's standpoint. Sanctification means being made one with Jesus so that the disposition that ruled Him will rule us. Are we prepared for what that will cost? It will cost everything that is not of God in us.

Are we prepared to be caught up into the swing of this prayer of the apostle Paul's? Are we prepared to say —"Lord, make me as holy as You can make a sinner saved by grace"? Jesus has prayed that we might be one with Him as He is one with the Father. The one and only characteristic of the Holy Ghost in a man is a strong family likeness to Jesus Christ, and freedom from everything that is unlike Him. Are we prepared to set ourselves apart for the Holy Spirit's ministrations in us?

And Abraham stretched forth his hand, and took the knife to slay his son. (Genesis 22:10)

Sacrifice in the Bible means that we give to God the best we have; it is the finest form of worship. Sacrifice is not giving up things, but giving to God with joy the best we have. We have dragged down the idea of surrender and of sacrifice, we have taken the life out of the words and made them mean something sad and weary and despicable; in the Bible they mean the very opposite. To go out in surrender to God means the surrendering of the miserable sense of my own un-importance: Am I willing to surrender that mean little sense for the great big idea God has for me? Am I willing to surrender the fact that I am an ignorant, useless, worthless, too-old person? There is more hindrance to God's work because people cling to a sense of unworthiness than because of conceit. *'Who am I?'* Instantly the trend of the mind is to say—'Oh well, I have not had any education'; 'I did not begin soon enough.' Am I willing to surrender the whole thing, and go out in surrender to God? to go out of the carnal mind into the spiritual?—'fools for Christ's sake'?

Abraham surrendered himself entirely to the supernatural God. Have you got hold of a supernatural God? not, do you know what God is going to do? You cannot know, but you have faith in Him, and therefore He can do what He likes.

NP 148

ARE YOU EXHAUSTED SPIRITUALLY?

The everlasting God . . . fainteth not, neither is weary.
(Isa. 40:28)

Exhaustion means that the vital forces are worn right out.
Spiritual exhaustion never comes through sin but only through
service, and whether or not you are exhausted will depend
upon where you get your supplies. Jesus said to Peter—"Feed
My sheep," but He gave him nothing to feed them with. The
process of being made broken bread and poured out wine
means that *you* have to be the nourishment for other souls until
they learn to feed on God. They must drain you to the dregs.
Be careful that you get your supply, or before long you will be
utterly exhausted. Before other souls learn to draw on the life
of the Lord Jesus direct, they have to draw on it through you;
you have to be literally "sucked," until they learn to take their
nourishment from God. We owe it to God to be our best for
His lambs and His sheep as well as for Himself.

   Has the way in which you have been serving God betrayed
you into exhaustion? If so, then rally your affections. Where
did you start the service from? From your own sympathy or
from the basis of the Redemption of Jesus Christ? Continually
go back to the foundation of your affections and recollect where
the source of power is. You have no right to say—"O Lord, I
am so exhausted." He saved and sanctified you in order to
exhaust you. Be exhausted for God, but remember that your
supply comes from Him. "All my fresh springs shall be in Thee."

Thou therefore endure hardness, as a good soldier of Jesus Christ.
(2 Timothy 2:3)

The first requirement of the worker is discipline voluntarily entered into. It is easy to be passionate, easy to be thrilled by spiritual influences, but it takes a heart in love with Jesus Christ to put the feet in His footprints, and to square the life to a steady 'going up to Jerusalem' with Him. Discipline is the one thing the modern Christian knows nothing of, we won't stand discipline nowadays. God has given me an experience of His life and grace, therefore I am a law unto myself.

The discipline of a worker is not in order to develop his own life, but for the purposes of his Commander. The reason there is so much failure is because we forget that we are here for that one thing, loyalty to Jesus Christ; otherwise we have no business to have taken the vows of God upon us. If a soldier is not prepared to be killed, he has no business to have enlisted as a soldier. The only way to keep true to God is by a steady persistent refusal to be interested in Christian work and to be interested alone in Jesus Christ.

A disciplined life means three things—a supreme aim incorporated into the life itself; an external law binding on the life from its Commander; and the absolute loyalty to God and His word as the ingrained attitude of heart and mind. There must be no insubordination; every impulse, every emotion, every illumination must be rigorously handled and checked if it is not in accordance with God and His word.

Our Lord Himself is the example of a disciplined life. He lived a holy life by sacrificing Himself to His Father; His words and His thinking were holy because He submitted His intelligence to His Father's word, and He worked the works of God because He steadily submitted His will to His Father's will; and as is the Master, so is the disciple.

AUG 64

IS YOUR IMAGINATION
OF GOD STARVED?

Lift up your eyes on high, and behold who hath created these things. (Isa. 40:26)

The people of God in Isaiah's day had starved their imagination by looking on the face of idols, and Isaiah made them look up at the heavens, that is, he made them begin to use their imagination aright. Nature to a saint is sacramental. If we are children of God, we have a tremendous treasure in Nature. In every wind that blows, in every night and day of the year, in every sign of the sky, in every blossoming and in every withering of the earth, there is a real coming of God to us if we will simply use our starved imagination to realize it.

The test of spiritual concentration is bringing the imagination into captivity. Is your imagination looking on the face of an idol? Is the idol yourself? Your work? Your conception of what a worker should be? Your experience of salvation and sanctification? Then your imagination of God is starved, and when you are up against difficulties you have no power, you can only endure in darkness. If your imagination is starved, do not look back to your own experience; it is God Whom you need. Go right out of yourself, away from the face of your idols, away from everything that has been starving your imagination. Rouse yourself, take the gibe that Isaiah gave the people, and deliberately turn your imagination to God.

One of the reasons of stultification in prayer is that there is no imagination, no power of putting ourselves deliberately before God. We have to learn how to be broken bread and poured out wine on the line of intercession more than on the line of personal contact. Imagination is the power God gives a saint to posit himself out of himself into relationships he never was in.

But, inasmuch as ye are partakers of Christ's sufferings, rejoice.
(1 Peter 4:13)

If we are going to be used by God, He will take us through a multitude of experiences that are not meant for us at all, but meant to make us useful in His hands. There are things we go through which are unexplainable on any other line, and the nearer we get to God the more inexplicable the way seems. It is only on looking back and by getting an explanation from God's Word that we understand His dealings with us.

PH 34

Not only does God waste His saints according to the judgments of men, He seems to bruise them most mercilessly. You say, 'But it could never be God's will to bruise me': if it pleased the Lord to bruise His own Son, why should He not bruise you? To choose suffering is a disease; but to choose God's will even though it means suffering is to suffer as Jesus did—'according to the will of God'.

In the Bible it is never the idealizing of the sufferer that is brought out, but the glorifying of God. God always serves Himself out of the saint's personal experience of suffering.

SHL 121

IS YOUR HOPE IN GOD
FAINT AND DYING?

Thou wilt keep him in perfect peace whose imagination is stayed on Thee. (Isa. 26:3 R.V. MARG.)

Is your imagination stayed on God or is it starved? The starvation of the imagination is one of the most fruitful sources of exhaustion and sapping in a worker's life. If you have never used your imagination to put yourself before God, begin to do it now. It is no use waiting for God to come; you must put your imagination away from the face of idols and look unto Him and be saved. Imagination is the greatest gift God has given us and it ought to be devoted entirely to Him. If you have been bringing every thought into captivity to the obedience of Christ, it will be one of the greatest assets to faith when the time of trial comes, because your faith and the Spirit of God will work together. Learn to associate ideas worthy of God with all that happens in Nature—the sunrises and the sunsets, the sun and the stars, the changing seasons, and your imagination will never be at the mercy of your impulses, but will always be at the service of God.

"We have sinned with our fathers;. . . and have forgotten"— then put a stiletto in the place where you have gone to sleep. "God is not talking to me just now," but He ought to be. Remember Whose you are and Whom you serve. Provoke yourself by recollection, and your affection for God will increase tenfold; your imagination will not be starved any longer, but will be quick and enthusiastic, and your hope will be inexpressibly bright.

I count all things but loss for the excellency of the knowledge of Christ Jesus my Lord. (Philippians 3:8)

The first thing the Spirit of God does in us is to efface the things we rely upon naturally. Paul argues this out in Philippians 3, he catalogues who he is and the things in which he might have confidence; 'but,' he says, 'I deliberately renounce all these things that I may gain Christ.' The continual demand to consecrate our gifts to God is the devil's counterfeit for sanctification. We have a way of saying—'What a wonderful power that man or woman would be in God's service.' Reasoning on man's broken virtues makes us fix on the wrong thing. The only way any man or woman can ever be of service to God is when he or she is willing to renounce all their natural excellencies and determine to be weak in Him—'I am here for one thing only, for Jesus Christ to manifest Himself in me.' That is to be the steadfast habit of a Christian's life. Whenever we think we are of use to God, we hinder Him. We have to form the habit of letting God carry on His work through us without let or hindrance as He did through Jesus, and He will use us in ways He dare not let us see. We have to efface every other thought but that of Jesus Christ. It is not done once for all; we have to be always doing it. If once you have seen that Jesus Christ is All in all, make the habit of letting Him be All in all. It will mean that you not only have implicit faith that He is All in all, but that you go through the trial of your faith and prove that He is. After sanctification God delights to put us into places where He can make us wealthy. Jesus Christ counts as service not what we do for Him, but what we are to Him, and the inner secret of that is identity with Him in person. *'That I may know Him.'*

MFL 106

MUST I LISTEN?

And they said unto Moses, Speak thou with us and we will hear:
but let not God speak with us, lest we die. (Ex. 20:19)

We do not consciously disobey God, we simply do not heed Him. God has given us His commands; there they are, but we do not pay any attention to them, not because of wilful disobedience but because we do not love and respect Him. "If ye love Me, ye will keep My commandments." When once we realize that we have been "disrespecting" God all the time, we are covered with shame and humiliation because we have not heeded Him.

"Speak thou with us . . . but let not God speak with us." We show how little we love God by preferring to listen to His servants only. We like to listen to personal testimonies, but we do not desire that God Himself should speak to us. Why are we so terrified lest God should speak to us? Because we know that if God does speak, either the thing must be done or we must tell God we will not obey Him. If it is only the servant's voice we hear, we feel it is not imperative, we can say, "Well that is simply your own idea, though I don't deny it is probably God's truth."

Am I putting God in the humiliating position of having treated me as a child of His whilst all the time I have been ignoring Him? When I do hear Him, the humiliation I have put on Him comes back on me—"Lord, why was I so dull and so obstinate?" This is always the result when once we do hear God. The real delight of hearing Him is tempered with shame in having been so long in not hearing Him.

For he is an holy God . . . he will not forgive your transgressions or your sins. (Joshua 24:19)

Have you ever been convicted of sin by conscience through the Spirit of God? If you have, you know this—that God dare not forgive you and be God. There is a lot of sentimental talk about God forgiving because He is love: God is so holy that He cannot forgive. God can only destroy for ever the thing that is unlike Himself. The Atonement does not mean that God forgives a sinner and allows him to go on sinning and receiving forgiveness; it means that God saves the sinner and turns him into a saint, i.e. destroys the sinner out of him, and through his conscience he realizes that by the Atonement God has done what He never could have done apart from it. When people testify you can always tell whether they have been convicted by the Spirit of God or whether their equilibrium has been disturbed by doing wrong things. When a man is convicted of sin by the Spirit of God through his conscience, his relationship to other people is absolute child's play. If when you were convicted of sin, you had been told to go and lick the dust off the boots of your greatest enemy, you would have done it willingly. Your relationship to men is the last thing that bothers you. It is your relationship to God that bothers you. I am completely out of the love of God, out of the holiness of God, and I tremble with terror when I think of God drawing near.

PS 65

THE DEVOTION OF HEARING

Speak; for Thy servant heareth. (1 Sam. 3:10)

Because I have listened definitely to one thing from God, it does not follow that I will listen to everything He says. The way in which I show God that I neither love nor respect Him is by the obtuseness of my heart and mind towards what He says. If I love my friend, I intuitively detect what he wants, and Jesus says, "Ye are My friends." Have I disobeyed some command of my Lord's this week? If I had realized that it was a command of Jesus, I would not consciously have disobeyed it. But most of us show such disrespect to God that we do not even hear what He says; He might never have spoken.

The destiny of my spiritual life is such identification with Jesus Christ that I always hear God, and I know that God always hears me (John 11:41). If I am united with Jesus Christ, I hear God, by the devotion of hearing all the time. A lily, or a tree, or a servant of God, may convey God's message to me. What hinders me from hearing is that I am taken up with other things. It is not that I will not hear God, but I am not devoted in the right place. I am devoted to things, to service, to convictions, and God may say what He likes but I do not hear Him. The child attitude is always, "Speak, Lord, for Thy servant heareth." If I have not cultivated this devotion of hearing I can only hear God's voice at certain times; at other times I am taken up with things—things which I say I must do, and I become deaf to Him, I am not living the life of a child. Have I heard God's voice to-day?

If any man suffer as a Christian, let him not be ashamed.
(1 Peter 4:16)

To 'suffer as a Christian' is not to be marked peculiar because of your views, or because you will not bend to conventionality; these things are not Christian, but ordinary human traits from which all men suffer irrespective of creed or religion or no religion. To 'suffer as a Christian' is to suffer because there is an essential difference between you and the world which rouses the contempt of the world, and the disgust and hatred of the spirit that is in the world. To 'suffer as a Christian' is to have no answer when the world's satire is turned on you, as it was turned on Jesus Christ when He hung upon the cross, when they turned His words into jest and jeer; they will do the same to you. He gave no answer, neither can you.

' . . . but if a man suffer as a Christian, let him not be ashamed.' It was in the throes of this blinding, amazing problem that Peter staggered. Peter meant to go with his Lord to death, and he did go; but never at any moment did he imagine that he would have to go without Him—that he would see Jesus taken by the power of the world, 'as a lamb that is led to the slaughter', and have no answer, no word to explain—that froze him to the soul. That is what it means to 'suffer as a Christian'—to hear men taunt Him, see them tear His words to pieces, and feel you cannot answer; to smart under their merciless, pitying sarcasm because you belong to that contemptible sect of 'Christians' . . . But when you have been 'comforted by His rod and His staff, you count it all joy to go through this God-glorifying suffering.

DS 70

THE DISCIPLINE OF HEEDING

What I tell you in darkness, that speak ye in light: and what ye
hear in the ear, that preach ye upon the housetops. (Matt. 10:27)

At times God puts us through the discipline of darkness to teach us to heed Him. Song birds are taught to sing in the dark, and we are put into the shadow of God's hand until we learn to hear Him. "What I tell you in darkness"—watch where God puts you into darkness, and when you are there keep your mouth shut. Are you in the dark just now in your circumstances, or in your life with God? Then remain quiet. If you open your mouth in the dark, you will talk in the wrong mood: darkness is the time to listen. Don't talk to other people about it; don't read books to find out the reason of the darkness, but listen and heed. If you talk to other people, you cannot hear what God is saying. When you are in the dark, listen, and God will give you a very precious message for someone else when you get into the light.

After every time of darkness there comes a mixture of delight and humiliation (if there is delight only, I question whether we have heard God at all), delight in hearing God speak, but chiefly humiliation—What a long time I was in hearing that! How slow I have been in understanding that! And yet God has been saying it all these days and weeks. Now He gives you the gift of humiliation which brings the softness of heart that will always listen to God *now*.

*I indeed baptize you with water unto repentance . . . he shall
baptize you with the Holy Ghost, and with fire. (Matthew 3:11)*

I want to ask a very personal question—How much do you
want to be delivered from? You say, 'I want to be delivered
from wrong-doing'—then you don't need to come to Jesus
Christ. 'I want to walk in the right way according to the judgment of men'—then you don't need Jesus Christ. But some
heart cries out—'I want, God knows I want, that Jesus Christ
should do in me all He said He would do.' How many of us
'want' like that? God grant that this 'want' may increase until
it swamps every other desire of heart and life. Oh, the patience,
the gentleness, the longing of the Lord Jesus after lives, and
yet men are turning this way and that, and even saints who
once knew Him are turning aside, their eyes are fixed on other
things, on the blessings that come from the baptism with the
Holy Ghost and have forgotten the Baptizer Himself.

Do you know what this mighty baptism will mean? It will
mean being taken right out of every other setting in life but
God's. Are you willing for that? It will mean that sin in you is
put to death, not counteracted, but killed right out by identification with the death of Jesus; it will mean a blazing personal
holiness like His. Are you willing for that? Face Jesus Himself;
other lights are fading since He grew bright. You are getting tired
of life as it is, tired of yourself as you are, getting sour with regard to the setting of your life; lift your eyes for one moment to
Jesus Christ. Do you want, more than you want your food, more
than you want your sleep, more than you want anything under
heaven, or in heaven, that Jesus Christ might so identify you
with Himself that you are His first and last and for ever? God
grant that the great longing desire of your heart may begin to
awaken as it has never done, not only the desire for the forgiveness of sins, but for identification with Jesus Himself until
you say, 'I live; yet not I, but Christ liveth in me.'

GW 22

AM I MY BROTHER'S KEEPER?

None of us liveth to himself. (Rom. 14:7)

Has it ever dawned on you that you are responsible for other souls spiritually before God? For instance, if I allow any private deflection from God in my life, everyone about me suffers. We "sit *together* in heavenly places." "Whether one member suffers, all the members suffer with it." When once you allow physical selfishness, mental slovenliness, moral obtuseness, spiritual density, everyone belonging to your crowd will suffer. "But," you say, "who is sufficient for these things if you erect a standard like that?" "Our sufficiency is of God," and of Him alone.

"Ye shall be My witnesses." How many of us are willing to spend every ounce of nervous energy, of mental, moral and spiritual energy we have for Jesus Christ? That is the meaning of a *witness* in God's sense of the word. It takes time, be patient with yourself. God has left us on the earth—what for? to be saved and sanctified? No, to be at it for Him. Am I willing to be broken bread and poured out wine for Him? To be spoilt for this age, for this life, to be spoilt from every standpoint but one—saving as I can disciple men and women to the Lord Jesus Christ. My life as a worker is the way I say "thank you" to God for His unspeakable salvation. Remember it is quite possible for any one of us to be flung out as reprobate silver—". . . lest that by any means when I have preached to others, I myself should be a castaway."

*I indeed baptize you with water unto repentance . . . he shall
baptize you with the Holy Ghost and with fire. (Matthew 3:11)*

Another thing about this mighty baptism—it takes you out of
your individual life and fits you into God's purpose. Are some
of you realizing the awful loneliness of being alive? You cannot mix in with the worldly crowd you used to, and there is a
great hunger and longing after you know not what. Look to
the Lord Jesus and say, 'My God, I want to be so identified with
the Lord Jesus that I am pure with His purity, empowered with
His power, indwelt with His life.' Do you know what will happen? God will take your lonely, isolated, individual life and fit
it into a marvellous oneness, into the mystical Body of Christ.
Oh, the isolated, lonely, Christian lives! What is needed is this
mighty baptism with the Holy Ghost and with fire. 'I have been
seeking for it, fasting for it,' you say; listen, 'Come unto me,'
says Jesus. He is the Baptizer with the Holy Ghost, and with
fire.

Have you seen Jesus as 'the Lamb of God, which taketh away
the sin of the world'? What is the first step to take? Come to
Him just as you are and ask Him to give you the Holy Spirit.
He begins to awaken in you the tremendous 'want', overwhelming, all-absorbing, passionate in its impelling rush, to
be baptized with the Holy ghost and with fire. If you have never
received the Holy Spirit, why not receive Him now? Ask God
for His Spirit on the authority of Jesus, and He will lead you,
as you obey Him, straight to the place where you will be identified with the death of Jesus.

GW 23

THE INSPIRATION OF
SPIRITUAL INITIATIVE

Arise from the dead. (Eph. 5:14)

All initiative is not inspired. A man may say to you—"Buck up, take your disinclination by the throat, throw it overboard, and walk out into the thing!" That is ordinary human initiative. But when the Spirit of God comes in and says, in effect, "Buck up," we find that the initiative is inspired.

We all have any number of visions and ideals when we are young, but sooner or later we find that we have no power to make them real. We cannot do the things we long to do, and we are apt to settle down to the visions and ideals as dead, and God has to come and say —"Arise from the dead." When the inspiration of God does come, it comes with such miraculous power that we are able to arise from the dead and do the impossible thing. The remarkable thing about spiritual initiative is that the life comes after we do the "bucking up." God does not give us overcoming life; He gives us life *as we overcome*. When the inspiration of God comes, and He says—"Arise from the dead," we have to get up; God does not lift us up. Our Lord said to the man with the withered hand—"Stretch forth thy hand," and as soon as the man did so, his hand was healed, but he had to take the initiative. If we will do the overcoming, we shall find we are inspired of God because He gives life immediately.

I indeed baptize you with water unto repentance . . . he shall baptize you with the Holy Ghost, and with fire. (Matthew 3:11)

Where are we in regard to the personal experience of the baptism of the Holy Ghost? If Jesus Christ had said to us, 'All you need to do is to be as holy as you can, overcome sin as far as you can, and I will overlook the rest', no intelligent man under heaven would accept such a salvation. But He says—'Be ye perfect'; 'Love your enemies'; 'Be so pure that lust is an impossibility'. Instantly every heart calls back, 'My God, who is sufficient for these things?' Oceans of penitential tears, mountains of good works, all powers and energy sink down till they are under the feet of the Lord Jesus, and, incarnate in John the Baptist, they all point to Him—'Behold the Lamb of God, which taketh away the sin of the world!' If Jesus Christ cannot deliver from sin, if He cannot adjust us perfectly to God as He says He can, if He cannot fill us with the Holy Ghost until there is nothing that can ever appeal again in sin or the world or the flesh, then He has misled us. But blessed be the Name of God, He can! He can so purify, so indwell, so merge with Himself, that only the things that appeal to Him appeal to you, to all other appeals there is the sentence of death, you have nothing to answer. When you come amongst those whose morality and uprightness crown them the lord of their own lives, there is no affinity with you, and they leave you alone.

GW 23

THE INITIATIVE AGAINST DEPRESSION

Arise and eat. (1 Kings 19:5)

The angel did not give Elijah a vision, or explain the Scriptures to him, or do anything remarkable; he told Elijah to do the most ordinary thing, viz., to get up and eat. If we were never depressed we should not be alive; it is the nature of a crystal never to be depressed. A human being is capable of depression, otherwise there would be no capacity for exaltation. There are things that are calculated to depress, things that are of the nature of death; and in taking an estimate of yourself, always take into account the capacity for depression.

When the Spirit of God comes He does not give us visions, He tells us to do the most ordinary things conceivable. Depression is apt to turn us away from the ordinary commonplace things of God's creation, but whenever God comes, the inspiration is to do the most natural simple things—the things we would never have imagined God was in, and as we do them we find He is there. The inspiration which comes to us in this way is an initiative against depression; we have to do the next thing and do it in the inspiration of God. If we do a thing in order to overcome depression, we deepen the depression; but if the Spirit of God makes us feel intuitively that we must do the thing, and we do it, the depression is gone. Immediately we arise and obey, we enter on a higher plane of life.

Put on the whole armour of God . . . and, having done all, to stand. (Ephesians 6:11–13)

Paul is writing from prison; he knows all about the Roman soldier whose armour he is describing, for he was chained to one of them. 'I am an ambassador in a chain,' he says.

These verses are not a picture of how to fight, but of how not to fight. If you have not put on the armour, you will have to fight; but 'having put on the whole armour of God, then *stand*', says Paul. There are times when God's servants are sent out to attack, to storm the citadel, but the counsel given here is as to how we are to hold the position which has been gained. We need to learn this conservation of energy, 'having done all, to stand', manifesting the full power of God.

'For we wrestle not against flesh and blood'—if we do, we are 'out of it'; our warfare is against 'the spiritual hosts of wickedness' which the world does not see. We are apt to forget that the enemy is unseen and that he is supernatural (cf. Daniel 10:12–13). 'Don't make any mistake,' says Paul, 'you are not wrestling against flesh and blood, you are wrestling against tremendous powers you will never be able to withstand unless you put on the whole armour of God. When you see men doing terrible things, remember you are not wrestling against them, they are the cat's-paw of the rulers of the darkness of this world.' We are to be taken up with a much more difficult wrestling, viz., the wrestling against the spiritual hosts of wickedness in the heavenly places which prevent us from seeing God . . .

'Praying always . . . for all saints.' It is not always a time of triumph; there are not only times of taking strongholds by storm, but times when spiritual darkness falls, when the great powers in the heavenlies are at work, when no one understands the wiles of Satan but God; at such times we have to stand steadily shoulder to shoulder for God. How often the Spirit of God emphasizes the 'together-ness' of the saints!

GW 98

THE INITIATIVE AGAINST DESPAIR

Rise, let us be going. (Matt. 26:46)

The disciples went to sleep when they should have kept awake, and when they realized what they had done it produced despair. The sense of the irreparable is apt to make us despair, and we say—"It is all up now, it is no use trying any more." If we imagine that this kind of despair is exceptional, we are mistaken, it is a very ordinary human experience. Whenever we realize that we have not done that which we had a magnificent opportunity of doing, then we are apt to sink into despair; and Jesus Christ comes and says—"Sleep on now, that opportunity is lost for ever, you cannot alter it, but arise and go to the next thing." Let the past sleep, but let it sleep on the bosom of Christ, and go out into the irresistible future with Him.

There are experiences like this in each of our lives. We are in despair, the despair that comes from actualities, and we cannot lift ourselves out of it. The disciples in this instance had done a downright unforgivable thing; they had gone to sleep instead of watching with Jesus, but He came with a spiritual initiative against their despair and said—"Arise and do the next thing." If we are inspired of God, what is the next thing? To trust Him absolutely and to pray on the ground of His Redemption.

Never let the sense of failure corrupt your new action.

. . . and she brake the cruse, and poured it over his head.
(Mark 14:3)

It was an act no one else saw any occasion for, they said it was
'a waste'. It was not an extraordinary occasion, and yet Mary
broke the box of ointment and spilt the whole thing. It was
not a useful thing, but an act of extravagant devotion, and Jesus
commended her and said wherever His gospel was preached,
this also should be spoken of for a memorial of her.

God spilt the life of His Son that the world might be saved.
Am I prepared to spill my life out for Him? Our Lord is carried
beyond Himself with delight when He sees any of us doing what
Mary did, extravagantly wasting our substance for him; not
set for this or that economy, but being abandoned to Him.

In the Bible there is always a oneness between the spiritual
and the material. It takes the incarnation of the Holy Ghost in
a man's body to make him what Jesus Christ wants him to be.
Unless the blessings of God can deal with our bodies and make
them the temples of the Holy Ghost, then the religion of Jesus
Christ is in the clouds. If I cannot exhibit the sentiment of the
Holy Ghost in the sordid actualities of life and in doing mental
things from the highest motive, I am not learning to pour out
unto the Lord.

'He that believeth on me . . . out of him shall flow . . .'—not,
he shall gain, but hundreds of others shall be continually refreshed. It is time now to break the life, to cease craving for
satisfaction, and to spill the thing out. The Lord is asking for
thousands of us to do it for Him.

PH 130

THE INITIATIVE AGAINST DRUDGERY

Arise, shine. (Isa. 60:1)

We have to take the first step as though there were no God. It is no use to wait for God to help us, He will not; but immediately we arise we find He is there. Whenever God inspires, the initiative is a moral one. We must do the thing and not lie like a log. If we will arise and shine, drudgery becomes divinely transfigured.

Drudgery is one of the finest touchstones of character there is. Drudgery is work that is very far removed from anything to do with the ideal—the utterly mean grubby things; and when we come in contact with them we know instantly whether or not we are spiritually real. Read John 13. We see there the Incarnate God doing the most desperate piece of drudgery, washing fishermen's feet, and He says—"If I then, your Lord and Master, have washed your feet, ye also ought to wash one another's feet." It requires the inspiration of God to go through drudgery with the light of God upon it. Some people do a certain thing and the way in which they do it hallows that thing for ever afterwards. It may be the most commonplace thing, but after we have seen them do it, it becomes different. When the Lord does a thing through us, He always transfigures it. Our Lord took on Him our human flesh and transfigured it, and it has become for every saint the temple of the Holy Ghost.

Wherein ye greatly rejoice, though now for a little while, if need be, ye have been put to grief in manifold temptations. (1 Peter 1:6)

If you know a man who has a good spiritual banking account, borrow from him for all you are worth, because he will give you all you want and never look to be paid back. Here is the reason a saint goes through the things he does go through— God wants to know if He can make him good 'bread' to feed other people with. The man who has gone through the crucible is going to be a tremendous support to hundreds of others . . .

If you have a trial of faith, endure it till you get through. If you have been through trials of faith in the past, God is bringing across your path immature souls, and you have no business to despise them but rather to help them through—be to them something that has to be 'sucked'. 'He perceived that virtue had gone out of him', and you will feel the same thing: there are people who spiritually and morally have to suck the vitals out of you, and if you don't keep up the supply from the life of Jesus Christ, you will be like an exhausted volcano before long. You must keep that up and let them nourish themselves from you until they are able to stand on their own feet and take direct life from Him.

PH 204, 206

THE INITIATIVE AGAINST DREAMING

Arise, let us go hence. (John 14:31)

Dreaming about a thing in order to do it properly is right; but dreaming about it when we should be doing it is wrong. After Our Lord had said those wonderful things to His disciples, we might have expected that He would tell them to go away and meditate over them all; but Our Lord never allowed "mooning." When we are getting into contact with God in order to find out what He wants, dreaming is right; but when we are inclined to spend our time in dreaming over what we have been told to do, it is a bad thing and God's blessing is never on it. God's initiative is always in the nature of a stab against this kind of dreaming, the stab that bids us "neither sit nor stand but go."

If we are quietly waiting before God and He has said —"Come ye yourselves apart," then that is meditation before God in order to get at the line He wants; but always beware of giving over to mere dreaming when once God has spoken. Leave Him to be the source of all your dreams and joys and delights, and go out and obey what He has said. If you are in love, you do not sit down and dream about the one you love all the time, you go and do something for him; and that is what Jesus Christ expects us to do. Dreaming after God has spoken is an indication that we do not trust Him.

> *It is written, Man shall not live by bread alone, but by every word*
> *that proceedeth out of the mouth of God. (Matthew 4:4)*

Our natural reactions are not wrong, although they may be used to express the wrong disposition. God never contradicts our natural reactions; He wants them to be made spiritual. When we are saved God does not alter the construction of our bodily life, but He does expect us to manifest in our bodily life the alteration He has made. We express ourselves naturally through our bodies, and we express the supernatural life of God in the same way, but it can only be done by the sacrifice of the natural. How many of us are spiritual in eating and drinking and sleeping? Those acts were spiritual in our Lord; His relationship to the Father was such that all His natural life was obedient to Him, and when He saw that His Father's will was for Him not to obey a natural reaction, He instantly obeyed His Father (see Matthew 4:1–4).

If our Lord had been fanatical He would have said—'I have been so long without food, I will never eat again.' That would have been to obey a principle instead of God. When God is educating us along the line of turning the natural into the spiritual, we are apt to become fanatical. Because by God's grace things have been done which are miraculous, we become devoted to the miracle and forget God, then when difficulties come we say it is the antagonism of the devil. The fact is we are grossly ignorant of the way God has made us. All that we need is a little of what we understand by pluck in the natural world put into the spiritual. Don't let your body get on top and and say there is nothing after all in what God said. Stand up to the difficulty, and all that you ever believed about the transforming grace of God will be proved in your bodily life.

MFL 68

HAVE YOU EVER BEEN CARRIED AWAY FOR HIM?

She hath wrought a good work on Me. (Mark 14:6)

If human love does not carry a man beyond himself, it is not love. If love is always discreet, always wise, always sensible and calculating never carried beyond itself, it is not love at all. It may be affection, it may be warmth of feeling, but it has not the true nature of love in it.

Have I ever been carried away to do something for God not because it was my duty, not because it was useful, nor because there was anything in it all beyond the fact that I love Him? Have I ever realized that I can bring to God things which are of value to Him, or am I mooning round the magnitude of His Redemption whilst there are any number of things I might be doing? Not Divine, colossal things which could be recorded as marvelous, but ordinary, simple human things which will give evidence to God that I am abandoned to Him? Have I ever produced in the heart of the Lord Jesus what Mary of Bethany produced?

There are times when it seems as if God watches to see if we will give Him the abandoned tokens of how genuinely we do love Him. Abandon to God is of more value than personal holiness. Personal holiness focuses the eye on our own whiteness; we are greatly concerned about the way we walk and talk and look, fearful lest we offend Him. Perfect love casts out all that when once we are abandoned to God. We have to get rid of this notion—"Am I of any use?" and make up our minds that we are not, and we may be near the truth. It is never a question of being of use, but of being of value to God Himself. When we are abandoned to God, He works through us all the time.

Is not this the carpenter's son? is not his mother called Mary? and his brethren, James, and Joses, and Simon, and Judas? And his sisters, are they not all with us? Whence then hath this man all these things?
(Matthew 13:55–56 [See also Mark 3:21; Luke 2:51; John 7:5])

These were the intimates our Lord grew up with in His own historic life. We say, 'Oh, but the Lord must have had a sweet and delightful home life.' But we are wrong: He had an exceedingly difficult home life. Jesus Christ's intimates were brothers and sisters who did not believe in Him, and He says that the disciple is not above his Master (Luke 6:40). The next time you feel inclined to grouse over uncongenial companions, remember that Jesus Christ had a devil in His company for three years.

Our Lord preached His first public sermon in the place where He was brought up, where He was most intimately known, and they smashed up His service and tried to kill Him. 'Oh, but,' we say, 'I expected that when I was saved and sanctified, my father and mother and brothers and sisters would be made right, but instead they seem to be all wrong.' If the mother of our Lord misunderstood Him, and His brethren did not believe in Him, the same things will happen to His life in us, and we must not think it strange concerning the misunderstandings of others. The life of the Son of God in us is brought into the same kind of circumstances that the historic life of Jesus Christ was brought into, and what was true of Him will be true also of His life in us.

PR 44

THE DISCIPLINE OF SPIRITUAL TENACITY

Be still, and know that I am God. (Ps. 46:10)

Tenacity is more than endurance, it is endurance combined with the absolute certainty that what we are looking for is going to transpire. Tenacity is more than hanging on, which may be but the weakness of being too afraid to fall off. Tenacity is the supreme effort of a man refusing to believe that his hero is going to be conquered. The greatest fear a man has is not that he will be damned, but that Jesus Christ will be worsted, that the things He stood for—love and justice and forgiveness and kindness among men—will not win out in the end; the things He stands for look like will-o'-the-wisps. Then comes the call to spiritual tenacity, not to hang on and do nothing, but to work deliberately on the certainty that God is not going to be worsted.

If our hopes are being disappointed just now, it means that they are being purified. There is nothing noble the human mind has ever hoped for or dreamed of that will not be fulfilled. One of the greatest strains in life is the strain of waiting for God. "Because thou has kept the word of my patience."

Remain spiritually tenacious.

Present your bodies a living sacrifice. (Romans 12:1)

If we do not resolutely cast out the natural, the supernatural can never become natural in us. There are some Christians in whom the supernatural and the natural seem one and the same, and you say—Well, they are not one with me, I find the natural at 'loggerheads' with the spiritual. The reason is that the other life has gone through the fanatical stage of cutting off the right arm, gone through the discipline of maiming the natural, completely casting it out, and God has brought it back into its right relationship with the spiritual on top, and the spiritual manifests itself in a life which knows no division into sacred and secular. There is no royal road there, each one has it entirely in his own hands; it is not a question of praying but of performing . . .

'Present your bodies a living sacrifice'—go to the funeral of your own independence. It is not a question of giving up sin, but of giving up my right to myself, my natural independence and self-assertiveness. Immediately I do, the natural cries out and goes through terrific suffering. There are things in me which must go through death or they will abide alone and ruin the personal life (cf. John 12:24). But if I sternly put them through death, God will bring them back into the right inheritance. Jesus says 'If any man will be my disciple, let him deny himself', i.e., deny his right to himself, and a man has to realize Who Jesus Christ is before he will do it. It is the things that are right and noble and good from the natural standpoint that keep us back from God's best. To discern that the natural virtues antagonize surrender to God, is to begin to see where the battle lies. It is going to cost the natural everything, not something.

NKW 104

THE DETERMINATION TO SERVE

The Son of Man came not to be ministered unto, but to minister.
(Matt. 20:28)

Paul's idea of service is the same as Our Lord's: "I am among you as He that serveth," "ourselves your servants for Jesus' sake." We have the idea that a man called to the ministry is called to be a different kind of being from other men. According to Jesus Christ, he is called to be the "doormat" of other men; their spiritual leader, but never their superior. "I know how to be abased," says Paul. This is Paul's idea of service—"I will spend myself to the last ebb for you; you may give me praise or give me blame, it will make no difference." So long as there is a human being who does not know Jesus Christ, I am his debtor to serve him until he does. The mainspring of Paul's service is not love for men, but love for Jesus Christ. If we are devoted to the cause of humanity, we shall soon be crushed and broken-hearted, for we shall often meet with more ingratitude from men than we would from a dog; but if our motive is love to God, no ingratitude can hinder us from serving our fellow men.

Paul's realization of how Jesus Christ had dealt with him is the secret of his determination to serve others. "I was before a perjurer, a blasphemer, an injurious person"—no matter how men may treat me, they will never treat me with the spite and hatred with which I treated Jesus Christ. When we realize that Jesus Christ has served us to the end of our meanness, our selfishness, and sin, nothing that we meet with from others can exhaust our determination to serve men for His sake.

And Jesus called a little child unto him . . . and said . . . Except ye . . . become as little children . . . (Matthew 18:2–3)

A healthy man does not know what health is: a sick man knows what health is, because he has lost it; and a saint rightly related to God does not know what the will of God is because he *is* the will of God. A disobedient soul knows what the will of God is because he has disobeyed. The illustration Jesus gives to His disciples of a saintly life is a little child. Jesus did not put up a child as an ideal, but to show them that ambition has no place whatever in the disposition of a Christian. The life of a child is unconscious in its fullness of life, and the source of its life is implicit love. To be made children over again causes pain because we have to reconstruct our mental ways of looking at things after God has dealt with our heart experience. Some of us retain our old ways of looking at things, and the deliverance is painful. Paul urges that we allow the pain—'Let this mind be in you, which was also in Christ Jesus'; 'bringing into captivity every thought to the obedience of Christ'. It is hard to do it. In the beginning we are so anxious—'Lord, give me a message for this meeting', until we learn that if we live in the centre of God's will, He will give us messages when He likes and withhold them when He likes. We try to help God help Himself to us; we have to get out of the way and God will help Himself to our lives in every detail. Have we learned to form the mind of Christ by the pain of deliverance till we know we are drawing on Him for everything?

IWP 46

THE DELIGHT OF SACRIFICE

I will very gladly spend and be spent for you. (2 Cor. 12:15)

When the Spirit of God has shed abroad the love of God in our hearts, we begin deliberately to identify ourselves with Jesus Christ's interests in other people, and Jesus Christ is interested in every kind of man there is. We have no right in Christian work to be guided by our affinities; this is one of the biggest tests of our relationship to Jesus Christ. The delight of sacrifice is that I lay down my life for my Friend, not fling it away, but deliberately lay my life out for Him and His interests in other people, not for a cause. Paul spent himself for one purpose only—that he might win men to Jesus Christ. Paul attracted to Jesus all the time, never to himself. "I am made all things to all men, that I might by all means save some." When a man says he must develop a holy life alone with God, he is of no more use to his fellow men: he puts himself on a pedestal, away from the common run of men. Paul became a sacramental personality; wherever he went, Jesus Christ helped Himself to his life. Many of us are after our own ends, and Jesus Christ cannot help Himself to our lives. If we are abandoned to Jesus, we have no ends of our own to serve. Paul said he knew how to be a "doormat" without resenting it, because the mainspring of his life was devotion to Jesus. We are apt to be devoted, not to Jesus Christ, but to the things which emancipate us spiritually. That was not Paul's motive. "I could wish myself were accursed from Christ for my brethren"—wild, extravagant—is it? When a man is in love it is not an exaggeration to talk in that way, and Paul is in love with Jesus Christ.

O Lord, thou hast searched me, and known me . . . (Psalm 139:1)

The 139th Psalm ought to be the personal experience of every Christian. My own introspection, or exploration of myself, will lead me astray, but when I realize not only that God knows me, but that He is the only One who does, I see the vital importance of intercessory introspection. Every man is too big for himself, thank God for everyone who realizes it and, like the Psalmist, hands himself over to be searched out by God. We only know ourselves as God searches us. 'God knows me' is different from 'God is omniscient'; the latter is a mere theological statement; the former is a child of God's most precious possession—'O Lord, thou hast searched *me*, and known *me*.'

. . . The Psalmist implies—'Thou art the God of the early mornings, the God of the late at nights; the God of the mountain peaks, the God of the sea; but my God, my soul has further horizons than the early mornings, deeper darkness than the nights of the earth, higher peaks than any mountain, greater depths than any sea—Thou who art the God of all these, be my God. I cannot search to the heights or to the depths; there are motives I cannot trace, dreams I cannot get at; my God, search me out and explore me, and let me know that thou hast.' Look back over your past history with God and you will see that this is the place He has been bringing you to—'God knows me, and I know He does.' You can't shift the man who knows that; there is the sanity of almighty God about him. It is an interpretation of what Jesus Christ said—'The very hairs of your head are all numbered. Fear not therefore . . . '

BE 85, 86

THE DESTITUTION OF SERVICE

Though the more abundantly I love you, the less I be loved.
(2 Cor. 12:15)

Natural love expects some return, but Paul says —I do not care whether you love me or not, I am willing to destitute myself completely, not merely for your sakes, but that I may get you to God. "For ye know the grace of our Lord Jesus Christ, that, though He was rich, yet for your sakes He became poor." Paul's idea of service is exactly along that line—I do not care with what extravagance I spend myself, and I will do it gladly. It was a joyful thing to Paul.

The ecclesiastical idea of a servant of God is not Jesus Christ's idea. His idea is that we serve Him by being the servants of other men. Jesus Christ out-socialists the socialists. He says that in His Kingdom he that is greatest shall be the servant of all. The real test of the saint is not preaching the gospel, but washing disciples' feet, that is, doing the things that do not count in the actual estimate of men but count everything in the estimate of God. Paul delighted to spend himself out for God's interests in other people, and he did not care what it cost. We come in with our economical notions—"Suppose God wants me to go there—what about the salary? What about the climate? How shall I be looked after? A man must consider these things." All that is an indication that we are serving God with a reserve. Paul focuses Jesus Christ's idea of a New Testament saint in his life, viz.: not one who proclaims the Gospel merely, but one who becomes broken bread and poured out wine in the hands of Jesus Christ for other lives.

And thine ears shall hear a word behind thee saying, This is the way, walk ye in it; when ye turn to the right hand, and when ye turn to the left. (Isaiah 30:21)

The surest test of maturity is the power to look back without blinking anything. When we look back we get either hopelessly despairing or hopelessly conceited. The difference between the natural backward look and the spiritual backward look is in what we forget. Forgetting in the natural domain is the outcome of vanity—the only things I intend to remember are those in which I figure as being a very fine person! Forgetting in the spiritual domain is the gift of God. The Spirit of God never allows us to forget what we have been, but He does make us forget what we have attained to, which is quite unnatural. The surest sign that you are growing in mature appreciation of your salvation is that as you look back you never think now of the things you used to bank on before. Think of the difference between your first realization of God's forgiveness, and your realization of what it cost God to forgive you; the hilarity in the one case has been merged into holiness, you have become intensely devoted to God who forgave you.

CHI 86

INFERIOR MISGIVINGS ABOUT JESUS

Sir, Thou hast nothing to draw with. (John 4:11)

"I am impressed with the wonder of what God says, but He cannot expect me really to live it out in the details of my life!" When it comes to facing Jesus Christ on His own merits, our attitude is one of pious superiority—Your ideals are high and they impress us, but in touch with actual things, it cannot be done. Each of us thinks about Jesus in this way in some particular. These misgivings about Jesus start from the amused questions put to us when we talk of our transactions with God—Where are you going to get your money from? How are you going to be looked after? Or they start from ourselves when we tell Jesus that our case is a bit too hard for Him. It is all very well to say "Trust in the Lord," but a man must live, and Jesus has nothing to draw with—nothing whereby to give us these things. Beware of the pious fraud in you which says—I have no misgivings about Jesus, only about myself. None of us ever had misgivings about ourselves; we know exactly what we cannot do, but we do have misgivings about Jesus. We are rather hurt at the idea that He can do what we cannot.

My misgivings arise from the fact that I ransack my own person to find out how He will be able to do it. My questions spring from the depths of my own inferiority. If I detect these misgivings in myself, let me bring them to the light and confess them—"Lord, I have had misgivings about Thee, I have not believed in Thy wits apart from my own; I have not believed in Thine almighty power apart from my finite understanding of it."

Submit yourself to every ordinance of man for the Lord's sake.
(1 Peter 2:13)

Peter's statements in these verses are remarkable, and they are statements the modern Christian does not like. He is outlining what is to be the conduct of saints in relation to the moral institutions based on the government of man by man. No matter, he says, what may be the condition of the community to which you belong, behave yourself as a saint in it. Many people are righteous in connection with human institutions. Paul continually dealt with insubordination in spiritual people. Degeneration in the Christian life comes in because of this refusal to recognize the insistence God places on obedience to human institutions. Take the institution of home life. Home is God's institution, and He says, 'Honour thy father and they mother'; are we fulfilling our duty to our parents as laid down in God's Book? Guard well the central institutions ordained by God, and there will be fewer problems in civilized life. We have to maintain spiritual reality wherever we are placed by the engineering of our circumstances by God; as servants we are to be subject to our masters, to the froward master as well as to the good and gentle.

BE 23

IMPOVERISHED MINISTRY OF JESUS

From whence then hast Thou that living water? (John 4:11)

"The well is deep"—and a great deal deeper than the Samaritan woman knew! Think of the depths of human nature, of human life, think of the depths of the "wells" in you. Have you been impoverishing the ministry of Jesus so that He cannot do anything? Suppose there is a well of fathomless trouble inside your heart, and Jesus comes and says—"Let not your heart be troubled"; and you shrug your shoulders and say, "But, Lord, the well is deep; You cannot draw up quietness and comfort out of it." No, He will bring them down from above. Jesus does not bring anything up from the wells of human nature. We limit the Holy One of Israel by remembering what we have allowed Him to do for us in the past, and by saying, "Of course I cannot expect God to do this thing." The thing that taxes almightiness is the very thing which we as disciples of Jesus ought to believe He will do. We impoverish His ministry the moment we forget He is Almighty; the impoverishment is in us, not in Him. We will come to Jesus as Comforter or as Sympathizer, but we will not come to Him as Almighty.

The reason some of us are such poor specimens of Christianity is because we have no Almighty Christ. We have Christian attributes and experiences, but there is no abandonment to Jesus Christ. When we get into difficult circumstances, we impoverish His ministry by saying—"Of course He cannot do anything," and we struggle down to the deeps and try to get the water for ourselves. Beware of the satisfaction of sinking back and saying—"It can't be done"; you know it can be done if you look to Jesus. The well of your incompleteness is deep, but make the effort and look away to Him.

Bring forth therefore fruits meet for repentance. (Matthew 3:8)

The experimental aspect of Redemption is repentance; the only proof that a man is born from above is that he brings forth 'fruits meet for repentance'. That is the one characteristic of New Testament regeneration, and it hits desperately hard because the Holy Spirit brings conviction on the most humiliating lines. Many a powerless, fruitless Christian life is the result of a refusal to obey in some insignificant thing—'first go'. It is extraordinary what we are brought up against when the Holy Spirit is at work in us, and the thing that fights longest against His demands is my prideful claim to my right to myself. The only sign of regeneration in practical experience is that we begin to make our life in accordance with the demands of God. Jesus Christ did not only come to present what God's normal man should be, He came to make the way for everyone of us to get there, and the gateway is His Cross. I cannot begin by imitating Jesus Christ, but only by being born into His Kingdom; then when I have been regenerated and have received the heredity of the Son of God, I find that His teaching belongs to that heredity, not to my human nature.

All this means great deliberation on our part. God does not expect us to understand these things in order to be saved, salvation is of God's free grace; but He does expect us to do our bit in appreciation of His 'so great salvation'.

CHI 23

DO YE NOW BELIEVE?

By this we believe. . . Jesus answered, Do ye now believe?
(John 16:30-31)

Now we believe. Jesus says—Do you? The time is coming when you will leave Me alone. Many a Christian worker has left Jesus Christ alone and gone into work from a sense of duty, or from a sense of need arising out of his own particular discernment. The reason for this is the absence of the resurrection life of Jesus. The soul has got out of intimate contact with God by leaning to its own religious understanding. There is no sin in it, and no punishment attached to it; but when the soul realizes how he has hindered his understanding of Jesus Christ, and produced for himself perplexities and sorrows and difficulties, it is with shame and contrition he has to come back.

We need to rely on the resurrection life of Jesus much deeper down than we do, to get into the habit of steadily referring everything back to Him; instead of this we make our common-sense decisions and ask God to bless them. He cannot, it is not in His domain, it is severed from reality. If we do a thing from a sense of duty, we are putting up a standard in competition with Jesus Christ. We become a "superior person," and say— "Now in this matter I must do this and that." We have put our sense of duty on the throne instead of the resurrection life of Jesus. We are not told to walk in the light of conscience or of a sense of duty, but to walk in the light as God is in the light. When we do anything from a sense of duty, we can back it up by argument; when we do anything in obedience to the Lord, there is no argument possible; that is why a saint can be easily ridiculed.

Work out your own salvation. (Philippians 2:12)

Our Lord warns that the devout life of a disciple is not a dream, but a decided discipline which calls for the use of all our powers. No amount of determination can give me the new life of God, that is a gift; where the determination comes in is in letting that new life work itself out according to Christ's standard. We are always in danger of confounding what we can do with what we cannot do. We cannot save ourselves, or sanctify ourselves, or give ourselves the Holy Spirit; only God can do that. Confusion continually occurs when we try to do what God alone can do, and try to persuade ourselves that God will do what we alone can do. We imagine that God is going to make us walk in the light; God will not; it is we who must walk in the light. God gives us the power to do it, but we have to see that we use the power. God puts the power and the life into us and fills us with His Spirit, but we have to work it out. 'Work out your own salvation,' says Paul, not, 'work for your salvation', but *'work it out'*; and as we do, we realize that the noble life of a disciple is gloriously difficult and the difficulty of it rouses us up to overcome, not faint and cave in. It is always necessary to make an effort to be noble.

SSM 94

WHAT DO YOU WANT THE LORD TO DO FOR YOU?

Lord, that I may receive my sight. (Luke 18:41)

What is the thing that not only disturbs you but makes you a disturbance? It is always something you cannot deal with yourself. "They rebuked him that he should hold his peace . . . but he cried so much the more." Persist in the disturbance until you get face to face with the Lord Himself; do not deify common sense. When Jesus asks us what we want Him to do for us in regard to the incredible thing with which we are faced, remember that He does not work in common sense ways, but in supernatural ways.

Watch how we limit the Lord by remembering what we have allowed Him to do for us in the past: I always failed there, and I always shall; consequently we do not ask for what we want. "It is ridiculous to ask God to do this." If it is an impossibility, it is the thing we have to ask. If it is not an impossible thing, it is not a real disturbance. God will do the absolutely impossible.

This man received his sight. The most impossible thing to you is that you should be so identified with the Lord that there is nothing of the old life left. He will do it if you ask Him. But you have to come to the place where you believe Him to be Almighty. Faith is not in what Jesus says but in Himself; if we only look at what He says we shall never believe. When once we see Jesus, He does the impossible thing as naturally as breathing. Our agony comes through the wilful stupidity of our own heart. We won't believe, we won't cut the shore line, we prefer to worry on.

Why beholdest thou the mote that is in thy brother's eye, but considerest not the beam that is in thine own eye? (Matthew 7:3)

We are all shrewd in pointing out the mote in our brother's eye. It puts us in a superior position, we are finer spiritual characters than they. Where do we find that characteristic? In the Lord Jesus? Never! . . .

We cannot get away from the penetration of Jesus Christ. If I see the mote in my brother's eye, it is because I have a beam in my own. It is a most home-coming statement. If I have let God remove the beam from my own outlook by His mighty grace, I will carry with me the implicit sunlight confidence that what God has done for me He can easily do for you, because you have only a splinter, I had a log of wood! This is the confidence God's salvation gives us, we are so amazed at the way God has altered us that we can despair of no one.

SSM 81

MARCH

THE UNDEVIATING QUESTION

Lovest thou Me? (John 21:17)

Peter declares nothing now (cf. Matthew 26:33-35). Natural individuality professes and declares; the love of the personality is only discovered by the hurt of the question of Jesus Christ. Peter loved Jesus in the way in which any natural man loves a good man. That is temperamental love; it may go deep into the individuality, but it does not touch the centre of the person. True love never professes anything. Jesus said —"Whosoever shall *confess* Me before men," i.e., confess his love not merely by his words, but by everything he does.

Unless we get hurt right out of every deception about ourselves, the word of God is not having its way with us. The word of God hurts as no sin can ever hurt, because sin blunts feeling. The question of the Lord intensifies feeling, until to be hurt by Jesus is the most exquisite hurt conceivable. It hurts not only in the natural way but in the profound personal way. The word of the Lord pierces even to the dividing asunder of soul and spirit; there is no deception left. There is no possibility of being sentimental with the Lord's question; you cannot say nice things when the Lord speaks directly to you, the hurt is too terrific. It is such a hurt that it stings every other concern out of account. There never can be any mistake about the hurt of the Lord's word when it comes to His child; but the point of the hurt is the great point of revelation.

And it came to pass in those days, that he went out into a mountain to pray, and continued all night in prayer to God. And when it was day, he called unto him his disciples. (Luke 6:12–13)

It is not a haphazard thing, but in the constitution of God, that there are certain times of the day when it not only seems easier, but it *is* easier, to meet God. If you have ever prayed in the dawn you will ask yourself why you were so foolish as not to do it always: it is difficult to get into communion with God in the midst of the hurly-burly of the day. George MacDonald said that if he did not open wide the door of his mind to God in the early morning he worked on the finite all the rest of the day— 'stand on the finite, act upon the wrong'. It is not sentiment but an implicit reality that the conditions of dawn and communion with God go together. When the day of God appears there will be no night, always dawn and day. There is nothing of the nature of strain in God's Day, it is all free and beautiful and fine. 'And there shall be night no more' . . .

We all know when we are at our best intellectually, and if instead of giving that time to God we give it to our own development, we not only rob God, but rob ourselves of the possibility of His life thriving in us. We heard it said that we shall suffer if we do not pray; I question it. What will suffer if we do not pray is the life of God in us; but when we do pray and devote the dawns to God His nature in us develops, there is less self-realization and more Christ-realization.

HGM 87, 88

HAVE YOU FELT THE HURT
OF THE LORD?

Jesus said unto him the third time, Lovest thou Me? (John 21:17)

Have you felt the hurt of the Lord to the uncovered quick, the place where the real sensitiveness of your life is lodged? The devil never hurts there, neither sin nor human affection hurts there, nothing goes through to that place but the word of God. "Peter was grieved because Jesus said unto him the third time. . ." He was awakening to the fact that in the real true centre of his personal life he was devoted to Jesus, and he began to see what the patient questioning meant. There was not the slightest strand of delusion left in Peter's mind, he never could be deluded again. There was no room for passionate utterance, no room for exhilaration or sentiment. It was a revelation to him to realize how much he did love the Lord, and with amazement he said—"Lord, Thou knowest all things." Peter began to see how much he did love Jesus; but he did not say—"Look at this or that to confirm it." Peter was beginning to discover to himself how much he did love the Lord, that there was no one in heaven above or upon earth beneath beside Jesus Christ; but he did not know it until the probing, hurting questions of the Lord came. The Lord's questions always reveal me to myself.

The patient directness and skill of Jesus Christ with Peter! Our Lord never asks questions until the right time. Rarely, but probably at least once, He will get us into a corner where He will hurt us with His undeviating questions, and we will realize that we do love Him far more deeply than any profession can ever show.

Jesus . . . leadeth them up into a high mountain apart by them-selves: and he was transfigured before them. (Mark 9:2)

We all have what are called 'brilliant moments'. We are not always dull, not always contented with eating and drinking. There are times when we are unlike our usual selves, both in the way of depression and of brilliance, when one moment stands out from every other, and we suddenly see the way which we should go. And there is the counterpart in spiritual experience of those times in the natural life. There are tides of the spirit, immortal moments, moments of amazing clearness of vision, and it is by these moments and by what we see then, that we are to be judged. 'While ye have the light, believe on the light,' said Jesus—do not believe what you see when you are not in the light. God is going to judge us by the times when we have been in living communion with Him, not by what we feel like today. God judges us entirely by what we have seen. We are not judged by the fact that we live up to the light of our conscience; we are judged by the Light, Jesus Christ. 'I am the light of the world'; and if we do not know Jesus Christ, we are to blame. The only reason we do not know Him is because we have not bothered our heads about Him. Honestly, does it matter to us whether Jesus lived and died, or did anything at all? 'But there are so many humbugs.' There is no counterfeit without the reality. Is Jesus Christ a fraud? We are to be judged by Him. 'This is the condemnation, that light is come into the world, and men loved the darkness rather than the light.' We are not judged by the light we have, but by the light we have refused to accept. God holds us responsible for what we will not look at. A man is never the same after he has seen Jesus. We are judged by our immortal moments, the moments in which we have seen the light of God.

PH 119

THE UNRELIEVED QUEST

Feed My sheep. (John 21:17)

This is love in the making. The love of God is un-made, it is God's nature. When we receive the Holy Spirit He unites us with God so that His love is manifested in us. When the soul is united to God by the indwelling Holy Spirit, that is not the end; the end is that we may be one with the Father as Jesus was. What kind of oneness had Jesus Christ with the Father? Such a oneness that the Father sent Him down here to be spent for us, and He says—"As the Father hath sent Me, even so send I you."

Peter realizes now with the revelation of the Lord's hurting question that he does love Him; then comes the point—"Spend it out." Don't testify how much you love Me, don't profess about the marvelous revelation you have had, but—"Feed My sheep." And Jesus has some extraordinarily funny sheep, some bedraggled, dirty sheep, some awkward, butting sheep, some sheep that have gone astray! It is impossible to weary God's love, and it is impossible to weary that love in me if it springs from the one centre. The love of God pays no attention to the distinctions made by natural individuality. If I love my Lord I have no business to be guided by natural temperament; I have to feed His sheep. There is no relief and no release from this commission. Beware of counterfeiting the love of God by working along the line of natural human sympathy, because that will end in blaspheming the love of God.

Come unto me. (Matthew 11:28)

We make covenants with ourselves, or with our experiences, or with our transactions—I came out to the penitent form; or, I surrendered to God. That is a covenant of self-idolatry, an attempt to consecrate our earnest consecration to God. It is never a question of covenanting to keep our vows before God, but of our relationship to God Who makes the covenant with us. In the matter of salvation it is God's honour that is at stake, not our honour. Few of us have faith in God, the whole thing is a solemn vow with our religious selves. We promise that we will do what God wants; we vow that we will remain true to Him, and we solemnly mark a text to this effect; but no human being can do it. We have to steadily refuse to promise anything and give ourselves over to God's promise, flinging ourselves entirely on to Him, which is the only possible act of the faith that comes as God's gift. It is a personal relation to God's faith—'between me and thee'. 'Come unto me,' said Jesus. The thing that keeps us from coming is religious self-idolatry.

NKW 63

COULD THIS BE TRUE OF ME?

But none of these things move me, neither count I my life dear unto myself. (Acts 20:24)

It is easier to serve God without a vision, easier to work for God without a call, because then you are not bothered by what God requires; common sense is your guide, veneered over with Christian sentiment. You will be more prosperous and success-ful, more leisure-hearted, if you never realize the call of God. But if once you receive a commission from Jesus Christ, the memory of what God wants will always come like a goad; you will no longer be able to work for Him on the common-sense basis.

What do I really count dear? If I have not been gripped by Jesus Christ, I will count service dear, time given to God dear, my life dear unto myself. Paul says he counted his life dear only in order that he might fulfil the ministry he had received; he refused to use his energy for any other thing. Acts 20:24 states Paul's almost sublime annoyance at being asked to consider himself; he was absolutely indifferent to any consideration other than that of fulfilling the ministry he had received. Prac-tical work may be a competitor against abandonment to God, because practical work is based on this argument—Remem-ber how useful you are here, or—Think how much value you would be in that particular type of work. That attitude does not put Jesus Christ as the Guide as to where we should go, but our judgment as to where we are of most use. Never con-sider whether you are of use; but ever consider that you are not your own but His.

> *. . . the love of God is shed abroad in our hearts by the Holy Ghost which is given unto us. (Romans 5:5)*

This does not mean that when we receive the Holy Spirit He enables us to have the capacity for loving God, but that He sheds abroad in our hearts *the love of God*, a much more fundamental and marvellous thing. It is pathetic the number of people who are piously trying to make their poor human hearts love God! The Holy Spirit sheds abroad in my heart, not the power to love God, but the very nature of God; and the nature of God coming into me makes me part of God's consciousness, not God part of my consciousness. I am unconscious of God because I have been taken up into His consciousness. Paul puts it in Galatians 2:20 (a verse with which we are perfectly familiar, but which none of us will ever fathom, no matter how long we live, or how much we experience of God's grace): 'I am crucified with Christ; nevertheless I live; yet not I, but Christ liveth in me.' . . .

In the Sermon on the Mount Jesus Christ says, in effect, that when as His disciples we have been initiated into the kind of life He lives, we are based on the knowledge that God is our heavenly Father and that He is love. Then there comes the wonderful working out of this knowledge in our lives; it is not that we *won't* worry, but that we have come to the place where we *cannot* worry, because the Holy Spirit has shed abroad the love of God in our hearts, and we find that we can never think of anything our heavenly Father will forget. Although great clouds and perplexities may come, as they did in the case of Job, and of the Apostle Paul, and in the case of every saint, yet they never touch 'the secret place of the Most High'. 'Therefore will not we fear, though the earth be removed, and though the mountains be carried into the midst of the sea.' The Spirit of God has so centred us in God and everything is so rightly adjusted that we do not fear.

BP 218

IS HE REALLY LORD?

. . . so that I might finish my course with joy, and the ministry,
which I have received of the Lord Jesus. (Acts 20:24)

Joy means the perfect fulfillment of that for which I was created and regenerated, not the successful doing of a thing. The joy Our Lord had lay in doing what the Father sent Him to do, and He says—"As My Father hath sent Me, even so am I sending you." Have I received a ministry from the Lord? If so, I have to be loyal to it, to count my life precious only for the fulfilling of that ministry. Think of the satisfaction it will be to hear Jesus say—"Well done, good and faithful servant"; to know that you have done what He sent you to do. We have all to find our niche in life, and spiritually we find it when we receive our ministry from the Lord. In order to do this we must have companied with Jesus; we must know Him as more than a personal Saviour. "I will show him how great things he must suffer *for My sake*."

"Lovest thou Me?" Then—"Feed My sheep." There is no choice of service, only absolute loyalty to Our Lord's commission; loyalty to what you discern when you are in closest contact with God. If you have received a ministry from the Lord Jesus, you will know that the need is never the call: the need is the opportunity. The call is loyalty to the ministry you received when you were in real touch with Him. This does not imply that there is a campaign of service marked out for you, but it does mean that you will have to ignore the demands for service along other lines.

. . . for he himself knew what was in man. (John 2:25)

Our Lord seemed to go so easily and calmly amongst all kinds of men—when He met a man who could sink to the level of Judas He never turned cynical, never lost heart or got discouraged; and when He met a loyal loving heart like John's He was not unduly elated, He never overpraised him. When we meet extra goodness we feel amazingly hopeful about everybody, and when we meet extra badness we feel exactly the opposite; but Jesus 'knew what was in man'. He knew exactly what human beings were like and what they needed; and he saw in them something no one else ever saw—hope for the most degraded. Jesus had a tremendous hopefulness about man.

CHI 96

In Matthew 15, our Lord tells His disciples what the human heart is like—'Out of the heart proceed . . . ' and then follows the ugly catalogue. We say, 'I never felt any of those things in my heart', and we prefer to trust our innocent ignorance rather than Jesus Christ's penetration. Either Jesus Christ must be the supreme Authority on the human heart, or He is not worth listening to. If I make conscious innocence the test, I am likely to come to a place where I will find with a shuddering awakening that what Jesus said is true, and I will be appalled at the possibility of evil in me. If I have never been a blackguard, the reason is a mixture of cowardice and the protection of civilized life; but when I am undressed before God I find that Jesus Christ is right in His diagnosis. As long as I remain under the refuge of innocence, I am living in a fool's paradise.

SSM 27

AMID A CROWD OF PALTRY THINGS

. . . in much patience, in afflictions, in necessities, in distresses.
(2 Cor. 6:4)

It takes Almighty grace to take the next step when there is no vision and no spectator—the next step in devotion, the next step in your study, in your reading, in your kitchen; the next step in your duty, when there is no vision from God, no enthusiasm and no spectator. It takes far more of the grace of God, far more conscious drawing upon God to take that step, than it does to preach the Gospel.

Every Christian has to partake of what was the essence of the Incarnation, he must bring the thing down into flesh and blood actualities and work it out through the finger tips. We flag when there is no vision, no uplift, but just the common round, the trivial task. The thing that tells in the long run for God and for men is the steady persevering work in the unseen, and the only way to keep the life uncrushed is to live looking to God. Ask God to keep the eyes of your spirit open to the Risen Christ, and it will be impossible for drudgery to damp you. Continually get away from pettiness and paltriness of mind and thought out into the thirteenth chapter of St. John's Gospel.

And he, when he is come, will convict the world in respect of sin
. . . because they believe not on me. (John 16:8, 9)

Note what causes you the deepest concern before God. Does social evil produce a deeper concern than the fact that people do not believe on Jesus Christ? It was not social evil that brought Jesus Christ down from heaven, it was the great primal sin of independence of God that brought God's Son to Calvary. Sin is not measured by a law or by a social standard, but by a Person. The Holy Spirit is unmistakable in His working: 'and he, when he is come, will convict the world in respect of sin . . . *because they believe not on me.*' That is the very essence of sin. The Holy Spirit brings moral conviction on that line, and on no other. A man does not need the Holy Spirit to tell him that external sins are wrong, ordinary culture and education will do that; but it does take the Holy Spirit to convict us of sin as our Lord defined it—'*because they believe not on me*'. Sin is not measured by a standard of moral rectitude and uprightness, but by my relationship to Jesus Christ. The point is, am I morally convinced that the only sin there is in the sight of the Holy Ghost, is disbelief in Jesus?

TGR 107

UNDAUNTED RADIANCE

Nay, in all these things, we are more than conquerors through
Him that loved us. (Rom. 8:37)

Paul is speaking of the things that might seem likely to separate or wedge in between the saint and the love of God; but the remarkable thing is that nothing *can* wedge in between the love of God and the saint. These things can and do come in between the devotional exercises of the soul and God and separate individual life from God; but none of them is able to wedge in between the love of God and the soul of the saint. The bedrock of our Christian faith is the unmerited, fathomless marvel of the love of God exhibited on the Cross of Calvary, a love we never can and never shall merit. Paul says this is the reason we are more than conquerors in all these things, supervictors, with a joy we would not have but for the very things which look as if they are going to overwhelm us.

The surf that distresses the ordinary swimmer produces in the surf-rider the super-joy of going clean through it. Apply that to our own circumstances, these very things—tribulation, distress, persecution, produce in us the super-joy; they are not things to fight. We are more than conquerors through Him *in* all these things, not in spite of them, but in the midst of them. The saint never knows the joy of the Lord in spite of tribulation, but *because* of it—"I am exceeding joyful in all our tribulation," says Paul.

Undaunted radiance is not built on anything passing, but on the love of God that nothing can alter. The experiences of life, terrible or monotonous, are impotent to touch the love of God, which is in Christ Jesus our Lord.

I have set watchmen upon thy walls, O Jerusalem; they shall never hold their peace day nor night: ye that are the Lord's remembrancers, take ye no rest, and give him no rest, till he establish, and till he make Jerusalem a praise in the earth. (Isaiah 62:6–7)

Do I know anything experimentally about this aspect of things? Have I ever spent one minute before God in intercessory importunity over the sins of other people? If we take this statement of the prophet and turn the searchlight on ourselves, we will be covered with shame and confusion because of our miserably selfish, self-centred Christianity.

How many of us have ever entered into this Ministry of the Interior where we become identified with our Lord and with the Holy Spirit in intercession? It is a threefold intercession: at the Throne of God, Jesus Christ; within the saint, the Holy Ghost; outside the saint, common-sense circumstances and common-sense people, and as these are brought before God in prayer the Holy Spirit gets a chance to make intercession according to the will of God. That is the meaning of personal sanctification, and that is why the barriers of personal testimony must be broken away and effaced by the realization of why we are sanctified—not to be fussy workers for God, but to be His servants, and this is the work, vicarious intercession.

One of the first lessons we learn in the Ministry of the Interior is to talk things out before God in soliloquy—tell God what you know He knows in order that you may get to know it as He does. All the harshness will go and the suffering sadness of God's Spirit will take its place, and gradually you will be brought into sympathy with His point of view.

When God puts a weight on you for intercession for souls don't shirk it by talking to them. It is much easier to talk to them than to talk to God about them—much easier to talk to them than to take it before God and let the weight crush the life out of you until gradually and patiently God lifts the life out of the mire. That is where very few of us go.

GW 20

THE RELINQUISHED LIFE

I am crucified with Christ. (Gal. 2:20)

No one is ever united with Jesus Christ until he is willing to relinquish not sin only, but his whole way of looking at things. To be born from above of the Spirit of God means that we must let go before we lay hold, and in the first stages it is the relinquishing of all pretence. What Our Lord wants us to present to Him is not goodness, nor honesty, nor endeavour, but real solid sin; that is all He can take from us. And what does He give in exchange for our sin? Real solid righteousness. But we must relinquish all pretence of being anything all claim of being worthy of God's consideration.

Then the Spirit of God will show us what further there is to relinquish. There will have to be the relinquishing of my claim to my right to myself in every phase. Am I willing to relinquish my hold on all I possess, my hold on my affections, and on everything, and to be identified with the death of Jesus Christ?

There is always a sharp painful disillusionment to go through before we do relinquish. When a man really sees himself as the Lord sees him, it is not the abominable sins of the flesh that shock him, but the awful nature of the pride of his own heart against Jesus Christ. When he sees himself in the light of the Lord, the shame and the horror and the desperate conviction come home.

If you are up against the question of relinquishing, go through the crisis, relinquish all, and God will make you fit for all that He requires of you.

Ye believe in God, believe also in me. (John 14:1)

We begin our religious life by believing our beliefs, we accept what we are taught without questioning; but when we come up against things we begin to be critical, and find out that the beliefs, however right, are not right for us because we have not bought them by suffering. What we take for granted is never ours until we have bought it by pain. A thing is worth just what it costs. When we go through the suffering of experience we seem to lose everything, but bit by bit we get it back.

It is absurd to tell a man he must believe this and that; in the meantime he can't! Scepticism is produced by telling men what to believe. We are in danger of putting the cart before the horse and saying a man must believe certain things before he can be a Christian; his beliefs are the effect of his being a Christian, not the cause of it. Our Lord's word 'believe' does not refer to an intellectual act, but to a moral act. With Him 'to believe' means 'to commit'. 'Commit yourself to me,' He says, and it takes a man all he is worth to believe in Jesus Christ. The man who has been through a crisis is more likely to commit himself to a Person, he sees more clearly; before the crisis comes we are certain, because we are shallow.

AUG 78

THE TIME OF RELAPSE

Will ye also go away? (John 6:67)

A penetrating question. Our Lord's words come home most when He talks in the most simple way. We know Who Jesus is, but in spite of that He says—"Will ye also go away?" We have to maintain a venturing attitude toward Him all the time.

"From that time many of His disciples went back, and walked no more with Him." They went back from walking with Jesus, not into sin, but they relapsed. Many to-day are spending and being spent in work for Jesus Christ, but they do not walk with Him. The one thing God keeps us to steadily is that we may be one with Jesus Christ. After sanctification the discipline of our spiritual life is along this line. If God gives a clear and emphatic realization to your soul of what He wants, do not try to keep yourself in that relationship by any particular method, but live a natural life of absolute dependence on Jesus Christ. Never try to live the life with God on any other line than God's line, and that line is absolute devotion to Him. The certainty that I do not know—that is the secret of going with Jesus.

Peter only saw in Jesus Someone to minister salvation to him and to the world. Our Lord wants us to be yoke-fellows with Him.

V. 70. Jesus answers the great lack in Peter. We cannot answer for others.

Consider the lilies, how they grow. (Luke 12:27)

Have you ever noticed the kind of pictures God gives to the saints? There are always pictures of creation, never pictures of men. God speaks of the unfailing stars and the upholding of the 'worm Jacob'. He talks about the marvels of creation, and makes His people forget the rush of business ideas that stamp the kingdoms of this world. The Spirit of God says—'Do not take your pattern and print from those; the God who holds you is the God who made the world—take your pattern from Him.'

Our Lord always took His illustrations from His Father's handiwork. In illustrating the spiritual life, our tendency is to catch the tricks of the world, to watch the energy of the business man, and to apply these methods to God's work. Jesus Christ tells us to take the lessons of our lives from the things men never look at—'Consider the lilies'; 'Behold the fowls of the air'. How often do we look at clouds, or grass, at sparrows, or flowers? Why, we have no time to look at them, we are in the rush of things—it is absurd to sit dreaming about sparrows and trees and clouds! Thank God, when He raises us to the heavenly places. He manifests in us the very mind that was in Christ Jesus, unhasting and unresting, calm, steady and strong.

OBH 33

HAVE A MESSAGE AND BE ONE

Preach the word. (2 Tim. 4:2)

We are not saved to be "channels only," but to be sons and daughters of God. We are not turned into spiritual mediums, but into spiritual messengers; the message must be part of ourselves. The Son of God was His own message, His words were spirit and life; and as His disciples our lives must be the sacrament of our message. The natural heart will do any amount of serving, but it takes the heart broken by conviction of sin, and baptized by the Holy Ghost, and crumpled into the purpose of God before the life becomes the sacrament of its message.

There is a difference between giving a testimony and preaching. A preacher is one who has realized the call of God and is determined to use his every power to proclaim God's truth. God takes us out of our own ideas for our lives and we are "batter'd to shape and use," as the disciples were after Pentecost. Pentecost did not teach the disciples anything; it made them the incarnation of what they preached—"Ye shall be witnesses unto Me."

Let God have perfect liberty when you speak. Before God's message can liberate other souls, the liberation must be real in you. Gather your material, and set it alight when you speak.

My heart consulted in me. (Nehemiah 5:7)

Meditation means getting to the middle of a thing; not being like a pebble in a brook letting the water of thought go over us; that is reverie, not meditation. Meditation is an intense spiritual activity, it means bringing every bit of the mind into harness and concentrating its powers; it includes both deliberation and reflection. Deliberation means being able to weigh well what we think, conscious all the time that we are deliberating and meditating. 'My heart consulted in me' (Nehemiah 5:7, marg.)—that is exactly the meaning of meditation, also—'But Mary kept all these things, pondering them in her heart' (Luke 2:19, RV marg.).

A great many delightful people mistake meditation for prayer; meditation often accompanies prayer, but it is not prayer, it is simply the power of the natural heart to get to the middle of things. Prayer is asking, whereby God puts processes to work and creates things which are not in existence until we ask. Prayer is definite talk to God, around which God puts an atmosphere, and we get answers back. Meditation has a reflex action; men without an ounce of the Spirit of God in them can meditate, but that is not prayer. This fundamental distinction is frequently obscured. Mary 'pondered' these things in her heart, i.e., she meditated on them, got right to the centre of the revelations about her Son, but as far as we know, she did not utter a word to anyone. But read St John's Gospel, and a wonder will occur to you. St Augustine has called John's Gospel 'the Heart of Jesus Christ'. Recall what Jesus said to His mother about John: 'Woman, behold, thy son!' and to John about Mary, 'Behold, thy mother! And from that hour the disciple took her unto his own home.' It is surely quite legitimate to think that Mary's meditations found marvellous expression to John under the guidance of the Spirit of God, and found a place in his Gospel and Epistles.

BP 112
145

VISION

I was not disobedient unto the heavenly vision. (Acts 26:19)

If we lose the vision, we alone are responsible, and the way we lose the vision is by spiritual leakage. If we do not run our belief about God into practical issues, it is all up with the vision God has given. The only way to be obedient to the heavenly vision is to give our utmost for God's highest, and this can only be done by continually and resolutely recalling the vision. The test is the sixty seconds of every minute, and the sixty minutes of every hour, not our times of prayer and devotional meetings.

"Though it tarry, wait for it." We cannot attain to a vision, we must live in the inspiration of it until it accomplishes itself. We get so practical that we forget the vision. At the beginning we saw it but did not wait for it; we rushed off into practical work, and when the vision was fulfilled, we did not see it. Waiting for the vision that tarries is the test of our loyalty to God. It is at the peril of our soul's welfare that we get caught up in practical work and miss the fulfillment of the vision.

Watch God's cyclones. The only way God sows His saints is by His whirlwind. Are you going to prove an empty pod? It will depend on whether or not you are actually living in the light of what you have seen. Let God fling you out, and do not go until He does. If you select your own spot, you will prove an empty pod. If God sows you, you will bring forth fruit.

It is essential to practise the walk of the feet in the light of the vision.

And God said . . . Let it not be grievous in thy sight. (Genesis 21:12)

The dilemmas of our personal life with God are few if we obey and many if we are wilful. Spiritually the dilemma arises from the disinclination for discipline; every time I refuse to discipline my natural self, I become less and less of a person and more and more of an independent, impertinent individual. Individuality is the characteristic of the natural man; personality is the characteristic of the spiritual man. That is why our Lord can never be defined in terms of individuality, but only in terms of personality. Individuality is the characteristic of the child, it is the husk of the personal life. It is all 'elbows', it separates and isolates; personality can merge and be blended. The shell of individuality is God's created covering for the protection of the personal life, but individuality must go in order that the personal life may be brought out into fellowship with God— 'that they may be one, even as We are one'.

NKW 101

If we have never been hurt by a statement of Jesus, it is questionable whether we have ever really heard Him speak. Jesus Christ has no tenderness whatever towards anything that is ultimately going to ruin a man for the service of God. If the Spirit of God brings to our mind a word of the Lord that hurts, we may be perfectly certain there is something He wants to hurt to death.

SSY 50

ABANDONMENT

*Then Peter began to say unto Him, Lo, we have left all, and have
followed Thee. (Mark 10:28)*

Our Lord replies in effect, that abandonment is for Himself, and
not for what the disciples themselves will get from it. Beware
of an abandonment which has the commercial spirit in it—"I
am going to give myself to God because I want to be delivered
from sin, because I want to be made holy." All that is the result of being right with God, but that spirit is not of the essential nature of Christianity. Abandonment is not for anything
at all. We have got so commercialized that we only go to God
for something from Him, and not for Himself. It is like saying
"No, Lord, I don't want Thee, I want myself; but I want myself
clean and filled with the Holy Ghost; I want to be put in Thy
showroom and be able to say—'This is what God has done for
me.'" If we only give up something to God because we want
more back, there is nothing of the Holy Spirit in our abandonment; it is miserable commercial self-interest. That we gain
heaven, that we are delivered from sin, that we are made useful to God—these things never enter as considerations into real
abandonment, which is a personal sovereign preference for
Jesus Christ Himself.

When we come up against the barriers of natural relationship, where is Jesus Christ? Most of us desert Him—"Yes, Lord,
I did hear Thy call; but my mother is in the road, my wife, my
self-interest, and I can go no further." "Then," Jesus says, "you
cannot be My disciple."

The test of abandonment is always over the neck of natural
devotion. Go over it, and God's own abandonment will embrace all those you had to hurt in abandoning. Beware of stopping short of abandonment to God. Most of us know abandonment in vision only.

As the Father taught me, I speak these things. (John 8:28 [RV])

The secret of our Lord's holy speech was that He habitually submitted His intelligence to His Father. Whenever problems pressed on the human side, as they did in the temptation, our Lord had within Himself the Divine remembrance that every problem had been solved in counsel with His Father before He became Incarnate (cf. Revelation 13:8), and that therefore the one thing for Him was to do the will of His Father, and to do it in His Father's way. Satan tried to hasten Him, tried to make Him face the problems as a Man and do God's will in His own way: 'The Son can do nothing of himself, but what he seeth the Father doing' (John 5:19, RV).

Are we intellectually insubordinate, spiritually stiffnecked, dictating to God in pious phraseology what we intend to let Him make us, hunting through the Bible to back up our pet theories? Or have we learned the secret of submitting our intelligence and our reasoning to Jesus Christ's word and will as He submitted His mind to His Father?

The danger with us is that we will only submit our minds to New Testament teaching where the light of our experience shines. 'If we walk in the light'—as our experience is in the light? No, 'if we walk in the light *as he is in the light* . . . ' We have to keep in the light that God is in, not in the rays of the light of our experience. There are phases of God's truth that cannot be experienced, and as long as we stay in the narrow grooves of our experience we shall never become God-like, but specialists of certain doctrines—Christian oddities. We have to be specialists in devotion to Jesus Christ and in nothing else. If we want to know Jesus Christ's idea of a saint and to find out what holiness means, we must not only read pamphlets about sanctification, we must face ourselves with Jesus Christ, and as we do so He will make us face ourselves with God.

MFL 109

THE ABANDONMENT OF GOD

God so loved the world that He gave . . . (John 3:16)

Salvation is not merely deliverance from sin, nor the experience of personal holiness; the salvation of God is deliverance out of self entirely into union with Himself. My experimental knowledge of salvation will be along the line of deliverance from sin and of personal holiness; but salvation means that the Spirit of God has brought me into touch with God's personality, and I am thrilled with something infinitely greater than myself, I am caught up into the abandonment of God.

To say that we are called to preach holiness or sanctification, is to get into a side eddy. We are called to proclaim Jesus Christ. The fact that He saves from sin and makes us holy is part of the effect of the wonderful abandonment of God.

Abandonment never produces the consciousness of its own effort, because the whole life is taken up with the One to Whom we abandon. Beware of talking about abandonment if you know nothing about it, and you will never know anything about it until you have realized that John 3:16 means that God gave Himself absolutely. In our abandonment we give ourselves over to God just as God gave Himself for us, without any calculation. The consequence of abandonment never enters into our outlook because our life is taken up with Him.

The young man saith unto him, All these things have I kept from my youth up: what lack I yet? (Matthew 19:20)

In listening to some evangelical addresses the practical conclusion one is driven to is that we have to be great sinners before we can be saved; and the majority of men are not great sinners. The rich young man was an upright, sterling, religious man; it would be absurd to talk to him about sin, he was not in the place where he could understand what it meant. There are hundreds of clean-living, upright men who are not convicted of sin, I mean sin in the light of the commandments Jesus mentioned. We need to revise the place we put conviction of sin in and the place the Spirit of God puts it in. There is no mention of sin in the apprehension of Saul of Tarsus, yet no one understood sin more fundamentally than the Apostle Paul, if we reverse God's order and refuse to put the recognition of who Jesus is first, we present a lame type of Christianity which excludes for ever the kind of man represented by this rich young ruler. The most staggering thing about Jesus Christ is that He makes human destiny depend not on goodness or badness, not on things done or not done, but on who we say He is.

IWP 116

OBEDIENCE

His servants ye are to whom ye obey. (Rom. 6:16)

The first thing to do in examining the power that dominates me is to take hold of the unwelcome fact that I am responsible for being thus dominated. If I am a slave to myself, I am to blame because at a point a way back I yielded to myself. Likewise, if I obey God I do so because I have yielded myself to Him.

Yield in childhood to selfishness, and you will find it the most enchaining tyranny on earth. There is no power in the human soul of itself to break the bondage of a disposition formed by yielding. Yield for one second to anything in the nature of lust (remember what lust is: "I must have it at once," whether it be the lust of the flesh or the lust of the mind)—once yield and though you may hate yourself for having yielded, you are a bondslave to that thing. There is no release in human power at all but only in the Redemption. You must yield yourself in utter humiliation to the only One Who can break the dominating power, viz., the Lord Jesus Christ —"He hath anointed me. . . to preach deliverance to all captives."

You find this out in the most ridiculously small ways —"Oh, I can give that habit up when I like." You cannot, you will find that the habit absolutely dominates you because you yielded to it willingly. It is easy to sing—"He will break every fetter" and at the same time be living a life of obvious slavery to yourself. Yielding to Jesus will break every form of slavery in any human life.

. . . ourselves your servants for Christ's sake. (2 Corinthians 4:5)

We make the mistake of imagining that service for others springs from love of others; the fundamental fact is that supreme love for our Lord alone gives us the motive power of service to any extent for others—'ourselves your servants for Jesus' sake'. That means I have to identify myself with God's interests in other people, and God is interested in some extraordinary people, viz., in you and in me, and He is just as interested in the person you dislike as He is in you. I don't know what your natural heart was like before God saved you, but I know what mine was like. I was misunderstood and misrepresented; everybody else was wrong and I was right. Then when God came and gave me a spring-cleaning, dealt with my sin, and filled me with the Holy Spirit, I began to find an extraordinary alteration in myself. I still think the great marvel of the experience of salvation is not the alteration others see in you, but the alteration you find in yourself. When you come across certain people and things and remember what you used to be like in connection with them, and realize what you are now by the grace of God, you are filled with astonishment and joy; where there used to be a well of resentment and bitterness, there is now a well of sweetness.

CHI 90

THE DISCIPLINE OF DISMAY

And as they followed, they were afraid. (Mark 10:32)

At the beginning we were sure we knew all about Jesus Christ, it was a delight to sell all and to fling ourselves out in a hardihood of love; but now we are not quite so sure. Jesus is out in front and He looks strange: "Jesus went before them and they were amazed."

There is an aspect of Jesus that chills the heart of a disciple to the core and makes the whole spiritual life gasp for breath. This strange Being with His face "set like a flint" and His striding determination, strikes terror into me. He is no longer Counsellor and Comrade, He is taken up with a point of view I know nothing about, and I am amazed at Him. At first I was confident that I understood Him, but now I am not so sure. I begin to realize there is a distance between Jesus Christ and me; I can no longer be familiar with Him. He is ahead of me and He never turns round; I have no idea where He is going, and the goal has become strangely far off.

Jesus Christ had to fathom every sin and every sorrow man could experience, and that is what makes Him seem strange. When we see Him in this aspect we do not know Him, we do not recognize one feature of His life, and we do not know how to begin to follow Him. He is out in front, a Leader Who is very strange, and we have no comradeship with Him.

The discipline of dismay is essential in the life of discipleship. The danger is to get back to a little fire of our own and kindle enthusiasm at it (cf. Isa. 1:10-11). When the darkness of dismay comes, endure until it is over, because out of it will come that following of Jesus which is an unspeakable joy.

What I tell you in the darkness, speak ye in the light: and what ye hear in the ear, proclaim upon the housetops. (Matthew 10:27)

'What I tell you in the darkness . . . ' Let it be understood that the darkness our Lord speaks of is not darkness caused by sin or disobedience, but rather darkness caused from excess of light. There are times in the life of every disciple when things are not clear or easy, when it is not possible to know what to do or say. Such times of darkness come as a discipline to the character and as the means of fuller knowledge of the Lord. Such darkness is a time for listening, not for speaking. This aspect of darkness as a necessary side to fellowship with God is not unusual in the Bible (see Isaiah 5:30; 50:10; 1 Peter 1:6–7). The Lord shares the darkness with His disciple—'What I tell you in the darkness' . . . He is there. He knows all about it. The sense of mystery must always be, for mystery means being guided by obedience to Someone Who knows more than I do. On the Mount of Transfiguration this darkness from excess of light is brought out—'They feared as they entered into the cloud', but in the cloud 'they saw no one any more, save Jesus only with themselves.'

PH 10

THE MASTER ASSIZES

For we must all appear before the judgment seat of Christ.
(2 Cor. 5:10)

Paul says that we must all, preacher and people alike, "appear before the judgment seat of Christ." If you learn to live in the white light of Christ here and now, judgment finally will cause you to delight in the work of God in you. Keep yourself steadily faced by the judgment seat of Christ; walk now in the light of the holiest you know. A wrong temper of mind about another soul will end in the spirit of the devil, no matter how saintly you are. One carnal judgment, and the end of it is hell in you. Drag it to the light at once and say—"My God, I have been guilty there." If you don't, hardness will come all through. The penalty of sin is confirmation in sin. It is not only God who punishes for sin; sin confirms itself in the sinner and gives back full pay. No struggling nor praying will enable you to stop doing some things, and the penalty of sin is that gradually you get used to it and do not know that it is sin. No power save the incoming of the Holy Ghost can alter the inherent consequences of sin.

"But if we walk in the light *as He is in the light.*" Walking in the light means for many of us walking according to our standard for another person. The deadliest Pharisaism to-day is not hypocrisy, but unconscious unreality.

I will give thee the treasures of darkness. (Isaiah 45:3)

We would never have suspected that treasures were hidden there, and in order to get them we have to go through things that involve us in perplexity. There is nothing more wearying to the eye than perpetual sunshine, and the same is true spiritually. The valley of the shadow gives us time to reflect, and we learn to praise God for the valley because in it our soul was restored in its communion with God. God gives us a new revelation of His kindness in the valley of the shadow. What are the days and the experiences that have furthered us most? The days of green pastures, of absolute ease? No, they have their value; but the days that have furthered us most in character are the days of stress and cloud, the days when we could not see our way but had to stand still and wait; and as we waited, the comforting and sustaining and restoring of God came in a way we never imagined possible before.

PH 84

THE WORKER'S RULING PASSION

Wherefore we labour that . . . we may be accepted of Him.
(2 Cor. 5:9)

"Wherefore we *labour* . . ." It is arduous work to keep the master ambition in front. It means holding one's self to the high ideal year in and year out, not being ambitious to win souls or to establish churches or to have revivals, but being ambitious only to be "accepted of Him." It is not lack of spiritual experience that leads to failure, but lack of labouring to keep the ideal right. Once a week at least take stock before God and see whether you are keeping your life up to the standard He wishes. Paul is like a musician who does not need the approval of the audience if he can catch the look of approval from his Master.

Any ambition which is in the tiniest degree away from this central one of being "approved unto God" may end in our being castaways. Learn to discern where the ambition leads, and you will see why it is so necessary to live facing the Lord Jesus Christ. Paul says—"Lest my body should make me take another line, I am constantly watching so that I may bring it into subjection and keep it under" (1 Cor. 9:27).

I have to learn to relate everything to the master ambition, and to maintain it without any cessation. My worth to God in public is what I am in private. Is my master ambition to please Him and be acceptable to Him, or is it something less, no matter how noble?

> *Whosoever shall come after me, let him deny himself, and take up his cross, and follow me. For whosoever will save his life shall lose it: but whosoever shall lose his life for my sake and the gospel's, the same shall save it. (Mark 8:34–5)*

Jesus says if a man gains himself, he loses himself; and if he loses himself for His sake, he gains himself.

Beware of introducing the idea of time; the instant the Spirit of God touches your spirit, it is manifested in the body. Do not get the idea of a three-storied building with a vague, mysterious, ethereal upper story called spirit, a middle story called soul, and a lower story called body. We are personality, which shows itself in three phases—spirit, soul, and body. Never think that what energizes the spirit takes time before it gets into the soul and body, it shows itself instantly, from the crown of the head to the soles of the feet.

Jesus says that men are capable of missing the supreme good and His point of view is not acceptable to us because we do not believe we are capable of missing it. We are far removed from Jesus Christ's point of view today, we take the natural rationalistic line, and His teaching is no good whatever unless we believe the main gist of His gospel, viz., that we have to have something planted into us by supernatural grace. Jesus Christ's point of view is that a man may miss the chief good; we like to believe we will end all right somehow, but Jesus says we won't. If my feet are going in one direction, I cannot advance one step in the opposite direction unless I turn right round.

HG 62

SHALL I ROUSE MYSELF UP TO THIS?

Perfecting holiness in the fear of God. (2 Cor. 7:1)

"Having therefore these promises." I claim the fulfillment of God's promises, and rightly, but that is only the human side; the Divine side is that through the promises I recognize God's claim on me. For instance, am I realizing that my body is the temple of the Holy Ghost, or have I a habit of body that plainly will not bear the light of God on it? By sanctification the Son of God is formed in me, then I have to transform my natural life into a spiritual life by obedience to Him. God educates us down to the scruple. When He begins to check, do not confer with flesh and blood, cleanse yourself at once. Keep yourself cleansed in your daily walk.

I have to cleanse myself from all filthiness of the flesh and spirit until both are in accord with the nature of God. Is the mind of my spirit in perfect agreement with the life of the Son of God in me, or am I insubordinate in intellect? Am I forming the mind of Christ, Who never spoke from His right to Himself, but maintained an inner watchfulness whereby He continually submitted His spirit to His Father? I have the responsibility of keeping my spirit in agreement with His Spirit, and by degrees Jesus lifts me up to where He lived—in perfect consecration to His Father's will, paying no attention to any other thing. Am I perfecting this type of holiness in the fear of God? Is God getting His way with me, and are other people beginning to see God in my life more and more?

Be serious with God and leave the rest gaily alone. Put God first literally.

The waters wear the stones: thou washest away the things which grow out of the dust of the earth: and thou destroyest the hope of man. (Job 14:19)

In physical nature there is something akin to habit. Flowing water hollows out for itself a channel which grows broader and deeper, and after having ceased to flow for a time, it will resume again the path traced before. It is never as easy to fold a piece of paper the first time as after, for after the first time it folds naturally. The process of habit runs all through physical nature, and our brain is physical. When once we understand the bodily machine with which we have to work out what God works in, we find that our body becomes the greatest ally of our spiritual life. The difference between a sentimental Christian and a sanctified saint is just here. The sanctified saint is one who has disciplined the body into perfect obedience to the dictates of the Spirit of God, consequently his body does with the greatest of ease whatever God wants him to do. The sentimental type of Christian is the sighing, tear-flowing, beginning-over-again Christian who always has to go to prayer meetings, always has to be stirred up, or to be soothed and put in bandages, because he has never formed the habit of obedience to the Spirit of God. Our spiritual life does not grow *in spite of* the body, but *because* of the body. 'Of the earth, earthy—is man's glory, not his shame; and it is in the 'earth, earthy' that the full regenerating work of Jesus Christ has its ultimate reach.

MFL 39

THE WAY OF ABRAHAM IN FAITH

·He went out, not knowing whither he went. (Heb. 11:8)

In the Old Testament, personal relationship with God showed itself in separation, and this is symbolized in the life of Abraham by his separation from his country and from his kith and kin. To-day the separation is more of a mental and moral separation from the way that those who are dearest to us look at things, that is, if they have not a personal relationship with God. Jesus Christ emphasized this (see Luke 14:26).

Faith never knows where it is being led, but it loves and knows the One Who is leading. It is a life of *faith*, not of intellect and reason, but a life of knowing Who makes us "go." The root of faith is the knowledge of a Person, and one of the biggest snares is the idea that God is sure to lead us to success.

The final stage in the life of faith is attainment of character. There are many passing transfigurations of character; when we pray we feel the blessing of God enwrapping us and for the time being we are changed, then we get back to the ordinary days and ways and the glory vanishes. The life of faith is not a life of mounting up with wings, but a life of walking and not fainting. It is not a question of sanctification; but of something infinitely further on than sanctification, of faith that has been tried and proved and has stood the test. Abraham is not a type of sanctification, but a type of the life of faith, a tried faith built on a real God. *"Abraham believed God."*

If thou be the Son of God, command that these stones become bread. (Matthew 4:3)

It is this temptation which has betaken the Christian Church today. We worship Man, and God is looked upon as a blessing machine for humanity. We find it in the most spiritual movements of all. For instance, watch how subtly the missionary call has changed. It is not now the watchword of the Moravian call, which saw behind every suffering heathen the Face of Christ: the need has come to be the call. It is not that Jesus Christ said 'Go', but that the heathen will not be saved if we do not go. It is a subtle change that is sagacious, but not spiritual. The need is never the call: the need is the opportunity. Jesus Christ's first obedience was to the will of His Father— 'Lo, in the volume of the Book it is written of me. I delight to do thy will', and, 'As the Father hath sent me, even so send I you.' The saint has to remain loyal to God in the midst of the machinery of successful civilization, in the midst of worldly prosperity, and in the face of crushing defeat . . .

The insinuation of putting men's needs first, success first, has entered into the very domain of evangelism, and has substituted 'the passion for souls' for 'the passion for Christ', and we experience shame when we realize how completely we have muddled the whole thing by not maintaining steadfast loyalty to Jesus Christ.

SHL 95–7

FRIENDSHIP WITH GOD

Shall I hide from Abraham that thing which I do? (Gen. 18:17)

Its Delights. This chapter brings out the delight of real friendship with God as compared with occasional feelings of His presence in prayer. To be so much in contact with God that you never need to ask Him to show you His will, is to be nearing the final stage of your discipline in the life of faith. When you are rightly related to God, it is a life of freedom and liberty and delight, you are God's will, and all your commonsense decisions are His will for you unless He checks. You decide things in perfect delightful friendship with God, knowing that if your decisions are wrong He will always check; when He checks, stop at once.

Its Difficulties. Why did Abraham stop praying when he did? He was not intimate enough yet to go boldly on until God granted his desire, there was something yet to be desired in his relationship to God. Whenever we stop short in prayer and say—"Well, I don't know; perhaps it is not God's will," there is still another stage to go. We are not so intimately acquainted with God as Jesus was, and as He wants us to be—"That they may be one even as we are one." Think of the last thing you prayed about—were you devoted to your desire or to God? Determined to get some gift of the Spirit or to get at God? "Your Heavenly Father knoweth what things ye have need of before ye ask Him." The point of asking is that you may get to know God better. "Delight thyself also in the Lord; and He shall give thee the desires of thine heart." Keep praying in order to get a perfect understanding of God Himself.

Every one that asketh receiveth. (Matthew 7:8)

It appears as if God were sometimes most unnatural; we ask Him to bless our lives and bring benedictions, and what immediately follows turns everything into actual ruin. The reason is that before God can make the heart into a garden of the Lord, He has to plough it, and that will take away a great deal of natural beauty. If we interpret God's designs by our desires, we will say He gave us a scorpion when we asked an egg, and a serpent when we asked a fish, and a stone when we asked for bread. But our Lord indicates that such thinking and speaking is too hasty, it is not born of faith or reliance on God. 'Everyone that asketh receiveth.'

DPR 48

'In everything give thanks,' says Paul, not—Give thanks *for* everything, but give thanks that in everything that transpires there abides the real Presence of God. God is more real than the actual things—'therefore will we not fear, though the earth be removed'. We think that our actual life is profound until something happens—a war or a bereavement, and we are flung clean abroad, then through the agony of the mystery of life we cry out to God and there comes the voice of Jesus—'Come unto Me.'

PH 135

INTEREST OR IDENTIFICATION?

I have been crucified with Christ. (Gal. 2:20)

The imperative need spiritually is to sign the death warrant of the disposition of sin, to turn all emotional impressions and intellectual beliefs into a moral verdict against the disposition of sin, viz., my claim to my right to myself. Paul says—"I have been crucified with Christ"; he does not say—"I have determined to imitate Jesus Christ," or, "I will endeavour to follow Him"—but—"I have been *identified* with Him in His death." When I come to such a moral decision and act upon it, then all that Christ wrought *for* me on the Cross is wrought *in* me. The free committal of myself to God gives the Holy Spirit the chance to impart to me the holiness of Jesus Christ.

". . . nevertheless I live . . ." The individuality remains, but the mainspring, the ruling disposition, is radically altered. The same human body remains, but the old satanic right to myself is destroyed.

"And the life which I now live in the flesh. . .," not the life which I long to live and pray to live, but the life I now live in my mortal flesh, the life which men can see, "I live by the faith of the Son of God." This faith is not Paul's faith in Jesus Christ, but the faith that the Son of God has imparted to him—"*the faith of the Son of God.*" It is no longer faith in faith, but faith which has overleapt all conscious bounds, the identical faith of the Son of God.

I have heard of thee by the hearing of the ear; but now mine eye seeth thee. Wherefore I abhor myself, and repent in dust and ashes. (Job 42:5–6)

Because a man has altered his life it does not necessarily mean that he has repented. A man may have lived a bad life and suddenly stopped being bad, not because he has repented, but because he is like an exhausted volcano. The fact that he has become good is no sign of his having become a Christian. The bedrock of Christianity is repentance. The apostle Paul never forgot what he had been; when he speaks of 'forgetting those things which are behind', he is referring to what he has attained to; the Holy Spirit never allowed him to forget what he had been (see 1 Corinthians 15:9, Ephesians 3:8, 1 Timothy 1:13–15). Repentance means that I estimate exactly what I am in God's sight and I am sorry for it, and on the basis of the Redemption I become the opposite. The only repentant man is the holy man, i.e., the one who becomes the opposite of what he was because something has entered into him. Any man who knows himself knows that he cannot be holy, therefore if he does become holy, it is because God has 'shipped' something into him; he is now 'presenced with Divinity', and can begin to bring forth 'fruits meet for repentance' . . .

'Now mine eye seeth thee,' said Job, 'wherefore I abhor myself' ('I loathe my words' RV marg.) 'and repent in dust and ashes.' When I enthrone Jesus Christ I say the thing that is violently opposed to the old rule. I deny my old ways as entirely as Peter denied his Lord.

Jesus Christ's claim is that He can put a new disposition, His own disposition, Holy Spirit, into any man, and it will be manifested in all that he does. But the disposition of the Son of God can only enter my life by the way of repentance.

BFB 103

THE BURNING HEART

Did not our heart burn within us? (Luke 24:32)

We need to learn this secret of the burning heart. Suddenly Jesus appears to us, the fires are kindled, we have wonderful visions, then we have to learn to keep the secret of the burning heart that will go through anything. It is the dull, bald, dreary, commonplace day, with commonplace duties and people, that kills the burning heart unless we have learned the secret of abiding in Jesus.

Much of our distress as Christians comes not because of sin, but because we are ignorant of the laws of our own nature. For instance, the only test as to whether we ought to allow an emotion to have its way is to see what the outcome of the emotion will be. Push it to its logical conclusion, and if the outcome is something God would condemn, allow it no more way. But if it be an emotion kindled by the Spirit of God and you do not let that emotion have its right issue in your life, it will react on a lower level. That is the way sentimentalists are made. The higher the emotion is, the deeper the degradation will be, if it is not worked out on its proper level. If the Spirit of God has stirred you, make as many things inevitable as possible, let the consequences be what they will. We cannot stay on the mount of transfiguration, but we must obey the light we received there, we must act it out. When God gives a vision, transact business on that line, no matter what it costs.

> We cannot kindle when we will
>   The fire which in the heart resides,
> The spirit bloweth and is still,
>   In mystery our soul abides;
>   But tasks in hours of insight will'd
>   Can be through hours of gloom fulfill'd.

---

*Though our outward man perish, yet the inward man is renewed
day by day. (2 Corinthians 4:16)*

Paul faces the possibility of old age, of decay, and of death, with
no rebellion and no sadness. Paul never hid from himself the
effect which his work had upon him, he knew it was killing
him, and, like his Master, he was old before his time; but there
was no whining and no retiring from the work. Paul was not
a fool, he did not waste his energy ridiculously, neither did he
ignore the fact that it was his genuine apostolic work and
nothing else that was wearing him out. Michelangelo said a
wonderful thing—'the more the marble wears, the better the
image grows', and it is an illustration of this very truth. Every
wasting of nerve and brain in work for God brings a corresponding uplift and strengthening to spiritual muscle and fibre.

MIC 81

AM I CARNALLY MINDED?

Whereas there is among you jealousy and strife, are ye not carnal? (1 Cor. 3:3)

No natural man knows anything about carnality. The flesh lusting against the Spirit that came in at regeneration, and the Spirit lusting against the flesh, produces carnality. "Walk in the Spirit," says Paul, "and ye shall not fulfil the lusts of the flesh"; and carnality will disappear.

Are you contentious, easily troubled about trifles? "Oh, but no one who is a Christian ever is!" Paul says they are, he connects these things with carnality. Is there a truth in the Bible that instantly awakens petulance in you? That is a proof that you are yet carnal. If sanctification is being worked out, there is no trace of that spirit left.

If the Spirit of God detects anything in you that is wrong, He does not ask you to put it right; He asks you to accept the light, and He will put it right. A child of the light confesses instantly and stands bared before God; a child of the darkness says—"Oh, I can explain that away." When once the light breaks and the conviction of wrong comes, be a child of the light, and confess, and God will deal with what is wrong if you vindicate yourself, you prove yourself to be a child of the darkness.

What is the proof that carnality has gone? Never deceive yourself; when carnality is gone it is the most real thing imaginable. God will see that you have any number of opportunities to prove to yourself the marvel of His grace. The practical test is the only proof. "Why," you say, "if this had happened before, there would have been the spirit of resentment!" You will never cease to be the most amazed person on earth at what God has done for you on the inside.

Moreover if thy brother shall trespass against thee, go and tell him his fault between thee and him alone: if he shall hear thee, thou hast gained thy brother. (Matthew 18:15)

It would be an immoral thing to forgive a man who did not say he was sorry. If a man sins against you and you go to him and point out that he has done wrong—if he hears you, then you can forgive him; but if he is obstinate you can do nothing; you cannot say 'I forgive you', you must bring him to a sense of justice. Jesus Christ said, 'I say unto you, Love your enemies', but He also said the most appallingly stern things that were ever uttered, e.g., ' . . . neither will your Father forgive your trespasses.' I cannot forgive my enemies and remain just unless they cease to be my enemies and give proof of their sorrow, which must be expressed in repentance. I have to remain steadfastly true to God's justice. There are times when it would be easier to say, 'Oh well, it does not matter, I forgive you', but Jesus insists that the uttermost farthing must be paid. The love of God is based on justice and holiness, and I must forgive on the same basis.

HGM 104

DECREASING INTO HIS PURPOSE

He must increase, but I must decrease. (John 3:30)

If you become a necessity to a soul, you are out of God's order. As a worker, your great responsibility is to be a friend of the Bridegroom. When once you see a soul in sight of the claims of Jesus Christ, you know that your influence has been in the right direction, and instead of putting out a hand to prevent the throes, pray that they grow ten times stronger until there is no power on earth or in hell that can hold that soul away from Jesus Christ. Over and over again, we become amateur providences, we come in and prevent God; and say—"This and that must not be." Instead of proving friends of the Bridegroom, we put our sympathy in the way, and the soul will one day say—"That one was a thief, he stole my affections from Jesus, and I lost my vision of Him."

Beware of rejoicing with a soul in the wrong thing, but see that you do rejoice in the right thing. "The friend of the Bridegroom. . . rejoiceth greatly because of the Bridegroom's voice: this my joy therefore is fulfilled. He must increase, but I must decrease." This is spoken with joy and not with sadness—at last they are to see the Bridegroom! And John says this is his joy. It is the absolute effacement of the worker, he is never thought of again.

Watch for all you are worth until you hear the Bridegroom's voice in the life of another. Never mind what havoc it brings, what upsets, what crumblings of health, rejoice with divine hilarity when once His voice is heard. You may often see Jesus Christ wreck a life before He saves it. (Cf. Matt. 1034.)

Jesus said unto them, Come ye after me. (Mark 1:17)

We have come to the conclusion nowadays that a man must be a conscious sinner before Jesus Christ can do anything for him. The early disciples were not attracted to Jesus because they wanted to be saved from sin; they had no conception that they needed saving. They were attracted to Him by a dominating sincerity, by sentiments other than those which we say make men come to Jesus. There was nothing theological in their following, no consciousness of passing from death unto life, no knowledge of what Jesus meant when He talked about His Cross. . . . They did not follow Jesus because they wanted to be saved, but because they could not help following. Three years later when again Jesus said, 'Follow me,' it was a different matter; many things had happened during these years. The first 'Follow me' meant an external following; now it was to be a following in internal martydom (see John 21:18–19).

MC 102

THE MOST DELICATE
MISSION ON EARTH

The friend of the Bridegroom. (John 3:29)

Goodness and purity ought never to attract attention to themselves, they ought simply to be magnets to draw to Jesus Christ. If my holiness is not drawing towards Him, it is not holiness of the right order, but an influence that will awaken inordinate affection and lead souls away into side-eddies. A beautiful saint may be a hindrance if he does not present Jesus Christ but only what Christ has done for him. He will leave the impression— "What a fine character that man is!" That is not being a true friend of the Bridegroom; I am increasing all the time, He is not.

In order to maintain this friendship and loyalty to the Bridegroom, we have to be more careful of our moral and vital relationship to Him than of any other thing, even of obedience. Sometimes there is nothing to obey, the only thing to do is to maintain a vital connection with Jesus Christ, to see that nothing interferes with that. Only occasionally do we have to obey. When a crisis arises we have to find out what God's will is, but the greater part of the life is not conscious obedience but the maintenance of this relationship—the friend of the Bridegroom. Christian work may be a means of evading the soul's concentration on Jesus Christ. Instead of being friends of the Bridegroom, we may become amateur providences, and may work against Him whilst we use His weapons.

Blessed be the God and Father of our Lord Jesus Christ, who hath blessed us with all spiritual blessings in heavenly places in Christ. (Ephesians 1:3)

The sanctified saint has to alter the horizon of other people's lives, and he does it by showing that they can be lifted on to a higher plane by the grace of God, viz., into the heavenly places in Christ Jesus. If you look at the Horizon from the sea shore you will not see much of the sea, but climb higher up the cliff, and as you rise higher the horizon keeps level with your eye and you see more in between. Paul is seated in the heavenly places and he can see the whole world mapped out in God's plan. He is looking ahead like a watchman, and his words convey the calm, triumphant contemplation of a conqueror. Some of us get distracted because we have not this world-wide outlook, we see only the little bit inside our own 'bandbox'. The apostle Paul has burst his bandbox, he has been lifted up on to a new plane in Christ Jesus and he sees now from His standpoint. The preacher and the worker must learn to look at life as a whole.

MIC 86

Always keep in contact with those books and those people that enlarge your horizon and make it possible for you to stretch yourself mentally. The Spirit of God is always the spirit of liberty; the spirit that is not of God is the spirit of bondage, the spirit of oppression and depression. The Spirit of God convicts vividly and tensely, but He is always the Spirit of liberty. God Who made the birds never made bird-cages; it is men who make bird-cages, and after a while we become cramped and can do nothing but chirp and stand on one leg. When we get out into God's great free life, we discover that that is the way God means us to live 'the glorious liberty of the children of God'.

MFL 92

VISION BY PERSONAL PURITY

Blessed are the pure in heart; for they shall see God. (Matt. 5:8)

Purity is not innocence, it is much more. Purity is the outcome of sustained spiritual sympathy with God. We have to grow in purity. The life with God may be right and the inner purity remain unsullied, and yet every now and again the bloom on the outside may be sullied. God does not shield us from this possibility, because in this way we realize the necessity of maintaining the vision by personal purity. If the spiritual bloom of our life with God is getting impaired in the tiniest degree, we must leave off everything and get it put right. Remember that vision depends on character—*the pure in heart* see God.

God makes us pure by His sovereign grace, but we have something to look after, this bodily life by which we come in contact with other people and with other points of view, it is these that are apt to sully. Not only must the inner sanctuary be kept right with God, but the outer courts as well are to be brought into perfect accord with the purity God gives us by His grace. The spiritual understanding is blurred immediately the outer court is sullied. If we are going to retain personal contact with the Lord Jesus Christ, it will mean there are some things we must scorn to do or to think, some legitimate things we must scorn to touch.

A practical way of keeping personal purity unsullied in relation to other people is to say to yourself—That man, that woman, *perfect in Christ Jesus*! That friend, that relative, *perfect in Christ Jesus*!

Be still, and know that I am God. (Psalm 46:10)

It is only when our lives are hid with Christ in God that we learn how to be silent unto God, not silent about Him, but silent with the strong restful certainty that all is well, behind everything stands God, and the strength of the soul is that it knows it. There are no panics intellectual or moral. What a lot of panicky sparrows we are, we cannot hear His voice at all—until we learn that wonderful life and music of the Lord Jesus telling us that our heavenly Father is the God of the sparrows, and by the marvellous transformation of grace He can turn the sparrows into His nightingales that can sing through every night of sorrow. A sparrow cannot sing through a night of sorrow, and no soul can sing through a night of sorrow unless it has learned to be silent unto God—one look, one thought about my Father in heaven, and it is all right.

IWP 91

VISION BY PERSONAL CHARACTER

Come up hither, and I will shew thee things. (Rev. 4:1)

An elevated mood can only come out of an elevated habit of personal character. If in the externals of your life you live up to the highest you know, God will continually say—"Friend, go up higher." The golden rule in temptation is—Go higher. When you get higher up, you face other temptations and characteristics. Satan uses the strategy of elevation in temptation, and God does the same, but the effect is different. When the devil puts you into an elevated place, he makes you screw your idea of holiness beyond what flesh and blood could ever bear, it is a spiritual acrobatic performance, you are just poised and dare not move; but when God elevates you by His grace into the heavenly places, instead of finding a pinnacle to cling to, you find a great table-land where it is easy to move.

Compare this week in your spiritual history with the same week last year and see how God has called you up higher. We have all been brought to see from a higher standpoint. Never let God give you one point of truth which you do not instantly live up to. Always work it out, keep in the light of it.

Growth in grace is measured not by the fact that you have not gone back, but that you have an insight into where you are spiritually; you have heard God say "Come up higher," not to you personally, but to the insight of your character.

"Shall I hide from Abraham that thing which I do?" God has to hide from us what He does until by personal character we get to the place where He can reveal it.

Ye are the salt of the earth. (Matthew 5:13)

Some modern teachers seem to think our Lord said 'Ye are the *sugar* of the earth', meaning that gentleness and winsomeness without curative-ness is the ideal of the Christian. It is a disadvantage to be salt. Think of the action of salt on a wound, and you will realize this. If you get salt into a wound, it hurts, and when God's children are amongst those who are 'raw' towards God, their presence hurts. The man who is wrong with God is like an open wound, and when 'salt' gets in it causes annoyance and distress and he is spiteful and bitter. The disciples of Jesus in the present dispensation preserve society from corruption; the 'salt' causes excessive irritation which spells persecution for the saint.

SSM 19

The Spirit of God will not work for the cure of some souls without you, and God is going to hold to the account of some of us the souls that have gone uncured, unhealed, untouched by Jesus Christ because we have refused to keep our souls open towards Him, and when the sensual, selfish, wrong lives came around we were not ready to present the Lord Jesus Christ to them by the power of the Holy Spirit.

WG 28

ISN'T THERE SOME MISUNDERSTANDING?

Let us go into Judea. His disciples say unto Him . . . Goest Thou thither again? (John 11:7-8)

I may not understand what Jesus Christ says, but it is dangerous to say that therefore He was mistaken in what He said. It is never right to think that my obedience to a word of God will bring dishonour to Jesus. The only thing that will bring dishonour is not obeying Him. To put my view of His honour in place of what He is plainly impelling me to do is never right, although it may arise from a real desire to prevent Him being put to open shame. I know when the proposition comes from God because of its quiet persistence: When I have to weigh the pros and cons, and doubt and debate come in, I am bringing in an element that is not of God, and I come to the conclusion that the suggestion was not a right one. Many of us are loyal to our notions of Jesus Christ, but how many of us are loyal to Him? Loyalty to Jesus means I have to step out where I do not see anything (cf. Matt. 14:29); loyalty to my notions means that I clear the ground first by my intelligence. Faith is not intelligent understanding, faith is deliberate commitment to a Person where I see no way.

Are you debating whether to take a step in faith in Jesus or to wait until you can see how to do the thing yourself? Obey Him with glad reckless joy. When He says something and you begin to debate, it is because you have a conception of His honour which is not His honour. Are you loyal to Jesus or loyal to your notion of Him? Are you loyal to what He says, or are you trying to compromise with conceptions which never came from Him? "Whatsoever He saith unto you, *do it.*"

Blessed are they which do hunger and thirst after righteousness:
for they shall be filled. (Matthew 5:6)
Blessed are they which are persecuted for righteousness sake: for
theirs is the kingdom of heaven. (Matthew 5:10)

The majority of us know nothing whatever about the righteousness that is gifted to us in Jesus Christ, we are still trying to bring human nature up to a pitch it cannot reach because there is something wrong with human nature. The old Puritanism which we are apt to ridicule did the same service for men that Pharisaism did for Saul, and that Roman Catholicism did for Luther; but nowadays we have no 'iron' in us anywhere; we have no idea of righteousness, we do not care whether we are righteous or not. We have not only lost Jesus Christ's idea of righteousness, but we laugh at the Bible idea of righteousness; our god is the conventional righteousness of the society to which we belong.

The claim that our Lord was original is hopelessly wrong. He most emphatically took care not to be; He states that He came to fulfil what was already here but undiscerned. 'Think not that I am come to destroy the law, or the prophets: I am come not to destroy, but to fulfil.' That is why it is so absurd to put our Lord as a Teacher first, He is not first a Teacher, He is a Saviour first. He did not come to give us a new code of morals: He came to enable us to keep a moral code we had not been able to fulfil. Jesus did not teach new things; He taught 'as one having authority'—with power to make men into accordance with what He taught. Jesus Christ came to make us holy, not to tell us to be holy: He came to do for us what we could not do for ourselves.

HG 56

OUR LORD'S SURPRISE VISITS

Be ye therefore ready also. (Luke 12:40)

The great need for the Christian worker is to be ready to face Jesus Christ at any and every turn. This is not easy, no matter what our experience is. The battle is not against sin or difficulties or circumstances, but against being so absorbed in work that we are not ready to face Jesus Christ at every turn. That is the one great need, not the facing of our belief, or our creed, or the question whether we are of any use, but to face *Him*.

Jesus rarely comes where we expect Him; He appears where we least expect Him, and always in the most illogical connections. The only way a worker can keep true to God is by being ready for the Lord's surprise visits. It is not service that matters, but intense spiritual reality, expecting Jesus Christ at every turn. This will give our life the attitude of child-wonder which He wants it to have. If we are going to be ready for Jesus Christ, we have to stop being religious (that is, using religion as a higher kind of culture) and be spiritually real.

If you are "looking off unto Jesus," avoiding the call of the religious age you live in, and setting your heart on what He wants, on thinking on His line—you will be called unpractical and dreamy; but when He appears in the burden and the heat of the day, you will be the only one who is ready. Trust no one, not even the finest saint who ever walked this earth, ignore him, if he hinders your sight of Jesus Christ.

In all things approving ourselves as the ministers of God.
(2 Corinthians 6:4)

One of the greatest proofs that you are drawing on the grace of God is that you can be humiliated without manifesting the slightest trace of anything but His grace in you.

2 Corinthians 6, verses 4–10, are Paul's spiritual diary, they describe the outward hardships which proved the hot-bed for the graces of the Spirit—the working together of outward hardships and inward grace. You have been asking the Lord to give you the graces of the Spirit and then some set of circumstances has come and given you a sharp twinge, and you say—'Well, I have asked God to bring out in me the graces of the Spirit, but every time the devil seems to get the better of me.' What you are calling 'the devil' is the very thing God is using to manifest the graces of the Spirit in you.

MIC 96

HOLINESS V. HARDNESS
TOWARDS GOD

And He . . . wondered that there was no intercessor. (Isa. 59:16)

The reason many of us leave off praying and become hard towards God is because we have only a sentimental interest in prayer. It sounds right to say that we pray; we read books on prayer which tell us that prayer is beneficial, that our minds are quieted and our souls uplifted when we pray; but Isaiah implies that God is amazed at such thoughts of prayer.

Worship and intercession must go together, the one is impossible without the other. Intercession means that we rouse ourselves up to get the mind of Christ about the one for whom we pray. Too often instead of worshipping God, we construct statements as to how prayer works. Are we worshipping or are we in dispute with God—'I don't see how You are going to do it." This is a sure sign that we are not worshipping. When we lose sight of God we become hard and dogmatic. We hurl our own petitions at God's throne and dictate to Him as to what we wish Him to do. We do not worship God, nor do we seek to form the mind of Christ. If we are hard towards God, we will become hard towards other people.

Are we so worshipping God that we rouse ourselves up to lay hold on Him so that we may be brought into contact with His mind about the ones for whom we pray? Are we living in a holy relationship to God, or are we hard and dogmatic?

"But there is no one interceding properly"—then be that one yourself, be the one who worships God and who lives in holy relationship to Him. Get into the real work of intercession, and remember it is a work that taxes every power; but a work which has no snare. Preaching the gospel has a snare; intercessory prayer has none.

Jesus of Nazareth, a man approved of God among you . . . Him ye have taken and by wicked hands have crucified and slain. (Acts 2:22–3)

The basis of Christ's character appeals to us all. One of the dangers of denominational teaching is that we are told that before we can be Christians we must believe that Jesus Christ is the Son of God, and that the Bible is the Word of God from Genesis to Revelation. Creeds are the effect of our belief, not the cause of it. I do not have to believe all that before I can be a Christian; but after I have become a Christian I begin to try and expound to myself Who Jesus Christ is, and to do that I must first of all take into consideration the New Testament explanation. 'Blessed art thou, Simon Bar-jona, for flesh and blood hath not revealed it unto thee, but my Father which is in heaven.' The *character* of Jesus Christ was lived on an ordinary plane, and exhibits one side only. To ten men who talk about the character of Jesus there is only one who will talk about His Cross. 'I like the story of Jesus Christ's life. I like the things He said. The Sermon on the Mount is beautiful, and I like to read of the things Jesus did; but immediately you begin to talk about the Cross, about forgiveness of sins, about being born from above, it is out of it.' The New Testament reveals that Jesus Christ is God manifest in the flesh, not a Being with two personalities; He is Son of God (the exact expression of Almighty God) and Son of Man (the presentation of God's normal man). As Son of God He reveals what God is like (John 14:9); as Son of Man He mirrors what the human race will be like on the basis of Redemption—a perfect oneness between God and man (Ephesians 4:13). But when we come to the *Cross* of Jesus Christ, that is outside our domain. If Jesus Christ was only a martyr, the New Testament teaching is stupid.

SA 34

HEEDFULNESS V. HYPOCRISY
IN OURSELVES

*If any man see his brother sin a sin which is not unto death, he
shall ask, and He shall give him life for them that sin not unto
death. (1 John 5:16)*

If we are not heedful of the way the Spirit of God works in us,
we will become spiritual hypocrites. We see where other folks
are failing and we turn our discernment into the gibe of criticism instead of into intercession on their behalf. The revelation is made to us not through the acuteness of our minds, but
by the direct penetration of the Spirit of God, and if we are
not heedful of the source of the revelation, we will become
criticizing centres and forget that God says—". . . he shall ask,
and He shall give him life for them that sin not unto death."
Take care lest you play the hypocrite by spending all your time
trying to get others right before you worship God yourself.

One of the subtlest burdens God ever puts on us as saints is
this burden of discernment concerning other souls. He reveals
things in order that we may take the burden of these souls
before Him and form the mind of Christ about them, and as
we intercede on His line, God says He will give us "life for them
that sin not unto death." It is not that we bring God into touch
with our minds, but that we rouse ourselves until God is able
to convey His mind to us about the one for whom we intercede.

Is Jesus Christ seeing the travail of His soul in us? He cannot
unless we are so identified with Himself that we are roused up
to get His view about the people for whom we pray. May we
learn to intercede so wholeheartedly that Jesus Christ will be
abundantly satisfied with us as intercessors.

The law is spiritual: but I am carnal, sold under sin.
(Romans 7:14)

Talk about conviction of sin! I wonder how many of us have ever had one five minutes' conviction of sin. It is the rarest thing to know of a man or woman who has been convicted of sin. I am not sure but that if in a meeting one or two people came under the tremendous conviction of the Holy Ghost, the majority of us would not advocate they should be put in a lunatic asylum, instead of referring them to the Cross of Christ. We are unfamiliar nowadays with this tremendous conviction of sin, which Paul refers to as being 'sold under sin', but it is not a bit too strong to say that when once the Spirit of God convicts a man of sin, it is either suicide or the Cross of Christ, no man can stand such conviction long. We have any amount of conviction about pride and wrong dealing with one another, but when the Holy Ghost convicts He does not bother us on that line, He gives us the deep conviction that we are living in independence of God, of a death away from God, and we find all our virtues and goodness and religion has been based on a ruinous thing, viz., the boundless inheritance of covetousness. That is what the Fall means. Let it soak into your thinking, and you will understand the marvel of the salvation of Jesus Christ which means deliverance from covetousness, root and branch. Never lay the flattering unction to your soul that because you are not covetous for money or wordly possessions, you are not covetous for anything. The fuss and distress of owning anything is the last remnant of the disposition of sin. Jesus Christ possessed nothing for Himself (see 2 Corinthians 8:9). Right through the warp and woof of human nature is the ruin caused by the disposition of covetousness which entered into the human race through the Fall, and it is this disposition which the Holy Spirit convicts of.

IWP 25

APRIL

HEARTINESS V. HEARTLESSNESS
TOWARDS OTHERS

*It is Christ . . . who also maketh intercession for us. The Spirit
. . . maketh intercession for the saints. (Rom. 8:34, 27)*

Do we need any more argument than this to become intercessors—that Christ "ever liveth to make intercession;" that the Holy Spirit "maketh intercession for the saints"? Are we living in such a vital relationship to our fellow men that we do the work of intercession as the Spirit-taught children of God? Begin with the circumstances we are in—our homes, our business, our country, the present crisis as it touches us and others—are these things crushing us? Are they badgering us out of the presence of God and leaving us no time for worship? Then let us call a halt, and get into such living relationship with God that our relationship to others may be maintained on the line of intercession whereby God works His marvels.

Beware of outstripping God by your very longing to do His will. We run ahead of Him in a thousand and one activities, consequently we get so burdened with persons and with difficulties that we do not worship God, we do not intercede. If once the burden and the pressure come upon us and we are not in the worshipping attitude, it will produce not only hardness toward God but despair in our own souls. God continually introduces us to people for whom we have no affinity, and unless we are worshipping God, the most natural thing to do is to treat them heartlessly, to give them a text like the jab of a spear, or leave them with a rapped-out counsel of God and go. A heartless Christian must be a terrible grief to Our Lord.

Are we in the direct line of the intercession of Our Lord and of the Holy Spirit?

And they come unto thee as the people cometh, and they sit be-fore thee as my people, and they hear thy words, but do them not. (Ezekiel 33:31 [RV])

There are many today who like to hear the word of God spoken straightly and ruggedly; they listen to, and are delighted with, the stern truth about holiness, about the baptism of the Holy Ghost, and deliverance from sin; they say to one another, 'Come, I pray you, and hear what is the word that cometh forth from the Lord.' They take up a pose of religion, but they are not penitent; they change the truth God requires into a mere attitude. God not only requires us to have a right attitude to Him, He requires us to allow His truth to so react in us that we are actively related to Him. These people flocked to Ezekiel like disciples to a teacher, they looked exactly like God's children, the difference was not on the outside but on the inside, and it would take the penetration of God to see it; but it was all pose, they were not real. The real attitude of sin in the heart towards God is that of being without God; it is pride, the worship of myself, that is the great atheistic fact in human life.

I wonder if any of us are among the enchanted but un-changed crowd? We follow any man or woman who speaks the truth of God; in fact, we are so enchanted that we say, 'If you come and hear this man or woman, you will hear the word of God.' But has it ever altered us into an active, living rela-tionship with God or is it altogether pose? If any of us have got the pose of the people of God but are not real, may God deal with us until He brings us into a right relationship to Him-self through the Atonement of the Lord Jesus Christ.

GW 90

THE GLORY THAT EXCELS

The Lord . . . hath sent me that thou mightest receive thy sight.
(Acts 9:17)

When Paul received his sight, he received spiritually an insight into the Person of Jesus Christ, and the whole of his subsequent life and preaching was nothing but Jesus Christ—"I determined not to know anything among you, save Jesus Christ, and Him crucified." No attraction was ever allowed to hold the mind and soul of Paul save the face of Jesus Christ.

We have to learn to maintain an unimpaired state of character up to the last notch revealed in the vision of Jesus Christ.

The abiding characteristic of a spiritual man is the interpretation of the Lord Jesus Christ to himself, and the interpretation to others of the purposes of God. The one concentrated passion of the life is Jesus Christ. Whenever you meet this note in a man, you feel he is a man after God's own heart.

Never allow anything to deflect you from insight into Jesus Christ. It is the test of whether you are spiritual or not. To be unspiritual means that other things have a growing fascination for you.

> Since mine eyes have looked on Jesus,
>   I've lost sight of all beside,
> So enchained my spirit's vision,
>   Gazing on the Crucified.

I live; and yet no longer I, but Christ liveth in me.
(Galatians 2:20)

As long as we use the image of our experience, of our feelings, of our answers to prayer, we shall never begin to understand what the Apostle Paul means when he says, 'I live; and yet no longer I, but Christ liveth in me.' The whole exercise of man's essential reason is drawing on God as the source of life. The hindrance comes when we begin to keep sensuous images spiritually in our minds. Those of us who have never had visions or ecstasies ought to be very thankful. Visions, and any emotions at all, are the greatest snare to a spiritual life, because immediately we get them we are apt to build them round our reasoning, and our reasoning round them and go no further. Over and over again sanctified people stagnate, they do not go back and they do not go on, they stagnate, they become stiller and stiller, and muddier and muddier, spiritually not morally, until ultimately there comes a sort of scum over the spiritual life and you wonder what is the matter with them. They are still true to God, still true to their testimony of what God has done for them, but they have never exercised the great God-given reason that is in them and got beyond the images of their experience into the knowledge that 'God alone is life'—transcending all we call experience. It is because people will not take the labour to think that the snare gets hold of them, and remember, thinking is a tremendous labour (see 2 Corinthians 10:5).

IWP 74

IF THOU HADST KNOWN!

*If thou hadst known . . . in this thy day, the things which belong
unto thy peace! but now they are hid from thine eyes.
(Luke 19:42)*

Jesus had entered into Jerusalem in triumph, the city was
stirred to its foundations; but a strange god was there, the pride
of Pharisaism; it was religious and upright, but a "whited sepulchre."

What is it that blinds me in this "my day"? Have I a strange
god—not a disgusting monster, but a disposition that rules me?
More than once God has brought me face to face with the
strange god and I thought I should have to yield, but I did not
do it. I got through the crisis by the skin of my teeth and I find
myself in the possession of the strange god still; I am blind to
the things which belong to my peace. It is an appalling thing
that we can be in the place where the Spirit of God should be
getting at us unhinderedly, and yet increase our condemnation in God's sight.

"If thou hadst known"—God goes direct to the heart, with
the tears of Jesus behind. These words imply culpable responsibility; God holds us responsible for what we do not see. "Now
they are hid from thine eyes"—because the disposition has
never been yielded. The unfathomable sadness of the "might
have been!" God never opens doors that have been closed. He
opens other doors, but He reminds us that there are doors
which we have shut, doors which need never have been shut,
imaginations which need never have been sullied. Never be
afraid when God brings back the past. Let memory have its way.
It is a minister of God with its rebuke and chastisement and
sorrow. God will turn the "might have been" into a wonderful
culture for the future.

194

Whatsoever a man soweth, that shall he also reap.
(Galatians 6:7)

The words our Lord uttered in reference to Himself are true of every seed that is sown—'Except a corn of wheat fall into the ground and die, it abideth alone; but if it die, it bringeth forth much fruit.' All Christian work, if it is spiritual, must follow that law, because it is the only way God's fruit can be brought forth.

Be endlessly patient. There is nothing more impertinent than our crass infidelity in God. If He does not make us ploughers and sowers and reapers all at once, we lose faith in Him. Modern evangelism makes the mistake of thinking that a worker must plough his field, sow the seed, and reap the harvest in half an hour. Our Lord was never in a hurry with the disciples, He kept on sowing the seed and paid no attention to whether they understood Him or not. He spoke the truth of God, and by His own life produced the right atmosphere for it to grow, and then left it alone, because He knew well that the seed had in it all the germinating power of God and would bring forth fruit after its kind once it was put in the right soil. We are never the same after listening to the truth; we may forget it, but we will meet it again. Sow the Word of God, and everyone who listens will get to God. If you sow vows, resolutions, aspirations, emotions, you will reap nothing but exhaustion '. . . and ye shall sow your seed in vain, for your enemies shall eat it' (Leviticus 26:16); but sow the Word of God, and as sure as God is God, it will bring forth fruit. . . . A man may not grasp all that is said, but something in him is intuitively held by it. See that you sow the real seed of the Word of God, and then leave it alone.

SHL 114

THOSE BORDERS OF DISTRUST

Behold, the hour cometh . . . that ye shall be scattered.
(John 16:32)

Jesus is not rebuking the disciples, their faith was real, but it was disturbed; it was not at work in actual things. The disciples were scattered to their own interests, alive to interests that never were in Jesus Christ. After we have been perfectly related to God in sanctification, our faith has to be worked out in actualities. We shall be scattered, not into work, but into inner desolations and made to know what internal death to God's blessings means. Are we prepared for this? It is not that we choose it, but that God engineers our circumstances so that we are brought there. Until we have been through that experience, our faith is bolstered up by feelings and by blessings. When once we get there, no matter where God places us or what the inner desolations are, we can praise God that all is well. That is faith being worked out in actualities.

". . . and shall leave Me alone." Have we left Jesus alone by the scattering of His providence? Because we do not see God in our circumstances? Darkness comes by the sovereignty of God. Are we prepared to let God do as He likes with us—prepared to be separated from conscious blessings? Until Jesus Christ is Lord, we all have ends of our own to serve; our faith is real, but it is not permanent yet. God is never in a hurry; if we wait, we shall see that God is pointing out that we have not been interested in Himself but only in His blessings. The sense of God's blessing is elemental.

"Be of good cheer, I have overcome the world." Spiritual grit is what we need.

They that are whole need not a physician but they that are sick.
(Luke 5:31)

There is a type of suffering caused because we do not see the way out. A man may say that the basis of things is rational—'Get to the bottom of things and you will find it all simple and easy of explanation'—well, that simply is not true. The basis of things is not rational, but tragic, and when you enter the domain of suffering and sorrow you find that reason and logic are your guide amongst things as they are, but nothing more. Is it rational that I should be born with an heredity over which I have no control? Is it rational that nations that are nominally Christian should be at war? The basis of things is tragic, and the only way out is through the Redemption. Many a man in mental stress of weather is driven to utter what sounds like blasphemy, and yet he may be nearer God than in his complacent acceptance of beliefs that have never been tried. Never be afraid of the man who seems to you to talk blasphemously, he is up against problems you may never have met with; instead of being wrathful, be patient with him. The man to be afraid of is the one who is indifferent, what morality he has got is well within his own grasp, and Jesus Christ is of no account at all.

BE 93

HIS AGONY AND OUR FELLOWSHIP

Then cometh Jesus with them unto a place called Gethsemane,
and saith unto the disciples, . . . tarry ye here, and watch with
Me. (Matt. 26:36, 38)

We can never fathom the agony in Gethsemane, but at least we need not misunderstand it. It is the agony of God and Man in one, face to face with sin. We know nothing about Gethsemane in personal experience. Gethsemane and Calvary stand for something unique; they are the gateway into Life for us.

It was not the death on the cross that Jesus feared in Gethsemane; He stated most emphatically that He came on purpose to die. In Gethsemane He feared lest He might not get through as Son of Man. He would get through as Son of God— Satan could not touch Him there; but Satan's onslaught was that He would get through as an isolated Figure only; and that would mean that He could be no Saviour. Read the record of the agony in the light of the temptation: "Then the devil leaveth Him for a season." In Gethsemane Satan came back and was again overthrown. Satan's final onslaught against our Lord as *Son of Man* is in Gethsemane.

The agony in Gethsemane is the agony of the Son of God in fulfilling His destiny as the Saviour of the world. The veil is drawn aside to reveal all it cost Him to make it possible for us to become sons of God. His agony is the basis of the simplicity of our salvation. The Cross of Christ is a triumph for the *Son of Man*. It was not only a sign that Our Lord had triumphed, but that He had triumphed to save the human race. Every human being can get through into the presence of God now because of what the Son of Man went through.

Ye are they which have continued with me in my temptations.
(Luke 22:28)

Jesus Christ looked upon His life as one of temptation; and He goes through the same kind of temptation in us as He went through in the days of His flesh. The essence of Christianity is that we give the Son of God a chance to live and move and have His being in us, and the meaning of all spiritual growth is that He has an increasing opportunity to manifest Himself in our mortal flesh. The temptations of Jesus are not those of a Man as man, but the temptations of God as Man. 'Wherefore it behoved Him in all things to be made like unto His brethren' (Hebrews 2:17). Jesus Christ's temptations and ours move in different spheres until we become His brethren by being born from above. 'For both He that sanctifieth and they that are sanctified are all of one; for which cause He is not ashamed to call them brethren' (Hebrews 2:11). By regeneration the Son of God is formed in me and He has the same setting in my life as He had when on earth. The honour of Jesus Christ is at stake in my bodily life; am I remaining loyal to Him in the temptations which beset His life in me?

PH 34

Put away the reverential blasphemy that what Jesus Christ feared in Gethsemane was death on the cross. There was no element of fear in His mind about it; He stated most emphatically that He came on purpose for the Cross (Matthew 16:21). His fear in Gethsemane was that He might not get through as Son of Man. Satan's onslaught was that although He would get through as Son of God, it would only be as an isolated Figure; and this would mean that He could be no Saviour.

PR 85

THE COLLISION OF GOD AND SIN

Who His own self bare our sins in His own body on the tree.
(1 Peter 2:24)

The Cross of Jesus is the revelation of God's judgment on sin. Never tolerate the idea of martyrdom about the Cross of Jesus Christ. The Cross was a superb triumph in which the foundations of hell were shaken. There is nothing more certain in Time or Eternity than what Jesus Christ did on the Cross: He switched the whole of the human race back into a right relationship with God. He made Redemption the basis of human life, that is, He made a way for every son of man to get into communion with God.

The Cross did not happen to Jesus: He came on purpose for it. He is "the Lamb slain from the foundation of the world." The whole meaning of the Incarnation is the Cross. Beware of separating God manifest in the flesh from the Son becoming sin. The Incarnation was for the purpose of Redemption. God became incarnate for the purpose of putting away sin; not for the purpose of Self-realization. The Cross is the centre of Time and of Eternity, the answer to the enigmas of both.

The Cross is not the cross of a man but the Cross of God, and the Cross of God can never be realized in human experience. The Cross is the exhibition of the nature of God, the gateway whereby any individual of the human race can enter into union with God. When we get to the Cross, we do not go through it; we abide in the life to which the Cross is the gateway.

The centre of salvation is the Cross of Jesus, and the reason it is so easy to obtain salvation is because it cost God so much. The Cross is the point where God and sinful man merge with a crash and the way to life is opened—but the crash is on the heart of God.

We preach Christ crucified. (1 Corinthians 1:23)

Never confuse the Cross of Christ with the benefits that flow from it. For all Paul's doctrine, his one great passion was the Cross of Christ, not salvation, nor sanctification, but the greatest truth that God so loved the world that He gave His only begotten Son; consequently you never find him artificial, or making a feeble statement. Every doctrine Paul taught had the blood and the power of God in it. There is an amazing force of spirit in all he said because the great passion behind was not that he wanted men to be holy, that was secondary, but that he had come to understand what God meant by the Cross of Christ. If we have the only idea of personal holiness, of being put in God's showroom, we shall never come anywhere near seeing what God wants; but when once we have come where Paul is and God is enabling us to understand what the Cross of Christ means, then nothing can ever turn us (Romans 8:35–9) . . .

Most of our emphasis today is on what our Lord's death means to us: the thing that is of importance is that we understand what God means in the Cross. Paul did not understand the Cross in order that he might receive the life of God; but by understanding the Cross, he received the life. Study the Cross for no other sake than God's sake, and you will be holy without knowing it.

AUG 54, 56

WHY ARE WE NOT TOLD PLAINLY?

*He charged them that they should tell no man what things they
had seen, till the Son of man were risen from the dead.
(Mark 9:9)*

Say nothing until the Son of Man is risen in you—until the life
of the risen Christ so dominates you that you understand what
the historic Christ taught. When you get to the right state on
the inside, the word which Jesus has spoken is so plain that
you are amazed you did not see it before. You could not understand it before, you were not in the place in disposition where
it could be borne.

Our Lord does not hide these things; they are unbearable
until we get into a fit condition of spiritual life. "I have yet many
things to say unto you, but ye cannot bear them now." There
must be communion with His risen life before a particular word
can be borne by us. Do we know anything about the impartation of the risen life of Jesus? The evidence that we do is that
His word is becoming interpretable to us. God cannot reveal
anything to us if we have not His Spirit. An obstinate outlook
will effectually hinder God from revealing anything to us. If
we have made up our minds about a doctrine, the light of God
will come no more to us on that line, we cannot get it. This
obtuse stage will end immediately His resurrection life has its
way with us.

"Tell no man. . ."—so many do tell what they saw on the
mount of transfiguration. They have had the vision and they
testify to it, but the life does not tally with it, the Son of man
is not yet risen in them. I wonder when He is going to be formed
in you and in me?

202

And he, bearing his cross, went forth . . . (John 19:17)

The Cross of Jesus is often wrongly taken as a type of the cross we have to carry. Jesus did not say, 'If any man will come after me, let him take up *my* cross', but, 'let him deny himself, and take up his cross, and follow me'. Our cross becomes our divinely appointed privilege by means of His Cross. We are never called upon to carry His Cross. We have so hallowed the Cross by twenty centuries of emotion and sentiment that it sounds a very beautiful and pathetic thing to talk about carrying our cross. But a wooden cross with iron nails in it is a clumsy thing to carry. The real cross was like that, and do we imagine that the external cross was more ugly than our actual one? Or that the thing that tore our Lord's hands and feet was not really so terrible as our imagination of it?

PR 100

The Cross of Jesus Christ stands unique and alone. His Cross is not our cross. Our cross is that we manifest before the world the fact that we are sanctified to do nothing but the will of God. By means of His Cross, our cross becomes our divinely appointed privilege. It is necessary to emphasize this because there is so much right feeling and wrong teaching abroad on the subject. We are never called upon to carry Christ's Cross: His Cross is the centre of Time and Eternity; the answer to the enigmas of both.

DS 90

HIS RESURRECTION DESTINY

Ought not Christ to have suffered these things, and to enter into His glory? (Luke 24:26)

Our Lord's Cross is the gateway into His life: His Resurrection means that He has power now to convey His life to me. When I am born again from above, I receive from the Risen Lord His very life.

Our Lord's Resurrection destiny is to bring "many sons unto glory." The fulfilling of His destiny gives Him the right to make us sons and daughters of God. We are never in the relationship to God that the Son of God is in; but we are brought by the Son into the relation of sonship. When Our Lord rose from the dead, He rose to an absolutely new life, to a life He did not live before He was incarnate. He rose to a life that had never been before; and His resurrection means for us that we are raised to His risen life, not to our old life. One day we shall have a body like unto His glorious body, but we can know now the efficacy of His resurrection and walk in newness of life. "I would know Him *in the power of His resurrection*."

"As Thou hast given Him power over all flesh, that He should give eternal life to as many as Thou hast given Him." "Holy Spirit" is the experimental name for Eternal Life working in human beings here and now. The Holy Spirit is the Deity in proceeding power Who applies the Atonement to our experience. Thank God it is gloriously and majestically true that the Holy Ghost can work in us the very nature of Jesus if we will obey Him.

For hereunto were ye called: because Christ also suffered for us,
leaving us an example, that ye should follow his steps.
(1 Peter 2:21)

This is the essence of fellowship with His sufferings. 'He suffered for you.' Are you suffering on account of someone else,
or for someone else? Are your agonizing prayers and suffering before the Lord on behalf of that 'distressing case' because
it hurts you, discomforts you, makes you long for release? If
so, you are not in fellowship with His suffering, nor anything
like it. But if your soul, out of love for God, longs for others
and bears with them in a voluntary, vicarious way, then you
have a fellowship Divine indeed.

DS 90

The devotion of the saint is to 'fill up that which is behind of
the afflictions of Christ for His body's sake' . . . How can we fill
up the sufferings that remain behind? 1 John 5:16 is an indication of one way, viz., that of intercession. Remember, no man
has time to pray, he has to take time from other things that
are valuable in order to understand how necessary time for
prayer is. The things that act like thorns and stings in our personal lives will go instantly we pray; we won't feel the smart
any more, because we have got God's point of view about them.
Prayer means that we get into union with God's view of other
people. Our devotion as saints is to identify ourselves with
God's interests in other lives. God pays no attention to our
personal affinities; He expects us to identify ourselves with *His*
interests in others.

PR 96

HAVE I SEEN HIM?

After that He appeared in another form unto two of them.
(Mark 16:12)

Being saved and seeing Jesus are not the same thing. Many are partakers of God's grace who have never seen Jesus. When once you have seen Jesus, you can never be the same, other things do not appeal as they used to do.

Always distinguish between what you see Jesus to be, and what He has done for you. If you only know what He has done for you, you have not a big enough God; but if you have had a vision of Jesus as He is, experiences can come and go, you will endure "as seeing Him Who is invisible." The man blind from his birth did not know Who Jesus was until He appeared and revealed Himself to him. Jesus appears to those for whom He has done something; but we cannot dictate when He will come. Suddenly at any turn He may come. "Now I see Him!"

Jesus must appear to your friend as well as to you; no one can see Jesus with your eyes. Severance takes place where one and not the other has seen Jesus. You cannot bring your friend unless God brings him. Have you seen Jesus? Then you will want others to see Him too. "And they went and told it unto the residue, neither believed they them." You must tell, although they do not believe.

O could I tell, ye surely would believe it!
O could I only say what I have seen!
How should I tell or how can ye receive it,
How, till He bringeth you where I have been?

And when Jesus had received the vinegar, he said, It is finished:
and he bowed his head, and gave up the ghost. (John 19:30)

Death is a great dread. It is easy to say that God is love until death has snatched away your dearest friend, then I defy you to say that God is love unless God's grace has done a work in your soul. Death means extinction of life as we understand it; our dead are gone and have left an aching void behind them. They do not talk to us, we do not feel their touch, and when the bereaved heart cries out, nothing comes back but the hollow echo of its own cry. The heart is raw, no pious chatter, no scientific cant can touch it. It is the physical calamity of death *plus* the thing behind which no man can grasp, that makes death so terrible. We have so taken for granted the comfort that Jesus Christ brings in the hour of death that we forget the awful condition of men apart from that revelation. Do strip your mind and imagination of the idea that we have comfort about the departed apart from the Bible; we have not. Every attempt to comfort a bereaved soul apart from the revelation Jesus Christ brings is a vain speculation. We know nothing about the mystery of death apart from what Jesus Christ tells us; but blessed be the Name of God, what He tells us makes us more than conquerors, so that we can shout the victory through the darkest valley of the shadow that ever a human being can go through.

SHL 24

MORAL DECISION ABOUT SIN

Knowing this, that our old man is crucified with Him, that the body of sin might be destroyed, that henceforth we should not serve sin. (Rom. 6:6)

Co-Crucifixion. Have I made this decision about sin—that it must be killed right out in me? It takes a long time to come to a moral decision about sin, but it is the great moment in my life when I do decide that just as Jesus Christ died for the sin of the world, so sin must die out in me, not be curbed or suppressed or counteracted, but crucified. No one can bring anyone else to this decision. We may be earnestly convinced, and religiously convinced, but what we need to do is to come to the decision which Paul forces here.

Haul yourself up, take a time alone with God, make the moral decision and say—"Lord, identify me with Thy death until I know that sin is dead in me." Make the moral decision that sin in you must be put to death.

It was not a divine anticipation on the part of Paul, but a very radical and definite experience. Am I prepared to let the Spirit of God search me until I know what the disposition of sin is—the thing that lusts against the Spirit of God in me? Then if so, will I agree with God's verdict on that disposition of sin— that it should be identified with the death of Jesus? I cannot reckon myself "dead indeed unto sin" unless I have been through this radical issue of will before God.

Have I entered into the glorious privilege of being crucified with Christ until all that is left is the life of Christ in my flesh and blood? "I am crucified with Christ; nevertheless I live; yet not I, but Christ liveth in me."

For I determined not to know any thing among you, save Jesus Christ, and Him crucified. (1 Corinthians 2:2)

The death of Jesus is the only entrance into the life He lived. We cannot get into His life by admiring Him, or by saying what a beautiful life His was, so pure and holy. To dwell only on His life would drive us to despair. We enter into His life by means of His death. Until the Holy Spirit has had His way with us spiritually, the death of Jesus Christ is an insignificant thing, and we are amazed that the New Testament should make so much of it. The death of Jesus Christ is always a puzzle to unsaved human nature. Why should the Apostle Paul say, 'For I determined not to know any thing among you, save Jesus Christ, and Him crucified'? Because unless the death of Jesus has the meaning the Apostle Paul gave to it, viz., that it is the entrance into His life, the Resurrection has no meaning for us either. The life of Jesus is a wonderful example of a perfect human life, but what is the good of that to us? . . .

We walk about imitating Jesus, but isn't it highly absurd! Before we have taken three steps, we come across lust, pride, envy, jealousy, hatred, malice, anger—things that never were in Him, and we get disheartened and say there is nothing in it. If Jesus Christ came to *teach* the human race only, He had better have stayed away. But if we know Him first as Saviour by being born again, we know that He did not come to teach merely: He came to *make* us what He teaches we should be; He came to *make* us sons of God. He came to give us the right disposition, not to tell us that we ought not to have the wrong one; and the way into all these benedictions is by means of His death.

PR 79–80

MORAL DIVINITY

For if we have been planted together in the likeness of His death,
we shall be also in the likeness of His resurrection. (Rom. 6:5)

Co-Resurrection. The proof that I have been through crucifixion with Jesus is that I have a decided likeness to Him. The incoming of the Spirit of Jesus into me readjusts my personal life to God. The resurrection of Jesus has given Him authority to impart the life of God to me, and my experimental life must be constructed on the basis of His life. I can have the resurrection life of Jesus now, and it will show itself in holiness.

The idea all through the apostle Paul's writings is that after the moral decision to be identified with Jesus in His death has been made, the resurrection life of Jesus invades every bit of my human nature. It takes omnipotence to live the life of the Son of God in mortal flesh. The Holy Spirit cannot be located as a Guest in a house, He invades everything. When once I decide that my "old man" (i.e., the heredity of sin) should be identified with the death of Jesus, then the Holy Spirit invades me. He takes charge of everything, my part is to walk in the light and to obey all that He reveals. When I have made the moral decision about sin, it is easy to reckon actually that I am dead unto sin, because I find the life of Jesus there all the time. Just as there is only one stamp of humanity, so there is only one stamp of holiness, the holiness of Jesus, and it is His holiness that is gifted to me. God puts the holiness of His Son into me, and I belong to a new order spiritually.

Woman, why weepest thou? (John 20:15)

Mary Magdalene was weeping at the sepulchre—what was she asking for? The dead body of Jesus. Of whom did she ask it? Of Jesus Himself, and she did not know Him! Did Jesus give her what she asked for? He gave her something infinitely grander than she had ever conceived—a risen, living impossible-to-die Lord. How many of us have been blind in our prayers? Look back and think of the prayers you thought had not been answered, but now you find God has answered them with a bigger manifestation than you ever dreamed. God has trusted you in the most intimate way He could trust you, with an absolute silence, not of despair but of pleasure, because He saw you could stand a much bigger revelation than you had at the time. Some prayers are followed by silence because they are wrong, others because they are bigger than we can understand. It will be a wonderful moment for some of us when we stand before God and find that the prayers we clamoured for in early days and imagined were never answered, have been answered in the most amazing way, and that God's silence has been the sign of the answer.

IYA 49

MORAL DOMINION

Death hath no more dominion over Him . . . in that He liveth,
He liveth unto God. Likewise reckon ye also yourselves to be dead
indeed unto sin, but alive unto God. (Rom. 6:9-11)

Co-Eternal Life. Eternal life was the life which Jesus Christ exhibited on the human plane, and it is the same life, not a copy of it, which is manifested in our mortal flesh when we are born of God. Eternal life is not a gift from God, eternal life is the gift *of God*. The energy and the power which was manifested in Jesus will be manifested in us by the sheer sovereign grace of God when once we have made the moral decision about sin.

"Ye shall receive the power of the Holy Ghost"—not power as a gift from the Holy Ghost; the power is the Holy Ghost, not something which He imparts. The life that was in Jesus is made ours by means of His Cross when once we make the decision to be identified with Him. If it is difficult to get right with God, it is because we will not decide definitely about sin. Immediately we do decide, the full life of God comes in. Jesus came to give us endless supplies of life: "that ye might be filled with all the fullness of God." Eternal Life has nothing to do with Time, it is the life which Jesus lived when He was down here. The only source of Life is the Lord Jesus Christ.

The weakest saint can experience the power of the Deity of the Son of God if once he is willing to "let go." Any strand of our own energy will blur the life of Jesus. We have to keep letting go, and slowly and surely the great full life of God will invade us in every part, and men will take knowledge of us that we have been with Jesus.

He saith unto him, Feed my sheep. (John 21:17)

After the Resurrection, Jesus Christ did not invite the disciples to a time of communion on the Mount of Transfiguration, He said—'Feed my sheep.' When God gives a man work to do, it is seldom work that seems at all proportionate to his natural ability. Paul, lion-hearted genius though he was, spent his time teaching the most ignorant people. The evidence that we are in love with God is that we identify ourselves with His interests in others, and other people are the exact expression of what we ourselves are; that is the humiliating thing! Jesus Christ came down to a most miserably insignificant people in order to redeem them. When He has lifted us into relationship with Himself, He expects us to identify ourselves with His interests in others.

PR 107

WHAT TO DO UNDER THE CONDITIONS

Cast thy burden upon the Lord. (Ps. 55:22)

We must distinguish between the burden-bearing that is right and the burden-bearing that is wrong. We ought never to bear the burden of sin or of doubt, but there are burdens placed on us by God which He does not intend to lift off, He wants us to roll them back on Him. "Cast that He hath given thee upon the Lord" (R.V. MARG.). If we undertake work for God and get out of touch with Him, the sense of responsibility will be overwhelmingly crushing; but if we roll back on God that which He has put upon us, He takes away the sense of responsibility by bringing in the realization of Himself.

Many workers have gone out with high courage and fine impulses, but with no intimate fellowship with Jesus Christ, and before long they are crushed. They do not know what to do with the burden, it produces weariness, and people say—"What an embittered end to such a beginning!"

"Roll thy burden upon the Lord"—you have been bearing it all; deliberately put one end on the shoulders of God. "The government shall be upon His shoulder." Commit to God "that He hath given thee"; not fling it off, but put it over onto Him and yourself with it, and the burden is lightened by the sense of companionship. Never disassociate yourself from the burden.

Blessed are ye. (Matthew 5:11)

The first time we read the Beatitudes, they appear to be simple and beautiful and un-startling statements, and they go unobserved into the subconscious mind. We are so used to the sayings of Jesus that they slip over us unheeded, they sound sweet and pious and wonderfully simple, but they are in reality like spiritual torpedoes that burst and explode in the subconcious mind, and when the Holy Spirit brings them back to our conscious minds we realize what startling statements they are . . .

The test of discipleship is obedience to the light when these truths are brought to the conscious mind. We do not hunt through the Bible for some precept to obey—Jesus Christ's teaching never leads to making ourselves moral prigs, but we live so in touch with God that the Holy Spirit can continually bring some word of His and apply it to the circumstances we are in. We are not brought to the test until the Holy Spirit brings the word back.

Neither is it a question of applying the Beatitudes literally, but of allowing the life of God to invade us by regeneration, and then soaking our minds in the teaching of Jesus Christ which slips down into the subconscious mind. By and by a set of circumstances will arise when one of Jesus Christ's statements emerges, and instantly we have to decide whether we will accept the tremendous spiritual revolution that will be produced if we do obey this precept of His. If we do obey it, our actual life will become different, and we shall find we have the power to obey if we will. That is the way the Holy Spirit works in the heart of a disciple.

SSM 14

INSPIRED INVINCIBILITY

Take My yoke upon you, and learn of Me. (Matt. 11:29)

"Whom the Lord loveth, He chasteneth." How petty our complaining is! Our Lord begins to bring us into the place where we can have communion with Him, and we groan and say— "O Lord, let me be like other people!" Jesus is asking us to take one end of the yoke—"My yoke is easy, get alongside Me and we will pull together." Are you identified with the Lord Jesus like that? If so, you will thank God for the pressure of His hand.

"To them that have no might He increaseth strength." God comes and takes us out of our sentimentality, and our complaining turns into a paean of praise. The only way to know the strength of God is to take the yoke of Jesus upon us and learn of Him.

"The joy of the Lord is your strength." Where do the saints get their joy from? If we did not know some saints, we would say—"Oh, he, or she, has nothing to bear." Lift the veil. The fact that the peace and the light and the joy of God are there is proof that the burden is there too. The burden God places squeezes the grapes and out comes the wine; most of us see the wine only. No power on earth or in hell can conquer the Spirit of God in a human spirit, it is an inner unconquerableness.

If you have the whine in you, kick it out ruthlessly. It is a positive crime to be weak in God's strength.

Pray ye therefore . . . (Matthew 9:38)

Prayer is simple, prayer is supernatural, and to anyone not related to our Lord Jesus Christ, prayer is apt to look stupid. It does sound unreasonable to say that God will do things in answer to prayer, yet our Lord said that He would. Our Lord bases everything on prayer, then the key to all our work as Christians is, 'Pray ye therefore.'

When we pray for others the Spirit of God works in the unconscious domain of their being that we know nothing about, and the one we are praying for knows nothing about, but after the passing of time the conscious life of the one prayed for begins to show signs of unrest and disquiet. We may have spoken until we are worn out, but have never come anywhere near, and we have given up in despair. But if we have been praying, we find on meeting them one day that there is the beginning of a softening in an enquiry and a desire to know something. It is that kind of intercession that does most damage to Satan's kingdom. It is so slight, so feeble in its initial stages that if reason is not wedded to the light of the Holy Spirit, we will never obey it, and yet it is that kind of intercession that the New Testament places most emphasis on, though it has so little to show for it. It seems stupid to think that we can pray and all that will happen, but remember to whom we pray, we pray to a God who understands the unconscious depths of personality about which we know nothing, and He has told us to pray. The great Master of the human heart said, 'Greater works than these shall he do . . . And whatsoever ye shall ask in my name, that will I do.'

IYA 93

THE RELAPSE OF CONCENTRATION

But the high places were not taken away out of Israel; neverthe-
less the heart of Asa was perfect all his days. (2 Chron. 15:17)

Asa was incomplete in his external obedience; he was right in
the main but not entirely right. Beware of the thing of which
you say—"Oh, that does not matter much." The fact that it does
not matter much to you may mean that it matters a very great
deal to God. Nothing is a light matter with a child of God. How
much longer are some of us going to keep God trying to teach
us one thing? He never loses patience. You say—"I know I am
right with God"; but still the "high places" remain, there is
something over which you have not obeyed. Are you protest-
ing that your heart is right with God, and yet is there something in your life about which He has caused you to doubt?
Whenever there is doubt, quit immediately, no matter what it
is. Nothing is a mere detail.

Are there some things in connection with your bodily life,
your intellectual life, upon which you are not concentrating
at all? You are all right in the main but you are slipshod; there
is a relapse on the line of concentration. You no more need a
holiday from spiritual concentration than your heart needs a
holiday from beating. You cannot have a moral holiday and
remain moral, nor can you have a spiritual holiday and remain
spiritual. God wants you to be entirely His, and this means that
you have to watch to keep yourself fit. It takes a tremendous
amount of time. Some of us expect to "clear the numberless
ascensions" in about two minutes.

Who can understand his errors? cleanse thou me from secret faults. (Psalm 19:12)

Is there some fault God has been checking you about and you have left it alone? Be careful lest it end in a dominant sin. The errors are silent, they creep in on us, and when we stand in the light of Jesus Christ we are amazed to find the conclusions we have come to. The reason is that we have deluded ourselves. This self-security keeps us entirely ignorant of what we really are, ignorant of the things that make the salvation of Jesus Christ necessary. When we say to ourselves—'Oh well, I am no worse than anyone else', that is the beginning; we shall soon produce blindness to our own defects and entrench ourselves around with a fictitious security. Jesus Christ has no chance whatever with the man who has the silent security of self-ignorance. When he hears anyone speak about deliverance from sin, he is untouched—'I have no need to be delivered'. Paul says, 'If our gospel be hid, it is hid to those in whom the god of this world hath blinded their minds'—blinded to everything Jesus Christ stands for, and a man is to blame for getting there.

SHL 56

CAN YOU COME DOWN?

While ye have light, believe in the light. (John 12:36)

We all have moments when we feel better than our best, and we say—"I feel fit for anything; if only I could be like this always!" We are not meant to be. Those moments are moments of insight which we have to live up to when we do not feel like it. Many of us are no good for this workaday world when there is no high hour. We must bring our commonplace life up to the standard revealed in the high hour.

Never allow a feeling which was stirred in you in the high hour to evaporate. Don't put your mental feet on the mantelpiece and say—"What a marvelous state of mind to be in!" Act immediately, do something, if only because you would rather not do it. If in a prayer meeting God has shown you something to do, don't say —"I'll do it": *do it*! Take yourself by the scruff of the neck and shake off your incarnate laziness. Laziness is always seen in cravings for the high hour; we talk about working up to a time on the mount. We have to learn to live in the grey day according to what we saw on the mount.

Don't cave in because you have been baffled once, get at it again. Burn your bridges behind you, and stand committed to God by your own act. Never revise your decisions, but see that you make your decisions in the light of the high hour.

Ye are my friends, if ye do whatsoever I command you.
(John 15:14)

God created man to be His friend. If we are the friends of Jesus we have deliberately and carefully to lay down our life for Him. It is difficult, and thank God it is! When once the relationship of being the friends of Jesus is understood, we shall be called upon to exhibit to everyone we meet the love He has shown to us. Watch the kind of people God brings across your path, you will find it is His way of picturing to you the kind of person you have been to Him.—'You are My child, the friend of My Son, now exhibit to that "hedgehoggy" person the love I exhibited to you when you were like that towards Me; exhibit to that mean, selfish person exactly the love I showed you when you were mean and selfish.' We shall find ample room to eat 'humble pie' all the days of our life. The thing that keeps us going is to recognize the humour of our heavenly Father in it all, and we shall meet the disagreeable person with a spiritual chuckle because we know what God is doing, He is giving us a mirror that we may see what we have been like towards Him; now we have the chance to prove ourselves His friends, and the other person will be amazed and say—'Why, the more I poke her, the sweeter she gets!' and will tumble in where we tumbled in, into the grace of God.

AHW 109

NECK OR NOTHING

Now when Simon Peter heard that it was the Lord he girt his
fisher's coat unto him . . . and did cast himself into the sea.
(John 21:7)

Have you ever had a crisis in which you deliberately and emphatically and recklessly abandoned everything? It is a crisis
of will. You may come up to it many times externally, but it
amounts to nothing. The real deep crisis of abandonment is
reached internally, not externally. The giving up of external
things may be an indication of being in total bondage.

Have you deliberately committed your will to Jesus Christ?
It is a transaction of will, not of emotion; the emotion is simply the gilt-edge of the transaction. If you allow emotion first,
you will never make the transaction. Do not ask God what the
transaction is to be, but make it in regard to the thing you do
see, either in the shallow or the profound place.

If you have heard Jesus Christ's voice on the billows, let your
convictions go to the winds, let your consistency go to the
winds, but maintain your relationship to Him.

If thou seest the oppression of the poor, and violent perverting of judgment and justice in a province, marvel not at the matter: for he that is higher than the highest regardeth; and there be higher than they. (Ecclesiastes 5:8)

All through the Bible the difference between God's order and God's permissive will is brought out. God's permissive will is the things that are now, whether they are right or wrong. If you are looking for justice, you will come to the conclusion that God is the devil; and if the providential order of things today were God's order, then that conclusion would be right. But if the order of things today is God's permissive will, that is quite another matter. God's order is no sin, no Satan, no wrong, no suffering, no pain, no death, no sickness and no limitation: God's providential will is every one of these things—sin, sickness, death, the devil, you and me, and things as they are. God's permissive will is the haphazard things that are on just now in which we have to fight and make character in, or else be damned by. We may kick and yell and say God is unjust, but we are all 'in the soup'. It is no use saying things are not as they are; it is no use being amazed at the providential order to tyranny, it is there. In personal life and in national life God's order is reached through pain, and never in any other way. Why it should be so is another matter, but that it is so is obvious. '. . . though he were a Son, yet learned he obedience by the things which he suffered.'

We have to get hold of God's order in the midst of His permissive will. God is bringing many 'sons' to glory. A son is one who has been through the fight and stood the test and come out sterlingly worthy. The Bible attitude to things is absolutely robust, there is not the tiniest whine about it; there is no possibility of lying like a limp jellyfish on God's providence, it is never allowed for a second. There is always a sting and a kick all through the Bible.

SHH 59

READINESS

God called unto him . . . and he said, Here am I. (Ex. 3:4)

When God speaks, many of us are like men in a fog, we give no answer. Moses' reply revealed that he was somewhere. Readiness means a right relationship to God and a knowledge of where we are at present. We are so busy telling God where we would like to go. The man or woman who is ready for God and His work is the one who carries off the prize when the summons comes. We wait with the idea of some great opportunity, something sensational, and when it comes we are quick to cry—"Here am I." Whenever Jesus Christ is in the ascendant, we are there, but we are not ready for an obscure duty.

Readiness for God means that we are ready to do the tiniest little thing or the great big thing it makes no difference. We have no choice in what we want to do, whatever God's programme may be we are there, ready. When any duty presents itself we hear God's voice as Our Lord heard His Father's voice, and we are ready for it with all the alertness of our love for Him. Jesus Christ expects to do with us as His Father did with Him. He can put us where He likes, in pleasant duties or in mean duties, because the union is that of the Father and Himself. "That they may be one, even as We are one."

Be ready for the sudden surprise visits of God. A ready person never needs to get ready. Think of the time we waste trying to get ready when God has called! The burning bush is a symbol of everything that surrounds the ready soul, it is ablaze with the presence of God.

. . . they saw no man any more, save Jesus only with themselves.
(Mark 9:8)

It was not that they saw no one else, but they saw no one else without seeing Jesus. The identified meaning of life is that we see 'every man perfect in Christ Jesus'. We do not need a trans-figuration experience to see meanness, because we are mean; we do not need a transfiguration experience to see sin, because we are sinners; but we do need a transfiguration experience to see Christ Jesus in the mean, in the sinner, in the all-but-lost, in the wrong and in the evil, so that it can be true of the experience of every saint—'they saw no one any more, save Jesus only with themselves'. That is what contact with Jesus means. It is easy to see the specks and the wrong in others, because we see in others that of which we are guilty ourselves. 'Wherefore thou art without excuse, O man, whosoever thou art that judgest: for wherein thou judgest another, thou condemnest thyself; for thou that judgest dost practise the same things' (Romans 2:1). The greatest cure for spiritual conceit is for God to give us a dose of the 'plague of our own heart'.

What a wonderful thing it will be for us if we enter into the transfigured experience of life! There is never any snare in the man or woman who has seen Jesus. Have you anyone 'save Jesus only' in your cloud? If you have, then it will get darker. You must get to the place where there is 'no one any more, save Jesus only'.

PH 116

IS IT NOT IN THE LEAST LIKELY?

For Joab had turned after Adonijah, though he turned not after Absalom. (1 Kings 2:28)

Joab stood the big test, he remained absolutely loyal and true to David and did not turn after the fascinating and ambitious Absalom, but yet towards the end of his life he turned after the craven Adonijah. Always remain alert to the fact that where one man has gone back is exactly where anyone may go back (see 1 Cor. 10:13). You have gone through the big crisis, now be alert over the least things; take into calculation the "retired sphere of the leasts."

We are apt to say—"It is not in the least likely that having been through the supreme crisis, I shall turn now to the things of the world." Do not forecast where the temptation will come, it is the least likely thing that is the peril. In the aftermath of a great spiritual transaction the "retired sphere of the leasts" begins to tell; it is not dominant, but remember it is there, and if you are not warned, it will trip you up. You have remained true to God under great and intense trials, now beware of the undercurrent. Do not be morbidly introspective, looking forward with dread, but keep alert; keep your memory bright before God. Unguarded strength is double weakness because that is where the "retired sphere of the leasts" saps. The Bible characters fell on their strong points, never on their weak ones.

"Kept by the power of God"—that is the only safety.

*Yea doubtless, and I count all things but loss for the excellency
of the knowledge of Christ Jesus my Lord . . . (Philippians 3:8)*

Paul goes on to state that he not only *estimated* the cost, he experienced it—'for whom I have suffered the loss of all things . . . that I may win Christ, and be found in him, not having mine own righteousness . . . ' Imagine anyone who has seen Jesus Christ transfigured saying he is sorry to find himself mean and ignoble! The more I whine about being a miserable sinner, the more I am hurting the Holy Spirit. It simply means I don't agree with God's judgment of me, I think after all I am rather desirable: God thought me so undesirable that He sent His Son to save me. To discover I am what God says I am ought to make me glad; if I am glad over anything I discover in myself, I am very short-sighted. The only point of rest is in the Lord Himself.

CHI 127

CAN A SAINT SLANDER GOD?

For all the promises of God in Him are yea, and in Him Amen.
(2 Cor. 1:20)

Jesus told the parable of the talents recorded in Matthew 25 as a warning that it is possible for us to misjudge our capacity. This parable has not to do with natural gifts, but with the Pentecostal gift of the Holy Ghost. We must not measure our spiritual capacity by education or by intellect; our capacity in spiritual things is measured by the promises of God. If we get less than God wants us to have, before long we will slander Him as the servant slandered his master "You expect more than You give me power to do; You demand too much of me, I cannot stand true to You where I am placed." When it is a question of God's Almighty Spirit, never say "I can't." Never let the limitation of natural ability come in. If we have received the Holy Spirit, God expects the work of the Holy Spirit to be manifested in us.

The servant justified himself in everything he did and condemned his lord on every point—"Your demand is out of all proportion to what you give." Have we been slandering God by daring to worry when He has said: "Seek ye first the Kingdom of God, and His righteousness; and all these things shall be added unto you"? Worrying means exactly what this servant implied—"I haven't had a decent chance," and the one who is lazy spiritually is captious with God. Lazy people always strike out on an independent line.

Never forget that our capacity in spiritual matters is measured by the promises of God. Is God able to fulfil His promises? Our answer depends on whether we have received the Holy Spirit.

With the mouth confession is made unto salvation. (Romans 10:10)

In the Bible confession and testimony are put in a prominent place, and the test of a man's moral calibre is the 'say so'. I may try and make myself believe a hundred and one things, but they will never be mine until I 'say so'. If I say with my self what I believe and confess it with my mouth, I am lifted into the domain of that thing. This is always the price of spiritual emancipation . . .

'When ye pray, say, Our Father.' 'But I don't feel that God is my Father': Jesus said, 'Say it'—'*say*, Our Father', and you will suddenly discover that He is. The safeguard against moral imprisonment is prayer. Don't pray according to your moods, but resolutely launch out on God, say 'Our Father', and before you know where you are, you are in a larger room. The door into a moral or spiritual emancipation which you wish to enter is a word. Immediately you are prepared to abandon your reserve and say the word, the door opens and in rushes the Godward side of things and you are lifted on to another platform immediately. 'Speech maketh a full man.' If you want to encourage your own life in spiritual things, talk about them. Beware of the reserve that keeps to itself, that wants to develop spirituality alone; spirituality must be developed in the open. Shyness is often unmitigated conceit, an unconscious over-estimate of your own worth; you are not prepared to speak until you have a proper audience. If you talk in the wrong mood, you will remain in the wrong mood and put the 'bastard self' on the throne; but if you talk in the mood which comes from revelation, emancipation will be yours.

PH 209

NOW DON'T HURT THE LORD!

Have I been so long time with you, and yet hast thou not known Me, Philip? (John 14:9)

Our Lord must be repeatedly astounded at us—astounded at how un-simple we are. It is opinions of our own which make us stupid; when we are simple we are never stupid, we discern all the time. Philip expected the revelation of a tremendous mystery, but not in the One Whom he knew. The mystery of God is not in what is going to be, it is now; we look for it presently, in some cataclysmic event. We have no reluctance in obeying Jesus, but it is probable that we are hurting Him by the questions we ask. "Lord, show us the Father." His answer comes straight back—"There He is, always here or nowhere." We look for God to manifest Himself to His children: God only manifests Himself *in* His children. Other people see the manifestation, the child of God does not. We want to be conscious of God; we cannot be conscious of our consciousness and remain sane. If we are asking God to give us experiences, or if conscious experience is in the road, we hurt the Lord. The very questions we ask hurt Jesus because they are not the questions of a child.

"Let not your heart be troubled"—then am I hurting Jesus by allowing my heart to be troubled? If I believe the character of Jesus, am I living up to my belief? Am I allowing anything to perturb my heart, any morbid questions to come in? I have to get to the implicit relationship that takes everything as it comes from Him. God never guides presently, but always now. Realize that the Lord is here *now*, and the emancipation is immediate.

Come unto me. (Matthew 11:28)

The questions that matter in life are remarkably few, and they are all answered by these words 'Come unto me'. Not—'Do this' and 'Don't do that', but 'Come' . . .

Have you ever come to Jesus? Watch the stubbornness of your heart and mind, you will find you will do anything rather than the one simple, childlike thing—Come. Be stupid enough to come, and commit yourself to what Jesus says. The attitude of coming is that the will resolutely lets go of everything and deliberately commits the whole thing to Jesus. At the most unexpected moments there comes the whisper of the Lord— 'Come unto me', and we are drawn to Him. Personal contact with Jesus alters everything. He meets our sins, our sorrows, and our difficulties with the one word—'Come'.

AHW 106

Come after me. (Mark 1:17)

If you do come after Jesus, you will realize that He pays no attention whatever to your natural affinities. One of the greatest hindrances to our coming to Jesus is the talk about temperament, I have never seen the Spirit of God pay any attention to a man's temperament, but over and over again I have seen people make their temperament and their natural affinities a barrier to coming to Jesus. We have to learn that our Lord does not heed our selective natural affinities. The idea that He does heed them has grown from the notion that we have to consecrate our gifts to God. We cannot consecrate what is not ours. The only thing I can give to God is 'my right to myself' (Romans 12:1). If I will give God that, He will make a holy experiment out of me, and God's experiments always succeed. The one mark of a disciple is moral originality. The Spirit of God is a well of water in the disciple, perennially fresh. When once the saint begins to realize that God engineers circumstances, there will be no more whine, but only a reckless abandon to Jesus. Never make a principle out of your own experience; let God be as original with other people as He is with you.

AHW 104

THE LIGHT THAT FAILS

We all with open face beholding . . . the glory of the Lord.
(2 Cor. 3:18)

A servant of God must stand so much alone that he never knows he is alone. In the first phases of Christian life disheartenments come, people who used to be lights flicker out, and those who used to stand with us pass away. We have to get so used to it that we never know we are standing alone. "All men forsook me. . . notwithstanding the Lord stood with me" (2 Tim. 4:16-17). We must build our faith, not on the fading light, but on the light that never fails. When "big" men go we are sad, until we see that they are meant to go, the one thing that remains is looking in the face of God for ourselves.

Allow nothing to keep you from looking God sternly in the face about yourself and about your doctrine, and every time you preach see that you look God in the face about things first, then the glory will remain all through. A Christian worker is one who perpetually looks in the face of God and then goes forth to talk to people. The characteristic of the ministry of Christ is that of unconscious glory that abides. "Moses wist not that the skin of his face shone while he talked with Him."

We are never called on to parade our doubts or to express the hidden ecstasies of our life with God. The secret of the worker's life is that he keeps in tune with God all the time.

And the chapters that were on top of the pillars were of lily work.
(1 Kings 7:19)

The lily work added nothing to the strength of the building; many would notice the strength and the majesty of the whole building, but the inspiration of it all was in the detail, in the 'lily work'. In architecture it is not so much the massive strength that counts as the finely proportioned ornament, and that is never obtrusive. If we look at men and women who have been long at work for God and have been going through chastening, we notice that they have lost their individual harshness, lost a great deal of their apparent go-aheadness for God; but they have acquired something else, viz., the most exquisite 'lily work' in their lives, and this after all is the thing most like Jesus Christ. It is the quiet, undisturbable Divinity that is characteristic of Jesus, not aggressiveness, and the same is true of God's children.

MU 39

THE WORSHIP OF THE WORK

Labourers together with God. (1 Cor. 3:9)

Beware of any work for God which enables you to evade concentration on Him. A great many Christian workers worship their work. The one concern of a worker should be concentration on God, and this will mean that all the other margins of life, mental, moral and spiritual, are free with the freedom of a child, a worshipping child, not a wayward child. A worker without this solemn dominant note of concentration on God is apt to get his work on his neck; there is no margin of body, mind or spirit free, consequently he becomes spent out and crushed. There is no freedom, no delight in life; nerves, mind and heart are so crushingly burdened that God's blessing cannot rest. But the other side is just as true—when once the concentration is on God, all the margins of life are free and under the dominance of God alone. There is no responsibility on you for the work; the only responsibility you have is to keep in living constant touch with God, and to see that you allow nothing to hinder your cooperation with Him. The freedom after sanctification is the freedom of a child, the things that used to keep the life pinned down are gone. But be careful to remember that you are freed for one thing only—to be absolutely devoted to your co-Worker.

We have no right to judge where we should be put, or to have preconceived notions as to what God is fitting us for. God engineers everything; wherever He puts us our one great aim is to pour out a whole-hearted devotion to Him in that particular work. "Whatsoever thy hand findeth to do, do it with thy might."

And we know that all things work together for good to them that love God, to them who are the called according to his purpose. (Romans 8:28)

The shrine of our conscious life is placed in a sacredness of circumstances engineered by God whereby He secures our effectual calling. That God engineers our circumstances for us if we accept His purpose in Christ Jesus is a thought of great practical moment.

Allow yourself to think for a little that you are to be a walking, living edition of the prayers of the Holy Spirit. No wonder God urges us to walk in the light! No wonder His Spirit prays in us and makes intercessions with groanings we cannot utter. We may feel burdened or we may not; we may consciously know nothing about it; the point is that God puts us into circumstances where He can answer the prayers of His Son and of the Holy Spirit. Remember the prayer of Jesus is 'that they may be one, even as we are one'. That is a oneness of personality in which individuality is completely transfigured; it is independence lost and identity revealed.

It is well to remember that it is the 'together' of circumstances that works for good. God changes our circumstances; sometimes they are bright, sometimes they are the opposite; but God makes them work together for our good, so that in each particular set of circumstances we are in, the Spirit of God has a better chance to pray the particular prayers that suit His designs, and the reason is only known to God, not to us.

DPR 55

THE WARNING AGAINST
WANTONING

Notwithstanding in this rejoice not, that the spirits are subject
unto you. (Luke 10:20)

As Christian workers, worldliness is not our snare, sin is not our snare, but spiritual wantoning is, viz.: taking the pattern and print of the religious age we live in, making eyes at spiritual success. Never court anything other than the approval of God, go "without the camp, bearing His reproach." Jesus told the disciples not to rejoice in successful service, and yet this seems to be the one thing in which most of us do rejoice. We have the commercial view—so many souls saved and sanctified, thank God, now it is all right. Our work begins where God's grace has laid the foundation; we are not to save souls, but to disciple them. Salvation and sanctification are the work of God's sovereign grace; our work as His disciples is to disciple lives until they are wholly yielded to God. One life wholly devoted to God is of more value to God than one hundred lives simply awakened by His Spirit. As workers for God we must reproduce our own kind spiritually, and that will be God's witness to us as workers. God brings us to a standard of life by His grace, and we are responsible for reproducing that standard in others.

Unless the worker lives a life hidden with Christ in God, he is apt to become an irritating dictator instead of an indwelling disciple. Many of us are dictators, we dictate to people and to meetings. Jesus never dictates to us in that way. Whenever Our Lord talked about discipleship, He always prefaced it with an "IF," never with an emphatic assertion—"You must." Discipleship carries an option with it.

Be ye therefore followers of God. (Ephesians 5:1)

The one striking thing about following is we must not find our own way, for when we take the initiative we cease to follow. In the natural world everything depends upon our taking the initiative, but if we are followers of God, we cannot take the initiative, we cannot choose our own work or say what we will do; we have not to find out at all, we have just to follow . . .

In following Our Lord Jesus Christ we are not following His followers. When Paul said, 'who shall bring you into the remembrance of my ways', he was careful to add, 'which be in Christ' (1 Corinthians 4:17). We are not called to follow in all the footsteps of the saints, but only in so far as they followed their Lord.

DF 61

Discipleship must always be a personal matter; we can never become disciples in crowds, or even in twos. It is so easy to talk about what 'we' mean to do—'we' are going to do marvellous things, and it ends in none of us doing anything. The great element of discipleship is the personal one.

IWP 104

INSTANT IN SEASON

Be instant in season, out of season. (2 Tim. 4:2)

Many of us suffer from the morbid tendency to be instant "out of season." The season does not refer to time, but to us—"Be instant in season, out of season," whether we feel like it or not. If we do only what we feel inclined to do, some of us would do nothing for ever and ever. There are unemployables in the spiritual domain, spiritually decrepit people, who refuse to do anything unless they are supernaturally inspired. The proof that we are rightly related to God is that we do our best whether we feel inspired or not.

One of the great snares of the Christian worker is to make a fetish of his rare moments. When the Spirit of God gives you a time of inspiration and insight, you say —"Now I will always be like this for God." No, you will not, God will take care you are not. Those times are the gift of God entirely. You cannot give them to yourself when you choose. If you say you will only be at your best, you become an intolerable drag on God; you will never do anything unless God keeps you consciously inspired. If you make a god of your best moments, you will find that God will fade out of your life and never come back until you do the duty that lies nearest, and have learned not to make a fetish of your rare moments.

That which hath been is named already, and it is known that it is man: neither may he contend with him that is mightier than he ... For who can tell a man what shall be after him under the sun? (Ecclesiastes 6:10, 12)

In order to estimate man properly in the 'soup' he is in just now, we must remember what he was in the beginning. God created man in His own image, a son of God. Adam was to have control over the life in the air and on the earth and in the sea, on one condition—that he allowed God to rule him absolutely. Man was to develop the earth and his own life until he was transfigured. But instead there came the introduction of sin, man took the rule over himself, he became his own god, and thereby lost control over everything else. It is this that accounts for the condition of things as they are now.

If we are going to have a sympathetic understanding of the Bible, we must rid ourselves of the abominable conceit that we are the wisest people that have ever been on the earth; we must stop our patronage of Jesus Christ and of the Bible, and have a bigger respect for the fundamental conception of life as it is. At the basis of Hebrew wisdom first of all, is confidence in God; and second, a terrific sigh and sob over the human race as a magnificent ruin of what God designed it to be. Modern wisdom says that man is a magnificent promise of what he is going to be. If that point of view is right, then there is no need to talk about sin and Redemption, and the Bible is a cunningly devised fable. But the Bible point of view seems to cover most of the facts.

SHH 76

THE SUPREME CLIMB

Take now thy son . . . and offer him there for a burnt offering upon one of the mountains which I will tell thee of. (Gen. 22:2)

Character determines how a man interprets God's will (cf. Psalm 18:25-26). Abraham interpreted God's command to mean that he had to kill his son, and he could only leave this tradition behind by the pain of a tremendous ordeal. God could purify his faith in no other way. If we obey what God says according to our sincere belief, God will break us from those traditions that misrepresent Him. There are many such beliefs to be got rid of, e.g., that God removes a child because the mother loves him too much—a devil's lie! and a travesty of the true nature of God. If the devil can hinder us from taking the supreme climb and getting rid of wrong traditions about God, he will do so; but if we keep true to God, God will take us through an ordeal which will bring us out into a better knowledge of Himself.

The great point of Abraham's faith in God was that he was prepared to do anything for God. He was there to obey God, no matter to what belief he went contrary. Abraham was not a devotee of his convictions, or he would have slain Isaac and said that the voice of the angel was the voice of the devil. That is the attitude of a fanatic. If you will remain true to God, God will lead you straight through every barrier into the inner chamber of the knowledge of Himself; but there is always this point of giving up convictions and traditional beliefs. Don't ask God to test you. Never declare as Peter did—"I will do anything, I will go to death with Thee." Abraham did not make any such declaration; he remained true to God, and God purified his faith.

He that followeth me shall not walk in darkness, but shall have the light of life. (John 8:12)

Supposing you are walking over a moor at night, you know there is a path but it is too dark and obscure for you to see; then the moon struggles through the clouds and you see the path, a clear strip of white, straight across the hill; in a little while all is obscure again, but you have seen the path and you know the way to go. There are times in our experience when life is just like that. We do not see the path though we know it is there, then the light shines and we see it, and when darkness comes again we can step boldly. Sometimes the light is as the moonlight or the dawn, or it comes as a terrifying flash of lightning, when all of a sudden we see the way we should go. 'While ye have light, believe in the light, that ye may be the children of light' (John 12:36). Have we believed in the light we have had? Can we recall the time when the light of God in the Face of Jesus Christ was clearer to us than anything else has ever been, when we saw perfectly clearly and understood exactly what the Lord wanted? Did we believe in that light; and have we walked up to the light? Can we say, 'I was not disobedient unto the heavenly vision'? So many of us see the light, we see the way across the moor; by a sudden lightning flash of God's revealing grace we see the way to go, but we do not take it. We say, 'Oh, yes, I did receive the Spirit of God, and I thought that it would be like this and that, but it has not been.' The reason is that we did not believe in the light when it was given . . .

If we have entered into the heavenly places in Christ Jesus, the light has shone, and, this is the marvellous thing, as we begin to do what we know the Lord would have us do, we find He does not enable *us* to do it, He simply puts through us all His power and the thing is done in His way. Thank God for everyone who has seen the light, who has understood how the Lord Jesus Christ clears away the darkness and brings the light by showing His own characteristics through us.

OBH 39

WHAT DO YOU WANT?

Seekest thou great things for thyself? (Jer. 45:5)

Are you seeking great things for yourself? Not seeking to be a great one, but seeking great things from God for yourself. God wants you in a closer relationship to Himself than receiving His gifts, He wants you to get to know Him. A great thing is accidental, it comes and goes. God never gives us anything accidental. There is nothing easier than getting into a right relationship with God except when it is not God Whom you want but only what He gives.

If you have only come the length of asking God for things, you have never come to the first strand of abandonment, you have become a Christian from a standpoint of your own. "I did ask God for the Holy Spirit, but He did not give me the rest and the peace I expected." Instantly God puts His finger on the reason—you are not seeking the Lord at all, you are seeking something for yourself. Jesus says—"Ask, and it shall be given you." Ask God for what you want, and you cannot ask if you are not asking for a right thing. When you draw near to God, you cease from asking for things. "Your Father knoweth what things ye have need of, before ye ask Him." Then why ask? That you may get to know Him.

Are you seeking great things for yourself? "O Lord, baptize me with the Holy Ghost." If God does not, it is because you are not abandoned enough to Him, there is something you will not do. Are you prepared to ask yourself what it is you want from God and why you want it? God always ignores the present perfection for the ultimate perfection. He is not concerned about making you blessed and happy just now; He is working out His ultimate perfection all the time—"that they may be one even as We are."

I must work the works of him that sent me, while it is day: the
night cometh, when no man can work. (John 9:4)

Today we hold conferences and conventions and give reports
and make our programmes. None of these things were in the
life of Jesus, and yet every minute of His life He realized that
He was fulfilling the purpose of His Father. How did He do it?
By maintaining the one relationship, and it is that one relationship He insists on in His disciples, and it is the one we have
lost in the rubbish of modern civilization. If we try and live
the life Jesus Christ lived, modern civilization will fling us out
like waste material; we are no good, we do not add anything
to the hard cash of the times we live in, and the sooner we are
flung out the better.

In St John's Gospel this aspect of our Lord's life is more elabo-
rately worked out than anywhere else. It is indicated in the
other Gospels (see Luke 2:49, 13:32; 12:50). Jesus knew He
was here for His Father's purpose and He never allowed the
cares of civilization to bother Him. He did nothing to add to
the wealth of the civilization in which He lived. He earned
nothing, modern civilization would not have tolerated Him for
two minutes.

HG 71

WHAT YOU WILL GET

Thy life will I give thee for a prey in all places whither thou goest.
(Jer. 45:5)

This is the unshakable secret of the Lord to those who trust Him—"I will give thee thy life." What more does a man want than his life? It is the essential thing. "Thy life for a prey" means that wherever you may go, even if it is into hell, you will come out with your life, nothing can harm it. So many of us are caught up in the show of things, not in the way of property and possessions, but of blessings. All these have to go; but there is something grander that never can go—the life that is "hid with Christ in God."

Are you prepared to let God take you into union with Himself, and pay no more attention to what you call the great things? Are you prepared to abandon entirely and let go? The test of abandonment is in refusing to say—"Well, what about this?" Beware of suppositions. Immediately you allow—What about this?—it means you have not abandoned, you do not really trust God. Immediately you do abandon, you think no more about what God is going to do. Abandon means to refuse yourself the luxury of asking any questions. If you abandon entirely to God, He says at once, "Thy life will I give thee for a prey." The reason people are tired of life is because God has not given them anything, they have not got their life as a prey. The way to get out of that state is to abandon to God. When you do get through to abandonment to God, you will be the most surprised and delighted creature on earth; God has got you absolutely and has given you your life. If you are not there, it is either because of disobedience or a refusal to be simple enough.

Be filled with the Spirit. (Ephesians 5:18)

The sovereign emotions are guided and controlled by love, but bear in mind that love in its highest moral meaning is the preference of one person for another person. A Christian's love is personal, passionate devotion to Jesus Christ, and he learns to grip on the threshold of his mind as in a vice every sentiment awakened by wrong emotions. God holds the saints responsible for emotions they have not got and ought to have as well as for the emotions they have allowed which they ought not to have allowed. If we indulge in inordinate affection, anger, anxiety, God holds us responsible; but He also insists that we have to be passionately filled with the right emotions . . .

If we have no emotional life, then we have disobeyed God. 'Be filled with the Spirit'; it is as impossible to be filled with the Spirit and be free from emotion as it is for a man to be filled with wine and not show it. The reason some of us are so amazingly dull and get sleeping-sickness is that we have never once thought of paying attention to the stirring up the Spirit of God gives the mind and our emotional nature. How many of us are terrified out of our wits lest we should be emotional! Jesus Christ demands the whole nature, and He demands that part of our nature the devil uses most, viz., the emotional part.

BE 73–4

THE GRACIOUSNESS
OF UNCERTAINTY

It doth not yet appear what we shall be. (1 John 3:2)

Naturally, we are inclined to be so mathematical and calculating that we look upon uncertainty as a bad thing. We imagine that we have to reach some end, but that is not the nature of spiritual life. The nature of spiritual life is that we are certain in our uncertainty, consequently we do not make our nests anywhere. Common sense says—"Well, supposing I were in that condition . . ." We cannot suppose ourselves in any condition we have never been in.

Certainty is the mark of the common-sense life: gracious uncertainty is the mark of the spiritual life. To be certain of God means that we are uncertain in all our ways, we do not know what a day may bring forth. This is generally said with a sigh of sadness; it should be rather an expression of breathless expectation. We are uncertain of the next step, but we are certain of God. Immediately we abandon to God, and do the duty that lies nearest, He packs our life with surprises all the time. When we become advocates of a creed, something dies; we do not believe God, we only believe our belief about Him. Jesus said, "Except ye . . . become as little children." Spiritual life is the life of a child. We are not uncertain of God, but uncertain of what He is going to do next. If we are only certain in our beliefs, we get dignified and severe and have the ban of finality about our views; but when we are rightly related to God, life is full of spontaneous, joyful uncertainty and expectancy.

"Believe also in Me," said Jesus, not—"Believe certain things about Me." Leave the whole thing to Him, it is gloriously uncertain how He will come in, but He will come. Remain loyal to Him.

That they might have my joy fulfilled in themselves. (John 17:13)

All degrees of joy reside in the heart. How can a Christian be full of happiness (if happiness depends on the things that happen) when he is in a world where the devil is doing his best to twist souls away from God, where people are tortured physically, where some are downtrodden and do not get a chance? It would be the outcome of the most miserable selfishness to be happy under such conditions; but a joyful heart is never an insult, and joy is never touched by eternal conditions. Beware of preaching the gospel of temperament instead of the Gospel of God. Numbers of people today preach the gospel of temperament, the gospel of 'cheer up'. The word 'blessed' is sometimes translated 'happy', but it is a much deeper word; it includes all that we mean by joy in its full fruition. Happiness is the characteristic of a child, and God condemns us for taking happiness out of a child's life; but as men and women we should have done with happiness long ago, we should be facing the stern issues of life, knowing that the grace of God is sufficient for every problem the devil can present.

BP 115

THE SPONTANEITY OF LOVE

Love suffereth long, and is kind . . . (1 Cor. 13:4 8)

Love is not premeditated, it is spontaneous, i.e., it bursts up in extraordinary ways. There is nothing of mathematical certainty in Paul's category of love. We cannot say—"Now I am going to think no evil; I am going to believe all things." The characteristic of love is spontaneity. We do not set the statements of Jesus in front of us as a standard; but when His Spirit is having His way with us, we live according to His standard without knowing it, and on looking back we are amazed at the disinterestedness of a particular emotion, which is the evidence that the spontaneity of real love was there. In everything to do with the life of God in us, its nature is only discerned when it is past.

The springs of love are in God, not in us. It is absurd to look for the love of God in our hearts naturally, it is only there when it has been shed abroad in our hearts by the Holy Spirit.

If we try to prove to God how much we love Him, it is a sure sign that we do not love Him. The evidence of our love for Him is the absolute spontaneity of our love, it comes naturally. In looking back we cannot tell why we did certain things, we did them according to the spontaneous nature of His love in us. The life of God manifests itself in this spontaneous way because the springs of love are in the Holy Ghost (Romans 5:5).

How much more shall the blood of Christ . . . purge your con-
science from dead works to serve the living God. (Hebrews 9:14)

Has conscience the place in our salvation and sanctification that it ought to have? Hyper-conscientious people blind themselves to the realization of what the death of Jesus means by saying, 'No, I have wronged this person and I must put the thing right.' It springs from the panging remorse that we experience when we realize we have wronged another, 'All you say about the Cross may be true, but I have been so mean and so wrong that there are things I must put right first.' It sounds noble to talk like that, but it is the essence of the pride that put Jesus Christ to death. The only thing to do is to cast the whole thing aside: 'My God, this thing in me is worthy only of death, the awful death of crucifixion to the last strand of life. Lord, it is my sin, my wrong, not Jesus Christ, that ought to be on that Cross.' When we get there and abandon the whole thing, the blood of Christ cleanses our conscience and the freedom is ineffable and amazing . . .

It is freedom not only from sin and the damage sin has done, but emancipation from the impairing left by sin, from all the distortions left in mind and imagination. Then when our conscience has been cleansed from dead works, Jesus Christ gives us the marvellously healing ministry of intercession as 'a clearing-house for conscience'. Not only is all sense of past guilt removed, but we are given the very secret heart of God for the purpose of vicarious intercession (see Romans 8:26–7).

PS 20

MAY

INSIGHT NOT EMOTION

I have to lead my life in faith, without seeing Him.
(2 Cor. 5:7, MOFFAT)

For a time we are conscious of God's attentions, then, when God begins to use us in His enterprises, we take on a pathetic look and talk of the trials and the difficulties, and all the time God is trying to make us do our duty as obscure people. None of us would be obscure spiritually if we could help it. Can we do our duty when God has shut up heaven? Some of us always want to be illuminated saints with golden haloes and the flush of inspiration, and to have the saints of God dealing with us all the time. A gilt-edged saint is no good, he is abnormal, unfit for daily life, and altogether unlike God . We are here as men and women, not as half-fledged angels, to do the work of the world, and to do it with an infinitely greater power to stand the turmoil because we have been born from above.

If we try to re-introduce the rare moments of inspiration, it is a sign that it is not God we want. We are making a fetish of the moments when God did come and speak, and insisting that He must do it again; whereas what God wants us to do is to "walk by faith." How many of us have laid ourselves by, as it were, and said—"I cannot do any more until God appears to me." He never will, and without any inspiration, without any sudden touch of God, we will have to get up. Then comes the surprise—"Why, He was there all the time, and I never knew it!" Never live for the rare moments, they are surprises. God will give us touches of inspiration when He sees we are not in danger of being led away by them. We must never make our moments of inspiration our standard; our standard is our duty.

> *Whence then cometh wisdom? and where is the place of understanding? . . . Behold, the fear of the Lord, that is wisdom: and to depart from evil is understanding. (Job 4:20, 28)*

Neither logic nor science can explain the sublimities of Nature. Supposing a scientist with a diseased olfactory nerve says that there is no perfume in a rose, and to prove his statement he dissects the rose and tabulates every part, and then says, 'Where is the perfume? It is a fiction; I have demonstrated that there is none.' There is always one fact more that science cannot explain, and the best thing to do is not to deny it in order to preserve your sanity, but to say, as Job did, 'No, the one fact more which you cannot explain means that God must step in just there, or there is no explanation to be had.'

Every common-sense fact requires something for its explanation which common-sense cannot give. The facts of every day and night reveal things our own minds cannot explain. When a scientific man comes across a gap in his explanations, instead of saying, 'There is no gap here', let him recognize that there is a gap he cannot bridge, and that he must be reverent with what he cannot understand. The tendency is to deny that a fact has any existence because it cannot be fitted into any explanation as yet. That 'the exception proves the rule' is not true: the exception proves that the rule won't do; the rule is only useful in the greatest number of cases. When scientists treat a thesis as a fact they mean that it is based on the highest degree of probability. There are no 'infallible' findings, and the man who bows down to scientific findings may be as big a fool as the man who refuses to do so. The man who prays ceases to be a fool, while the man who refuses to pray nourishes a blind life within his own brain and he will find no way out that road. Job cries out that prayer is the only way out in all these matters.

BFB 79, 82

THE PASSION OF PATIENCE

Though it tarry, wait for it. (Hab. 2:3)

Patience is not indifference; patience conveys the idea of an immensely strong rock withstanding all onslaughts. The vision of God is the source of patience, because it imparts a moral inspiration. Moses endured, not because he had an ideal of right and duty, but because he had a vision of God. He "endured, as seeing Him Who is invisible." A man with the vision of God is not devoted to a cause or to any particular issue; he is devoted to God Himself. You always know when the vision is of God because of the inspiration that comes with it; things come with largeness and tonic to the life because everything is energized by God. If God gives you a time spiritually, as He gave His Son actually, of temptation in the wilderness, with no word from Himself at all, endure, and the power to endure is there because you see God.

"Though it tarry, wait for it." The proof that we have the vision is that we are reaching out for more than we have grasped. It is a bad thing to be satisfied spiritually. "What shall I render unto the Lord?" said the Psalmist. "I will *take* the cup of salvation." We are apt to look for satisfaction in ourselves— "Now I have got the thing; now I am entirely sanctified; now I can endure." Instantly we are on the road to ruin. Our reach must exceed our grasp. "Not as though I had already attained, either were already perfect." If we have only what we have experienced, we have nothing; if we have the inspiration of the vision of God, we have more than we can experience. Beware of the danger of relaxation spiritually.

Be ye not unwise, but understanding what the will of the Lord is. (Ephesians 5:17)

An artist is one who not only sees but is prepared to pay the price of acquiring the technical knowledge to express what he sees. An artistic person is one who has not enough art in him to make him work at the technique of art whereby he can express himself, he indulges in moods and tones and impressions; consequently there are more artistic people than there are artists. The same is true of poetry, there are many people with poetic notions, but very few poets. It is not enough for a man to feel the divine flame burning in him; unless he goes into the concentrated, slogging business of learning the technique of expression, his genius will be of no use to anyone. Apply these illustrations spiritually: if we have not enough of the life of God in us to overcome the difficulty of expressing it in our bodies, then we are living an impoverished spiritual life. Think of the illuminations the Spirit of God has given you; He expected you to bring your physical body which He made into obedience to the vision, and you never attempted to but let it drift, and when the crisis came and God looked for you to be His mouthpiece, you crumpled all to pieces. You had not formed the habit of apprehending; your physical machine was not under control. It is a terrible thing to sit down to anything.

Beware of being side-tracked by the idea that you can develop a spiritual life apart from physical accompaniments. It is a desperately dangerous thing to allow the spiritual vision to go ahead of physical obedience.

Do some practical obeying.

MFL 81

VITAL INTERCESSION

Praying always with all prayer and supplication in the Spirit.
(Eph. 6:18)

As we go on in intercession we may find that our obedience to God is going to cost other people more than we thought. The danger then is to begin to intercede in sympathy with those whom God was gradually lifting to a totally different sphere in answer to our prayers. Whenever we step back from identification with God's interest in others into sympathy with them, the vital connection with God has gone, we have put our sympathy, our consideration for them in the way, and this is a deliberate rebuke to God.

It is impossible to intercede vitally unless we are perfectly sure of God, and the greatest dissipator of our relationship to God is personal sympathy and personal prejudice. Identification is the key to intercession, and whenever we stop being identified with God, it is by sympathy, not by sin. It is not likely that sin will interfere with our relationship to God, but sympathy will, sympathy with ourselves or with others which makes us say —"I will not allow that thing to happen." Instantly we are out of vital connection with God.

Intercession leaves you neither time nor inclination to pray for your own "sad sweet self." The thought of yourself is not kept out, because it is not there to keep out; you are completely and entirely identified with God's interests in other lives.

Discernment is God's call to intercession, never to fault finding.

The sleep of a labouring man is sweet, whether he eat little or much; but the abundance of the rich will not suffer him to sleep. (Ecclesiastes 5:12)

The sleep of a labouring man is sweet, it recreates him. The Bible indicates that sleep is not meant only for the recuperation of a man's body, but that there is a tremendous furtherance of spiritual and moral life during sleep. According to the Bible, a great deal more than physical recuperation happens in the sleep of any man who has done his daily toil in actual work. 'He giveth *to* his beloved in sleep' (Psalm 127:2, RV, marg.). This is a phase that is cut out altogether, because we ignore the deeper issues.

'Whether he eat little or much.' Paul's counsel is that 'if any would not work, neither should he eat'. There are plenty of folks who eat but don't work, and they suffer for it. If we are physically healthy, the benefit of the food we eat corresponds to the work we do, and the same is true in mental, moral and spiritual health. The prayer Our Lord taught us is full of wisdom along this line, 'Give us this day our daily bread.' That does not mean that if we do not pray we shall not get it. The word 'give' has the sense of 'receiving'. When we become children of God we receive our daily bread from Him, the basis of blessing lies there, otherwise we take it as an animal with no discernment of God.

SHH 63

VICARIOUS INTERCESSION

Having therefore, brethren, boldness to enter into the holiest by the blood of Jesus. (Heb. 10:19)

Beware of imagining that intercession means bringing our personal sympathies into the presence of God and demanding that He does what we ask. Our approach to God is due entirely to the vicarious identification of our Lord with sin. We have "boldness to enter into the holiest *by the blood of Jesus.*"

Spiritual stubbornness is the most effectual hindrance to intercession, because it is based on sympathy with that in ourselves and in others that we do not think needs atoning for. We have the notion that there are certain right and virtuous things in us which do not need to be based on the Atonement, and just in the domain of "stodge" that is produced by this idea we cannot intercede. We do not identify ourselves with God's interest in others, we get petulant with God; we are always ready with our own ideas, and intercession becomes the glorification of our own natural sympathies. We have to realize that the identification of Jesus with sin means the radical alteration of all our sympathies. Vicarious intercession means that we deliberately substitute God's interests in others for our natural sympathy with them.

Am I stubborn or substituted? Petted or perfect in my relationship to God? Sulky or spiritual? Determined to have my own way or determined to be identified with Him?

It is good and comely for one to eat and to drink, and to enjoy the good of all his labour that he taketh under the sun all the days of his life, which God giveth him: for it is his portion. (Ecclesiastes 5:18)

The Bible makes much of man's body. The teaching of Christianity on this point has been twisted by the influence of Plato's teaching, which says that a man can only further his moral and spiritual life by despising his body. The Bible teaches that the body is the temple of the Holy Ghost, it was moulded by God of the dust of the ground and is man's chief glory, not his shame. When God became Incarnate 'he took not on him the nature of angels', but was made 'in the likeness of men', and it is man's body that is yet to manifest the glory of God on earth. Material things are going to be translucent with the light of God.

Jesus Christ 'came eating and drinking', and from Genesis to Revelation eating and drinking, and labouring in the ordinary toil of life in the condition of things as they are, are the things in which man will find his right relationship to life and to God.

SHH 67

JUDGMENT ON THE ABYSS OF LOVE

For the time is come that judgment must begin at the house of God. (1 Peter 4:17)

The Christian worker must never forget that salvation is God's thought, not man's; therefore it is an unfathomable abyss. Salvation is the great thought of God, not an experience. Experience is only a gateway by which salvation comes into our conscious life. Never preach the experience; preach the great thought of God behind. When we preach we are not proclaiming how man can be saved from hell and be made moral and pure; we are conveying good news about God.

In the teachings of Jesus Christ the element of judgment is always brought out, it is the sign of God's love. Never sympathize with a soul who finds it difficult to get to God, God is not to blame. It is not for us to find out the reason why it is difficult, but so to present the truth of God that the Spirit of God will show what is wrong. The great sterling test in preaching is that it brings everyone to judgment. The Spirit of God locates each one to himself.

If Jesus ever gave us a command He could not enable us to fulfil, He would be a liar; and if we make our inability a barrier to obedience, it means we are telling God there is something He has not taken into account. Every element of self-reliance must be slain by the power of God. Complete weakness and dependence will always be the occasion for the Spirit of God to manifest His power.

*. . . for a man's life consisteth not in the abundance of the things
which he possesseth. (Luke 12:15)*

The whole teaching of Jesus is opposed to the idea of civilization, viz., possessing things for myself—'This is mine.' The sense of property is connected, not with the lasting element of our personality, but with that which has to do with sin; it is the sense of property that makes me want to gratify myself. Jesus Christ had no sense of property, there was never any attempt to gratify Himself by possessing things for Himself—'the Son of man hath not where to lay his head'. What was His, He gave—'I lay down my life . . . I lay it down of myself.' The thing that leads me wrong always and every time is what I am persuaded I possess. The thing that is mine is the thing I have with the power to give it. All that I want to possess without the power to give, is of the nature of sin. . . .

According to Jesus Christ a man's life does not consist in the abundance of the things he possesses—not only in the way of goods and chattels, but in the way of a good name, a virtuous character; these things are a man's inheritance, but not his *life*. When the Holy Spirit begins to try and break into the house of our possessions in order to grant us the real life of God, we look on Him as a robber, as a disturber of our peace, because when He comes He reveals the things which are not of God and must go; and they are the things which constituted our life before He came in, our golden affections were carefully nested in them. The thing that hurts shows where we live. If God hurts it is because we are not living rightly related to Him.

GW 29

LIBERTY ON THE ABYSS
OF THE GOSPEL

Stand fast therefore in the liberty wherewith Christ hath made us free. (Gal. 5:1)

A spiritually minded man will never come to you with the demand—"Believe this and that;" but with the demand that you square your life with the standards of Jesus. We are not asked to believe the Bible, but to believe the One Whom the Bible reveals (cf. John 5:39-40). We are called to present liberty of conscience, not liberty of view. If we are free with the liberty of Christ, others will be brought into that same liberty —the liberty of realizing the dominance of Jesus Christ.

Always keep your life measured by the standards of Jesus. Bow your neck to His yoke alone, and to no other yoke whatever; and be careful to see that you never bind a yoke on others that is not placed by Jesus Christ. It takes God a long time to get us out of the way of thinking that unless everyone sees as we do, they must be wrong. That is never God's view. There is only one liberty, the liberty of Jesus at work in our conscience enabling us to do what is right.

Don't get impatient, remember how God dealt with you— with patience and with gentleness; but never water down the truth of God. Let it have its way and never apologize for it. Jesus said, "Go and make *disciples*," not "make converts to your opinions."

Sell all that thou hast, and distribute unto the poor.
(Matthew 19:21)

There is a general principle here and a particular reference. We are always in a danger of taking the particular reference for the general principle and evading the general principle. The particular reference here is to selling material goods. The rich young ruler had deliberately to be destitute, deliberately to distribute, deliberately to discern where his treasure was, and devote himself to Jesus Christ. The principle underlying it is that I must detach myself from everything I possess. Many of us suppress our sense of property, we don't starve it, we suppress it. Undress yourself morally before God of everything that might be a possession until you are a mere conscious human being, and then give God that. That is where the battle is fought—in the domain of the will before God; it is not fought in external things at all. Is He sovereign Lord or is He not? Am I more devoted to my notion of what Jesus Christ wants than to Himself? If so, I am likely to hear one of His hard sayings that will produce sorrow in me. What Jesus says *is* hard, it is only easy when it comes to those who really are His disciples. Beware of allowing anything to soften a hard word of Jesus . . .

I can be so rich in poverty, so rich in the consciousness that I am nobody, that I will never be a disciple of Jesus Christ; and I can be so rich in the consciousness that I am somebody that I will never be a disciple. Am I willing to be destitute of the sense that I am destitute? It is not giving up outside things, but making yourself destitute to yourself, and that is where the discouragement comes in.

GW 78

BUILDING FOR ETERNITY

*For which of you, intending to build a tower, sitteth not down
first, and counteth the cost, whether he have sufficient to finish
it? (Luke 14:28)*

Our Lord refers not to a cost we have to count, but to a cost
which He has counted. The cost was those thirty years in
Nazareth, those three years of popularity, scandal and hatred,
the deep unfathomable agony in Gethsemane, and the onslaught at Calvary—the pivot upon which the whole of Time
and Eternity turns. Jesus Christ has counted the cost. Men are
not going to laugh at Him at last and say—"This man began to
build, and was not able to finish."

The conditions of discipleship laid down by Our Lord in vv.
26, 27 and 33 mean that the men and women He is going to
use in His mighty building enterprises are those in whom He
has done everything. "If any man come to Me, and hate not
. . . , *he cannot be My disciple.*" Our Lord implies that the only
men and women He will use in His building enterprises are
those who love Him personally, passionately and devotedly
beyond any of the closest ties on earth. The conditions are stern,
but they are glorious.

All that we build is going to be inspected by God. Is God going
to detect in His searching fire that we have built on the foundation of Jesus some enterprise of our own? These are days of
tremendous enterprises, days when we are trying to work for
God, and therein is the snare. Profoundly speaking, we can
never work for God . Jesus takes us over for His enterprises,
His building schemes entirely, and no soul has any right to
claim where he shall be put.

As sorrowful, yet always rejoicing; as poor, yet making many rich;
as having nothing, and yet possessing all things.
(2 Corinthians 6:10)

As we draw on the grace of God He increases voluntary poverty all along the line. Always give the best you have got every time; never think about who you are giving it to, let other people take it or leave it as they choose. Pour out the best you have, and always be poor. Never reserve anything; never be diplomatic and careful about the treasure God gives.

AUG 128

'Give to him that asketh thee.' Why do we always make this mean money? Our Lord makes no mention of money. The blood of most of us seems to run in gold. The reason we make it mean money is because that is where our heart is. Peter said, 'Silver and gold have I none; but such as I have give I thee.' God grant we may understand that the spring of giving is not impulse nor inclination, but the inspiration of the Holy Spirit, I give because Jesus tells me to . . .

The way Christians wriggle and twist and compromise over this verse springs from infidelity in the ruling providence of our Heavenly Father. We enthrone common-sense as God and say, 'It is absurd; if I give to every one that asks, every beggar in the place will be at my door.' Try it, I have yet to find the man who obeyed Jesus Christ's command and did not realize that God restrains those who beg.

SSM 46

THE PATIENCE OF FAITH

Because thou hast kept the word of My patience. (Rev. 3:10)

Patience is more than endurance. A saint's life is in the hands of God like a bow and arrow in the hands of an archer. God is aiming at something the saint cannot see, and He stretches and strains, and every now and again the saint says—"I cannot stand any more." God does not heed, He goes on stretching till His purpose is in sight, then He lets fly. Trust yourself in God's hands. For what have you need of patience just now? Maintain your relationship to Jesus Christ by the patience of faith. "Though He slay me, yet will I wait for Him."

Faith is not a pathetic sentiment, but robust vigorous confidence built on the fact that God is holy love. You cannot see Him just now, you cannot understand what He is doing, but you know *Him*. Shipwreck occurs where there is not that mental poise which comes from being established on the eternal truth that God is holy love. Faith is the heroic effort of your life; you fling yourself in reckless confidence on God.

God has ventured all in Jesus Christ to save us, now He wants us to venture our all in abandoned confidence in Him. There are spots where that faith has not worked in us as yet, places untouched by the life of God. There were none of those spots in Jesus Christ's life, and there are to be none in ours. "This is life eternal, that they might know Thee." The real meaning of eternal life is a life that can face anything it has to face without wavering. If we take this view, life becomes one great romance, a glorious opportunity for seeing marvelous things all the time. God is disciplining us to get us into this central place of power.

Whatsoever thy hand findeth to do, do it with thy might: for there is no work nor device, nor knowledge, nor wisdom, in the grave, whither thou goest. (Ecclesiastes 9:10)

The Bible nowhere teaches us to work for work's sake. That is one of the greatest bugbears of the anti-Christian movement in the heart of Christianity today. It is Work with a capital W in which the worship of Jesus Christ is lost sight of. People will sacrifice themselves endlessly for *the work*. Perspiration is mistaken for inspiration. Our guidance with regard to work is to remember that its value is in what it does for us. It is difficult not to let ulterior considerations come in—'What's the good of doing this, we are only here for a short time, why should we do it as if it were to last for ever?' Solomon's counsel is—'Whatsoever thy hand attaineth to do by thy strength *that do*' (RV, marg.). He is not recommending work for work's sake, but because through the drudgery of work the man himself is developed. When you deify work, you apostatize from Jesus Christ. In the private spiritual life of many a Christian it is work that has hindered concentration on God. When work is out of its real relation it becomes a means of evading concentration on God. Carlyle pointed out that the weariness and sickness of modern life is shown in the restlessness of work. When a man is not well he is always doing things, an eternal fidget. Intense activity may be the sign of physical weariness. When a man is healthy his work is so much part of himself that you never know he is doing it; he does it with his might, and that makes no fuss. We lose by the way we do our work the very thing it is intended to bring us.

At the back of all is the one thing God is after, what a man is, not what he does, and Solomon keeps that in view all the time. It is what we are in our relation to things that counts not what we attain to in them. If you put attainment as the end you may reap a broken heart and find that all your outlay ends in disaster, death cuts it short, or disease, or ruin.

SHH 128

GRASP WITHOUT REACH

Where there is no vision, the people cast off restraint.
(Prov. 29:18, RV).

There is a difference between an ideal and a vision. An ideal has not moral inspiration; a vision has. The people who give themselves over to ideals rarely *do* anything. A man's conception of Deity may be used to justify his deliberate neglect of his duty. Jonah argued that because God was a God of justice and of mercy, therefore everything would be all right. I may have a right conception of God, and that may be the very reason why I do not do my duty. But wherever there is vision, there is also a life of rectitude because the vision imparts moral incentive.

Ideals may lull to ruin. Take stock of yourself spiritually and see whether you have ideals only or if you have vision.

Ah, but a man's reach should exceed his grasp,

Or what's a heaven for?

"Where there is no vision . . ." When once we lose sight of God, we begin to be reckless, we cast off certain restraints, we cast off praying, we cast off the vision of God in little things, and begin to act on our own initiative. If we are eating what we have out of our own hand, doing things on our own initiative without expecting God to come in, we are on the downward path, we have lost the vision. Is our attitude to-day an attitude that springs from our vision of God? Are we expecting God to do greater things than He has ever done? Is there a freshness and vigour in our spiritual outlook?

I am the living bread which came down out of heaven: if any man eat of this bread, he shall live for ever: yea and the bread which I will give is my flesh, for the life of the world. (John 6:51)

Good corn is not bread; if we are compelled to eat corn we will suffer for it. Corn must be ground and mixed and kneaded and baked, and baked sufficiently, before it is fit to be eaten. When the husk is away and the kernel garnered, we are apt to think that all is done; but the process has only just begun. A granary of corn is not bread; people cannot eat handfuls of corn and be nourished, something must be done to the corn first. Apply that illustration to the life of a sanctified saint. The afflictions after sanctification are not meant to purify us, but to make us broken bread in the hands of our Lord to nourish others. Many Christian workers are like Ephraim, 'a cake not turned'; they are faddists and cranks, and when they are given out for distribution they produce indigestion instead of giving nourishment.

SHL 111

Jesus Christ was made broken bread and poured out wine for us, and He expects us to be made broken bread and poured out wine in His hands for others. If we are not thoroughly baked, we will produce indigestion because we are dough instead of bread. We have to be made into good nutritious stuff for other people. The reason we are going through the things we are is that God wants to know whether He can make us good bread with which to feed others. The stuff of our lives, not simply of our talk, is to be the nutriment of those who know us.

MU 48

TAKE THE INITIATIVE

*Add to your faith virtue ... (Furnish your faith with resolu-
tion. MOFFAT) (2 Peter 1:5)*

"Add" means there is something we have to do. We are in danger of forgetting that we cannot do what God does, and that
God will not do what we can do. We cannot save ourselves nor
sanctify ourselves, God does that; but God will not give us good
habits, He will not give us character, He will not make us walk
aright. We have to do all that ourselves, we have to work out
the salvation God has worked in. "Add" means to get into the
habit of doing things, and in the initial stages it is difficult. To
take the initiative is to make a beginning, to instruct yourself
in the way you have to go.

Beware of the tendency of asking the way when you know
it perfectly well. Take the initiative, stop hesitating, and take
the first step. Be resolute when God speaks, act in faith immediately on what He says, and never revise your decisions. If
you hesitate when God tells you to do a thing you endanger
your standing in grace. Take the initiative, take it yourself, take
the step with your will now, make it impossible to go back.
Burn your bridges behind you—"I *will* write that letter"; "I *will*
pay that debt." Make the thing inevitable.

We have to get into the habit of hearkening to God about
everything, to form the habit of finding out what God says. If
when a crisis comes, we instinctively turn to God, we know
that the habit has been formed. We have to take the initiative
where we *are*, not where we are not.

*Thou shalt love the Lord thy God with all thy heart, and with
all thy soul, and with all thy mind. This is the first and great
commandment. (Matthew 22:37–8)
If ye love me, keep my commandments. (John 14:15)*

Before we can love God we must have the Lover of God in us,
viz., the Holy Spirit. When the Holy Spirit has shed abroad the
love of God in our hearts, then that love requires cultivation.
No love on earth will develop without being cultivated. We
have to dedicate ourselves to love, which means identifying
ourselves with God's interests in other people, and God is interested in some funny people, viz., in you and in me! We must
beware of letting natural affinities hinder our walking in love.
One of the most cruel ways of killing love is by disdain built
on natural affinities. To be guided by our affinities is a natural
tendency, but spiritually this tendency must be denied, and as
we deny it we find that God gives us affinity with those for
whom we have no natural affinity. Is there anyone in your life
who would not be there if you were not a Christian? The love
of God is not mere sentimentality; it is a most practical thing
for the saint to love as God loves. The springs of love are in
God, not in us. The love of God is only in us when it has been
shed abroad in our hearts by the Holy Spirit, and the evidence
that it is there is the spontaneous way in which it is manifested.

AHW 117

YOU WON'T REACH IT ON TIPTOE

Add to your brotherliness . . . love. (2 Peter 1:7)

Love is indefinite to most of us, we do not know what we mean when we talk about love. Love is the sovereign preference of one person for another, and spiritually Jesus demands that that preference be for Himself (cf. Luke 14:26). When the love of God is shed abroad in our hearts by the Holy Ghost, Jesus Christ is easily first; then we must practise the working out of these things mentioned by Peter.

The first thing God does is to knock pretence and the pious pose right out of me. The Holy Spirit reveals that God loved me not because I was lovable, but because it was His nature to do so. Now, He says to me, show the same love to others—"Love as I have loved you." "I will bring any number of people about you whom you cannot respect, and you must exhibit My love to them as I have exhibited it to you." You won't reach it on tiptoe. Some of us have tried to, but we were soon tired.

"The Lord suffereth long . . ." Let me look within and see His dealings with me. The knowledge that God has loved me to the uttermost, to the end of all my sin and meanness and selfishness and wrong, will send me forth into the world to love in the same way. God's love to me is inexhaustible, and I must love others from the bedrock of God's love to me. Growth in grace stops the moment I get huffed. I get huffed because I have a peculiar person to live with. Just think how disagreeable I have been to God! Am I prepared to be so identified with the Lord Jesus that His life and His sweetness are being poured out all the time? Neither natural love nor Divine love will remain unless it is cultivated. Love is spontaneous, but it has to be maintained by discipline.

And the second is like unto it, Thou shalt love thy neighbour as thyself. (Matthew 22:39)

Everything our Lord taught about the duty of man to man might be summed up in the one law of giving. It is as if He set Himself to contradict the natural counsel of the human heart, which is to acquire and keep. A child will say of a gift, 'Is it my own?' When a man is born again that instinct is replaced by another, the instinct of giving. The law of the life of a disciple is Give, Give, Give (e.g., Luke 6:38). As Christians our giving is to be proportionate to all we have received of the infinite giving of God. 'Freely ye have received, freely give.' Not how much we give, but what we do not give, is the test of our Christianity. When we speak of giving we nearly always think only of money. Money is the life-blood of most of us. We have a remarkable trick—when we give money we don't give sympathy; and when we give sympathy we don't give money. The only way to get insight into the meaning for ourselves of what Jesus taught is by being indwelt by the Holy Spirit, because He enables us first of all to understand our Lord's life; unless we do that, we will exploit His teaching, take out of it only what we agree with. There is one aspect of giving we think little about, but which had a prominent place in our Lord's life, viz., that of social intercourse. He accepted hospitality on the right hand and on the left, from publicans and from the Pharisees, so much so that they said He was 'a gluttonous man, and a wine bibber, a friend of publicans and sinners!' He spent Himself with one lodestar all the time, to seek and to save that which was lost, and Paul says, 'I am become all things to all men, that I might by all means save some.' How few of us ever think of giving socially! We are so parsimonious that we won't spend a thing in conversation unless it is on a line that helps us!

CHI 77–8

MAKE A HABIT OF
HAVING NO HABITS

*For if these things are yours and abound, they make you to be
not idle nor unfruitful. (2 Peter 1:8, RV)*

When we begin to form a habit we are conscious of it. There
are times when we are conscious of becoming virtuous and patient and godly, but it is only a stage; if we stop there we shall
get the strut of the spiritual prig. The right thing to do with
habits is to lose them in the life of the Lord, until every habit
is so practised that there is no conscious habit at all. Our spiritual life continually resolves into introspection because there
are some qualities we have not added as yet. Ultimately the
relationship is to be a completely simple one.

Your god may be your little Christian habit, the habit of
prayer at stated times, or the habit of Bible reading. Watch how
your Father will upset those times if you begin to worship your
habit instead of what the habit symbolizes—I can't do that just
now, I am praying; it is my hour with God. No, it is your hour
with your habit. There is a quality that is lacking in you. Recognize the defect and then look for the opportunity of exer-
cising yourself along the line of the quality to be added.

Love means that there is no habit visible, you have come to
the place where the habit is lost, and by practice you do the
thing unconsciously. If you are consciously holy, there are certain things you imagine you cannot do, certain relationships
in which you are far from simple; that means there is something to be added. The only supernatural life is the life the Lord
Jesus lived, and He was at home with God anywhere. Is there
anywhere where you are not at home with God? Let God press
through in that particular circumstance until you gain Him,
and life becomes the simple life of a child.

Give a portion to seven, and also to eight; for thou knowest not what evil shall be upon the earth. If the clouds be full of rain, they empty themselves upon the earth: and if the tree fall toward the south or toward the north, in the places where the tree falleth, there it shall be. (Ecclesiastes 11:2)

'Economy is doing without what you want just now in case a time may come when you will want what you don't want now.' It is possible to be so economical that you venture nothing. We have deified economy, placed insurance and economy on the throne, consequently we will do nothing on the line of adventure or extravagance. To use the word 'economy' in connection with God is to belittle and misunderstand Him. Where is the economy of God in His sunsets and sunrises, in the grass and flowers and trees? God has made a superabounding number of things that are of no *use* to anyone. How many of us bother our heads about the sunrises and sunsets? Yet they go on just the same. Lavish extravagance to an extraordinary degree is the characteristic of God, never economy. Grace is the overflowing favour of God. Imagine a man who is in love being economical! The characteristic of a man when he is awake is never that he is calculating and sensible.

Today we are so afraid of poverty that we never dream of doing anything that might involve us in being poor. We are out of the running of the mediaeval monks who took on the vow of poverty. Many of us are poor, but none of us chooses to be. These men chose to be poor, they believed it was the only way they could perfect their own inner life. Our attitude is that if we are extravagant, a rainy day will come for which we have not laid up. You cannot lay up for a rainy day and justify it in the light of Jesus Christ's teaching. We are not Christians at heart, we don't believe in the wisdom of God, but only in our own. We go in for insurance and economy and speculation, everything that makes us secure in our own wisdom.

SHH 142

THE HABIT OF A GOOD CONSCIENCE

A conscience void of offence toward God, and toward men.
(Acts 24:16)

God's commands are given to the life of His Son in us, consequently to the human nature in which His Son has been formed, His commands are difficult, but immediately we obey they become divinely easy.

Conscience is that faculty in me which attaches itself to the highest that I know, and tells me what the highest I know demands that I do. It is the eye of the soul which looks out either towards God or towards what it regards as the highest, and therefore conscience records differently in different people. If I am in the habit of steadily facing myself with God, my conscience will always introduce God's perfect law and indicate what I should do. The point is, will I obey? I have to make an effort to keep my conscience so sensitive that I walk without offence. I should be living in such perfect sympathy with God's Son, that in every circumstance the spirit of my mind is renewed, and I "make out" at once "what is that good, and acceptable, and perfect, will of God."

God always educates us down to the scruple. Is my ear so keen to hear the tiniest whisper of the Spirit that I know what I should do? "Grieve not the Holy Spirit." He does not come with a voice like thunder; His voice is so gentle that it is easy to ignore it. The one thing that keeps the conscience sensitive to Him is the continual habit of being open to God on the inside. When there is any debate, quit. "Why shouldn't I do this?" You are on the wrong track. There is no debate possible when conscience speaks. At your peril, you allow one thing to obscure your inner communion with God. Drop it, whatever it is, and see that you keep your inner vision clear.

Your body is the temple of the Holy Ghost. (1 Corinthians 6:19)

Have I ever realized that the most wonderful thing in the world is the thing that is nearest to me, viz., my body? Who made it? Almighty God. Do I pay the remotest attention to my body as being the temple of the Holy Ghost? Remember our Lord lived in a body like ours. The next reality that I come in contact with by my body is other people's bodies. All our relationships in life, all the joys and all the miseries, all the hells and all the heavens, are based on bodies; and the reality of Jesus Christ's salvation brings us down to the Mother Earth we live on, and makes us see by the regenerating power of God's grace how amazingly precious are the ordinary things that are always with us. Master that, and you have mastered everything. We imagine that our bodies are a hindrance to our development, whereas it is only through our bodies that we develop. We cannot express a character without a body.

MFL 62

THE HABIT OF ENJOYING
THE DISAGREEABLE

That life also of Jesus might be made manifest in our mortal flesh.
(2 Cor. 4:10)

We have to form habits to express what God's grace has done in us. It is not a question of being saved from hell, but of being saved in order to manifest the life of the Son of God in our mortal flesh, and it is the disagreeable things which make us exhibit whether or not we are manifesting His life. Do I manifest the essential sweetness of the Son of God, or the essential irritation of "myself" apart from Him? The only thing that will enable me to enjoy the disagreeable is the keen enthusiasm of letting the life of the Son of God manifest itself in me. No matter how disagreeable a thing may be, say—"Lord, I am delighted to obey Thee in this matter," and instantly the Son of God will press to the front, and there will be manifested in my human life that which glorifies Jesus.

There must be no debate. The moment you obey the light, the Son of God presses through you in that particular; but if you debate you grieve the Spirit of God. You must keep yourself fit to let the life of the Son of God be manifested, and you cannot keep yourself fit if you give way to self-pity. Our circumstances are the means of manifesting how wonderfully perfect and extraordinarily pure the Son of God is. The thing that ought to make the heart beat is a new way of manifesting the Son of God. It is one thing to choose the disagreeable, and another thing to go into the disagreeable by God's engineering. If God puts you there, He is amply sufficient.

Keep your soul fit to manifest the life of the Son of God. Never live on memories; let the word of God be always living and active in you.

Your body is the temple of the Holy Ghost. (1 Corinthians 6:19)

The instinct of ownership is a right one, though the disposition expressed through it may be wrong. In a saint the idea of ownership is that we have the power to glorify God by good works (see Matthew 5:16). What we own is the honour of Jesus Christ. Have I ever realized that His honour is at stake in my bodily life? 'What? know ye not that your body is the temple of the Holy Ghost which is in you . . . ?' Do I own my body for that one purpose? Do I own my brain to think God's thoughts after Him? We have to be intensely and personally God's.

The Spirit of God brings us into the realization of our ownership, and the instinct of ownership becomes a tremendous wealth in the life. 'All things are yours', and Paul prays that the eyes of our understanding may be enlightened that we may know what is ours in Christ Jesus.

No personality, from a tiny child to Almighty God, is without this sense of ownership. How wonderfully sprightly a dog looks when he is owned! How weary and hang-dog we become when we are convicted of sin; but when we experience God's salvation, we straighten up immediately, everything is altered, we can fling our heads back and look the world in the face because the Lord Jesus Christ is ours and we are His. A dominant ownership, such as the ownership of the Lord means that we own everything He owns. 'The meek shall inherit the earth.'

MFL 75

THE HABIT OF RISING TO THE OCCASION

That ye may know what is the hope of His calling . . . (Eph. 1:18)

Remember what you are saved for—that the Son of God might be manifested in your mortal flesh. Bend the whole energy of your powers to realize your election as a child of God; rise to the occasion every time.

You cannot do anything for your salvation, but you must do something to manifest it, you must work out what God has worked in. Are you working it out with your tongue, and your brain and your nerves? If you are still the same miserable crosspatch, set on your own way, then it is a lie to say that God has saved and sanctified you.

God is the Master Engineer, He allows the difficulties to come in order to see if you can vault over them properly—"By my God have I leaped over a wall." God will never shield you from any of the requirements of a son or daughter of His. Peter says—"Think it not strange concerning the fiery trial which is to try you." Rise to the occasion; do the thing. It does not matter how it hurts as long as it gives God the chance to manifest Himself in your mortal flesh.

May God not find the whine in us any more, but may He find us full of spiritual pluck and athleticism, ready to face anything He brings. We have to exercise ourselves in order that the Son of God may be manifested in our mortal flesh. God never has museums. The only aim of the life is that the Son of God may be manifested, and all dictation to God vanishes. Our Lord never dictated to His Father, and we are not here to dictate to God; we are here to submit to His will so that He may work through us what He wants. When we realize this, He will make us broken bread and poured-out wine to feed and nourish others.

> *Truly the light is sweet, and a pleasant thing it is for the eyes to behold the sun: Yea, if a man live many years, let him rejoice in them all: but let him remember the days of darkness, for they shall be many. All that cometh is vanity. (Ecclesiastes 11:7–8)*

Solomon is stating the practical attitude to things in the midst of the haphazard. You have to live this actual life, he says, with our confidence based on God, and see that you keep your day full of the joy and the light of life; enjoy things as they come. When we have a particularly good time, we are apt to say, 'Oh well, it can't last long.' We expect the worst. When we have one trouble, we expect more. The Bible counsels us to rejoice— 'yet let him remember the days of darkness'.

The Bible talks about drinking wine when we are glad (see Psalm 104:15); this is different from the modern view. It is bad to drink wine when you are in the dumps. Solomon is amazingly keen that a man should enjoy the pleasant things, remembering that that is why they are here. The universe is meant for enjoyment. '. . . God, who giveth us richly all things to enjoy.' 'Whatsoever ye do whether ye eat or drink, do all to the glory of God.' We argue on the rational line—Don't do this or that because it is wrong. Paul argues in this way: Don't do it, not because it is wrong, but because the man who follows you will stumble if he does it, therefore cut it out, never let him see you do it any more (cf. 1 Corinthians 8:9–13). Solomon's attitude is a safe and sane one, that when a man is rightly related to God he has to see that he enjoys his own life and that others do too.

SHH 145

THE HABIT OF WEALTH

Partakers of the divine nature. (2 Peter 1:4)

We are made partakers of the Divine nature through the promises; then we have to "manipulate" the Divine nature in our human nature by habits, and the first habit to form is the habit of realizing the provision God has made. "Oh, I can't afford it," we say—one of the worst lies is tucked up in that phrase. It is ungovernably bad taste to talk about money in the natural domain, and so it is spiritually, and yet we talk as if our Heavenly Father had cut us off without a shilling! We think it a sign of real modesty to say at the end of a day—"Oh, well, I have just got through, but it has been a severe tussle." And all the Almighty God is ours in the Lord Jesus! And He will tax the last grain of sand and the remotest star to bless us if we will obey Him. What does it matter if external circumstances are hard? Why should they not be! If we give way to self-pity and indulge in the luxury of misery, we banish God's riches from our own lives and hinder others from entering into His provision. No sin is worse than the sin of self-pity, because it obliterates God and puts self-interest upon the throne. It opens our mouths to spit out murmurings and our lives become craving spiritual sponges; there is nothing lovely or generous about them.

When God is beginning to be satisfied with us He will impoverish everything in the nature of fictitious wealth, until we learn that all our fresh springs are in Him. If the majesty and grace and power of God are not being manifested in us (not to our consciousness), God holds us responsible. "God is able to make all grace abound"; then learn to lavish the grace of God on others. Be stamped with God's nature, and His blessing will come through you all the time.

Take no thought for your life . . . (Matthew 6:25)

Immediately we look at these words of our Lord, we find them the most revolutionary of statements. We argue in exactly the opposite way, even the most spiritual of us—'I *must* live, I *must* make so much money, I *must* be clothed and fed.' That is how it begins; the great concern of the life is not God, but how we are going to fit ourselves to live. Jesus Christ says, 'Reverse the order, get rightly related to Me first, see that you maintain that as the great care of your life, and never put the concentration of your care on the other things.' It is a severe discipline to allow the Holy Spirit to bring us into harmony with the teaching of Jesus in these verses.

SSM 68

If after you have received the Holy Spirit, you try and put other things first instead of God, you will find confusion. The Holy Spirit presses through and says—'Where does God come in in this new relationship? in this mapped-out holiday? in these new books you are buying?' The Holy Spirit always presses that point until we learn to make concentration on God our first consideration. It is not only wrong to worry, it is real infidelity because it means we do not believe God can look after the little practical details of our lives, it is never anything else that worries us. Notice what Jesus said would choke the word He puts in—the devil? No, the cares of this world. That is how infidelity begins. It is 'the little foxes that spoil the vines', the little worries always. The great cure for infidelity is obedience to the Spirit of God.

SSM 72

HIS ASCENSION AND OUR UNION

And it came to pass, while He blessed them, He was parted from them, and carried up into heaven. (Luke 24:51)

We have no corresponding experience to the events in Our Lord's life after the Transfiguration. From then onwards Our Lord's life was altogether vicarious. Up to the time of the Transfiguration He had exhibited the normal perfect life of a man; from the Transfiguration onwards—Gethsemane, the Cross, the Resurrection—everything is unfamiliar to us. His Cross is the door by which every member of the human race can enter into the life of God; by His Resurrection He has the right to give eternal life to any man, and by His Ascension Our Lord enters heaven and keeps the door open for humanity.

On the Mount of Ascension the Transfiguration is completed. If Jesus had gone to heaven from the Mount of Transfiguration, He would have gone alone; He would have been nothing more to us than a glorious Figure. But He turned His back on the glory, and came down from the Mount to identify Himself with fallen humanity.

The Ascension is the consummation of the Transfiguration. Our Lord does now go back into His primal glory; but He does not go back simply as Son of God; He goes back to God as Son of Man as well as Son of God. There is now freedom of access for anyone straight to the very throne of God by the Ascension of the Son of Man. As Son of Man Jesus Christ deliberately limited omnipotence, omnipresence and omniscience in Himself. Now they are His in absolute full power. As Son of Man Jesus Christ has all power at the throne of God. He is King of kings and Lords of lords from the day of His Ascension until now.

Take no thought saying, What shall we eat? or What shall we drink? or, Wherewithal shall we be clothed? (Matthew 6:31)

Today we enthrone insurance and economy, but it is striking to recall that the one thing Jesus Christ commended was extravagance. Our Lord only called one work 'good', and that was the act of Mary of Bethany when she broke the alabaster box of ointment. It was neither useful nor her duty, it sprang from her devotion to Jesus, and He said of it—'Wheresoever this gospel shall be preached throughout the whole world, this also that she hath done shall be spoken of for a memorial of her.'

The object of a man's life is not to hoard; he has to get enough for his brute life and no more; the best of his life is to be spent in confidence in God. Man is meant to utilize the earth and its products for food and the nourishment of his body, but he must not live in order to make his existence. If the children of Israel gathered more manna than they needed, it turned into dry rot, and that law still holds good.

SHH 73

CAREFUL UNREASONABLENESS

Behold the fowls of the air . . . Consider the lilies of the field.
(Matt. 6:26, 28)

Consider the lilies of the field, how they grow; they simply *are*!
Think of the sea, the air, the sun, the stars and the moon—all
these *are*, and what a ministration they exert. So often we mar
God's designed influence through us by our self-conscious effort to be consistent and useful. Jesus says that there is only
one way to develop spiritually, and that is by concentration
on God. "Do not bother about being of use to others; believe
on Me"—pay attention to the Source, and out of you will flow
rivers of living water. We cannot get at the springs of our natural life by common sense, and Jesus is teaching that growth in
spiritual life does not depend on our Father in heaven. Our
heavenly Father knows the circumstances we are in, and if we
keep concentrated on Him we will grow spiritually as the lilies.

The people who influence us most are not those who but-
tonhole us and talk to us, but those who live their lives like
the stars in heaven and the lilies in the field, perfectly simply
and unaffectedly. Those are the lives that mould us.

If you want to be of use to God, get rightly related to Jesus
Christ and He will make you of use unconsciously every minute
you live.

> *When ye come into the land which I give you, then shall the land*
> *keep a sabbath unto the Lord . . . in the seventh year shall be a*
> *sabbath of solemn rest for the land, a sabbath unto the Lord.*
> *(Leviticus 25:1–4)*

The twenty-fifth chapter of Leviticus is the great classic on the rights of the land. The establishment of men's rights on the earth is limited by the rights of the earth itself. If you keep taking from the land, never giving it any rest, in time it will stop giving to you. We talk about the rights of the land, and make it mean our right to grab as much from it as we can. In God's sight the land has rights just as human beings have, and many of the theories which are being advanced today go back to God's original prescription for the land. When God ordained 'a sabbath of solemn rest for the land', it was a reiteration of the instructions given to Adam in the Garden of Eden—'Be fruitful, and multiply, and replenish the earth, and subdue it' (Genesis 1:28). Man was intended to replenish the earth by looking after it, being its lord not its tyrant; sin has made man its tyrant (cf. Romans 8:19). The rights of the land will probably only be fully realized in the Millennium, because in this dispensation men ignore obedience to God's laws.

BE 24

"OUT OF THE WRECK I RISE"

Who shall separate us from the love of Christ? (Rom. 8:35)

God does not keep a man immune from trouble; He says—"I will be with him in trouble." It does not matter what actual troubles in the most extreme form get hold of a man's life, not one of them can separate him from his relationship to God. We are "more than conquerors in all these things." Paul is not talking of imaginary things, but of things that are desperately actual; and he says we are super-victors in the midst of them, not by our ingenuity, or by our courage, or by anything other than the fact that not one of them affects our relationship to God in Jesus Christ. Rightly or wrongly, we are where we are, exactly in the condition we are in. I am sorry for the Christian who has not something in his circumstances he wishes was not there.

"Shall tribulation . . .?" Tribulation is never a noble thing but let tribulation be what it may—exhausting, galling, fatiguing, it is not able to separate us from the love of God. Never let cares or tribulations separate you from the fact that God loves you.

"Shall anguish . . .?"—can God's love hold when everything says that His love is a lie, and that there is no such thing as justice?

"Shall famine . . .?"—can we not only believe in the love of God but be more than conquerors, even while we are being starved?

Either Jesus Christ is a deceiver and Paul is deluded, or some extraordinary thing happens to a man who holds on to the love of God when the odds are all against God's character. Logic is silenced in the face of every one of these things. Only one thing can account for it—the love of God in Christ Jesus. "Out of the wreck I rise" every time.

I have uttered that I understood not: things too wonderful for me, which I knew not. (Job 42:3)

Everything a man takes to be the key to a problem is apt to turn out another lock. For instance, the theory of evolution was supposed to be the key to the problem of the universe, but instead it has turned out a lock. Again, the atomic theory was thought to be the key; then it was discovered that the atom itself was composed of electrons, and each electron was found to be a universe of its own, and that theory too becomes a lock and not a key. Everything that man attempts as a simplification of life, other than a personal relationship to God, turns out to be a lock, and we should be alert to recognize when a thing turns from a key to a lock. The creed Job held, which pretended to be a key to the character of God, turned out to be a lock, and Job is realizing that the only key to life is not a statement of faith in God, nor an intellectual conception of God, but a personal relationship to Him. God Himself is the key to the riddle of the universe, and the basis of things is to be found only in Him. If a man leaves out God and takes any scientific explanation as the key, he only succeeds in finding another lock.

BFB 99

THE REALM OF THE REAL

In your patience possess ye your souls. (Luke 21:19)

When a man is born again, there is not the same robustness in his thinking or reasoning for a time as formerly. We have to make an expression of the new life, to form the mind of Christ. "Acquire your soul with patience." Many of us prefer to stay at the threshold of the Christian life instead of going on to construct a soul in accordance with the new life God has put within. We fail because we are ignorant of the way we are made, we put things down to the devil instead of our own undisciplined natures. Think what we can be when we are roused!

There are certain things we must not pray about—moods, for instance. Moods never go by praying moods go by kicking. A mood nearly always has its seat in the physical condition, not in the moral. It is a continual effort not to listen to the moods which arise from a physical condition; never submit to them for a second. We have to take ourselves by the scruff of the neck and shake ourselves, and we will find that we can do what we said we could not. The curse with most of us is that we *won't*. The Christian life is one of incarnate spiritual pluck.

Except ye see signs and wonders, ye will not believe. (John 4:48)

A miracle is a work done by one who has fuller knowledge and authority than we have. Things that were called miracles a hundred years ago are not thought of as miracles today because men have come to a fuller knowledge. The miracles of Jesus were an exhibition of the power of God, that is, they were simply mirrors of what God Almighty is doing gradually and everywhere and all the time; but every miracle Jesus performed had a tremendous lesson behind it. It was not merely an exhibition of the power of God, there was always a moral meaning behind for the individual. That is why God does not heal some people. We are apt to confine life to one phase only, the physical: there are three phases—physical, psychical and spiritual. Whenever Jesus touched the physical domain a miracle happened in the other phases as well. If a miracle is wrought by any other power in the physical it leaves no corresponding stamp of truth in the other domains of soul and spirit.

SHL 32

DIVINE REASONINGS OF FAITH

*But seek ye first the kingdom of God, and His righteousness, and
all these things shall be added unto you. (Matt. 6:33)*

Immediately we look at these words of Jesus, we find them
the most revolutionary statement human ears ever listened to.
"Seek ye first the kingdom of God." We argue in exactly the
opposite way, even the most spiritually-minded of us—"But I
must live; I must make so much money; I must be clothed; I
must be fed." The great concern of our lives is not the kingdom of God, but how we are to fit ourselves to live. Jesus re-
verses the order: Get rightly related to God first, maintain that
as the great care of your life, and never put the concern of your
care on the other things.

"Take no thought for your life . . ." Our Lord points out the
utter unreasonableness from His standpoint of being so anxious over the means of living. Jesus is not saying that the man
who takes thought for nothing is blessed—that man is a fool.
Jesus taught that a disciple has to make his relationship to God
the dominating concentration of his life, and to be carefully
careless about everything else in comparison to that. Jesus is
saying—"Don't make the ruling factor of your life what you
shall eat and what you shall drink, but be concentrated absolutely on God." Some people are careless over what they eat
and drink, and they suffer for it; they are careless about what
they wear, and they look as they have no business to look; they
are careless about their earthly affairs, and God holds them
responsible. Jesus is saying that the great care of the life is to
put the relationship to God first, and everything else second.

It is one of the severest disciplines of the Christian life to
allow the Holy Spirit to bring us into harmony with the teaching of Jesus in these verses.

The Son of Man hath not where to lay His head. (Matthew 8:20)

The poverty of our Lord and of His disciples is the exact expression of the nature of the religion of Jesus Christ—just man and God; man possessing nothing, professing nothing; yet when the Lord asks at some dawn, after a heart-breaking failure, 'Lovest thou me?' the soul confesses, 'Yea, Lord, thou knowest that I love thee.' And when that poverty is a disgust to the full-fed religious world, the disciple does not *profess*, but confesses, with aching hands and bleeding feet, 'I love Him', and goes 'outside the camp, bearing his reproach'.

We have grown literally afraid of being poor. We despise anyone who elects to be poor in order to simplify and save his inner life. If he does not join the general scramble, and pant with the money-making street, we deem him spiritless and lacking in ambition. We have lost the power of imagining what the ancient idealization of poverty could have meant—the liberation from material attachments, the unbribed soul, the manlier indifference, the paying our way by what we are to do, and not by what we have; the right to fling away our life at any moment irresponsibly, the more athletic trim, in short, the moral fighting shape.

DL 76, 77

NOW THIS EXPLAINS IT

That they all may be one; as thou, Father, art in me, and I in thee, that they also may be one in us. (John 17:21)

If you are going through a solitary way, read John 17, it will explain exactly why you are where you are—Jesus has prayed that you may be one with the Father as He is. Are you helping God to answer that prayer, or have you some other end for your life? Since you became a disciple you cannot be as independent as you used to be.

The purpose of God is not to answer our prayers, but by our prayers we come to discern the mind of God, and this is revealed in John 17. There is one prayer God must answer, and that is the prayer of Jesus—"that they may be one, even as We are One." Are we as close to Jesus Christ as that?

God is not concerned about our plans; He does not say—Do you want to go through this bereavement; this upset? He allows these things for His own purpose. The things we are going through are either making us sweeter, better, nobler men and women; or they are making us more captious and fault-finding, more insistent upon our own way. The things that happen either make us fiends, or they make us saints; it depends entirely upon the relationship we are in to God. If we say—"Thy will be done," we get the consolation of John 17, the consolation of knowing that our Father is working according to His own wisdom. When we understand what God is after we will not get mean and cynical. Jesus has prayed nothing less for us than absolute oneness with Himself as He was one with the Father. Some of us are far off it, and yet God will not leave us alone until we are one with Him, because Jesus has prayed that we may be.

Then the lust, when it hath conceived, beareth sin: and the sin, when it is full grown, bringeth forth death. (James 1:15 [RV]).

How do we think about sin habitually, as Christians? If we have light views about sin we are not students in the school of Christ. The fact of sin is the secret of Jesus Christ's Cross; its removal is the secret of His risen and ascended life. Do we think along these lines? It is quite possible to be living in union with God through the Atonement and yet be traitors mentally . . . .

If you read carefully the modern statements regarding sin you will be amazed to find how often we are much more in sympathy with them than with the Bible statements. We have to face the problem that our hearts may be right with God while our heads have a startling affinity with a great deal that is antagonistic to the Bible teaching. What we need, and what we get if we go on with God, is an intellectual re-birth as well as a heart re-birth.

The trouble with the modern statements regarding sin is that they make sin far too slight. Sin according to the modern view simply means selfishness, and preachers and teachers are as dead against selfishness as the New Testament is. Immediately we come to the Bible we find that sin is much deeper than that. According to the Bible, sin in its final analysis is not a defect but a defiance, a defiance that means death to the life of God in us. Sin is seen not only in selfishness, but in what men call unselfishness. It is possible to have such sympathy with our fellow-men as to be guilty of red-handed rebellion against God. Enthusiasm for humanity as it is, is quite a different thing from the enthusiasm for the saints which the Bible reveals, viz., enthusiasm for readjusted humanity.

BE 114–15

CAREFUL INFIDELITY

Take no thought for your life, what ye shall eat or what ye shall drink; nor yet for your body what ye shall put on. (Matt. 6:25)

Jesus sums up common-sense carefulness in a disciple as infidelity. If we have received the Spirit of God, He will press through and say—Now where does God come in in this relationship, in this mapped out holiday, until we learn to make Him our first consideration. Whenever we put other things first, there is confusion.

"Take no thought . . ." Don't take the pressure of forethought upon yourself. It is not only wrong to worry, it is infidelity, because worrying means that we do not think that God can look after the practical details of our lives, and it is never anything else that worries us. Have you ever noticed what Jesus said would choke the word He puts in? The devil? No, the cares of this world. It is the little worries always. I will not trust where I cannot see, that is where infidelity begins. The only cure for infidelity is obedience to the Spirit.

The great word of Jesus to His disciples is *abandon*.

Marvel not that I said unto thee, ye must be born again.
(John 3:7)

The reason we do not see the need to be born from above is that we have a vast capacity for ignoring facts. People talk about the evolution of the race. The writers of today seem to be incapable of a profound understanding of history, they write glibly about the way the race is developing, where are their eyes and their reading of human life as it is? We are not evolving and developing in any sense to justify what is known as evolution. We have developed in certain domains but not in all. We are nowhere near the massive, profound intellectual grasp of the men who lived before Christ was born. What brain today can come near Plato or Socrates? And yet people say we are developing and getting better, and we are laying the flattering unction to our souls that we have left Jesus Christ and His ideas twenty centuries behind. No wonder Jesus said that if we stand by Him and take His point of view, men will hate us as they hated Him.

HG 64

THE DELIGHT OF DESPAIR

And when I saw Him, I fell at His feet as dead. (Rev. 1:17)

It may be that like the apostle John you know Jesus Christ intimately, when suddenly He appears with no familiar characteristic at all, and the only thing you can do is to fall at His feet as dead. There are times when God cannot reveal Himself in any other way than in His majesty, and it is the awfulness of the vision which brings you to the delight of despair; if you are ever to be raised up, it must be by the hand of God.

"He laid His right hand upon me." In the midst of the awfulness, a touch comes, and you know it is the right hand of Jesus Christ. The right hand not of restraint nor of correction nor of chastisement, but the right hand of the Everlasting Father. Whenever His hand is laid upon you, it is ineffable peace and comfort, the sense that "underneath are the everlasting arms," full of sustaining and comfort and strength. When once His touch comes, nothing at all can cast you into fear again. In the midst of all His ascended glory the Lord Jesus comes to speak to an insignificant disciple, and to say—"Fear not." His tenderness is ineffably sweet. Do I know Him like that?

Watch some of the things that strike despair. There is despair in which there is no delight, no horizon, no hope of anything brighter; but the delight of despair comes when I know that "in me (that is, in my flesh) dwelleth no good thing." I delight to know that there is that in me which must fall prostrate before God when He manifests Himself, and if I am ever to be raised up it must be by the hand of God. God can do nothing for me until I get to the limit of the possible.

I am crucified with Christ: nevertheless I live; yet not I, but Christ liveth in me. (Galatians 2:20)

To imagine that Jesus Christ came to save and sanctify *me* is heresy: He came to save and sanctify me *into himself,* to be His absolute bondslave; so completely His bondslave that when He speaks there is no possibility of dispute. 'I reckon on you for extreme service, with no complaining on your part and no explanation on Mine.' We begin to debate and say, 'Why shouldn't I do this? I'm within my rights.' That idea is so foreign to our Lord's conception that He has made no provision for it. The passion of Christianity is that I deliberately sign away my own rights and become a bondslave of Jesus Christ. Any fool can insist on his rights, and any devil will see that he gets them; but the Sermon on the Mount means that the only right the saint will insist on is the right to give up his rights. That is the New Testament idea of sanctification, and that is why so few get anywhere near the baptism with the Holy Ghost. 'I want to be baptized with the Holy Ghost so that I may be of use'—then it is all up. We are baptized with the Holy Ghost not *for* anything at all, but entirely, as our Lord puts it, to be His witnesses, those with whom He can do exactly what He likes.

HGM 130

THE TEST OF SELF-INTEREST

If thou wilt take the left hand, then I will go to the right; or if thou depart to the right hand, then I will go to the left.
(Gen. 13:9)

As soon as you begin to live the life of faith in God, fascinating and luxurious prospects will open up before you, and these things are yours by right; but if you are living the life of faith you will exercise your right to waive your rights, and let God choose for you. God sometimes allows you to get into a place of testing where your own welfare would be the right and proper thing to consider if you were not living a life of faith; but if you are, you will joyfully waive your right and leave God to choose for you. This is the discipline by means of which the natural is transformed into the spiritual by obedience to the voice of God.

Whenever *right* is made the guidance in the life, it will blunt the spiritual insight. The great enemy of the life of faith in God is not sin, but the good which is not good enough. The good is always the enemy of the best. It would seem the wisest thing in the world for Abraham to choose, it was his right, and the people around would consider him a fool for not choosing. Many of us do not go on spiritually because we prefer to choose what is right instead of relying on God to choose for us. We have to learn to walk according to the standard which has its eye on God. *"Walk before Me."*

And without shedding of blood is no remission of sins.
(Hebrews 9:22)

The first fundamental reference in this verse is unquestionably
to our Lord's Atonement; and yet there is a direct reference to
ourselves. Do we begin to know what the Bible means by 'the
blood of Jesus Christ'? Blood and life are inseparable. In the
Bible the experiences of salvation and sanctification are never
separated as we separate them; they are separable in experience, but when God's Book speaks of being 'in Christ' it is
always in terms of entire sanctification. We are apt to look upon
the blood of Christ as a kind of magic-working thing, instead
of an impartation of His very life. The whole purpose of being
born again and being identified with the death of the Lord Jesus
is that His blood may flow through our mortal body; then the
tempers and the affections and dispositions which were manifested in the life of the Lord will be manifested in us in some
degree. . . . There are two sides to the Atonement—it is not only
the life of Christ *for* me but His life *in* me for my life; no Christ
for me if I do not have Christ *in* me. All through there is to
be this strenuous, glorious practising in our bodily life of the
changes which God has wrought in our soul through His Spirit,
and the only proof that we are in earnest is that we work out
what God works in. As we apply this truth to ourselves, we
shall find in practical experience that God does alter passions
and nerves and tempers. God alters every physical thing in a
human being so that these bodies can be used now as slaves to
the new disposition. We can make our eyes, and ears, and every
one of our bodily organs express as slaves the altered disposition of our soul.

BP 70

THINK AS JESUS TAUGHT

Pray without ceasing. (1 Thess. 5:17)

We think rightly or wrongly about prayer according to the conception we have in our minds of prayer. If we think of prayer as the breath in our lungs and the blood from our hearts, we think rightly. The blood flows ceaselessly, and breathing continues ceaselessly; we are not conscious of it, but it is always going on. We are not always conscious of Jesus keeping us in perfect joint with God, but if we are obeying Him, He always is. Prayer is not an exercise, it is the life. Beware of anything that stops ejaculatory prayer. "Pray without ceasing," keep the childlike habit of ejaculatory prayer in your heart to God all the time.

Jesus never mentioned unanswered prayer; He had the boundless certainty that prayer is always answered. Have we by the Spirit the unspeakable certainty that Jesus had about prayer, or do we think of the times when God does not seem to have answered prayer? "Every one that asketh receiveth." We say—"But . . . , but . . ." God answers prayer in the best way, not sometimes, but every time, although the immediate manifestation of the answer in the domain in which we want it may not always follow. Do we expect God to answer prayer?

The danger with us is that we want to water down the things that Jesus says and make them mean something in accordance with common sense; if it were only common sense, it was not worth while for Him to say it. The things Jesus says about prayer are supernatural revelations.

And there appeared unto them Elias and Moses: and they were talking with Jesus. (Mark 9:4)

Jesus was standing in the full blaze and glory of His pre-Incarnate glory while the two representatives of the Old Covenant talked with Him about the issue which He was about to accomplish at Jerusalem. Then He turned His back upon that glory, and came down from the Mount to be identified with fallen humanity, symbolized by the demon-possessed boy. Had He gone back into the glory which was His before the Incarnation having only reached the Mount of Transfiguration, He would have left the human race exactly where it was; His life would only have been a sublime ideal. There are many who look at the life of Jesus Christ as an ideal and nothing more— 'His teachings are so fine, we do not need to have anything to do with the Atonement, or with those crude doctrines of the apostle Paul's about the Cross and personal apprehension; it is quite enough for us to have the Sermon on the Mount.' I should think it was! If Jesus Christ came to be an Example only, He is the greatest torturer of the human race. But our Lord did not come primarily to teach us and give us an example; He came to lift us into a totally new kingdom, and to impart a new life to which His teachings would apply.

PR 78

THE LIFE THAT LIVES

*Tarry ye in the city of Jerusalem, until ye be endued with power
from on high. (Luke 24:49)*

The disciples had to tarry until the day of Pentecost not for their
own preparation only; they had to wait until the Lord was glorified historically. As soon as He was glorified, what happened?
"Therefore being by the right hand of God exalted, and having received of the Father the promise of the Holy Ghost, He
hath shed forth this, which ye now see and hear." The paren-
thesis in John 7:39 ("For the Holy Ghost was not yet given;
because that Jesus was not yet glorified") does not apply to us;
the Holy Ghost *has been* given, the Lord *is* glorified; the waiting
depends not on God's providence, but on our fitness.

The Holy Spirit's influence and power were at work before
Pentecost, but *He* was not there. Immediately Our Lord was
glorified in Ascension, the Holy Spirit came into this world, and
He has been here ever since. We have to receive the revelation that He is here. The reception of the Holy Spirit is the
maintained attitude of a believer. When we receive the Holy
Spirit, we receive quickening life from the ascended Lord.

It is not the baptism of the Holy Ghost which changes men,
but the power of the ascended Christ coming into men's lives
by the Holy Ghost that changes them. We too often divorce
what the New Testament never divorces. The baptism of the
Holy Ghost is not an experience apart from Jesus Christ: it is
the evidence of the ascended Christ.

The baptism of the Holy Ghost does not make you think of
Time or Eternity, it is one amazing glorious NOW. "This is life
eternal that they might know Thee." Begin to know Him now,
and finish never.

I will restore to you the years that the locust hath eaten.
(Joel 2:25)

The greatest problems of conscience are not the wrong things we have done, but wrong relationships. We may have become born again, but what about those we have wronged? It is of no use to sit down and say, 'It is irreparable now, I cannot alter it.' Thank God He can alter it! We may try to repair the damage in our own way, by apologizing, by writing letters; but it is not a simple easy matter of something to apologize for. Behind the veil of human lives God begins to reveal the tragedies of hell. Or we may say, 'I have been atoned for, therefore I do not need to think about the past.' If we are conscientious the Holy Spirit will make us think about the past, and it is just here that the tyranny of nerves and the bondage of Satan comes in. The shores of life are strewn with ruined friendships, irreparable severances through our own blame or others, and when the Holy Spirit begins to reveal the tremendous twist, then comes the strange distress, 'How can we repair it?' Many a sensitive soul has been driven into insanity through anguish of mind because he has never realized what Jesus Christ came to do, and all the asylums in the world will never touch them in the way of healing; the only thing that will is the realization of what the death of Jesus means, viz., that the damage we have done may be repaired through the efficiency of His Cross. Jesus Christ has atoned for all, and He can make it good in us, not only as a gift but by a participation on our part. The miracle of the grace of God is that He can make the past as though it had never been; He can 'restore the years that the locust hath eaten, the cankerworm, and the caterpillar, and the palmerworm'.

PS 21

UNQUESTIONED REVELATION

And in that day ye shall ask Me nothing. (John 16:23)

When is "that day"? When the Ascended Lord makes you one
with the Father. In that day you will be one with the Father as
Jesus is, and "in that day," Jesus says, "ye shall ask Me nothing." Until the resurrection life of Jesus is manifested in you,
you want to ask this and that; then after a while you find all
questions gone, you do not seem to have any left to ask. You
have come to the place of entire reliance on the resurrection
life of Jesus which brings you into perfect contact with the
purpose of God. Are you living that life now? If not, why
shouldn't you?

There may be any number of things dark to your understanding but they do not come in between your heart and God. "And
in that day ye shall ask Me no question"—you do not need to,
you are so certain that God will bring things out in accordance
with His will. John 14:1 has become the real state of your heart,
and there are no more questions to be asked. If anything is a
mystery to you and it is coming in between you and God, never
look for the explanation in your intellect, look for it in your
disposition, it is that which is wrong. When once your disposition is willing to submit to the life of Jesus, the understanding will be perfectly clear, and you will get to the place where
there is no distance between the Father and His child because
the Lord has made you one, and "in that day ye shall ask Me
no question."

God so loved the world . . . (John 3:16)

The Bible says that 'God so loved the world, that he gave his only begotten Son . . . ', and yet it says that if we are friends of the world we are enemies of God. 'Know ye not that the friendship of the world is enmity with God?' (James 4:4). The difference is that God loves the world so much that He goes all lengths to remove the wrong from it, and we must have the same kind of love. Any other kind of love for the world simply means that we take it as it is and are perfectly delighted with it. The world is all right and we are very happy in it; sin and evil and the devil are so many Orientalisms. It is that sentiment which is the enemy of God. Do we love the world in this sense sufficiently to spend and be spent so that God can manifest His grace through us until the wrong and the evil are removed?

BP 121

UNDISTURBED RELATIONSHIP

At that day ye shall ask in My name . . . The Father Himself
loveth you. (John 16:26, 27)

"At that day ye shall ask in My name," i.e., in My nature. Not—
"You shall use My name as a magic word," but—"You will be
so intimate with Me that you will be one with Me." "That day"
is not a day hereafter, but a day meant for here and now. "The
Father Himself loveth you"—the union is so complete and
absolute. Our Lord does not mean that life will be free from
external perplexities, but that just as He knew the Father's heart
and mind, so by the baptism of the Holy Ghost He can lift us
into the heavenly places where He can reveal the counsels of
God to us.

"Whatsoever ye shall ask the Father in My name . . ." "That
day" is a day of undisturbed relationship between God and the
saint. Just as Jesus stood unsullied in the presence of His Father, so by the mighty efficacy of the baptism of the Holy Ghost,
we can be lifted into that relationship—"that they may be one,
even as We are One."

" . . . He will give it you." Jesus says that God will recognize
our prayers. What a challenge! By the Resurrection and Ascension power of Jesus, by the sentdown Holy Ghost, we can
be lifted into such a relationship with the Father that we are
at one with the perfect sovereign will of God by our free choice
even as Jesus was. In that wonderful position, placed there by
Jesus Christ, we can pray to God in His name, in His nature,
which is gifted to us by the Holy Ghost, and Jesus says—"Whatsoever ye shall ask the Father in My name, He will give it you."
The sovereign character of Jesus Christ is tested by His own
statements.

Consider the lilies. (Matthew 6:28)

When Jesus said 'Consider the lilies of the field, how they grow', He was referring to the new life in us. If we make His words apply to the natural life only, we make Him appear foolish. If we are born of God and are obeying Him, the unconscious life is forming in us just where we are. God knows exactly the kind of garden to put His lilies in, and they grow and take form unconsciously. What is it that deforms natural beauty? Overmuch cultivation; and overmuch denominational teaching will deform beauty in the spiritual world . . .

The new life must go on and take form unconsciously. God is looking after it, He knows exactly the kind of nourishment as well as the kind of disintegration that is necessary. Be careful that you do not bury the new life, or put it into circumstances where it cannot grow. A lily can only grow in the surroundings that suit it, and in the same way God engineers the circumstances that are best fitted for the development of the life of His Son in us.

PR 40

"YES—BUT . . .!"

Lord, I will follow Thee; but . . . (Luke 9:61)

Supposing God tells you to do something which is an enormous test to your common sense, what are you going to do? Hang back? If you get into the habit of doing a thing in the physical domain, you will do it every time until you break the habit determinedly; and the same is true spiritually. Again and again you will get up to what Jesus Christ wants, and every time you will turn back when it comes to the point, until you abandon resolutely. "Yes, but—supposing I do obey God in this matter, what about . . .?" "Yes, I will obey God if He will let me use my common sense, but don't ask me to take a step in the dark." Jesus Christ demands of the man who trusts Him the same reckless sporting spirit that the natural man exhibits. If a man is going to do anything worth while, there are times when he has to risk everything on his leap, and in the spiritual domain Jesus Christ demands that you risk everything you hold by common sense and leap into what He says, and immediately you do, you find that what He says fits on as solidly as common sense. At the bar of common sense Jesus Christ's statements may seem mad; but bring them to the bar of faith, and you begin to find with awestruck spirit that they are the words of God. Trust entirely in God, and when He brings you to the venture, see that you take it. We act like pagans in a crisis, only one out of a crowd is daring enough to bank his faith in the character of God.

Whatsoever I speak therefore, even as the Father said unto me, so I speak. (John 12:50)

Jesus Christ said He always spoke as His Father wished Him to. Did His Father write out the words and tell Him to learn them by heart? No, the mainspring of the heart of Jesus Christ was the mainspring of the heart of God the Father, consequently the words Jesus Christ spoke were the exact expression of God's thought. In our Lord the tongue was in its right place; He never spoke from His head, but always from His heart. 'If any man among you seem to be religious, and bridleth not his tongue . . . this man's religion is vain' (James 1:26), there is nothing in it. The tongue and the brain are under our control, not God's . . .

Sometimes Jesus Christ's speech sounded anything but nice to natural ears, e.g. Matthew 23. Some of the words He used, and some applications He made of His truth were terrible and rugged. Read our Lord's description of the heart: 'Out of the heart,' says Jesus, 'proceed . . .'—and then comes the ugly catalogue (Matthew 15:19). Upright men and women of the world simply do not believe this. Jesus Christ did not speak as a man there. He spoke as the Master of men, with an absolute knowledge of what the human heart is like. That is why He so continually pleads with us to hand the keeping of our hearts over to Him.

BP 126

GOD FIRST

Jesus did not commit Himself unto them . . . for He knew what was in man. (John 2:24-25)

Put God First in Trust. Our Lord trusted no man; yet He was never suspicious, never bitter, never in despair about any man, because He put God first in trust; He trusted absolutely in what God's grace could do for any man. If I put my trust in human beings first, I will end in despairing of everyone; I will become bitter, because I have insisted on man being what no man ever can be—absolutely right. Never trust anything but the grace of God in yourself or in anyone else.

Put God's Needs First. "Lo, I come to do Thy will, O God" (Heb. 10:9).

A man's obedience is to what he sees to be a need; Our Lord's obedience was to the will of His Father. The cry to-day is— "We must get some work to do; the heathen are dying without God, we must go and tell them of Him." We have to see first of all that God's needs in us personally are being met. "Tarry ye until . . ." The purpose of this College is to get us rightly related to the needs of God. When God's needs in us have been met, then He will open the way for us to realize His needs elsewhere.

Put God's Trust First. "And whoso receiveth one such little child in my name receiveth Me" (Matt. 18:5).

God's trust is that He gives me Himself as a babe. God expects my personal life to be a "Bethlehem." Am I allowing my natural life to be slowly transfigured by the indwelling life of the Son of God? God's ultimate purpose is that His Son might be manifested in my mortal flesh.

Ye call me Master and Lord; and ye say well; for so I am.
(John 13:13)

Our Lord never takes measures to make us obey Him. Our obedience is the outcome of a oneness of spirit with Him through His Redemption.

Obedience to Jesus Christ is essential, but not compulsory; He never insists on being Master. We feel that if only He would insist, we should obey Him. But our Lord never enforces His 'thou shalt's' and 'thou shalt not's'; He never takes means to force us to do what he says; He never coerces. If we do not keep His commandments, He does not come and tell us we are wrong, we know it, we cannot get away from it. There is no ambiguity in our mind as to whether what He says is right. Our Lord never says 'you *must*', but if we are to be His disciples we know we must . . . .

'Ye call me Master and Lord: and ye say well; for so I am'— But *is* He? 'Master' and 'Lord' have very little place in our spiritual vocabulary; we prefer the words 'Saviour' and 'Sancitifer' and 'Healer'. In other words, we know very little about love as Jesus revealed it. It is seen in the way we use the word 'obey'. Our use of the word implies the submission of an inferior to a superior; obedience in our Lord's use of the word is the relationship of equals, a son and father. ' . . . though he was a Son, yet learned he obedience by the things which he suffered.' Our Lord was not a servant of God. He was His Son. The Son's obedience as Redeemer was *because He was* Son, not in order *to be* Son.

SSY 84

JUNE

THE STAGGERING QUESTION

Son of man, can these bones live? (Ezek. 37:3)

Can that sinner be turned into a saint? Can that twisted life be put right? There is only one answer: "O Lord, Thou knowest, I don't." Never trample in with religious common sense and say—"Oh, yes, with a little more Bible reading and devotion and prayer, I see how it can be done."

It is much easier to do something than to trust in God; we mistake panic for inspiration. That is why there are so few fellow workers with God and so many workers for Him. We would far rather work for God than believe in Him. Am I quite sure that God will do what I cannot do? I despair of men in the degree in which I have never realized that God has done anything for me. Is my experience such a wonderful realization of God's power and might that I can never despair of anyone I see? Have I had any spiritual work done in me at all? The degree of panic is the degree of the lack of personal spiritual experience.

"Behold, O my people, I will open your graves." When God wants to show you what human nature is like apart from Himself, He has to show it you in yourself. If the Spirit of God has given you a vision of what you are apart from the grace of God (and He only does it when His Spirit is at work), you know there is no criminal who is half so bad in actuality as you know yourself to be in possibility. My "grave" has been opened by God and "I know that in me (that is, in my flesh) dwelleth no good thing." God's Spirit continually reveals what human nature is like apart from His grace.

And behold, I send forth the promise of my Father upon you.
(Luke 24:49)

Do you say 'I am waiting for my Pentecost'? Who told you to wait? 'Oh, I am waiting as the disciples did in the upper room.' Not all the waiting on earth will ever gain you the baptism with the Holy Ghost. The baptism with the Holy Ghost is the infallible sign that Jesus has ascended to the right hand of God and has received of the Father the promise of the Holy Ghost. We too often divorce what the New Testament never divorces: the baptism with the Holy Ghost is not an experience apart from Christ, it is the evidence that He has ascended.

HGM 21

We are told by some that it is foolish to tell people to ask for the Holy Spirit because this is the dispensation of the Holy Spirit. Thank God it is! God's mighty Spirit is with all men, He impinges on their lives at all points and in unexpected ways, but the great need is to receive the Holy Spirit. There stands the promise for every one who will put it to the test: 'If ye then, being evil, know how to give good gifts to your children: how much more shall your heavenly Father give the Holy Spirit to them that ask Him?' The bedrock in Jesus Christ's kingdom is poverty, not possession; not decisions for Christ, but a sense of absolute futility—'I can't begin to do it.' That is the entrance; and it does take us a long while to believe we are poor. It is at the point of destitution that the bounty of God can be given.

HGM 17

WHAT ARE YOU HAUNTED BY?

What man is he that feareth the Lord? (Ps. 25:12)

What are you haunted by? You will say—By nothing, but we are all haunted by something, generally by ourselves, or, if we are Christians, by our experience. The Psalmist says we are to be haunted by God. The abiding consciousness of the life is to be God, not thinking about Him. The whole of our life inside and out is to be absolutely haunted by the presence of God. A child's consciousness is so mother-haunted that although the child is not consciously thinking of its mother, yet when calamity arises, the relationship that abides is that of the mother. So we are to live and move and have our being in God, to look at everything in relation to God, because the abiding consciousness of God pushes itself to the front all the time.

If we are haunted by God, nothing else can get in, no cares, no tribulation, no anxieties. We see now why Our Lord so emphasized the sin of worry. How can we dare be so utterly unbelieving when God is round about us? To be haunted by God is to have an effective barricade against all the onslaughts of the enemy.

"His soul shall dwell at ease." In tribulation, misunderstanding, slander, in the midst of all these things, if our life is hid with Christ in God, He will keep us at ease. We rob ourselves of the marvelous revelation of this abiding companionship of God. "God is our Refuge"—nothing can come through that shelter.

And when the day of Pentecost was now come . . . ('was being fulfilled', RV marg.). (Acts 2:1)

What an unspeakably wonderful day the Day of Pentecost was! There is only one Bethlehem, one Calvary, one Pentecost; these are the landmarks of Time and Eternity, everything and everyone is judged by them.

Beware of thinking of Pentecost in the light of personal experience only. The descent of the Holy Ghost can never be experimental, it is historical. The reception of the Holy Ghost into our hearts is experimental. Those who insist on the experimental line are in danger of forgetting the revelation and of putting all the emphasis on experience, while those who emphasize the revelation are in danger of forgetting the practical experience. In the New Testament the two are one; the experimental must be based on and regulated by the revelation. We imagine that we have the monopoly of the teaching about the holy Spirit when we deal with His work in individual lives, viz., His power to transform men on the inside—the most important phase to us, but in God's Book the tiniest phase of the work of the mighty Spirit of God.

GHM 20

THE SECRET OF THE LORD

The secret (friendship R.V.) of the Lord is with them that fear Him. (Ps. 25:14)

What is the sign of a friend? That he tells you secret sorrows? No, that he tells you secret joys. Many will confide to you their secret sorrows, but the last mark of intimacy is to confide secret joys. Have we ever let God tell us any of His joys, or are we telling God our secrets so continually that we leave no room for Him to talk to us? At the beginning of our Christian life we are full of requests to God, then we find that God wants to get us into relationship with Himself, to get us in touch with His purposes. Are we so wedded to Jesus Christ's idea of prayer— "Thy will be done"—that we catch the secrets of God? The things that make God dear to us are not so much His great big blessings as the tiny things, because they show His amazing intimacy with us; He knows every detail of our individual lives.

". . . him shall He teach in the way that He shall choose." At first we want the consciousness of being guided by God; then as we go on we live so much in the consciousness of God that we do not need to ask what His will is, because the thought of choosing any other will never occurs to us. If we are saved and sanctified God guides us by our ordinary choices, and if we are going to choose what He does not want, He will check, and we must heed. Whenever there is doubt, stop at once. Never reason it out and say—"I wonder why I shouldn't?" God instructs us in what we choose, that is, He guides our common sense, and we no longer hinder His Spirit by continually saying—"Now, Lord, what is Thy will?"

It is God which worketh in you. (Philippians 2:13)

We cannot give ourselves the Holy Spirit; the Holy Spirit is God Almighty's gift if we will simply become poor enough to ask for Him. 'If ye then, being evil, know how to give good gifts unto your children; how much more shall your heavenly Father give the Holy Spirit to them that ask him?' (Luke 9:13). But when the Holy Spirit has come in, there is something we can do and God cannot do, we can obey Him. If we do not obey Him, we shall grieve Him. 'And grieve not the Holy Spirit of God' (Ephesians 4:30). Over and over again we need to be reminded of Paul's counsel, 'Work out your own salvation with fear and trembling. For it is God that worketh in you both to will and to do of His good pleasure.' Thank God, it is gloriously and majestically true that the Holy Spirit can work in us the very nature of Jesus Christ if we will obey Him, until in and through our mortal flesh may be manifested works which will make men glorify our Father in heaven, and take knowledge of us that we have been with Jesus.

BP 220

THE NEVER-FAILING GOD

For He hath said, I will never leave thee, nor forsake thee.
(Heb. 13:5)

What line does my thought take? Does it turn to what God says or to what I fear? Am I learning to say not what God says, but to say something after I have heard what He says? "He hath said, I will never leave thee, nor forsake thee. So that we may boldly say, The Lord is my helper, and I will not fear what man shall do unto me."

"I will in no wise fail thee"—not for all my sin and selfishness and stubbornness and waywardness. Have I really let God say to me that He will never fail me? If I have listened to this say-so of God's, then let me listen again.

"Neither will I in any wise forsake thee." Sometimes it is not difficulty that makes me think God will forsake me, but drudgery. There is no Hill Difficulty to climb, no vision given, nothing wonderful or beautiful, just the commonplace day in and day out—can I hear God's say-so in these things?

We have the idea that God is going to do some exceptional thing that He is preparing and fitting us for some extraordinary thing by and by, but as we go on in grace we find that God is glorifying Himself here and now, in the present minute. If we have God's say-so behind us, the most amazing strength comes, and we learn to sing in the ordinary days and ways.

*If any man be in Christ, he is a new creature: old things are
passed away. (2 Corinthians 5:17)*

The way the Holy Spirit corrupts our natural virtues when He
comes in is one of the most devastating experiences. He does
not build up and transfigure what we possess in the way of
virtue and goodness by natural heredity; it is corrupted to
death, until we learn that we

> '. . . dare not trust the sweetest frame,
> But wholly lean on Jesus' name.'

It is a deep instruction to watch how natural virtues break
down. The Holy Spirit does not patch up our natural virtues,
for the simple reason that no natural virtue can come anywhere
near Jesus Christ's demands. God does not build up our natural virtues and transfigure them, He totally recreates us on the
inside. 'And every virtue we possess is His alone.' As we bring
every bit of our nature into harmony with the new life which
God puts in, what will be exhibited in us will be the virtues
that were characteristic of the Lord Jesus, not our natural virtues. The supernatural is made natural. The life that God plants
in us develops its own virtues, not the virtues of Adam but of
Jesus Christ, and Jesus Christ can never be described in terms
of the natural virtues.

AHW 98

GOD'S SAY-SO

He hath said . . . so that we may boldly say . . . (Heb. 13:5-6)

My say-so is to be built on God's say-so. God says—"I will never leave thee," then I can with good courage say—"The Lord is my helper, I will not fear—" I will not be haunted by apprehension. This does not mean that I will not be tempted to fear, but I will remember God's say-so. I will be full of courage, like a child "bucking himself up" to reach the standard his father wants. Faith in many a one falters when the apprehensions come; they forget the meaning of God's say-so, forget to take a deep breath spiritually. The only way to get the dread taken out of us is to listen to God's say-so.

What are you dreading? You are not a coward about it, you are going to face it, but there is a feeling of dread. When there is nothing and no one to help you, say—"But the Lord is my Helper, this second, in my present outlook." Are you learning to say things after listening to God, or are you saying things and trying to make God's word fit in? Get hold of the Father's say-so, and then say with good courage—"I will not fear." It does not matter what evil or wrong may be in the way, He has said—"I will never leave thee."

Frailty is another thing that gets in between God's say-so and ours. When we realize how feeble we are in facing difficulties, the difficulties become like giants, we become like grasshoppers, and God becomes a nonentity. Remember God's say-so—"*I will in no wise fail you.*" Have we learned to sing after hearing God's key-note? Are we always possessed with the courage to say—"The Lord is my helper," or are we succumbing?

Till we all attain . . . unto the measure of the stature of the fulness of Christ. (Ephesians 4:13)

The personal Holy Spirit builds us up into the body of Christ. All that Jesus Christ came to do is made ours experimentally by the Holy Spirit, and all His gifts are for the good of the whole body, not for individual exaltation. Individuality must go in order that the personal life may be brought out into fellowship with God. By the baptism of the Holy Ghost we are delivered from the husk of independent individuality, our personality is awakened and brought into communion with God. We too often divorce what the New Testament never divorces. The baptism of the Holy Ghost is not an experience apart from Christ: it is the evidence of the ascended Christ. It is not the baptism of the Holy Ghost that changes men, but the power of the ascended Christ coming into men's lives by the Holy Ghost that changes them. 'Ye shall be witnesses unto me.' This great Pentecostal phrase puts the truth for us in unforgettable words. Witnesses not so much of what Jesus Christ can do, but *witnesses unto me*, a delight to the heart of Jesus, a satisfaction to Him wherever He places us.

MC 131

WORK OUT WHAT GOD WORKS IN

Work out your own salvation. (Phil. 2:12-13)

Your will agrees with God, but in your flesh there is a disposition which renders you powerless to do what you know you ought to do. When the Lord is presented to the conscience, the first thing conscience does is to rouse the will, and the will always agrees with God. You say—"But I do not know whether my will is in agreement with God." Look to Jesus and you will find that your will and your conscience are in agreement with Him every time. The thing in you which makes you say "I shan't" is something less profound than your will; it is perversity, or obstinacy, and they are never in agreement with God. The profound thing in man is his will, not sin. Will is the essential element in God's creation of man: sin is a perverse disposition which entered into man. In a regenerated man the source of will is almighty. "For it is God which worketh in you both to will and to do of His good pleasure." You have to work out with concentration and care what God works in; not work your own salvation, but work it out, while you base resolutely in unshaken faith on the complete and perfect Redemption of the Lord. As you do this, you do not bring an opposed will to God's will, God's will is your will, and your natural choices are along the line of God's will, and the life is as natural as breathing. God is the source of your will, therefore you are able to work out His will. Obstinacy is an unintelligent "wadge" that refuses to be enlightened; the only thing is for it to be blown up with dynamite, and the dynamite is obedience to the Holy Spirit.

Do I believe that Almighty God is the source of my will? God not only expects me to do His will but He is in me to do it.

For by one Spirit are we all baptized into one body . . .
(1 Corinthians 12:13)

God is the Architect of the human body and He is also the Architect of the Body of Christ. There are two Bodies of Christ: the Historic Body and the Mystical Body. The historic Jesus was the habitation of the Holy Ghost (see Luke 3:22; John 1:32–3), and the Mystic Christ, i.e., the Body of Christ composed of those who have experienced regeneration and sanctification, is likewise the habitation of the Holy Ghost. When we are baptized with the Holy Ghost we are no longer isolated believers but part of the Mystical Body of Christ. Beware of attempting to live a holy life alone, it is impossible. Paul continually insists on the 'together' aspect—'God hath quickened us *together* . . . and hath raised us up *together*, and made us sit *together* . . .' (Ephesians 2:4–6). The 'together' aspect is always the work of the Holy Ghost.

HGM 25

'Be filled with the Spirit,' says Paul. We have all seen the seashore when the tide is out, with all its separate pools, how are those pools to be made one? By digging channels between them? No, wait till the tide comes in, and where are the pools? Absolutely lost, merged in one tremendous floodtide. That is exactly what happens when Christians are indwelt by the Holy Spirit. Once let people be filled with the Holy Spirit and you have the ideal of what the New Testament means by the Church. The Church is a separated band of people who are united to God by the regenerating power of the Spirit, and the bedrock of membership in the Church is that we know who Jesus is by a personal revelation of Him.

CHI 49

DON'T SLACK OFF

Whatever ye shall ask in My name, that will I do. (John14:13)

Am I fulfilling this ministry of the interior? There is no snare or any danger of infatuation or pride in intercession, it is a hidden ministry that brings forth fruit whereby the Father is glorified. Am I allowing my spiritual life to be frittered away, or am I bringing it all to one centre—the Atonement of my Lord? Is Jesus Christ more and more dominating every interest in my life? If the one central point, the great exerting influence in my life is the Atonement of the Lord, then every phase of my life will bear fruit for Him.

I must take time to realize what is the central point of power. Do I give one minute out of sixty to concentrate upon it? "If ye abide in Me"—continue to act and think and work from that centre—"ye shall ask what ye will, and it shall be done unto you." Am I abiding? Am I taking time to abide? What is the greatest factor of power in my life? Is it work, service, sacrifice for others, or trying to work for God? The thing that ought to exert the greatest power in my life is the Atonement of the Lord. It is not the thing we spend the most time on that moulds us most; the greatest element is the thing that exerts most power. We must determine to be limited and concentrate our affinities.

"Whatsoever ye shall ask in My name, that will I do." The disciple who abides in Jesus is the will of God, and his apparently free choices are God's fore-ordained decrees. Mysterious? Logically contradictory and absurd? Yes, but a glorious truth to a saint.

Listen, O isles, unto me: and hearken, ye people, from far: The Lord hath called me from the womb . . . and he hath made my mouth like a sharp sword. (Isaiah 49:1, 2)

A saint is made by God, 'He made me'. Then do not tell God He is a bungling workman. We do that whenever we say 'I can't'. To say 'I can't' literally means we are too strong in ourselves to depend on God. 'I can't pray in public; I can't talk in the open air.' Substitute 'I won't', and it will be nearer the truth. The thing that makes us say 'I can't' is that we forget that we must rely entirely on the creative purpose of God and on this characteristic of perfect finish for God.

Much of our difficulty comes because we choose our own work—'Oh well, this is what I am fitted for.' Remember that Jesus took a fisherman and turned him into a shepherd. That is symbolical of what He does all the time. The idea that we have to consecrate our gifts to God is a dangerous one. We cannot consecrate what is not ours (1 Corinthians 4:7). We have to consecrate ourselves, and leave our gifts alone. God does not ask us to do the thing that is easy to us naturally; He only asks us to do the thing we are perfectly fitted to do by grace, and the cross will always come along that line.

SSY 108

WHAT NEXT?

If ye know these things, happy are ye if ye do them. (John 13:17)

Determine to know more than others. If you do not cut the moorings, God will have to break them by a storm and send you out. Launch all on God, go out on the great swelling tide of His purpose, and you will get your eyes open. If you believe in Jesus, you are not to spend all your time in the smooth waters just inside the harbour bar, full of delight, but always moored; you have to get out through the harbour bar into the great deeps of God and begin to know for yourself, begin to have spiritual discernment.

When you know you should do a thing, and do it, immediately you know more. Revise where you have become stodgy spiritually, and you will find it goes back to a point where there was something you knew you should do, but you did not do it because there seemed no immediate call to, and now you have no perception, no discernment; at a time of crisis you are spiritually distracted instead of spiritually self-possessed. It is a dangerous thing to refuse to go on knowing.

The counterfeit of obedience is a state of mind in which you work up occasions to sacrifice yourself; ardour is mistaken for discernment. It is easier to sacrifice yourself than to fulfil your spiritual destiny, which is stated in Romans 12:1-2. It is a great deal better to fulfil the purpose of God in your life by discerning His will than to perform great acts of self-sacrifice. "To obey is better than sacrifice." Beware of harking back to what you were once when God wants you to be something you have never been. "If any man will do . . . he shall know."

But thou, when thou prayest . . . (Matthew 6:6)

'But it is so difficult to get time.' Of course it is, we have to make time, and that means effort, and effort makes us conscious of the need to re-organize our general ways. It will facilitate matters to remember, even if it humbles us, that we take time to eat our breakfast and our dinner, etc. Most of the difficulty in forming a special habit is that we will not discipline ourselves . . .

You say you cannot get up early in the morning; well, a very good thing to do is to get up in order to prove that you cannot! This does not contradict at all the notion that we must not put earnestness in the place of God; it means that we have to understand that our bodily mechanism is made by God, and that when we are regenerated He does not give us another body, we have the same body, and therefore the way we use our wits in order to learn a secular thing is the way to learn any spiritual thing. 'But thou, when thou prayest . . .' begin now.

DPR 30

THE NEXT BEST THING TO DO

For every one that asketh receiveth. (Luke 11:10)

Ask if you have not Received. There is nothing more difficult than to ask. We will long and desire and crave and suffer, but not until we are at the extreme limit will we *ask*. A sense of unreality makes us ask. Have you ever asked out of the depths of moral poverty? "If any of you lack wisdom, let him ask of God . . .," but be sure that you do lack wisdom. You cannot bring yourself up against Reality when you like. The next best thing to do if you are not spiritually real, is to ask God for the Holy Spirit on the word of Jesus Christ (see Luke 11:13). The Holy Spirit is the One Who makes real in you all that Jesus did for you.

"For every one that asketh receiveth." This does not mean you will not get if you do not ask (cf. Matt. 5:45), but until you get to the point of asking you *won't receive* from God. To receive means you have come into the relationship of a child of God, and now you perceive with intelligent and moral appreciation and spiritual understanding that these things come from God.

"If any of you lack wisdom . . ." If you realize you are lacking, it is because you have come in contact with spiritual reality; do not put your reasonable blinkers on again. People say—Preach us the simple gospel: don't tell us we have to be holy, because that produces a sense of abject poverty, and it is not nice to feel abjectly poor. "Ask" means *beg*. Some people are poor enough to be interested in their poverty, and some of us are like that spiritually. We will never receive if we ask with an end in view; if we ask, not out of our poverty but out of our lust. A pauper does not ask from any other reason than the abject panging condition of his poverty; he is not ashamed to beg.

—Blessed are the *paupers* in spirit.

The first (commandment) is . . . thou shalt love the Lord thy God with all thy heart, and with all thy soul, and with all thy mind, and with all thy strength ('from all thy heart . . .' RV marg.). (Mark 12:29–30)

My relationship to God embraces every faculty, I am to love Him with *all* my heart, *all* my soul, *all* my mind, *all* my strength, every detail is instinct with devotion to Him; if it is not I am disjointed somewhere. Think what you do for someone you love! The most amazingly minute details are perfectly transfigured because your whole nature is embraced, not one faculty only. You don't love a person with your heart and leave the rest of your nature out, you love with your whole being, from the crown of the head to the sole of the foot. That is the attitude of the New Testament all through. In 1 Corinthians 15 the Apostle Paul has been speaking about the stupendous mystery of the resurrection, and suddenly, like a swinging lamp in a mine, he rushes it right straight down and says, 'Now concerning the collection . . . ' The New Testament is continually doing it—'Jesus knowing . . . that the Father had given all things into His hands . . . began to wash the disciples' feet.' It takes God Incarnate to wash feet properly. It takes God Incarnate to do anything properly.

GW 9

THE NEXT BEST THING TO DO

Seek, and ye shall find. (Luke 11:9)

Seek if you have not Found. "Ye ask, and receive not, because ye ask amiss." If you ask for things from life instead of from God, you ask amiss, i.e., you ask from a desire for self-realization. The more you realize yourself the less will you seek God. "Seek, and ye shall find." Get to work, narrow your interests to this one. Have you ever sought God with your whole heart, or have you only given a languid cry to Him after a twinge of moral neuralgia? Seek, concentrate, and you will find.

"Ho, every one that thirsteth, come ye to the waters." Are you thirsty, or smugly indifferent—so satisfied with your experience that you want nothing more of God? Experience is a gateway, not an end. Beware of building your faith on experience, the metallic note will come in at once, the censorious note. You can never give another person that which you have found, but you can make him homesick for what you have.

"Knock, and it shall be opened unto you." "Draw nigh to God." Knock—the door is closed, and you suffer from palpitation as you knock. "Cleanse your hands"—knock a bit louder, you begin to find you are dirty. "Purify your heart"—this is more personal still, you are desperately in earnest now—you will do anything. "Be afflicted"—have you ever been afflicted before God at the state of your inner life? There is no strand of self-pity left, but a heartbreaking affliction of amazement to find you are the kind of person that you are. "Humble yourself"—it is a humbling business to knock at God's door—you have to knock with the crucified thief. "To him that knocketh, *it shall be opened.*"

He that hath ears to hear, let him hear. (Matthew 11:15)

We hear only what we listen for. Have we listened to what Jesus has to say? Have we paid any attention to finding out what He did say? Most of us do not know what He said. If we have only a smattering of religion, we talk a lot about the devil; but what hinders us spiritually is not the devil nearly so much as inattention. We may *hear* the sayings of Jesus Christ, but our wills are left untouched, we never *do* them. The understanding of the Bible only comes from the indwelling of the Holy Spirit making the universe of the Bible real to us.

SSM 107

Much is written about our Lord speaking so simply that anyone could understand, and we forget that while it remains true that the common people heard him gladly, no one, not even His own disciples, understood Him until after the Resurrection and the coming of the Holy Spirit, the reason being that a pure heart is the essential requirement for being 'of the truth'. 'Blessed are the pure in heart: for they shall see God.'

GW 34

GETTING THERE

Come unto Me. (Matt. 11:28)

Where the sin and the sorrow cease, and the song and the saint commence. Do I want to get there? I can now. The questions that matter in life are remarkably few, and they are all answered by the words—"Come unto Me." Not—Do this, or don't do that; but—"Come unto Me." If I will come to Jesus my actual life will be brought into accordance with my real desires; I will actually cease from sin, and actually find the song of the Lord begin.

Have you ever come to Jesus? Watch the stubbornness of your heart, you will do anything rather than the one simple childlike thing—"Come unto Me." If you want the actual experience of ceasing from sin, you must come to Jesus.

Jesus Christ makes Himself the touchstone. Watch how He used the word "Come." At the most unexpected moments there is the whisper of the Lord—"Come unto Me," and you are drawn immediately. Personal contact with Jesus alters everything. Be stupid enough to come and commit yourself to what He says. The attitude of coming is that the will resolutely lets go of everything and deliberately commits all to Him.

". . . and I will give you rest," i.e., I will stay you. Not —I will put you to bed and hold your hand and sing you to sleep; but—I will get you out of bed, out of the languor and exhaustion, out of the state of being half dead while you are alive; I will imbue you with the spirit of life, and you will be stayed by the perfection of vital activity. We get pathetic and talk about "suffering the will of the Lord!" Where is the majestic vitality and might of the Son of God about that?

Jesus said unto them, Verily, verily, I say unto you, Before Abraham was, I am. (John 8:58) (See also Matthew 18:3–5)

Spiritually we never grow old; through the passing of the years we grow so many years young. The characteristic of the spiritual life is its unageing youth, exactly the opposite of the natural life. 'I am . . . the First and the Last.' The Ancient of Days represents the Eternal Childhood. God Almighty became the weakest thing in His own creation, a Baby. When He comes into us in new birth we can easily kill His life in us, or else we can see to it that His life is nourished according to the dictates of the Spirit of God so that we grow 'unto the measure of the stature of the fulness of Christ'. The mature saint is just like a little child, absolutely simple and joyful and gay. Go on living the life that God would have you live and you will grow younger instead of older. There is a marvellous rejuvenescence when once you let God have His way. If you are feeling very old, then get born again and do more at it.

PR 47

GETTING THERE

Master, where dwellest Thou? . . . Come and see. Come with Me.
(John 1:39)

Where the self-interest sleeps and the real interest awakens. "They abode with Him that day." That is about all some of us ever do, then we wake up to actualities, self-interest arises and the abiding is passed. There is no condition of life in which we cannot abide in Jesus.

"Thou art Simon, thou shalt be called Cephas." God writes the new name on those places only in our lives where He has erased the pride and self-sufficiency and self-interest. Some of us have the new name in spots only, like spiritual measles. In sections we look all right. When we have our best spiritual mood on, you would think we were very high-toned saints; but don't look at us when we are not in that mood. The disciple is one who has the new name written all over him; self-interest and pride and self-sufficiency have been completely erased.

Pride is the deification of self, and this to-day in some of us is not of the order of the Pharisee, but of the publican. To say "Oh, I'm no saint," is acceptable to human pride, but it is unconscious blasphemy against God. It literally means that you defy God to make you a saint, "I am much too weak and hopeless, I am outside the reach of the Atonement." Humility before men may be unconscious blasphemy before God. Why are you not a saint? It is either that you do not want to be a saint, or that you do not believe God can make you one. It would be all right, you say, if God saved you and took you straight to heaven. That is just what He will do! "We will come unto him, and make our abode with him." Make no conditions, let Jesus be everything, and He will take you home with Him not only for a day, but for ever.

That they may be one, even as we are one. (John 17:22)

The conception which Jesus Christ had of society was that men might be one with Him as He was one with the Father. The full-orbed meaning of the term 'personality' in its fundamental aspect is a being created by God who has lived on this earth and formed his character. The majority of us are not personalities as yet, we are beginning to be, and our value to God in His Kingdom depends on the development and growth of our personality. There is a difference between being saved and sanctified by the sheer sovereign grace of God and choosing to be the choice ones, not for heaven, but down here. The average view of Christianity, that we only need to have faith and we are saved, is a stumbling block. How many of us care anything about being witnesses to Jesus Christ? How many of us are willing to spend every ounce of energy we have, every bit of mental, moral and spiritual life for Jesus Christ? That is the meaning of a worker in God's sense. God has left us on earth, what for? To be saved and sanctified? No, to be at it for Him . . .

My life as a worker is the way I say 'Thank you' to God for His unspeakable salvation.

AUG 18

GETTING THERE

Come ye after Me. (Mark 1:17)

Where the selective affinity dies and the sanctified abandon lives. One of the greatest hindrances in coming to Jesus is the excuse of temperament. We make our temperament and our natural affinities barriers to coming to Jesus. The first thing we realize when we come to Jesus is that He pays no attention whatever to our natural affinities. We have the notion that we can consecrate our gifts to God. You cannot consecrate what is not yours; there is only one thing you can consecrate to God, and that is your right to yourself (Romans 12:1). If you will give God your right to yourself, He will make a holy experiment out of you. God's experiments always succeed. The one mark of a saint is the moral originality which springs from abandonment to Jesus Christ. In the life of a saint there is this amazing wellspring of original life all the time; the Spirit of God is a well of water springing up, perennially fresh. The saint realizes that it is God Who engineers circumstances, consequently there is no whine, but a reckless abandon to Jesus. Never make a principle out of your experience; let God be as original with other people as He is with you.

If you abandon to Jesus, and come when He says "Come," He will continue to say "Come" through you; you will go out into life reproducing the echo of Christ's "Come." That is the result in every soul who has abandoned and come to Jesus.

Have I come to Jesus? Will I come *now*?

> *If a man therefore purge himself . . . he shall be a vessel unto*
> *honour, sanctified, and meet for the master's use.*
> *(2 Timothy 2:21)*

The vessels in a household have their honour from the use made of them by the head of the house. As a worker I have to separate myself for one purpose—for Jesus Christ to use me for what He likes. Imitation, doing what other people do, is an unmitigated curse. Am I allowing anyone to mould my ideas of Christian service? Am I taking my ideals from some servant of God or from God Himself? We are here for one thing only— to be vessels 'meet for the master's use'. We are not here to work for God because we have chosen to do so, but because God has apprehended us. Natural ability has nothing to do with service; consequently there is never any thought of, 'Oh well, I am not fitted for this.'

Is He going to help Himself to your life, or are you taken up with your conception of what you are going to do? God is responsible for our lives, and the one great keynote is reckless reliance upon Him.

Aug 34

GET A MOVE ON

Abide in Me. (John 15:4)

In the Matter of Determination. The Spirit of Jesus is put
into me by the Atonement, then I have to construct with patience the way of thinking that is exactly in accordance with
my Lord. God will not make me think like Jesus, I have to do
it myself; I have to bring every thought into captivity to the
obedience of Christ. "Abide in Me"—in intellectual matters,
in money matters, in every one of the matters that make
human life what it is. It is not a handbox life.

Am I preventing God from doing things in my circumstances
because I say it will hinder my communion with Him? That is
an impertinence. It does not matter what my circumstances are,
I can be as sure of abiding in Jesus in them as in a prayer meeting. I have not to change and arrange my circumstances myself. With Our Lord the inner abiding was unsullied; He was at
home with God wherever His body was placed. He never chose
His own circumstances, but was meek towards His Father's
dispensations for Him. Think of the amazing leisure of Our
Lord's life! We keep God at excitement point, there is none of
the serenity of the life hid with Christ in God about us.

Think of the things that take you out of abiding in Christ—
Yes, Lord, just a minute, I have got this to do; Yes, I will abide
when once this is finished; when this week is over, it will be
all right, I will abide then. *Get a move on*; begin to abide *now*. In
the initial stages it is a continual effort until it becomes so much
the law of life that you abide in Him unconsciously. Determine
to abide in Jesus wherever you are placed.

And it came to pass . . . that these made war . . . Twelve years they served Chedorlaomer, and in the thirteenth year they rebelled. (Genesis 14: 1–4)

Life without conflict is impossible, either in nature or in grace. This is an open fact of life. The basis of physical, mental, moral and spiritual life is antagonism. Physical life is maintained according to the power of fight in the corpuscles of the blood. If I have sufficient vital force within to overcome the forces without, I produce the balance of health. The same is true of mental life. If I want to maintain a clear, vigorous, mental life, I have to fight, and in this way I produce the balance of thought. Morally it is the same. Virtue is the result of fight; I am only virtuous according to the moral stability I have within. If I have sufficient moral fighting capacity, I produce the moral balance of virtue. We make virtue out of necessity, but no one is virtuous who is good because he cannot help it. Virtue is the outcome of conflict. And spiritually it is the same. 'In the world ye shall have tribulation'; i.e., everything that is not spiritual makes for my undoing; 'but be of good cheer; I have overcome the world.' When once this is understood it is a perfect delight to meet opposition, and as we learn to score off the things that come against us, we produce the balance of holiness. Faith must be tried, and it is the trial of faith that is precious. If you are faint-hearted, it is a sign you won't play the game, you are fit for neither God nor man because you will face nothing.

NKW 36

GET A MOVE ON

And beside this . . . add . . . (2 Peter 1:5)

In the Matter of Drudgery. You have inherited the Divine nature, says Peter (v. 4), now screw your attention down and form habits, give diligence, concentrate. "Add" means all that character means. No man is born either naturally or supernaturally with character, he has to make character. Nor are we born with habits; we have to form habits on the basis of the new life God has put into us. We are not meant to be illuminated versions, but the common stuff of ordinary life exhibiting the marvel of the grace of God. Drudgery is the touchstone of character. The great hindrance in spiritual life is that we will look for big things to do. "Jesus took a towel . . . and began to wash the disciples' feet."

There are times when there is no illumination and no thrill, but just the daily round, the common task. Routine is God's way of saving us between our times of inspiration. Do not expect God always to give you His thrilling minutes, but learn to live in the domain of drudgery by the power of God.

It is the "adding" that is difficult. We say we do not expect God to carry us to heaven on flowery beds of ease, and yet we act as if we did! The tiniest detail in which I obey has all the omnipotent power of the grace of God behind it. If I do my duty, not for duty's sake, but because I believe God is engineering my circumstances, then at the very point of my obedience the whole superb grace of God is mine through the Atonement.

344

Why dost thou not pardon my transgression, and take away mine iniquity? (Job 7:21)

Job gives utterance to a mood which is not foreign to us when he says, 'Am I a sea, or a whale, that thou settest a watch over me?' In certain moods of anguish the human heart says to God, 'I wish You would let me alone, why should I be used for things which have no appeal to me?' In the Christian life we are not being used for our own designs at all, but for the fulfillment of the prayer of Jesus Christ. He has prayed that we might be 'one with him as he is one with the Father', consequently God is concerned only about that one thing, and He never says 'By your leave'. Whether we like it or not, God will burn us in His fire until we are as pure as He is, and it is during the process that we cry, as Job did, 'I wish You would leave me alone.'

We have the idea that prosperity, or happiness, or morality, is the end of a man's existence; according to the Bible it is something other, viz., 'to glorify God and enjoy him for ever'. When a man is right with God, God puts His honour in that man's keeping. Job was one of those in whom God staked His honour, and it was during the process of His inexplicable ways that Job makes his appeal for mercy, and yet all through there comes out his implicit confidence in God. 'And blessed is he, whosoever shall not be offended in me,' said our Lord.

BFB 28

WHAT DO YOU MAKE OF THIS?

Greater love hath no man than this, that a man lay down his
life for his friend . . . I have called you friends. (John 15:13, 15)

Jesus does not ask me to die for Him, but to lay down my life for Him. Peter said—"I will lay down my life for Thy sake" and he meant it; his sense of the heroic was magnificent. It would be a bad thing to be incapable of making such a declaration as Peter made; the sense of our duty is only realized by our sense of the heroic. Has the Lord ever asked you—"Wilt thou lay down thy life for My sake?" It is far easier to die than to lay down the life day in and day out with the sense of the high calling. We are not made for brilliant moments, but we have to walk in the light of them in ordinary ways. There was only one brilliant moment in the life of Jesus, and that was on the Mount of Transfiguration; then He emptied Himself the second time of His glory, and came down into the demon-possessed valley. For thirty-three years Jesus laid out His life to do the will of His Father, and, John says, "we ought to lay down our lives for the brethren." It is contrary to human nature to do it.

If I am a friend of Jesus, I have deliberately and carefully to lay down my life for Him. It is difficult, and thank God it is difficult. Salvation is easy because it cost God so much, but the manifestation of it in my life is difficult. God saves a man and endues him with the Holy Spirit, and then says in effect—"Now work it out, be loyal to Me, whilst the nature of things round about you would make you disloyal." "I have called you friends." Stand loyal to your Friend, and remember that His honour is at stake in your bodily life.

Better is the sight of the eyes than the wandering of the desire:
this is also vanity and vexation of spirit. (Ecclesiastes 6:9)

Lust means literally—'I must have it at once, and I don't care what the consequences are.' It may be a low, animal lust, or it may be a mental lust, or a moral or spiritual lust; but it is a characteristic that does not belong to the life hid with Christ in God. Love is the opposite; love can wait endlessly. 'Better is the sight of the eyes, than the wandering of the desire.' One of the first things Jesus Christ does is to open a man's eyes and he sees things as they are. Until then he is not satisfied with the seeing of his eyes, he wants more, anything that is hidden he must drag to the light, and the wandering of desire is the burning waste of a man's life until he finds God. His heart lusts, his mind lusts, his eyes lust, everything in him lusts until he is related to God. It is the demand for an infinite satisfaction and it ends in the perdition of a man's life.

Jesus Christ says, 'Come unto me, and I will give you rest', i.e., I will put you in the place where your eyes are open. And notice what Jesus Christ says we will look at—lilies, and sparrows, and grass. What man in his senses bothers about these things! We consider aeroplanes and tanks and shells, because these demand our attention, the other things do not. The great emancipation in the salvation of God is that it gives a man the sight of his eyes, and he sees for the first time the handiwork of God in a daisy.

'But their eyes were holden that they should not know him.' . . . 'And their eyes were opened, and they knew him' (Luke 24:16, 31). The salvation of Jesus Christ enables a man to see for the first time in his life, and it is a wonderful thing.

SSH 72

THE UNCRITICAL TEMPER

Judge not, that ye be not judged. (Matt. 7:1)

Jesus says regarding judging—*Don't*. The average Christian is the most penetratingly critical individual. Criticism is a part of the ordinary faculty of man; but in the spiritual domain nothing is accomplished by criticism. The effect of criticism is a dividing up of the powers of the one criticized; the Holy Ghost is the only One in the true position to criticize, He alone is able to show what is wrong without hurting and wounding. It is impossible to enter into communion with God when you are in a critical temper; it makes you hard and vindictive and cruel, and leaves you with the flattering unction that you are a superior person. Jesus says, as a disciple cultivate the uncritical temper. It is not done once and for all. Beware of anything that puts you in the superior person's place.

There is no getting away from the penetration of Jesus. If I see the mote in your eye, it means I have a beam in my own. Every wrong thing that I see in you, God locates in me. Every time I judge, I condemn myself (see Romans 2:17-20). Stop having a measuring rod for other people. There is always one fact more in every man's case about which we know nothing. The first thing God does is to give us a spiritual spring-cleaning; there is no possibility of pride left in a man after that. I have never met the man I could despair of after discerning what lies in me apart from the grace of God.

---

*Many will say to me in that day, Lord, Lord, have we not proph-
esied in thy name? and in thy name have cast out devils? and in
thy name done many wonderful works? (Matthew 7:22)*

If we are able to cast out devils and to do wonderful works,
surely we are the servants of God? Not at all, says Jesus, our
lives must bear evidence in every detail. Our Lord warns here
against those who utilize His words and His ways to remedy
the evils of men whilst they are disloyal to Himself. 'Have we
not prophesied in thy name . . . cast out devils . . . done many
wonderful works'—not one word of confessing Jesus Christ;
one thing only, they have preached Him as a remedy. In Luke
10:20 our Lord told the disciples not to rejoice because the
devils were subject to them, but to rejoice because they were
rightly related to Himself. We are brought back to the one point
all the time—an unsullied relationship to Jesus Christ in every detail, private and public.

SSM 106

DON'T THINK NOW, TAKE THE ROAD

*And Peter . . . walked on the water to go to Jesus. But when he
saw the wind boisterous, he was afraid. (Matt. 14:29 30)*

The wind was actually boisterous, the waves were actually
high, but Peter did not see them at first He did not reckon with
them, he simply recognized his Lord and stepped out in recognition of Him, and walked on the water. Then he began to
reckon with the actual things, and down he went instantly.
Why could not our Lord have enabled him to walk at the bottom of the waves as well as on the top of them? Neither could
be done saving by recognition of the Lord Jesus.

We step right out on God over some things, then self-con-
sideration enters in and down we go. If you are recognizing
your Lord, you have no business with where He engineers your
circumstances. The actual things are, but immediately you look
at them you are overwhelmed, you cannot recognize Jesus,
and the rebuke comes: "Wherefore didst thou doubt?" Let actual circumstances be what they may, keep recognizing Jesus,
maintain complete reliance on Him.

If you debate for a second when God has spoken, it is all up.
Never begin to say—"Well, I wonder if He did speak?" Be reckless immediately, fling it all out on Him. You do not know when
His voice will come, but whenever the realization of God comes
in the faintest way imaginable, recklessly abandon. It is only
by abandon that you recognize Him. You will only realize His
voice more clearly by recklessness.

A time to keep silence, and a time to speak. (Ecclesiastes 3:7)

Sometimes it is cowardly to speak, and sometimes it is cowardly to keep silence. In the Bible the great test of a man's character is his tongue (see James 1:26). The tongue only came to its right place within the lips of the Lord Jesus Christ, because He never spoke from His right to Himself. He who was the Wisdom of God Incarnate, said 'the words that I speak unto you, I speak not of myself', i.e., from the disposition of my right to Myself, but from My relationship to My Father. We are either too hasty or too slow; either we won't speak at all, or we speak too much, or we speak in the wrong mood. The thing that makes us speak is the lust to vindicate ourselves. '. . . leaving you an example . . . who did no sin neither was guile found in his mouth.' Guile has the ingredient of self-vindication in it— My word, I'll make him smart for saying that about me! That spirit never was in Jesus Christ. The great deliverance for a man in time is to learn the programmes of speech and of silence.

SHH 27

SERVICE OF PASSIONATE DEVOTION

Lovest thou Me? . . . Feed My sheep. (John 21:16)

Jesus did not say—Make converts to your way of thinking, but look after My sheep, see that they get nourished in the knowledge of Me. We count as service what we do in the way of Christian work; Jesus Christ calls service what we are to Him, not what we do for Him. Discipleship is based on devotion to Jesus Christ, not on adherence to a belief or a creed. "If any man come to Me and hate not . . ., he cannot be My disciple." There is no argument and no compulsion, but simply—If you would be My disciple, you must be devoted to Me. A man touched by the Spirit of God suddenly says—"Now I see Who Jesus is," and that is the source of devotion.

To-day we have substituted credal belief for personal belief, and that is why so many are devoted to causes and so few devoted to Jesus Christ. People do not want to be devoted to Jesus, but only to the cause He started. Jesus Christ is a source of deep offence to the educated mind of to-day that does not want Him in any other way than as a Comrade. Our Lord's first obedience was to the will of His Father, not to the needs of men; the saving of men was the natural outcome of His obedience to the Father. If I am devoted to the cause of humanity only, I will soon be exhausted and come to the place where my love will falter; but if I love Jesus Christ personally and passionately, I can serve humanity though men treat me as a door-mat. The secret of a disciple's life is devotion to Jesus Christ, and the characteristic of the life is its unobtrusiveness. It is like a corn of wheat, which falls into the ground and dies, but presently it will spring up and alter the whole landscape (John 12:24).

That they may be one, even as we are one. (John 17:22)

Christianity is personal, therefore it is un-individual. An individual remains definitely segregated from every other individual; when you come to the teaching of our Lord there is no individuality in that sense at all, but only personality, 'that they may be *one*'. Two *individuals* can never merge; two *persons* can become one without losing their identity. Personality is the characteristic of the spiritual man as individuality is the characteristic of the natural man. When the holy Spirit comes in He emancipates our personal spirit into union with God, and individuality ultimately becomes so interdependent that it loses all its self-assertiveness. Jesus Christ prayed for our identification with Himself in His oneness with the Father—'that they may be one, *even as we are one*'. That is infinitely beyond experience. Identification is a revelation—the exposition of the experience. The standard Revelation with regard to identification is our Lord Himself, and you can never define Him in terms of individuality, but only in terms of personality. When Jesus Christ emancipates the personality individuality is not destroyed, it is transfigured, and the transfiguring, incalculable element is love, personal passionate devotion to Himself, and to others for His sake.

BE 31

HAVE YOU COME TO "WHEN" YET?

And the Lord turned the captivity of Job when he prayed for his friends. (Job 42:10)

The plaintive, self-centred, morbid kind of prayer, a dead-set that I want to be right, is never found in the New Testament. The fact that I am trying to be right with God is a sign that I am rebelling against the Atonement. "Lord, I will purify my heart if You will answer my prayer; I will walk rightly if You will help me." I *cannot* make myself right with God, I *cannot* make my life perfect; I can only be right with God if I accept the Atonement of the Lord Jesus Christ as an absolute gift. Am I humble enough to accept it? I have to resign every kind of claim and cease from every effort, and leave myself entirely alone in His hands, and then begin to pour out in the priestly work of intercession. There is much prayer that arises from real disbelief in the Atonement. Jesus is not beginning to save us, He has saved us, the thing is done, and it is an insult to ask Him to do it.

If you are not getting the hundredfold more, not getting insight into God's word, then start praying for your friends, enter into the ministry of the interior. "The Lord turned the captivity of Job *when he prayed for his friends.*" The real business of your life as a saved soul is intercessory prayer. Wherever God puts you in circumstances, pray immediately, pray that His Atonement may be realized in other lives as it has been in yours. Pray for your friends *now*; pray for those with whom you come in contact *now*.

I will be as the dew unto Israel: he shall blossom as the lily.
(Hosea 14:5) (RV)

The New Testament notices things which from our standpoint do not seem to count. For instance. Our Lord called only twelve disciples, but what about all those other disciples of His who were not specially called? The twelve disciples were called for a special purpose; but there were hundreds who followed Jesus and were sincere believers in Him who were unnoticed. We are apt to have a disproportionate view of a Christian because we look only at the exceptions. The exceptions stand out *as* exceptions. The extraordinary conversions and phenomenal experiences are magnificent specimen studies of what happens in the life of everyone, but not one in a million has an experience such as the Apostle Paul had. The majority of us are unnoticed and unnoticeable people. If we take the extraordinary experiences a a model for the Christian life, we erect a wrong standard without knowing it, and in the passing of the years we produce that worst abortion, the spiritual prig—an intolerable un-likeness to Jesus Christ. The man or woman who becomes a spiritual prig does so by imperceptible degrees, but the starting-point is a departure from the evangel of the New Testament and a building up on the evangel of Protestantism.

MU 35

THE MINISTRY OF THE INTERIOR

But ye are . . . a royal priesthood. (1 Peter 2:9)

By what right do we become "a royal priesthood"? By the right of the Atonement. Are we prepared to leave ourselves resolutely alone and to launch out into the priestly work of prayer? The continual grubbing on the inside to see whether we are what we ought to be generates a self-centred, morbid type of Christianity, not the robust, simple life of the child of God. Until we get into a right relationship to God, it is a case of hanging on by the skin of our teeth, and we say—What a wonderful victory I have got! There is nothing indicative of the miracle of Redemption in that. Launch out in reckless belief that the Redemption is complete, and then bother no more about yourself, but begin to do as Jesus Christ said—pray for the friend who comes to you at midnight, pray for the saints, pray for all men. Pray on the realization that you are only perfect in Christ Jesus, not on this plea—"O Lord, I have done my best, please hear me."

How long is it going to take God to free us from the morbid habit of thinking about ourselves? We must get sick unto death of ourselves, until there is no longer any surprise at anything God can tell us about ourselves. There is only one place where we are right, and that is in Christ Jesus. When we are there, then we have to pour out for all we are worth in this ministry of the interior.

O wretched man that I am! Who shall deliver me from the body of this death? (Romans 7:24)

Be careful not to be caught up in the clap-trap of today which says, 'I believe in the teachings of Jesus, but I don't see any need for the Atonement.' Men talk pleasant, patronizing things about Jesus Christ's teaching while they ignore His Cross. By all means let us study Christ's teaching, we do not think nearly enough along New Testament lines, we are swamped by pagan standards, and as Christians we ought to allow Jesus Christ's principles to work out in our brains as well as in our lives; but the teaching of Jesus apart from His Atonement simply adds an ideal that leads to despair. What is the good of telling me that only the pure in heart can see God when I am impure? of telling me to love my enemies when I hate them? I may keep it down but the spirit is there. Does Jesus Christ make it easier? He makes it a hundredfold more difficult! The purity God demands is impossible unless we can be re-made from within, and that is what Jesus Christ undertakes to do through the Atonement. Jesus Christ did not come to tell men they ought to be holy—there is an 'ought' in every man that tells him that, and whenever he sees a holy character he may bluster and excuse himself as he likes, but he knows that is what he ought to be: He came to put us in the place where we can be holy, that is, He came to *make* us what He teaches we should be, that is the difference.

BE 10–11

THE UNDEVIATING TEST

For with what judgment ye judge, ye shall be judged; and with
what measure ye mete, it shall be measured to you again.
(Matt. 7:2)

This statement is not a haphazard guess, it is an eternal law of God. Whatever judgment you give, it is measured to you again. There is a difference between retaliation and retribution. Jesus says that the basis of life is retribution—"with what measure ye mete, it shall be measured to you again." If you have been shrewd in finding out the defects in others, remember that will be exactly the measure given to you. Life serves back in the coin you pay. This law works from God's throne downwards (cf. Psalm 18:25-26).

Romans 2 applies it in a still more definite way, and says that the one who criticizes another is guilty of the very same thing. God looks not only at the act, He looks at the possibility. We do not believe the statements of the Bible to begin with. For instance, do we believe this statement, that the things we criticize in others we are guilty of ourselves? The reason we see hypocrisy and fraud and unreality in others is because they are all in our own hearts. The great characteristic of a saint is humility—Yes, all those things and other evils would have been manifested in me but for the grace of God, therefore I have no right to judge.

Jesus says—"Judge not, that ye be not judged"; if you do judge, it will be measured to you exactly as you have judged. Who of us would dare to stand before God and say—"My God, judge me as I have judged my fellow men"? We have judged our fellow men as sinners; if God should judge us like that we would be in hell. God judges us through the marvelous Atonement of Jesus Christ.

If thine eye offend thee, pluck it out. (Mark 9:47)

Sanctification means not only that we are delivered from sin, but that we start on a life of stern discipline. It is not a question of praying but of performing, of deliberately disciplining ourselves. There is no royal road there; we each have it entirely in our own hands. It is not wrong things that have to be sacrificed, but right things. 'The good is the enemy of the best', not the bad, but the good that is not good enough. The danger is to argue on the line of giving up only what is wrong; Jesus Christ selected things essential to a full orbed life—the right hand and the eye, these are not bad things, they are creations of God. Jesus Christ talked rugged, unmitigated truth. He was never ambiguous, and He says it is better to be maimed than damned. There was never a saint yet who did not have to start with a maimed life. Anyone will give up wrong things if he knows how to, but will I give up the best I have for Jesus Christ? If I am only willing to give up wrong things, never let me talk about being in love with Him! We say, 'Why shouldn't I do it, there is no harm in it?' For pity's sake, go and do it, but remember that the construction of a spiritual character is doomed once you take that line.

BE 48

ACQUAINTANCE WITH GRIEF

A Man of sorrows and acquainted with grief. (Isa. 53:3)

We are not acquainted with grief in the way in which Our Lord was acquainted with it; we endure it, we get through it, but we do not become intimate with it. At the beginning of life we do not reconcile ourselves to the fact of sin. We take a rational view of life and say that a man by controlling his instincts, and by educating himself, can produce a life which will slowly evolve into the life of God. But as we go on, we find the presence of something which we have not taken into consideration, viz., sin, and it upsets all our calculations. Sin has made the basis of things wild and not rational. We have to recognize that sin is a fact, not a defect; sin is red-handed mutiny against God. Either God or sin must die in my life. The New Testament brings us right down to this one issue. If sin rules in me, God's life in me will be killed; if God rules in me, sin in me will be killed. There is no possible ultimate but that. The climax of sin is that it crucified Jesus Christ, and what was true in the history of God on earth will be true in your history and in mine. In our mental outlook we have to reconcile ourselves to the fact of sin as the only explanation as to why Jesus Christ came, and as the explanation of the grief and sorrow in life.

These things saith he that is holy, he that is true. (Revelation 3:7)

The disciple's Lord is the supreme Authority in every relationship of life the disciple is in or can be in. That is a very obvious point, but think what it means—it means recognizing it as impertinent to say, 'Oh, well, Jesus Christ does not know my circumstances; the principles involved in His teachings are altogether impracticable for me where I am.' That thought never came from the Spirit of God, and it has to be gripped in a vice on the threshold of the mind and allowed no way. If as we obey God such a circumstance is possible where Jesus Christ's precepts and principles are impracticable, then He has misled us. The idea insinuates itself—'Oh, well, I can be justified from my present conduct because of—so and so.' We are never justified as disciples in taking any line of action other than that indicated by the teaching of our Lord and made possible for us by His Spirit. The providence of God fits us into various settings of life to see if we will be disciples in those relationships.

IWP 123

RECONCILING ONE'S SELF
TO THE FACT OF SIN

This is your hour, and the power of darkness. (Luke 22:53)

It is not being reconciled to the fact of sin that produces all the disasters in life. You may talk about the nobility of human nature, but there is something in human nature which will laugh in the face of every ideal you have. If you refuse to agree with the fact that there is vice and self-seeking, something downright spiteful and wrong in human beings, instead of reconciling yourself to it, when it strikes your life, you will compromise with it and say it is of no use to battle against it. Have you made allowance for this hour and the power of darkness, or do you take a recognition of yourself that misses out sin? In your bodily relationships and friendships do you reconcile yourself to the fact of sin? If not, you will be caught round the next corner and you will compromise with it. If you reconcile yourself to the fact of sin, you will realize the danger at once—Yes, I see what that would mean. The recognition of sin does not destroy the basis of friendship; it establishes a mutual regard for the fact that the basis of life is tragic. Always beware of an estimate of life which does not recognize the fact that there is sin.

Jesus Christ never trusted human nature, yet He was never cynical, never suspicious, because He trusted absolutely in what He could do for human nature. The pure man or woman, not the innocent, is the safeguarded man or woman. You are never safe with an innocent man or woman. Men and women have no business to be innocent; God demands that they be pure and virtuous. Innocence is the characteristic of a child; it is a blameworthy thing for a man or woman not to be reconciled to the fact of sin.

Philip saith unto him, Lord, shew us the Father, and it sufficeth us. (John 14:9)
And he findeth Philip, and Jesus saith unto him. Follow me. (John 1:43)

You may have had no reluctance in obeying the Lord's command, and yet it is probable you are hurting Him because you look for God to manifest Himself where He never can—'Lord, shew us the Father.' We look to God to manifest Himself to His children: God manifests Himself *in* His children, consequently the manifestation is seen by others, not by us. It is a snare to want to be conscious of God; you cannot be conscious of your consciousness and remain sane. You have obeyed Christ's command, then are you hurting Him by asking some profoundly perverse question? I believe our Lord is repeatedly astounded at the stupidity we display. It is notions of our own that make us stupid; when we are simple we are never stupid, we discern all the time. 'Lord, shew us the Father'; 'Shew me Thy face'; 'Expound this thing to me'; and His answer comes straight back to our heart: 'Have I been so long time with you, and yet hast thou not known *me*?'

GW 25

RECEIVING ONE'S SELF
IN THE FIRES OF SORROW

What shall I say? Father, save me from this hour? But for this
cause came I unto this hour. Father, glorify Thy name.
(John 12:27-29, R.V.)

My attitude as a saint to sorrow and difficulty is not to ask that they may be prevented, but to ask that I may preserve the self God created me to be through every fire of sorrow. Our Lord received Himself in the fire of sorrow, He was saved not *from* the hour, but *out of* the hour.

We say that there ought to be no sorrow, but there is sorrow, and we have to receive ourselves in its fires. If we try and evade sorrow, refuse to lay our account with it, we are foolish. Sorrow is one of the biggest facts in life; it is no use saying sorrow ought not to be. Sin and sorrow and suffering *are*, and it is not for us to say that God has made a mistake in allowing them.

Sorrow burns up a great amount of shallowness, but it does not always make a man better. Suffering either gives me my self or it destroys my self. You cannot receive your self in success, you lose your head; you cannot receive your self in monotony, you grouse. The way to find your self is in the fires of sorrow. Why it should be so is another matter, but that it is so is true in the Scriptures and in human experience. You always know the man who has been through the fires of sorrow and received himself, you are certain you can go to him in trouble and find that he has ample leisure for you. If a man has not been through the fires of sorrow, he is apt to be contemptuous, he has no time for you. If you receive yourself in the fires of sorrow, God will make you nourishment for other people.

And he must needs go through Samaria. (John 4:4)

One great thing to notice is that God's order comes to us in the haphazard. We try to plan our ways and work things out for ourselves, but they go wrong because there are more facts than we know; whereas if we just go on with the days as they come, we find that God's order comes to us in that apparently haphazard way. The man who does not know God depends entirely on his own wits and forecasting. If instead of arranging our own programmes we will trust to the wisdom of God and concentrate all our efforts on the duty that lies nearest, we shall find that we meet God in that way and in no other. When we become 'amateur providences' and arrange times and meetings, we may cause certain things to happen, but we very rarely meet God in that way; we meet Him most effectively as we go on in the ordinary ways. Where you look for God, He does not appear; where you do not look for Him, there He is— a trick of the weather, a letter, and suddenly you are face to face with the best thing you ever met. This comes out all through the life of Jesus Christ; it was the most natural thing for Him to go through Samaria.

HGM 31

ALWAYS NOW

We . . . beseech you that ye receive not the grace of God in vain.
(2 Cor. 6:1)

The grace you had yesterday will not do for today. Grace is the overflowing favour of God; you can always reckon it is there to draw upon. "In much patience, in afflictions, in necessities, in distresses"—that is where the test for patience comes. Are you failing the grace of God there? Are you saying—Oh, well, I won't count this time? It is not a question of praying and asking God to help you; it is taking the grace of God *now*. We make prayer the preparation for work, it is never that in the Bible. Prayer is the exercise of drawing on the grace of God. Don't say—I will endure this until I can get away and pray. Pray *now*; draw on the grace of God in the moment of need. Prayer is the most practical thing, it is not the reflex action of devotion. Prayer is the last thing in which we learn to draw on God's grace.

"In stripes, in imprisonments, in tumults, in labours"—in all these things manifest a drawing upon the grace of God that will make you a marvel to yourself and to others. Draw now, not presently. The one word in the spiritual vocabulary is *Now*. Let circumstances bring you where they will, keep drawing on the grace of God in every conceivable condition you may be in. One of the greatest proofs that you are drawing on the grace of God is that you can be humiliated without manifesting the slightest trace of anything but His grace.

"Having nothing . . ." Never reserve anything. Pour out the best you have, and always be poor. Never be diplomatic and careful about the treasure God gives. This is poverty triumphant.

There is an evil which I have seen under the sun, and it is common among men: a man to whom God has given riches, wealth, and honour, so that he wanteth nothing for his soul of all that he desireth, yet God giveth him not power to eat thereof, but a stranger eateth it: this is vanity, and it is an evil disease. (Ecclesiastes 6:1, 2)

The inevitable barriers are there in every one of our lives. They may not be of an intense order, such as a terrible maiming, or blindness, or deafness, or something that knocks a man out of fulfilling his ambitions, they may be hereditary incapabilities; but the peril is lest we lie down and whine and are of no more good. The thing to do is to recognize that the barriers are inscrutable, that they are there not by chance but entirely by God's permission, and they should be faced and not ignored. Was there ever a more severely handicapped life on this earth than Helen Keller's? The peril of the inevitable barriers is that if I have not faced the facts sufficiently, I am apt to blame God for them. There is one fact more that I do not know, and that fact lies entirely with God, not with me. It is no use to spend my time saying, I wish I was not like this, I am just like it. The practical point in Christianity is—Can Jesus Christ and His religion be of any use to me as I am, not as I am not? Can He deal with me where I am, in the condition I am in?

SHH 70

THE OVERSHADOWING
PERSONAL DELIVERANCE

I am with thee to deliver thee, saith the Lord. (Jer. 1:8)

God promised Jeremiah that He would deliver him personally—"Thy life will I give unto thee for a prey." That is all God promises His children. Wherever God sends us, He will guard our lives. Our personal property and possessions are a matter of indifference, we have to sit loosely to all those things; if we do not, there will be panic and heartbreak and distress. That is the inwardness of the overshadowing of personal deliverance.

The Sermon on the Mount indicates that when we are on Jesus Christ's errands, there is no time to stand up for ourselves. Jesus says, in effect, Do not be bothered with whether you are being justly dealt with or not. To look for justice is a sign of deflection from devotion to Him. Never look for justice in this world, but never cease to give it. If we look for justice, we will begin to grouse and to indulge in the discontent of self-pity—Why should I be treated like this? If we are devoted to Jesus Christ we have nothing to do with what we meet, whether it is just or unjust. Jesus says—Go steadily on with what I have told you to do and I will guard your life. If you try to guard it yourself, you remove yourself from My deliverance. The most devout among us become atheistic in this connection; we do not believe God, we enthrone common sense and tack the name of God on to it. We do lean to our own understanding, instead of trusting God with all our hearts.

And when he is come, he will reprove the world of sin, of righteousness and of judgment. (John 16:8)

The subject of human free will is nearly always either overstated or understated. There is a pre-determination in man's spirit which makes him will along certain lines; but no man has the power to make an act of pure free will. When the Spirit of God comes into a man, He brings His own generating will power and causes him to will with God, and we have the amazing revelation that the saint's free choices are the pre-determinations of God. That is a most wonderful thing in Christian psychology, viz., that a saint chooses exactly what God pre-determined he should choose. If you have never received the Spirit of God this will be one of the things which is 'foolishness' to you; but if you have received the Spirit and are obeying Him, you find He brings your spirit into complete harmony with God and the sound of your goings and the sound of God's goings are one and the same.

BP 215

APPREHENDED BY GOD

If that I may apprehend that for which also I am apprehended.
(Phil. 3:12)

Never choose to be a worker; but when once God has put His call on you, woe be to you if you turn to the right hand or to the left. We are not here to work for God because we have chosen to do so, but because God has apprehended us. There is never any thought of—"Oh, well, I am not fitted for this." What you are to preach is determined by God, not by your own natural inclinations. Keep your soul steadfastly related to God, and remember that you are called not to bear testimony only, but to preach the gospel. Every Christian must testify, but when it comes to the call to preach, there must be the agonizing grip of God's hand on you, your life is in the grip of God for that one thing. How many of us are held like that?

Never water down the word of God, preach it in its undiluted sternness; there must be unflinching loyalty to the word of God; but when you come to personal dealing with your fellow men, remember who you are—not a special being made up in heaven, but a sinner saved by grace.

"I count not myself to have apprehended: but *this one thing I do* . . ."

If I had not come and spoken unto them, they had not had sin: but now they have no cloke for their sin. (John 15:22)

We have, as Christian disciples, to continually recognize that much of what is called Christianity today is not the Christianity of the New Testament; it is distinctly different in generation and manifestation. Jesus is not the fountain-head of modern Christianity; He is scarcely thought about. Christian preachers, Sunday School teachers, religious books, all without any apology patronize Jesus Christ and put Him on one side. We have to learn that to stand true to Jesus Christ's point of view means ostracism, the ostracism that was brought on Him; most of us know nothing whatever about it. The modern view looks upon human nature as pathetic: men and women are poor ignorant babes in the wood who have lost themselves. Jesus Christ's view is totally different, He does not look on men and women as babes in the wood, but as sinners who need saving, and the modern mind detests His view. Our Lord's teaching is based on something we violently hate, viz., His doctrine of sin; we do not believe it unless we have had a radical dealing with God on the line of His teaching.

Remember that a disciple is committed to much more than belief in Jesus; he is committed to his Lord's view of the world, of men, of God and of sin. Take stock of your views and compare them with the New Testament, and never get tricked into thinking that the Bible does not mean what it says when it disagrees with you. Disagree with what our Lord says by all means if you like, but never say that the Bible does not mean what it says.

HG 63

DIRECTION OF DISCIPLINE

And if thy right hand offend thee, cut it off and cast it from thee:
for it is profitable for thee that one of thy members should perish
and not that thy whole body should be cast into hell. (Matt. 5:30)

Jesus did not say that everyone must cut off the right hand, but—If your right hand offends you in your walk with Me, cut it off. There are many things that are perfectly legitimate, but if you are going to concentrate on God you cannot do them. Your right hand is one of the best things you have, but, says Jesus, if it hinders you in following His precepts, cut it off. This line of discipline is the sternest one that ever struck mankind.

When God alters a man by regeneration, the characteristic of the life to begin with is that it is maimed. There are a hundred and one things you dare not do, things that to you and in the eyes of the world that knows you are as your right hand and your eye, and the unspiritual person says—Whatever is wrong in that? How absurd you are! There never has been a saint yet who did not have to live a maimed life to start with. But it is better to enter into life maimed and lovely in God's sight than to be lovely in man's sight and lame in God's. In the beginning Jesus Christ by His Spirit has to check you from doing a great many things that may be perfectly right for everyone else but not right for you. See that you do not use your limitations to criticize someone else.

It is a maimed life to begin with, but in v. 48 Jesus gives the picture of a perfectly full-orbed life—"Ye shall be *perfect*, as your heavenly Father is perfect."

Whosoever hateth his brother is a murderer. (1 John 3:15)

Few of us are actually murderers, but we are all criminals in potentiality; and one of the greatest humiliations in work for God is that we are never free from the reminder by the Holy Spirit of what we might be in actuality but for the grace of God.

CHI 24

The Bible never deals with proportionate sin; according to the Bible an impure thought is as bad as adultery; a covetous thought is as bad as a theft. It takes a long education in the things of God before we believe that is true. Never trust innocence when it is contradicted by the word of God. The tiniest bit of sin is an indication of the vast corruption that is in the human heart. ('For from within, out of the heart of man, proceed . . . ' Mark 7:21–3.) That is why we must keep in the light all the time. Never allow horror at crime to blind you to the fact that it is human nature like your own that committed it. A saint is never horror-stricken because although he knows that what our Lord says about the human heart is true, he knows also of a Saviour who can save to the uttermost.

CHI 71

DO IT NOW

Agree with thine adversary quickly. (Matt. 5:25)

Jesus Christ is laying down this principle—Do what you know you must do, now, and do it quickly; if you do not, the inevitable process will begin to work and you will have to pay to the last farthing in pain and agony and distress. God's laws are unalterable; there is no escape from them. The teaching of Jesus goes straight to the way we are made up.

To see that my adversary gives me my rights is natural; but Jesus says that it is a matter of eternal and imperative importance to me that I pay my adversary what I owe him. From our Lord's standpoint it does not matter whether I am defrauded or not; what does matter is that I do not defraud. Am I insisting on my rights, or am I paying what I owe from Jesus Christ's standpoint?

Do the thing quickly, bring yourself to judgment now. In moral and spiritual matters, you must do it at once; if you do not, the inexorable process will begin to work. God is determined to have His child as pure and clean and white as driven snow, and as long as there is disobedience in any point of His teaching, He will prevent none of the working of His spirit. Our insistence in proving that we are right is nearly always an indication that there has been some point of disobedience. No wonder the Spirit so strongly urges to keep steadfastly in the light!

"Agree with thine adversary quickly." Have you suddenly turned a corner in any relationship and found that you had anger in your heart? Confess it quickly, quickly put it right before God, be reconciled to that one—*do it now.*

For from within, out of the heart of men, proceed evil thoughts, adulteries, fornications, murders . . . (Mark 7:21–2)

This passage is detestable to an unspiritual person, it is in absolutely bad taste, nine out of every ten people do not believe it because they are grossly ignorant about the heart. In these verses Jesus Christ says, to put it in modern language. 'No crime has ever been committed that every human being is not capable of committing.' Do I believe that? Do you? If we do not, remember we pass a verdict straight off on the Lord Jesus Christ, we tell Him He does not know what He is talking about. We read that Jesus 'knew what was in man', meaning that He knew men's hearts; and the Apostle Paul emphasizes the same thing—'Don't glory in man; trust only the grace of God in yourself and in other people.' No wonder Jesus Christ pleads with us to give over the keeping of our hearts to Him so that He can fill them with a new life! Every characteristic seen in the life of Jesus Christ becomes possible in our lives when once we hand over our hearts to Him to be filled with the Holy Spirit.

BP 104

JULY

THE INEVITABLE PENALTY

Verily I say unto thee, Thou shalt by no means come out thence
till thou have paid the uttermost farthing. (Matt. 5:26)

There is no heaven with a little corner of hell in it. God is determined to make you pure and holy and right; He will not allow you to escape for one moment from the scrutiny of the Holy Spirit. He urged you to come to judgment right away when He convicted you, but you did not; the inevitable process began to work and now you are in prison, and you will only get out when you have paid the uttermost farthing. "Is this a God of mercy, and of love?" you say. Seen from God's side, it is a glorious ministry of love. God is going to bring you out pure and spotless and undefiled; but He wants you to recognize the disposition you were showing—the disposition of your right to yourself. The moment you are willing that God should alter your disposition, His recreating forces will begin to work. The moment you realize God's purpose, which is to get you rightly related to Himself and then to your fellow men, He will tax the last limit of the universe to help you take the right road. Decide it now—"Yes, Lord, I *will* write that letter to-night"; "I *will* be reconciled to that man now."

These messages of Jesus Christ are for the will and the conscience, not for the head. If you dispute the Sermon on the Mount with your head, you will blunt the appeal to your heart.

"I wonder why I don't go on with God?" Are you paying your debts from God's standpoint? Do *now* what you will have to do some day. Every moral call has an "ought" behind it.

Whatsoever things are pure. . . (Philippians 4:8)

Purity is not innocence, it is much more. Purity means stainlessness, an unblemishedness that has stood the test. Purity is learned in private, never in public. Jesus Christ demands purity of mind and imagination, chastity of bodily and mental habits. The only men and women it is safe to trust are those who have been tried and have stood the test; purity is the outcome of conflict, not of necessity. You cannot trust innocence or natural goodness; you cannot trust possibilities. This explains Jesus Christ's attitude. Our Lord trusted no man (see John 2:24–5), yet He was never suspicious, never bitter; His confidence in what God's grace could do for any man was so perfect that He never despaired of anyone. If our trust is placed in human beings, we will end in despairing of every one. But when we limit our thinking to the things of purity we shall think only of what God's grace has done in others, and put our confidence in that and in nothing else.

MFL 88

THE CONDITIONS OF DISCIPLESHIP

If any man come to Me, and hate not . . . he cannot be My disciple. (Luke 14:26, 27, 33)

If the closest relationships of life clash with the claims of Jesus Christ, He says it must be instant obedience to Himself. Discipleship means personal, passionate devotion to a Person, Our Lord Jesus Christ. There is a difference between devotion to a Person and devotion to principles or to a cause. Our Lord never proclaimed a cause; He proclaimed personal devotion to Himself. To be a disciple is to be a devoted love-slave of the Lord Jesus. Many of us who call ourselves Christians are not devoted to Jesus Christ. No man on earth has this passionate love to the Lord Jesus unless the Holy Ghost has imparted it to him. We may admire Him, we may respect Him and reverence Him, but we cannot love Him. The only Lover of the Lord Jesus is the Holy Ghost, and He sheds abroad the very love of God in our hearts. Whenever the Holy Ghost sees a chance of glorifying Jesus, He will take your heart, your nerves, your whole personality, and simply make you blaze and glow with devotion to Jesus Christ.

The Christian life is stamped by "moral spontaneous originality," consequently the disciple is open to the same charge that Jesus Christ was, viz., that of inconsistency. But Jesus Christ was always consistent to God, and the Christian must be consistent to the life of the Son of God in him, not consistent to hard and fast creeds. Men pour themselves into creeds, and God has to blast them out of their prejudices before they can become devoted to Jesus Christ.

Whatsoever things are lovely . . . (Philippians 4:8)

The things of loveliness, i.e., the things that are morally agreeable and pleasant. The word 'lovely' has the meaning of juicy and delicious. That is the definition given by Calvin, and he is supposed to be a moloch of severity! We have the idea that our duty must always be disagreeable, and we make any number of duties out of diseased sensibilities. If our duty is disagreeable, it is a sign that we are in a disjointed relationship to God. If God gave some people a fully sweet cup, they would go carefully into a churchyard and turn the cup upside down and empty it, and say, 'No, that could never be meant for me.' The idea has become incorporated into their make-up that their lot must always be miserable. Once we become rightly related to God, duty will never be a disagreeable thing of which we have to say with a sigh, 'Oh, well, I must do my duty.' Duty is the daughter of God. Never take your estimate of duty after a sleepless night, or after a dose of indigestion; take your sense of duty from the Spirit of God and the word of Jesus. There are people whose lives are diseased and twisted by a sense of duty which God never inspired; but once let them begin to think about the things of loveliness, and the healing forces that will come into their lives will be amazing. The very essence of godliness is in the things of loveliness; think about these things, says Paul.

MFL 89

THE CONCENTRATION
OF PERSONAL SIN

Woe is me! for I am undone; because I am a man of unclean lips.
(Isa. 6:5)

When I get into the presence of God, I do not realize that I am a sinner in an indefinite sense; I realize the concentration of sin in a particular feature of my life. A man will say easily— "Oh, yes, I know I am a sinner"; but when he gets into the presence of God he cannot get off with that statement. The conviction is concentrated on—I am this, or that, or the other. This is always the sign that a man or woman is in the presence of God. There is never any vague sense of sin, but the concentration of sin in some personal particular. God begins by convicting us of the one thing fixed on in the mind that is prompted by His Spirit; if we will yield to His conviction on that point, He will lead us down to the great disposition of sin underneath. That is the way God always deals with us when we are consciously in His presence.

This experience of the concentration of sin is true in the greatest and the least of saints as well as in the greatest and the least of sinners. When a man is on the first rung of the ladder of experience, he may say—I do not know where I have gone wrong, but the Spirit of God will point out some particular definite thing. The effect of the vision of the holiness of the Lord on Isaiah was to bring home to him that he was a man of unclean lips. "And he laid it upon my mouth, and said Lo, this hath touched thy lips; and thine iniquity is taken away, and thy sin purged." The cleansing fire had to be applied where the sin had been concentrated.

Whatsoever things are of good report . . . (Philippians 4:8)

When we do think about the things of good report we shall be astonished to realize where they are to be found; they are found where we only expected to find the opposite. When our eyes are fixed on Jesus Christ we begin to see qualities blossoming in the lives of others that we never saw there before. We see people whom we have tabooed and put on the other side exhibiting qualities we have never exhibited, although we call ourselves saved and sanctified. Never look for other people to be holy; it is a cruel thing to do, it distorts your view of yourself and of others. Could anyone have had a sterner view of sin than Jesus had, and yet had anyone a more loving, tender patience with the worst of men than He had? The difference in the attitude is that Jesus Christ never expected men to be holy; He knew they could not be: *He came to make men holy.* All He asks of men is that they acknowledge they are not right, then He will do all the rest—'Blessed are the poor in spirit'.

MFL 90

ONE OF GOD'S GREAT DON'TS

Fret not thyself, it tendeth only to evil doing. (Ps. 37:8, R.V.)

Fretting means getting out at elbows mentally or spiritually. It is one thing to say "Fret not," but a very different thing to have such a disposition that you find yourself able not to fret. It sounds so easy to talk about "resting in the Lord" and "waiting patiently for Him" until the nest is upset—until we live, as so many are doing, in tumult and anguish; is it possible then to rest in the Lord? If this "don't" does not work there, it will work nowhere. This "don't" must work in days of perplexity as well as in days of peace, or it never will work. And if it will not work in your particular case, it will not work in anyone else's case. Resting in the Lord does not depend on external circumstances at all, but on your relationship to God Himself.

Fussing always ends in sin. We imagine that a little anxiety and worry are an indication of how really wise we are; it is much more an indication of how really wicked we are. Fretting springs from a determination to get our own way. Our Lord never worried and He was never anxious, because He was not "out" to realize His own ideas; He was "out" to realize God's ideas. Fretting is wicked if you are a child of God.

Have you been bolstering up that stupid soul of yours with the idea that your circumstances are too much for God? Put all "supposing" on one side and dwell in the shadow of the Almighty. Deliberately tell God that you will not fret about that thing. All our fret and worry is caused by calculating without God.

I keep under my body, and bring it into subjection.
(1 Corinthians 9:27)

The way to examine whether we are doing what Jesus Christ wants us to do is to look at the habits of our life in three domains—physical, emotional, and intellectual. The best scrutiny we can give ourselves is along this line: Are my bodily habits chaste? is my emotional nature inordinate? is my intellectual life insubordinate? When we begin to work out what God has worked in, we are faced with the problem that this physical body, this mechanism, has been used by habit to obeying another rule called sin; when Jesus Christ delivers us from that rule, He does not give us a new body. He gives us power to break and then re-mould every habit formed while we were under the dominion of sin. Much of the misery in our Christian life comes not because the devil tackles us, but because we have never understood the simple laws of our make-up. We have to treat the body as the servant of Jesus Christ: when the body says 'Sit', and He says 'Go', go! When the body says 'Eat', and he says 'Fast', fast! When the body says 'Yawn', and He says 'Pray', pray!

BE 57

DON'T CALCULATE WITHOUT GOD

Commit thy way unto the Lord, trust also in Him, and He shall bring it to pass. (Ps. 37:5)

Don't calculate without God.

God seems to have a delightful way of upsetting the things we have calculated on without taking Him into account. We get into circumstances which were not chosen by God, and suddenly we find we have been calculating without God; He has not entered in as a living factor. The one thing that keeps us from the possibility of worrying is bringing God in as the greatest factor in all our calculations.

In our religion it is customary to put God first, but we are apt to think it is an impertinence to put Him first in the practical issues of our lives. If we imagine we have to put on our Sunday moods before we come near to God, we will never come near Him. We must come as we are.

Don't calculate with the evil in view.

Does God really mean us to take no account of the evil? "Love. . . taketh no account of the evil." Love is not ignorant of the existence of the evil, but it does not take it in as a calculating factor. Apart from God, we do reckon with evil; we calculate with it in view and work all our reasonings from that standpoint.

Don't calculate with the rainy day in view.

You cannot lay up for a rainy day if you are trusting Jesus Christ. Jesus said—"Let not your heart be troubled." God will not keep your heart from being troubled. It is a command—"*Let not. . .*" Haul yourself up a hundred and one times a day in order to do it, until you get into the habit of putting God first and calculating with Him in view.

Now unto him who is able . . . to present you faultless before the presence of his glory . . . (Jude 24)

There is no such thing as God overlooking sin. That is where people make a great mistake with regard to God's love; they say 'God is love and of course He will forgive sin': God is *holy* love and of course He *cannot* forgive sin. Therefore if God does forgive, there must be a reason that justifies Him in doing it. Unless there is a possibility of forgiveness establishing an order of holiness and rectitude in a man, it would be a mean and abominable thing to be forgiven. If I am forgiven without being altered by the forgiveness, forgiveness is a damage to me and a sign of unmitigated weakness on the part of God. A man has to clear God's character in forgiving him. The revelation of forgiveness in the Bible is not that God puts snow over a rubbish heap, but that He turns a man into the standard of Himself, the Forgiver. If I receive forgiveness and yet go on being bad, I prove that God is not justified in forgiving me. When God forgives a man He gives him the heredity of His own Son, and there is no man on earth but can be presented 'perfect in Christ Jesus'. Then on the ground of the Redemption, it is up to me to live as a son of God. The reason my sins are forgiven so easily is because the Redemption cost God so much.

HGM 102

VISION AND REALITY

And the parched ground shall become a pool. (Isa. 35:7)

We always have visions, before a thing is made real. When we
realize that although the vision is real, it is not real in us, then
is the time that Satan comes in with his temptations, and we
are apt to say it is no use to go on. Instead of the vision becoming real, there has come the valley of humiliation.

> Life is not as idle ore,
> But iron dug from central gloom,
> And batter'd by the shocks of doom
> To shape and use.

God gives us the vision, then He takes us down to the valley
to batter us into the shape of the vision, and it is in the valley
that so many of us faint and give way. Every vision will be made
real if we will have patience. Think of the enormous leisure of
God! He is never in a hurry. We are always in such a frantic
hurry. In the light of the glory of the vision we go forth to do
things, but the vision is not real in us yet; and God has to take
us into the valley, and put us through fires and floods to batter us into shape, until we get to the place where He can trust
us with the veritable reality. Ever since we had the vision God
has been at work, getting us into the shape of the ideal, and
over and over again we escape from His hand and try to batter
ourselves into our own shape.

The vision is not a castle in the air, but a vision of what God
wants you to be. Let Him put you on His wheel and whirl you
as He likes, and as sure as God is God and you are you, you
will turn out exactly in accordance with the vision. Don't lose
heart in the process. If you have ever had the vision of God,
you may try as you like to be satisfied on a lower level, but
God will never let you.

The kingdom of God is within you. (Luke 17:21)

The blessedness of the gospel of the kingdom of God in this dispensation is that a man is born from above while he is below, and he actually sees with the eyes of his spirit the rule of God in the devil's territory. You will see how far we have got away from Jesus Christ's teaching. We bring in all kinds of things, we talk about salvation and sanctification and forgiveness of sins; Jesus did not mention these things to Nicodemus (He mentioned them later to the disciples), He said, 'Be born from above and you will see the rule of God.' It is an attitude of essential simplicity all through. Preaching what we call the Gospel, i.e. salvation from hell does not appeal to men; but once get Jesus Christ to preach His own Gospel and the Spirit of God to expound it, then men are hauled up at once.

HG 51

ALL NOBLE THINGS ARE DIFFICULT

Enter ye in at the strait gate . . . because strait is the gate, and narrow is the way. . . . (Matt. 7:13-14)

If we are going to live as disciples of Jesus, we have to remember that all noble things are difficult. The Christian life is gloriously difficult, but the difficulty of it does not make us faint and cave in, it rouses us up to overcome. Do we so appreciate the marvelous salvation of Jesus Christ that we are our utmost for His highest?

God saves men by His sovereign grace through the Atonement of Jesus; He works in us to will and to do of His good pleasure; but we have to work out that salvation in practical living. If once we start on the basis of His Redemption to do what He commands, we find that we can do it. If we fail, it is because we have not practised. The crisis will reveal whether we have been practising or not. If we obey the Spirit of God and practise in our physical life what God has put in us by His Spirit, then when the crisis comes, we shall find that our own nature as well as the grace of God will stand by us.

Thank God He does give us difficult things to do! His salvation is a glad thing but it is also a heroic, holy thing. It tests us for all we are worth. Jesus is bringing many "sons" unto glory, and God will not shield us from the requirements of a son. God's grace turns out men and women with a strong family likeness to Jesus Christ, not milksops. It takes a tremendous amount of discipline to live the noble life of a disciple of Jesus in actual things. It is always necessary to make an effort to be noble.

For the word of God is quick and powerful and sharper than any two-edged sword, piercing even to the dividing asunder of soul and spirit, and of the joints and marrow, and is a discerner of the thoughts and intents of the heart. (Hebrews 4:12)

'Why should I believe a thing because it is in the Bible?' That is a perfectly legitimate question. There is no reason why you should believe it, it is only when the Spirit of God applies the Scriptures to the inward consciousness that a man begins to understand their living efficacy. If we try from the outside to fit the Bible to an external standard, or to a theory of verbal inspiration or any other theory, we are wrong. 'Ye search the scriptures, because ye think that in them ye have eternal life; and these are they which bear witness of me; and ye will not come to me, that ye may have life' (John 5:39–40).

There is another dangerous tendency, that of closing all questions by saying, 'Let us get back to the external authority of the Bible.' That attitude lacks courage and the power of the Spirit of God; it is a literalism that does not produce 'written epistles', but persons who are more or less incarnate dictionaries; it produces not saints but fossils, people without life, with none of the living reality of the Lord Jesus. There must be the Incarnate Word and the interpreting word, i.e. people whose lives back up what they preach, 'written epistles, known and real of all men'. Only when we receive the Holy Spirit and are lifted into a total readjustment to God do the words of God become 'quick and powerful' to us. The only way the words of God can be understood is by contact with the Word of God. The connection between our Lord Himself, who is the Word, and His spoken words is so close that to divorce them is fatal. 'The words that I speak unto you, they are spirit, and they are life.'

BE 122

THE WILL TO LOYALTY

Choose you this day whom ye will serve. (Josh. 24:15)

Will is the whole man active. I cannot *give up* my will, I must exercise it. I must *will* to obey, and I must *will* to receive God's Spirit. When God gives a vision of truth it is never a question of what He will do, but of what we will do. The Lord has been putting before us all some big propositions, and the best thing to do is to remember what you did when you were touched by God before—the time when you were saved, or first saw Jesus, or realized some truth. It was easy then to yield allegiance to God; recall those moments now as the Spirit of God brings before you some new proposition.

"Choose you this day whom ye will serve." It is a deliberate calculation, not something into which you drift easily; and everything else is in abeyance until you decide. The proposition is between you and God; do not confer with flesh and blood about it. With every new proposition other people get more and more "out of it;" that is where the strain comes. God allows the opinion of His saints to matter to you, and yet you are brought more and more out of the certainty that others understand the step you are taking. You have no business to find out where God is leading, the only thing God will explain to you is Himself.

Profess to Him—"I will be loyal." Immediately you choose to be loyal to Jesus Christ, you are a witness against yourself. Don't consult other Christians but profess before Him—I will serve Thee. *Will* to be loyal —and give other people credit for being loyal too.

And Jesus went into the temple, and began to cast out them that sold and them that bought in the temple, and overthrew the tables of the money-changers . . . (Mark 11:15 [cf. John 2:13–17])

We bring to the New Testament a sentimental conception of our Lord; we think of Him as the 'meek and mild and gentle Jesus' and make it mean that He was of no practical account whatever. Our Lord *was* 'meek and lowly in heart', yet watch Him in the Temple, meekness and gentleness were not the striking features there. We see instead a terrible Being with a whip of small cords in His hands, overturning the money-changers' tables and driving out men and cattle. Is He the 'meek and gentle Jesus' there? He is absolutely terrifying; no one dare interfere with Him. Why could He not have driven them out in a gentler way? Because passionate zeal had eaten Him up, with a detestation of everything that dared to call His Father's honour into disrepute. 'Make not my Father's house an house of merchandise'—the deification of commercial enterprise. Everything of the nature of wrong must go when Jesus Christ begins to cleanse His Father's house.

SHL 70

THE GREAT PROBING

Ye cannot serve the Lord. (Josh. 24:19)

Have you the slightest reliance on anything other than God? Is there a remnant of reliance left on any natural virtue, any set of circumstances? Are you relying on yourself in any particular in this new proposition which God has put before you? That is what the probing means. It is quite true to say—"I cannot live a holy life," but you can decide to let Jesus Christ make you holy. "Ye cannot serve the Lord God"; but you can put yourself in the place where God's almighty power will come through you. Are you sufficiently right with God to expect Him to manifest His wonderful life in you?

"Nay, but we will serve the Lord." It is not an impulse, but a deliberate commitment. You say—But God can never have called *me* to this, I am too unworthy, it can't mean *me*. It does mean you, and the weaker and feebler you are, the better. The one who has something to trust in is the last one to come anywhere near saying —"I will serve the Lord."

We say—"If I really could believe!" The point is—If I really *will* believe. No wonder Jesus Christ lays such emphasis on the sin of unbelief. "And He did not many mighty works there because of their unbelief." If we really believed that God meant what He said—what should we be like! Dare I really let God be to me all that He says He will be?

And they are they which testify of me. (John 5:39)
For had ye believed Moses, ye would have believed me, for he
wrote of me. (John 5:46)

To believe in Jesus means much more than the experience of salvation in any form, it entails a mental and moral commitment to our Lord Jesus Christ's view of God and man, of sin and the devil, and of the Scriptures.

How much intellectual impertinence there is today among many Christians relative to the Scriptures, because they forget that to 'believe also' in Jesus means that they are committed beforehand to His attitude to the Bible. He said that He was the context of the Scriptures. '. . . they are they which testify of me.' We hear much about 'key words' to the Scriptures, but there is only one 'key word' to the Scriptures for a believer, and that is our Lord Jesus Christ Himself. All the intellectual arrogance about the Bible is a clear proof of disbelief in Jesus. How many Sunday School teachers today believe as Jesus believed in the Old Testament? How many have succumbed to the insolence of intellectual partisanship about the Person of our Lord and His limitations, and say airily, 'Of course, there is no such thing as demon possession or hell, and no such being as the devil.' To 'believe also' in Jesus means that we submit our intelligence to Him as He submitted His intelligence to His Father. This does not mean that we do not exercise our reason, but it does mean that we exercise it in submission to Reason Incarnate. Beware of interpreters of the Scriptures who take any other context than our Lord Jesus Christ.

AUG 104

THE SPIRITUAL SLUGGARD

Let us consider one another to provoke unto love and to good works; not forsaking the assembling of ourselves together. (Heb. 10:24-25)

We are all capable of being spiritual sluggards; we do not want to mix with the rough and tumble of life as it is, our one object is to secure retirement. The note struck in Hebrews 10 is that of provoking one another and of keeping together—both of which require initiative, the initiative of Christrealization, not of self-realization. To live a remote, retired, secluded life is the antipodes of spirituality as Jesus Christ taught it.

The test of our spirituality comes when we come up against injustice and meanness and ingratitude and turmoil, all of which have the tendency to make us spiritual sluggards. We want to use prayer and Bible reading for the purpose of retirement. We utilize God for the sake of getting peace and joy, that is, we do not want to realize Jesus Christ, but only our enjoyment of Him. This is the first step in the wrong direction. All these things are effects and we try to make them causes.

"I think it meet," said Peter, ". . . to stir you up by putting you in remembrance." It is a most disturbing thing to be smitten in the ribs by some provoker of God, by someone who is full of spiritual activity. Active work and spiritual activity are not the same thing. Active work may be the counterfeit of spiritual activity. The danger of spiritual sluggishness is that we do not wish to be stirred up, all we want to hear about is spiritual retirement. Jesus Christ never encourages the idea of retirement—"Go tell My brethren . . ."

When Jesus came to the place, he looked up, and saw him, and said unto him, Zacchaeus, make haste, and come down; for to-day I must abide at thy house. (Luke 19:5)

The thing we have to learn by contact with Jesus Christ is this, that if the whole human race—everybody, good, bad and indifferent—is lost, we must have the boundless confidence of Jesus Christ Himself about us, that is, we must know that He can save anybody and everybody. There is a great deal of importance to be attached to this point. Just reflect in your mind and think of some lives you know that are frozen; there is no conviction of sin; they are dishonourable, and they know it; they are abnormal, off the main tract altogether, but they are not a bit troubled about it; talk to them about their wrong doing and they are totally indifferent to you. You have to learn how to introduce the atmosphere of the Lord Jesus Christ around those souls. As soon as you do, something happens. Look what happened to Zacchaeus—'And Zacchaeus stood, and said unto the Lord, Behold, Lord, the half of my goods I give to the poor; and if I have wrongfully exacted aught of any man, I restore him fourfold.' Who had been talking to him about his doings? Not a soul. Jesus had never said a word about his evil doings. What awakened him? What suddenly made him know where he was? The presence of Jesus!

WG 23

THE SPIRITUAL SAINT

That I may know Him. (Phil. 3:10)

The initiative of the saint is not towards self-realization, but towards knowing Jesus Christ. The spiritual saint never believes circumstances to be haphazard, or thinks of his life as secular and sacred; he sees everything he is dumped down in as the means of securing the knowledge of Jesus Christ. There is a reckless abandonment about him. The Holy Spirit is determined that we shall realize Jesus Christ in every domain of life, and He will bring us back to the same point again and again until we do. Self-realization leads to the enthronement of work. Whether it be eating or drinking or washing disciples' feet, whatever it is, we have to take the initiative of realizing Jesus Christ in it. Every phase of our actual life has its counterpart in the life of Jesus. Our Lord realized His relationship to the Father even in the most menial work. "Jesus knowing . . . that He was come from God, and went to God . . . took a towel . . . and began to wash the disciples' feet."

The aim of the spiritual saint is "that I may know Him." Do I know Him where I am to-day? If not, I am failing Him. I am here not to realize myself, but to know Jesus. In Christian work the initiative is too often the realization that something has to be done and I must do it. That is never the attitude of the spiritual saint; his aim is to secure the realization of Jesus Christ in every set of circumstances he is in.

But the Comforter, which is the Holy Ghost, whom the Father
will send in my name, he shall teach you all things, and bring
to your remembrance whatsoever I have said unto you.
(John 14:26)

Every mind has two compartments—conscious and subconscious. We say that the things we hear and read slip away from memory; they do not really, they pass into the subconscious mind. It is the work of the Holy Spirit to bring back into the conscious mind the things that are stored in the subconscious. In studying the Bible never think that because you do not understand it, therefore it is of no use. A truth may be of no use to you just now, but when the circumstances arise in which that truth is needed, the Holy Spirit will bring it back to your remembrance. This accounts for the curious emergence of the statements of Jesus; we say, 'I wonder where that word came from?' Jesus said that the Holy Spirit would 'bring all things to your remembrance, whatsoever I have said unto you'. The point is, will I obey Him when He does bring it to my remembrance? If I discuss the matter with someone else the probability is that I will not obey. 'Immediately I conferred not with flesh and blood. . .' Always trust the originality of the Holy Spirit when He brings a word to your remembrance.

                                                        SSM 13

THE SPIRITUAL SOCIETY

Till we all come . . . unto the measure of the stature of the fulness of Christ. (Eph. 4:13)

Rehabilitation means the putting back of the whole human race into the relationship God designed it to be in, and this is what Jesus Christ did in Redemption. The Church ceases to be a spiritual society when it is on the look-out for the development of its own organization. The rehabilitation of the human race on Jesus Christ's plan means the realization of Jesus Christ in corporate life as well as in individual life. Jesus Christ sent apostles and teachers for this purpose—that the corporate Personality might be realized. We are not here to develop a spiritual life of our own, or to enjoy spiritual retirement; we are here so to realize Jesus Christ that the Body of Christ may be built up.

Am I building up the Body of Christ, or am I looking for my own personal development only? The essential thing is my personal relationship to Jesus Christ—"That *I* may know *Him*." To fulfil God's design means entire abandonment to Him. Whenever I want things for myself, the relationship is distorted. It will be a big humiliation to realize that I have not been concerned about realizing Jesus Christ, but only about realizing what He has done for me.

My goal is God Himself, not joy nor peace,
Nor even blessing, but Himself, my God.

Am I measuring my life by this standard or by anything less?

But we have this treasure in earthen vessels, that the excellency of the power may be of God, and not of us. (2 Corinthians 4:7)

In the Incarnation we see the amalgam of the Divine and the human. Pure gold cannot be used as coin, it is too soft; in order to make gold serviceable for use it must be mixed with an alloy. The pure gold of the Divine is of no use in human affairs; there must be an alloy, and the alloy does not stand for sin, but for that which makes the Divine serviceable for use. God Almighty is nothing but a mental abstraction to me unless He can become actual, and the revelation of the New Testament is that God did become actual: 'the Word was made flesh'. Jesus Christ was not pure Divine, He was unique: Divine and human. . .

Holiness Movements are apt to ignore the human and bank all on the Divine; they tell us that human nature is sinful, forgetting that Jesus Christ took on Him our human nature, and 'in Him is no sin'. It was God who made human nature, not the devil; sin came into human nature and cut it off from the Divine, and Jesus Christ brings the pure Divine and the pure human together. Sin is a wrong thing altogether and is not to be allowed for a moment. Human nature is earthly, it is sordid, but it is not bad, the thing that makes it bad is sin.

No man is constituted to live a pure Divine life on earth; he is constituted to live a human life on earth presenced with Divinity. When the pure Divine comes into us we have the difficulty of making our human nature the obedient servant of the new disposition, it is difficult, and thank God it is! God gives us the fighting chance. A saint is not an ethereal creature too refined for life on this earth; a saint is a mixture of the Divine and the human that can stand anything.

BE 51–2

THE PRICE OF VISION

In the year that king Uzziah died, I saw also the Lord. (Isa. 6:1)

Our soul's history with God is frequently the history of the "passing of the hero." Over and over again God has to remove our friends in order to bring Himself in their place, and that is where we faint and fail and get discouraged. Take it personally: In the year that the one who stood to me for all that God was, died—I gave up everything? I became ill? I got disheartened? or—I saw the Lord?

My vision of God depends upon the state of my character. Character determines revelation. Before I can say 'I saw also the Lord," there must be something corresponding to God in my character. Until I am born again and begin to see the Kingdom of God, I see along the line of my prejudices only; I need the surgical operation of external events and an internal purification.

It must be God first, God second, and God third, until the life is faced steadily with God and no one else is of any account whatever. "In all the world there is none but thee, my God, there is none but thee."

Keep paying the price. Let God see that you are willing to live up to the vision.

A city that is set on an hill cannot be hid. (Matthew 5:14)

The illustrations our Lord uses are all conspicuous, viz., salt, light, and a city set on a hill. There is no possibility of mistaking them. Salt to preserve from corruption has to be placed in the midst of it, and before it can do its work it causes excessive irritation which spells persecution. Light attracts bats and night-moths, and points out the way for burglars as well as honest people: Jesus would have us remember that men will certainly defraud us. A city is a gathering place for all the human driftwood that will not work for its own living, and a Christian will have any number of parasites and ungrateful hangers-on. All these considerations form a powerful temptation to make us pretend we are not salt, to make us put our light under a bushel, and cover our city with a fog, but Jesus will have nothing in the nature of covert discipleship.

SSM 19–20

THE ACCOUNT WITH PERSECUTION

*But I say unto you, That ye resist not evil; but whosoever shall
smite thee on thy right cheek, turn to him the other also.
(Matt. 5:39, etc.)*

These verses reveal the humiliation of being a Christian. Naturally, if a man does not hit back, it is because he is a coward; but spiritually if a man does not hit back, it is a manifestation of the Son of God in him. When you are insulted, you must not only not resent it, but make it an occasion to exhibit the Son of God. You cannot imitate the disposition of Jesus; it is either there or it is not. To the saint personal insult becomes the occasion of revealing the incredible sweetness of the Lord Jesus.

The teaching of the Sermon on the Mount is not—Do your duty, but—Do what is not your duty. It is not your duty to go the second mile, to turn the other cheek, but Jesus says if we are His disciples we shall always do these things. There will be no spirit of—"Oh, well, I cannot do any more, I have been so misrepresented and misunderstood." Every time I insist upon my rights, I hurt the Son of God; whereas I can prevent Jesus from being hurt if I take the blow myself. That is the meaning of filling up that which is behind of the afflictions of Christ. The disciple realizes that it is his Lord's honour that is at stake in his life, not his own honour.

Never look for right in the other man, but never cease to be right yourself. We are always looking for justice; the teaching of the Sermon on the Mount is—Never look for justice, but never cease to give it.

Simon Peter answered him, Lord, to whom shall we go? Thou hast the words of eternal life. (John 6:68)

John 6 contains a description of the sifting out of the disciples from the crowd round about, until there were just the twelve left, and to them Jesus says—'Would ye also go away?' Some who had been following Jesus had not gone too far to turn back, and 'they went back, and walked no more with him'. But Peter has gone too far to turn back and he says, 'Lord, to whom shall we go?' There is a stage like that in our spiritual experience, we do not see the Guide ahead of us, we do not feel the joy of the Lord, there is no exhilaration, yet we have gone too far to go back, we are up against it now. It might be illustrated in the spiritual life by Tennyson's phrase, 'a white funeral'. When we go through the moral death to self-will we find we have committed ourselves, there are many things that must go the the 'white funeral'. At the first we have the idea that everything apart from Christ is bad; but there is much in our former life that is fascinating, any amount of paganism that is clear and vigorous, virtues that are good morally. But we have to discover they are not stamped with the right image and superscription, and if we are going to live the life of a saint we must go to the moral death of those things, make a termination of them, turn these good natural things into the spiritual.

PH 159

THE POINT OF SPIRITUAL HONOUR

I am debtor both to the Greeks, and to the barbarians.
(Rom. 1:14)

Paul was overwhelmed with the sense of his indebtedness to Jesus Christ, and he spent himself to express it. The great inspiration in Paul's life was his view of Jesus Christ as his spiritual creditor. Do I feel that sense of indebtedness to Christ in regard to every unsaved soul? The spiritual honour of my life as a saint is to fulfil my debt to Christ in relation to them. Every bit of my life that is of value I owe to the Redemption of Jesus Christ; am I doing anything to enable Him to bring His Redemption into actual manifestation in other lives? I can only do it as the Spirit of God works in me this sense of indebtedness.

I am not to be a superior person amongst men, but a bond-slave of the Lord Jesus. "Ye are not your own." Paul sold himself to Jesus Christ. He says—I am a debtor to everyone on the face of the earth because of the Gospel of Jesus; I am free to be an absolute slave only. That is the characteristic of the life when once this point of spiritual honour is realized. Quit praying about yourself and be spent for others as the bondslave of Jesus. That is the meaning of being made broken bread and poured out wine in reality.

And ye shall hear of wars and rumours of wars, see that ye be not troubled. (Matthew 24:6)

That is either the statement of a madman or of a Being who has power to put something into a man and keep him free from panic, even in the midst of the awful terror of war. The basis of panic is always cowardice. Our Lord teaches us to look things full in the face. He says—'When you hear of wars, don't be scared.' It is the most natural thing in the world to be scared, and the clearest evidence that God's grace is at work in our hearts is when we do not get into panics. Our Lord insists on the inevitableness of peril. He says, 'You must lay your account with war, with hatred, and with death.' Men may have lived undisturbed over a volcano for a long while, when suddenly an eruption occurs. Jesus Christ did not say—'You will understand why war has come,' but—'Don't be scared when it does come, do not be in a panic.' It is astonishing how we ignore Jesus Christ's words. He said that nations would end in war and bloodshed and havoc. We ignore His warnings; and when war comes we lose our wits and exhibit panic.

SA 54

THE NOTION OF DIVINE CONTROL

How much more shall your Father which is in heaven give good things to them that ask Him? (Matt. 7:11)

Jesus is laying down rules of conduct for those who have His Spirit. By the simple argument of these verses He urges us to keep our minds filled with the notion of God's control behind everything, which means that the disciple must maintain an attitude of perfect trust and an eagerness to ask and to seek.

Notion your mind with the idea that God is there. If once the mind is notioned along that line, then when you are in difficulties it is as easy as breathing to remember—Why, my Father knows all about it! It is not an effort, it comes naturally when perplexities press. Before, you used to go to this person and that, but now the notion of the Divine control is forming so powerfully in you that you go to God about it. Jesus is laying down the rules of conduct for those who have His Spirit, and it works on this principle—God is my Father, He loves me, I shall never think of anything He will forget, why should I worry?

There are times, says Jesus, when God cannot lift the darkness from you, but trust Him. God will appear like an unkind friend, but He is not; He will appear like an unnatural Father, but He is not; He will appear like an unjust judge, but He is not. Keep the notion of the mind of God behind all things strong and growing. Nothing happens in any particular unless God's will is behind it, therefore you can rest in perfect confidence in Him. Prayer is not only asking, but an attitude of mind which produces the atmosphere in which asking is perfectly natural. "Ask, and it shall be given you."

For we know that the law is spiritual: but I am carnal, sold under sin. For that which I do I allow not: for what I would, that I do not: but what I hate, that do I. (Romans 7:14–15)

A lot of tawdry stuff has been written on this chapter simply because Christians so misunderstand what conviction of sin really is. Conviction of sin such as the apostle Paul is describing does not come when a man is born again, nor even when he is sanctified, but long after, and then only to a few. It came to Paul as an apostle and saint, and he could diagnose sin as no other. Knowledge of what sin is is in inverse ratio to its presence; only as sin goes do you realize what it is; when it is present you do not realize what it is because the nature of sin is that it destroys the capacity to know you sin.

BE 75

When once a man really sees himself as the Lord Jesus Christ sees him, it is not the abominable social sins of the flesh that shock him, it is the awful nature of the pride of his own heart against the Lord Jesus Christ—the shame, the horror, the desperate conviction that comes when we realize ourselves in the light of Jesus Christ as the Spirit of God reveals Him to us. That is the true gift of repentance and the real meaning of it.

DP 131

THE MIRACLE OF BELIEF

My speech and my preaching was not with enticing words.
(1 Cor. 2:1-5)

Paul was a scholar and an orator of the first rank; he is not speaking out of abject humility, but saying that he would veil the power of God if, when he preached the gospel, he impressed people with his "excellency of speech." Belief in Jesus is a miracle produced only by the efficacy of Redemption, not by impressiveness of speech, not by wooing and winning, but by the sheer unaided power of God. The creative power of the Redemption comes through the preaching of the Gospel, but never because of the personality of the preacher. The real fasting of the preacher is not from food, but rather from eloquence, from impressiveness and exquisite diction, from everything that might hinder the gospel of God being presented. The preacher is there as the representative of God—"as though God did beseech you by us." He is there to present the Gospel of God. If it is only because of my preaching that people desire to be better, they will never get anywhere near Jesus Christ. Anything that flatters me in my preaching of the Gospel will end in making me a traitor to Jesus; I prevent the creative power of His Redemption from doing its work.

"*I, if I be lifted up. . ., will draw all men unto Me.*"

He that believeth on me, out of his belly shall flow rivers of living water. (John 7:38)

We must distinguish between the revelation of Redemption and the experience of regeneration. We don't *experience* life; we are alive. We don't *experience* Redemption; we experience regeneration, that is, we experience the life of God coming into our human nature, and immediately the life of God comes in it produces a surface of consciousness, but Redemption means a great deal more than a man is conscious of. The Redemption is not only for mankind, it is for the universe, for the material earth; everything that sin and the devil have touched and marred has been completely redeemed by Jesus Christ. There is a day coming when the Redemption will be actually manifested, when there will be 'a new heaven and a new earth', with a new humanity upon it. . . . What the Redemption deals with is the sin of the whole human race, not primarily with the sins of individuals, but something far more fundamental, viz., the heredity of sin. Pseudo-evangelism singles out the individual, it prostitutes the terrific meaning of the Redemption into an individual possession, the salvation of *my* soul.

CHI 9–10

THE MYSTERY OF BELIEVING

And he said, Who art Thou, Lord? (Acts 9:6)

By the miracle of Redemption Saul of Tarsus was turned in one second from a strong-willed, intense Pharisee into a humble, devoted slave of the Lord Jesus.

There is nothing miraculous about the things we can explain. We command what we are able to explain, consequently it is natural to seek to explain. It is not natural to obey; nor is it necessarily sinful to disobey. There is no moral virtue in obedience unless there is a recognition of a higher authority in the one who dictates. It is possibly an emancipation to the other person if he does not obey. If one man says to another—"You must," and—"You shall," he breaks the human spirit and unfits it for God. A man is a slave for obeying unless behind his obedience there is a recognition of a holy God. Many a soul begins to come to God when he flings off being religious, because there is only one Master of the human heart, and that is not religion but Jesus Christ. But woe be to me if when I see *Him* I say—I *will* not. He will never insist that I do, but I have begun to sign the death warrant of the Son of God in my soul. When I stand face to face with Jesus Christ and say—I will not, He will never insist; but I am backing away from the recreating power of His Redemption. It is a matter of indifference to God's grace how abominable I am if I come to the light; but woe be to me if I refuse the light (see John 3:19-21).

Faith cometh by hearing, and hearing by the word of God.
(Romans 10:17)

Our idea of faith has a good deal to do with the harmful way faith is often spoken of. Faith is looked upon as an attitude of mind whereby we assent to a testimony on the authority of the one who testifies. We say that because Jesus says these things, we believe in Him. The faith of the New Testament is infinitely more than that; it is the means by which sanctification is manifested, the means of introducing the life of God into us, not the effect of our understanding only. In Romans 3:24–5, Paul speaks about faith in the blood of Jesus, and faith is the instrument the Spirit of God uses. Faith is more than an attitude of the mind; faith is the complete, passionate, earnest trust of our whole nature in the Gospel of God's grace as it is presented in the Life and Death and Resurrection of our Lord Jesus Christ.

OBH 20

MASTERY OVER THE BELIEVER

Ye call Me Master and Lord: and ye say well; for so I am.
(John 13:13)

Our Lord never insists on having authority; He never says—
Thou shalt. He leaves us perfectly free—so free that we can spit
in His face, as men did; so free that we can put Him to death,
as men did; and He will never say a word. But when His life
has been created in me by His Redemption, I instantly recognize His right to absolute authority over me. It is a moral domination—"Thou art *worthy* . . ." It is only the unworthy in me
that refuses to bow down to the worthy. If when I meet a man
who is more holy than myself, I do not recognize his worthi-
ness and obey what comes through him, it is a revelation of
the unworthy in me. God educates us by means of people who
are a little better than we are, not intellectually but "holily,"
until we get under the domination of the Lord Himself, and
then the whole attitude of the life is one of obedience to Him.

If our Lord insisted upon obedience He would become a task-
master, and He would cease to have any authority. He never
insists on obedience, but when we do see Him we obey Him
instantly, He is easily Lord, and we live in adoration of Him
from morning till night. The revelation of my growth in grace
is the way in which I look upon obedience. We have to rescue
the word "obedience" from the mire. Obedience is only possible between equals; it is the relationship between father and
son, not between master and servant. "I and My Father are
one." "Though He were a Son, yet learned He obedience by
the things which He suffered." The Son's obedience was as
Redeemer, *because He was Son*, not in order to be Son.

414

And Peter answered and said to Jesus, Master, it is good for us to be here; and let us make three tabernacles; one for thee, and one for Moses, and one for Elias. (Mark 9:5)

The test of spiritual life is the power to descend; if we have power to rise only, there is something wrong. We all have had times on the mount when we have seen things from God's standpoint and we wanted to stay there; but if we are disciples of Jesus Christ, He will never allow us to stay there. Spiritual selfishness makes us want to stay on the mount; we feel so good, as if we could do anything—talk like angels and live like angels, if only we could stay there. But there must be the power to descend; the mountain is not the place for us to live, we were built for the valleys. This is one of the hardest things to learn because spiritual selfishness always wants repeated moments on the mount.

MU 51

Being seated together in heavenly places in Christ Jesus does not mean lolling about on the mount of transfiguration, singing ecstatic hymns, and letting demon-possessed boys go to the devil in the valley; it means being in the accursed places of this earth as far as the walk of the feet is concerned, but in undisturbed communion with God.

IWP 70

DEPENDENT ON GOD'S PRESENCE

They that wait upon the Lord . . . shall walk and not faint.
(Isa. 40:31)

There is no thrill in walking; it is the test of all the stable qualities. To "walk and not faint" is the highest reach possible for strength. The word "walk" is used in the Bible to express the character—"John looking on Jesus *as He walked*, said, Behold the Lamb of God!" There is never anything abstract in the Bible, it is always vivid and real. God does not say—Be spiritual, but— *"Walk before Me."*

When we are in an unhealthy state physically or emotionally, we always want thrills. In the physical domain this will lead to counterfeiting the Holy Ghost; in the emotional life it leads to inordinate affection and the destruction of morality; and in the spiritual domain if we insist on getting thrills, on mounting up with wings, it will end in the destruction of spirituality.

The reality of God's presence is not dependent on any place, but only dependent upon the determination to set the Lord always before us. Our problems come when we refuse to bank on the reality of His presence. The experience the Psalmist speaks of—"Therefore will we not fear, though . . ." will be ours when once we are based on Reality, not the consciousness of God's presence but the reality of it—Why, He has been here all the time!

At critical moments it is necessary to ask guidance, but it ought to be unnecessary to be saying always—"O Lord, direct me here, and there." Of course He will! If our common-sense decisions are not His order, He will press through them and check; then we must be quiet and wait for the direction of His presence.

As it is written, For thy sake we are killed all the day long; we are accounted as sheep for the slaughter. (Romans 8:36)

Life is a far greater danger than death. I want to say something, crudely, but very definitely: the Bible nowhere says that men are damned; the Bible says that men are damnable. There is always the possibility of damnation in any life, always the possibility of disobedience; but, thank God, there is also always the possibility of being made 'more than conqueror'. The possibilities of life are awful. Think—are you absolutely certain that you are not going to topple headlong over a moral precipice before you are three years older? Look back on your life and ask yourself how it was you escaped when you were set on the wrong course—the tiniest turn and you would have been a moral ruin? Disease cut off with a tremendous fell swoop your companions—why did it not cut you off? The men with you in your youth who were so brilliant—where are they now? Out in the gutter some of them, all but damned while they live. Why are you not there? Why am I not there? Oh, it does us good, although it frightens us, to look at the possibilities of life. May God help us to face the issues.

SHL 26

THE GATEWAY TO THE KINGDOM

Blessed are the poor in spirit. (Matt. 5:3)

Beware of placing Our Lord as a Teacher first. If Jesus is a Teacher only, then all He can do is to tantalize me by erecting a standard I cannot attain. What is the use of presenting me with an ideal I cannot possibly come near? I am happier without knowing it. What is the good of telling me to be what I never can be—to be pure in heart, to do more than my duty, to be perfectly devoted to God? I must know Jesus Christ as Saviour before His teaching has any meaning for me other than that of an ideal which leads to despair. But when I am born again of the Spirit of God, I know that Jesus Christ did not come to *teach* only: He came to *make me what He teaches I should be.* The Redemption means that Jesus Christ can put into any man the disposition that ruled His own life, and all the standards God gives are based on that disposition.

The teaching of the Sermon on the Mount produces despair in the natural man—the very thing Jesus means it to do. As long as we have a self-righteous, conceited notion that we can carry out Our Lord's teaching, God will allow us to go on until we break our ignorance over some obstacle, then we are willing to come to Him as paupers and receive from Him. "Blessed are the paupers in spirit," that is the first principle in the Kingdom of God. The bedrock in Jesus Christ's kingdom is poverty, not possession; not decisions for Jesus Christ, but a sense of absolute futility—I cannot begin to do it. Then Jesus says— Blessed are you. That is the entrance, and it does take us a long while to believe we are poor! The knowledge of our own poverty brings us to the moral frontier where Jesus Christ works.

Except your righteousness shall exceed the righteousness of the scribes and Pharisees, ye shall in no case enter into the kingdom of heaven. (Matthew 5:20)

The Sermon on the Mount is quite unlike the Ten Commandments in the sense of its being absolutely unworkable unless Jesus Christ can remake us.

There are teachers who argue that the Sermon on the Mount supersedes the Ten Commandments, and that, because 'we are not under law, but under grace', it does not matter whether we honour our father and mother, whether we covet, etc. Beware of statements like this: There is no need nowadays to observe giving the tenth either of money or of time; we are in a new dispensation and everything belongs to God. That, in practical application, is sentimental dust-throwing. The giving of the tenth is not a sign that all belongs to God, but a sign that the tenth belongs to God and the rest is ours, and we are held responsible for what we do with it. To be 'not under the law, but under grace' does not mean that we can do as we like.

SSM 21

SANCTIFICATION

This is the will of God, even your sanctification. (1 Thess. 4:3)

The Death Side. In sanctification God has to deal with us on the death side as well as on the life side. Many of us spend so much time in the place of death that we get sepulchral. There is always a battle royal before sanctification, always something that tugs with resentment against the demands of Jesus Christ. Immediately the Spirit of God begins to show us what sanctification means, the struggle begins. "If any man come to Me and hate not . . . his own life, he cannot be My disciple."

The Spirit of God in the process of sanctification will strip me until I am nothing but "myself," that is the place of death. Am I willing to be "myself," and nothing more—no friends, no father, no brother, no self-interest—simply ready for death? That is the condition of sanctification. No wonder Jesus said: "I came not to send peace, but a sword." This is where the battle comes, and where so many of us faint. We refuse to be identified with the death of Jesus on this point. "But it is so stern," we say; "He cannot wish me to do that." Our Lord is stern; and He does wish us to do that.

Am I willing to reduce myself simply to "me," determinedly to strip myself of all my friends think of me, of all I think of myself, and to hand that simple naked self over to God? Immediately I am, He will sanctify me wholly, and my life will be free from earnestness in connection with everything but God.

When I pray—"Lord, show me what sanctification means for me," He will show me. It means being made one with Jesus. Sanctification is not something Jesus Christ puts into me: it is Himself in me (1 Cor. 1:30).

And this is the condemnation, that light is come into the world,
and men loved darkness rather than light. (John 3:19)

I am not judged by the light I have, but by the light I have refused to accept. There is no man but can have the knowledge,
perfectly clearly obtainable, of the standard of Jesus Christ.
Whether I am a Christian or not, or whether I am conscientious or not, is not the question; it is whether I have refused
the light of the finest moral character who ever lived, Jesus
Christ. *This* is the condemnation, that the Light, Jesus Christ,
has come into the world, and I prefer darkness, i.e. my own
point of view. The characteristic of a man who begins to walk
in the light is that he drags himself into the light all the time.
He does not make excuses for things done in the dark, he brings
everything to the light, and says, 'This is to be condemned; this
does not belong to Jesus Christ', and so keeps in the light. . .

'But if we walk in the light, as he is in the light. . . ' (1 John
1:7); that is, don't have anything folded up, don't juggle things,
don't pretend you have not done anything shady. John says,
if you have committed sin, confess it; walk in the light, and
you will have fellowship with everyone else who is there.
Natural affinity does not count here at all. Watch how God has
altered your affinities since you were filled with the Spirit; you
have fellowship with people you have no natural affinity for
at all; you have fellowship with everybody who is in the light.
Light is the description of clear, beautiful, moral character from
God's standpoint, and if we walk in the light, 'the blood of Jesus
Christ cleanses us from all sin'; God Almighty can find nothing to censure.

SA 49, 52

SANCTIFICATION

Of Him are ye in Christ Jesus, who of God is made unto us . . .
sanctification. (1 Cor. 1:30)

The Life Side. The mystery of sanctification is that the perfections of Jesus Christ are imparted to me, not gradually, but instantly when by faith I enter into the realization that Jesus Christ is made unto me sanctification. Sanctification does not mean anything less than the holiness of Jesus being made mine manifestly.

The one marvelous secret of a holy life lies not in imitating Jesus, but in letting the perfections of Jesus manifest themselves in my mortal flesh. Sanctification is "Christ in you." It is *His* wonderful life that is imparted by faith as a sovereign gift of God's grace. Am I willing for God to make sanctification as real in me as it is in His word?

Sanctification means the impartation of the holy qualities of Jesus Christ. It is His patience, His love, His holiness, His faith, His purity, His godliness, that is manifested in and through every sanctified soul. Sanctification is not drawing from Jesus the power to be holy; it is drawing from Jesus the holiness that was manifested in Him, and He manifests it in me. Sanctification is an impartation, not an imitation. Imitation is on a different line. In Jesus Christ is the perfection of everything, and the mystery of sanctification is that all the perfections of Jesus are at my disposal, and slowly and surely I begin to live a life of ineffable order and sanity and holiness: "Kept by the power of God."

Lovest thou me . . . Feed my sheep. (John 21:16)

'If you love Me', says Jesus, 'Feed my sheep.' 'Don't make converts to your way of thinking, but look after My sheep, see that
they are nourished in the knowledge of Me.' Our Lord's first
obedience was to the will of His Father, and He said, 'As the
Father hath sent me, even so send I you.' It sounds the right
thing to say that Jesus Christ came here to help mankind: but
His great desire was to do the will of His Father, and our Lord
was misunderstood because He would not put the needs of men
first. He said the first commandment is 'Thou shalt love the
lord thy God with all thy heart, and with all thy soul, and with
all thy mind, and with all thy strength.'

Jesus Christ is a source of deep offence to the educated
trained mind of today that does not want Him in any other
way than as a Comrade. Many do not want to be devoted to
Him, but only to the cause He started. If I am only devoted to
the cause of humanity, I will soon be exhausted and come to
the point where my love will falter, but if I love Jesus Christ I
will serve humanity, though men and women treat me like a
door-mat.

PH 145

DISPOSITION AND DEEDS

Except your righteousness shall exceed the righteousness of the scribes and Pharisees ye shall in no case enter into the kingdom of heaven. (Matt. 5:20)

The characteristic of a disciple is not that he does good things, but that he is good in motive because he has been made good by the supernatural grace of God. The only thing that exceeds right-*doing* is right-*being*. Jesus Christ came to put into any man who would let Him a new heredity which would exceed the righteousness of the scribes and Pharisees. Jesus says—If you are My disciple you must be right not only in your living but in your motives, in your dreams, in the recesses of your mind. You must be so pure in your motives that God Almighty can see nothing to censure. Who can stand in the Eternal Light of God and have nothing for God to censure? Only the Son of God, and Jesus Christ claims that by His Redemption He can put into any man His own disposition, and make him as un-sullied and as simple as a child. The purity which God demands is impossible unless I can be remade within, and that is what Jesus has undertaken to do by His Redemption.

No man can make himself pure by obeying laws. Jesus Christ does not give us rules and regulations; His teachings are truths that can only be interpreted by the disposition He puts in. The great marvel of Jesus Christ's salvation is that He alters heredity. He does not alter human nature; He alters its mainspring.

Peter . . . walked upon the waters to come to Jesus.
(Matthew 14:29)

Passionate, genuine affection for Jesus will lead to all sorts of vows and promises which it is impossible to fulfil. It is an attitude of mind and heart that sees only the heroic. We are called to be unobtrusive disciples, not heroes. When we are right with God, the tiniest thing done out of love to Him is more precious to Him than any eloquent preaching of a sermon. . . . We all have a lurking desire to be exhibitions for God, to be put, as it were, in His show room. Jesus does not want us to be specimens. He wants us to be so taken up with Him that we never think about ourselves, and the only impression left on others by our life is that Jesus Christ is having unhindered way.

Walking on water is easy to impulsive pluck, but walking on dry land as a disciple of Jesus Christ is different. Peter walked on the water to go to Jesus, but he followed Him afar off on the land. We do not need the grace of God to stand crises; human nature and our pride will do it. We can buck up and face the music of a crisis magnificently, but it does require the supernatural grace of God to live twenty-four hours of the day as a saint, to go through drudgery as a saint, to go through poverty as a saint, to go through an ordinary, unobtrusive, ignored existence as a saint, unnoted and unnoticeable. The 'show business', which is so incorporated into our view of Christian work today, has caused us to drift far from our Lord's conception of discipleship. It is instilled in us to think that we have to do exceptional things for God; we have not. We have to be exceptional in ordinary things, to be holy in mean streets, among mean people, surrounded by sordid sinners. That is not learned in five minutes.

SSY 68

AM I BLESSED LIKE THIS?

Blessed are . . . (Matt. 5:3-10)

When we first read the statements of Jesus they seem wonderfully simple and unstartling, and they sink unobserved into our unconscious minds. For instance, the Beatitudes seem merely mild and beautiful precepts for all unworldly and useless people, but of very little practical use in the stern workaday world in which we live. We soon find, however, that the Beatitudes contain the dynamite of the Holy Ghost. They explode, as it were, when the circumstances of our lives cause them to do so. When the Holy Spirit brings to our remembrance one of these Beatitudes we say—"What a startling statement that is!" and we have to decide whether we will accept the tremendous spiritual upheaval that will be produced in our circumstances if we obey His words. That is the way the Spirit of God works. We do not need to be born again to apply the Sermon on the Mount literally. The literal interpretation of the Sermon on the Mount is child's play; the interpretation by the Spirit of God as He applies Our Lord's statements to our circumstances is the stern work of a saint.

The teaching of Jesus is out of all proportion to our natural way of looking at things and it comes with astonishing discomfort to begin with. We have slowly to form our walk and conversation on the line of the precepts of Jesus Christ as the Holy Spirit applies them to our circumstances. The Sermon on the Mount is not a set of rules and regulations; it is a statement of the life we will live when the Holy Spirit is getting His way with us.

The blood of Jesus Christ his Son cleanseth us from all sin.
(1 John 1:7)

When we speak of the blood of Jesus Christ cleansing us from all sin, we do not mean the physical blood shed on Calvary, but the whole life of the Son of God which was poured out to redeem the world. All the perfections of the essential nature of God were in that blood, and all the holiest attainments of mankind as well. It was the life of the perfection of Deity that was poured out on Calvary, '. . . the church of God, which he purchased with his own blood' (Acts 20:28). We are apt to look upon the blood of Jesus Christ as a magic-working power instead of its being the very life of the Son of God poured forth for men. The whole meaning of our being identified with the death of Jesus is that His blood may flow through our mortal bodies. Identification with the death of Jesus Christ means identification with Him to the death of everything that never was in Him, and it is the blood of Christ, in the sense of the whole personal life of the Son of God, that comes into us and 'cleanseth us from all sin'.

PH 162

THE ACCOUNT WITH PURITY

Out of the heart proceed . . . (Matt. 15:18-20)

We begin by trusting our ignorance and calling it innocence, by trusting our innocence and calling it purity; and when we hear these rugged statements of Our Lord's, we shrink and say—But I never felt any of those awful things in my heart. We resent what Jesus Christ reveals. Either Jesus Christ is the supreme Authority on the human heart, or He is not worth paying any attention to. Am I prepared to trust His penetration, or do I prefer to trust my innocent ignorance? If I make conscious innocence the test, I am likely to come to a place where I find with a shuddering awakening that what Jesus Christ said is true, and I shall be appalled at the possibility of evil and wrong in me. As long as I remain under the refuge of innocence I am living in a fool's paradise. If I have never been a blackguard, the reason is a mixture of cowardice and the protection of civilized life; but when I am undressed before God, I find that Jesus Christ is right in His diagnosis.

The only thing that safeguards is the Redemption of Jesus Christ. If I will hand myself over to Him, I need never experience the terrible possibilities that are in my heart. Purity is too deep down for me to get to naturally: but when the Holy Spirit comes in, He brings into the centre of my personal life the very Spirit that was manifested in the life of Jesus Christ, viz:, *Holy* Spirit, which is unsullied purity.

Whosoever shall keep the whole law, and yet offend in one point,
he is guilty of all. (James 2:10)

Every man has an imperative something with him which makes him say 'I ought,' even in the most degraded specimens of humanity the 'ought' is there, and the Bible tells us where it comes from—it comes from God. The modern tendency is to leave God out and make our standard what is most useful to man. The utilitarian says that these distinct laws of conduct have been evolved by man for the benefit of man—the greatest use to the greatest number. That is not the reason a thing is right; the reason a thing is right is that God is behind it. God's 'ought's' never alter; we never grow out of them. Our difficulty is that we find in ourselves this attitude—'I ought to do this, but I won't;' 'I ought to do that, but I don't want to.' That puts out of court the idea that if you teach men what is right they will do it—they won't; what is needed is a power which will enable a man to do what he knows is right. We may say 'Oh I won't count this time', but every bit of moral wrong is counted by God. The moral law exerts no coercion, neither does it allow any compromise. 'For whosoever shall keep the whole law, and yet offend in one point, he is guilt of all.' Once we realize this we see why it was necessary for Jesus Christ to come. The Redemption is the Reality which alters inability into ability.

BE 8

THE WAY TO KNOW

If any man will do His will, he shall know of the doctrine . . .
(John 7:17)

The golden rule for understanding spiritually is not intellect, but obedience. If a man wants scientific knowledge, intellectual curiosity is his guide; but if he wants insight into what Jesus Christ teaches, he can only get it by obedience. If things are dark to me, then I may be sure there is something I will not do. Intellectual darkness comes through ignorance; spiritual darkness comes because of something I do not intend to obey.

No man ever receives a word from God without instantly being put to the test over it. We disobey and then wonder why we don't go on spiritually. "If when you come to the altar," said Jesus, "there you remember your brother hath ought against you . . . don't say another word to Me, but first go and put that thing right." The teaching of Jesus hits us where we live. We cannot stand as humbugs before Him for one second. He educates us down to the scruple. The Spirit of God unearths the spirit of self-vindication; He makes us sensitive to things we never thought of before.

When Jesus brings a thing home by His word, don't shirk it. If you do, you will become a religious humbug. Watch the things you shrug your shoulders over, and you will know why you do not go on spiritually. *First go*—at the risk of being thought fanatical you must obey what God tells you.

When it was yet dark . . . (John 20:1)

There is twilight before night, and an infinitely deeper dark before dawn; but there are hours in spiritual experience darker than either of these, when the new day looks like disaster, and light and illumination have not yet come. There is no possible progress in personal life or national life without cataclysms, big crises, breaks. In our ordinary life we have the idea that things should gradually progress, but there comes a time when there is a tumble-up, a mixture of God and man and friends, of crime and abomination, and all our idea of steady progress is done for, although there may be progress in individual lives. In the Bible there is the same idea. For instance, take what our Lord says about new birth—'Verily, verily, I say unto thee, Except a man be born again, he cannot see the kingdom of God' (John 3:3). Some teachers make a new birth a simple and natural thing, they say it is necessary, but a necessity along the line of natural development. When Jesus Christ talks about it He implies that the need to be born again is an indication of something radically wrong—'Marvel not that I said unto thee, Ye must be born again.' It is a crisis. We like to talk about the light of God coming like the dawn, but it never does to begin with, it comes in a lightning flash, in terrific upheaval. Things do not go unless they are started, and the start of everything in history and in men's souls proves that the basis of things is not rational but tragic; consequently there must be a crisis.

HGM 54

AFTER OBEDIENCE—WHAT?

And straightway He constrained His disciples to get into the ship,
and to go to the other side . . . (Mark 6:45-52)

We are apt to imagine that if Jesus Christ constrains us, and we obey Him, He will lead us to great success. We must never put our dreams of success as God's purpose for us; His purpose may be exactly the opposite. We have an idea that God is leading us to a particular end, a desired goal; He is not. The question of getting to a particular end is a mere incident. What we call the process, God calls the end.

What is my dream of God's purpose? His purpose is that I depend on Him and on His power now. If I can stay in the middle of the turmoil calm and unperplexed, that is the end of the purpose of God. God is not working towards a particular finish; His end is the process—that I see Him walking on the waves, no shore in sight, no success, no goal, just the absolute certainty that it is all right because I see Him walking on the sea. It is the process, not the end, which is glorifying to God.

God's training is for now, not presently. His purpose is for this minute, not for something in the future. We have nothing to do with the afterwards of obedience; we get wrong when we think of the afterwards. What men call training and preparation, God calls the end.

God's end is to enable me to see that He can walk on the chaos of my life just now. If we have a further end in view, we do not pay sufficient attention to the immediate present: if we realize that obedience is the end, then each moment as it comes is precious.

Ye must be born again. (John 3:7)

The natural man does not want to be born again. If a man's morality is well within his own grasp and he has enough religion to give the right tone to his natural life, to talk about being born again seems utterly needless. The natural man is not in distress, he is not conscious of conviction of sin, or of any disharmony, he is quite contented and at peace. Conviction of sin is the realization that my natural life is based on a disposition that will not have Jesus Christ. The Gospel does not present what the natural man wants but what he needs, and the Gospel awakens an intense resentment as well as an intense craving. We will take God's blessings and loving-kindnesses and prosperities, but when it comes to the need of having our disposition altered, there is opposition at once.

No man can have his state of mind altered without suffering for it in his body, and that is why men do anything to avoid conviction of sin. When a worldly man who is happy, moral and upright, comes in contact with Jesus Christ, his 'beauty', i.e. the perfectly ordered completeness of his nature, is destroyed and that man must be persuaded that Jesus Christ has a better kind of life for him otherwise he feels he had better not have come across Him. . . . Thank God, we are coming to the end of the shallow presentation of Christianity that makes out that Jesus Christ came only to give us peace. Thousands of people are happy without God in this world, but that kind of happiness and peace is on a wrong level. Jesus Christ came to send a sword through every peace that is not based on a personal relationship to Himself. He came to put us right with God that His own peace might reign.

SHL 40–1

WHAT DO YOU SEE IN YOUR CLOUDS?

Behold, He cometh with clouds. (Rev. 1:7)

In the Bible clouds are always connected with God. Clouds are those sorrows or sufferings or providences, within or without our personal lives, which seem to dispute the rule of God. It is by those very clouds that the Spirit of God is teaching us how to walk by faith. If there were no clouds, we should have no faith. "The clouds are but the dust of our Father's feet." The clouds are a sign that He is there. What a revelation it is to know that sorrow and bereavement and suffering are the clouds that come along with God! God cannot come near without clouds, He does not come in clear shining.

It is not true to say that God wants to teach us something in our trials: through every cloud He brings, He wants us to *unlearn* something. His purpose in the cloud is to simplify our belief until our relationship to Him is exactly that of a child—God and my own soul, other people are shadows. Until other people become shadows, clouds and darkness will be mine every now and again. Is the relationship between myself and God getting simpler than ever it has been?

There is a connection between the strange providences of God and what we know of Him, and we have to learn to interpret the mysteries of life in the light of our knowledge of God. Unless we can look the darkest, blackest fact full in the face without damaging God's character, we do not yet know Him.

"They feared as they entered the cloud . . ." Is there anyone "save Jesus only" in your cloud? If so, it will get darker; you must get to the place where there is "no one any more save Jesus only."

The sun also ariseth, and the sun goeth down, and hasteneth to his place where he arose. The wind goeth toward the south, and turneth about unto the north; it whirleth about continually, and the wind returneth again according to his circuits.
(Ecclesiastes 1:5–6)

Everything that happens in Nature is continually being obliterated and beginning again. What Solomon says is not merely a poetical statement. A sunset or a sunrise may thrill you for half a minute, so may beautiful music or a song, but the sudden aftermath is a terrific, and almost eternal sadness. Lovers always think of what one would do if the other died; it is more than drivel. Immediately you strike the elemental in war or in Nature or in love, you come to the basis of ineffable sadness and tragedy. You feel that things ought to be full of joy and brightness, but they are not. You will never find the abiding order of joy in the haphazard, and yet the meaning of Christianity is that God's order comes to a man in the haphazard.

There is a difference between God's will and God's order. Take the case of two boys born in the slums, one determines to get out of it, and carves out for himself an honourable career, he gets at God's order in the middle of His permissive will. The other sinks down in despair and remains where he is. God's order is —no sin, no sickness, no devil, no war: His permissive will is things as they are.

SHH 6

THE DISCIPLINE OF DISILLUSIONMENT

*Jesus did not commit Himself unto them. . . for He knew what
was in man. (John 2:24-25)*

Disillusionment means that there are no more false judgments
in life. To be undeceived by disillusionment may leave us cynical and unkindly severe in our judgment of others, but the disillusionment which comes from God brings us to the place
where we see men and women as they really are, and yet there
is no cynicism, we have no stinging, bitter things to say. Many
of the cruel things in life spring from the fact that we suffer
from illusions. We are not true to one another as *facts*; we are
true only to our *ideas* of one another. Everything is either delightful and fine, or mean and dastardly, according to our idea.

The refusal to be disillusioned is the cause of much of the
suffering in human life. It works in this way—if we love a human being and do not love God, we demand of him every
perfection and every rectitude, and when we do not get it we
become cruel and vindictive; we are demanding of a human
being that which he or she cannot give. There is only one Being
Who can satisfy the last aching abyss of the human heart, and
that is the Lord Jesus Christ. Why Our Lord is apparently so
severe regarding every human relationship is because He
knows that every relationship not based on loyalty to Himself
will end in disaster. Our Lord trusted no man, yet He was never
suspicious, never bitter. Our Lord's confidence in God and in
what His grace could do for any man, was so perfect that He
despaired of no one. If our trust is placed in human beings, we
shall end in despairing of everyone.

> *Mortify therefore your members which are upon the earth; for-*
> *nication, uncleanness, passion, evil desire, and covetousness,*
> *which is idolatry. (Colossians 3:5)*

In this passage Paul mentions things that are of the nature of
rubbish, and he mentions them in their complete ugliness. They
are the abortion of the stuff human nature is made of, and he
says, 'Mortify them, destroy them by neglect.' Certain things
can only be dealt with by ignoring them; if you face them you
increase their power. It is absurd to say, Pray about them; when
once a thing is seen to be wrong, don't pray about it, it fixes
the mind on it; never for a second brood on it, destroy it by
neglect. We have no business to harbour an emotion which
we can see will end in any of the things Paul mentions. No
man or woman on earth is immune, each one of us knows the
things we should not think about, or pray about, but resolutely
neglect. It is a great thing for our moral character to have something to ignore. It is because these things are not understood
that there is so much inefficiency in spiritual life. What Christianity supplies is 'the expulsive power of a new affection'. We
cannot destroy sin by neglect; God deals with sin, and we can
get the effective measure of His dealing with it in our actual
life.

BE 47

TILL YOU ARE ENTIRELY HIS

Let your endurance be a finished product, so that you may be finished and complete, with never a defect. (James 1:4, MOFFAT)

Many of us are all right in the main, but there are some domains in which we are slovenly. It is not a question of sin, but of the remnants of the carnal life which are apt to make us slovenly. Slovenliness is an insult to the Holy Ghost. There should be nothing slovenly, whether it be in the way we eat and drink, or in the way we worship God.

Not only must our relationship to God be right, but the external expression of that relationship must be right. Ultimately God will let nothing escape, every detail is under His scrutiny. In numberless ways God will bring us back to the same point over and over again. He never tires of bringing us to the one point until we learn the lesson, because He is producing the finished product. It may be a question of impulse, and again and again, with the most persistent patience, God has brought us back to the one particular point; or it may be mental woolgathering, or independent individuality. God is trying to impress upon us the one thing that is not entirely right.

We have been having a wonderful time this Session over the revelation of God's Redemption, our hearts are perfect towards Him; His wonderful work in us makes us know that in the main we are right with Him. "Now," says the Spirit, through St. James, "let your endurance be a finished product." Watch the slipshod bits—"Oh, that will have to do for now." Whatever it is, God will point it out with persistence until we are entirely His.

Let not sin therefore reign in your mortal body, that ye should obey it in the lusts thereof. (Romans 6:12)

Paul is strong in urging us to realize what salvation means in our bodily lives; it means that we command our bodies to obey the new disposition. That is where you find the problems on the margins of the sanctified life. Paul argues in Romans 6:29, 'You are perfectly adjusted to God on the inside by a perfect Saviour, but your members have been used as servants of the wrong disposition; now begin to make those same members obey the new disposition.' As we go on, we find every place God brings us into is the means of enabling us to realize with growing joy that the life of Christ within is more than a match, not only for the enemy on the outside, but for the impaired body that comes between. Paul urges with passionate pleading, that we present our bodies a living sacrifice, and then realize, not presumptuously, but with slow, sure, overwhelming certainty that every command of Christ can be obeyed in our bodily life through the Atonement.

IWP 28

AUGUST

SOMETHING MORE ABOUT HIS WAYS

When Jesus had made an end of commanding his disciples, he departed thence to teach and to preach in their cities. (Matt. 11:1)

He comes where He commands us to leave. If when God said "Go," you stayed because you were so concerned about your people at home, you robbed them of the teaching and preaching of Jesus Christ Himself. When you obeyed and left all consequences to God, the Lord went into your city to teach; as long as you would not obey, you were in the way. Watch where you begin to debate and to put what you call duty in competition with your Lord's commands. "I know He told me to go, but then my duty was here;" that means you do not believe that Jesus means what He says.

He teaches where He instructs us not to.

"Master, . . . let us make three tabernacles."

Are we playing the spiritual amateur providence in other lives? Are we so noisy in our instruction of others that God cannot get anywhere near them? We have to keep our mouths shut and our spirits alert. God wants to instruct us in regard to His Son, He wants to turn our times of prayer into mounts of transfiguration, and we will not let Him. When we are certain of the way God is going to work, He will never work in that way any more.

He works where He sends us to wait.

"Tarry ye . . . until . . ."

Wait on God and He will work, but don't wait in spiritual sulks because you cannot see an inch in front of you! Are we detached enough from our own spiritual hysterics to wait on God? To wait is not to sit with folded hands, but to learn to do what we are told.

These are phases of His ways we rarely recognize.

> *What, could ye not watch with me one hour? Matthew 26:40*
> *For this cause many among you are weak and sickly, and not a*
> *few sleep. (1 Corinthians 11:30)*

There are many today who are suffering from spiritual sleeping sickness, and the sorrow of the world which works death is witnessed in all directions. If personal sorrow does not work itself out along the appropriate line, it will lull us to a pessimistic sleep. For instance, when we see our brother 'sinning a sin not unto death' do we get to prayer for him, probed by the searching sorrow of his sin? (see 1 John 5:16). Most of us are so shallow spiritually that when our Lord in answer to some outrageous request we have made, asks us—'Are ye able to drink the cup that I drink? or to be baptized with the baptism that I am baptized with?' we say 'We are able.' Then He begins to show us what the cup and the baptism meant to Him— 'But I have a baptism to be baptized with; and how am I straitened till it be accomplished!' (Luke 12:50). And Jesus said unto them, 'Ye shall indeed drink of the cup that I drink of; and with the baptism that I am baptized withal shall ye be baptized'— and there begins to dawn for the disciple the great solemn day of martyrdom which closes for ever the day of exuberant undisciplined service, and opens the patient pilgrimage of pain and joy, with 'more of the first than the last'.

HGM 119

THE DISCIPLINE OF DIFFICULTY

In the world ye shall have tribulation: but be of good cheer; I have overcome the world. (John 16:33)

An average view of the Christian life is that it means deliverance from trouble. It is deliverance *in* trouble, which is very different. "He that dwelleth in the secret place of the Most High . . . *there* shall no evil befall thee"—no plague can come nigh the place where you are at one with God.

If you are a child of God, there certainly will be troubles to meet, but Jesus says do not be surprised when they come. "In the world ye shall have tribulation: but be of good cheer, I have overcome the world, there is nothing for you to fear." Men who before they were saved would scorn to talk about troubles, often become "fushionless" after being born again because they have a wrong idea of a saint.

God does not give us overcoming life: He gives us life as we overcome. The strain is the strength. If there is no strain, there is no strength. Are you asking God to give you life and liberty and joy? He cannot, unless you will accept the strain. Immediately you face the strain, you will get the strength. Overcome your own timidity and take the step, and God will give you to eat of the tree of life and you will get nourishment. If you spend yourself out physically, you become exhausted; but spend yourself spiritually, and you get more strength. God never gives strength for to-morrow, or for the next hour, but only for the strain of the minute. The temptation is to face difficulties from a common-sense standpoint. The saint is hilarious when he is crushed with difficulties because the thing is so ludicrously impossible to anyone but God.

If thou wilt be perfect, go and sell that thou hast . . . and come and follow me. (Matthew 19:21)

Numbers of people say, 'I have asked God to sanctify me and He has not done it.' Of course He has not! Do we find one word in the Bible which tells us to pray, 'Lord, sanctify me?' What we do read is that God sanctifies what we give. An unconditional 'give up' is the condition of sanctification, not claiming something for ourselves. This is where unscriptural holiness teaching has played so much havoc with spiritual experience. We receive from God on one condition only, viz., that we yield ourselves to Him and are willing to receive nothing. Immediately we state conditions and say, 'I want to be filled with the Holy Spirit,' 'I want to be delivered from sin,' 'I want to be the means of saving souls'—we may pray to further orders, but an answer will never come that way. That is all the energy of the flesh, it has no thought of the claims of Jesus on the life. Are we willing to be baptized into His death? How much struggle is there in a dead man?

IWP 17

THE BIG COMPELLING OF GOD

Behold, we go up to Jerusalem. (Luke 18:31)

Jerusalem stands in the life of Our Lord as the place where He reached the climax of His Father's will. "I seek not Mine own will, but the will of the Father which hath sent Me." That was the one dominating interest all through our Lord's life, and the things He met with on the way, joy or sorrow, success or failure, never deterred Him from His purpose. "He stedfastly set His face to go to Jerusalem."

The great thing to remember is that we go up to Jerusalem to fulfill God's purpose, not our own. Naturally, our ambitions are our own; in the Christian life we have no aim of our own. There is so much said to-day about our decisions for Christ, our determination to be Christians, our decisions for this and that, but in the New Testament it is the aspect of God's compelling that is brought out. "Ye have not chosen Me, but I have chosen you." We are not taken up into conscious agreement with God's purpose, we are taken up into God's purpose without any consciousness at all. We have no conception of what God is aiming at, and as we go on it gets more and more vague. God's aim looks like missing the mark because we are too short-sighted to see what He is aiming at. At the beginning of the Christian life we have our own ideas as to what God's purpose is—"I am meant to go here or there," "God has called me to do this special work"; and we go and do the thing, and still the big compelling of God remains. The work we do is of no account, it is so much scaffolding compared with the big compelling of God. "He took unto Him the twelve," He takes us all the time. There is more than we have got at as yet.

446

Praying in the Holy Ghost . . . (Jude 20)

When we pray in the Holy Ghost we begin to have a more intimate conception of God; the Holy ghost brings all through us the sense of His resources. For instance, we may be called to a definite purpose for our life which the Holy Ghost reveals and we know that it means a decision, a reckless fling over on to God, a burning of our bridges behind us; and there is not a soul to advise us when we take that step saving the Holy Ghost. Our clingings come in this way—we put one foot on God's side and one on the side of human reasoning; then God widens the space until we either drop down in between or jump on to one side or the other. We have to take a leap, a reckless leap, and if we have learned to rely on the Holy ghost, it will be a reckless leap on to God's side. So many of us limit our praying because we are not reckless in our confidence in God. In the eyes of those who do not know God, it is madness to trust Him, but when we pray in the Holy Ghost we begin to realize the resources of God, that He is our perfect heavenly Father, and we are His children.

Always keep an inner recollectedness that God is our Father through the Lord Jesus Christ.

IYA 62

THE BRAVE COMRADESHIP OF GOD

Then He took unto Him the twelve. (Luke 18:31)

The bravery of God in trusting us! You say—"But He has been unwise to choose me, because there is nothing in me; I am not of any value." That is why He chose you. As long as you think there is something in you, He cannot choose you because you have ends of your own to serve; but if you have let Him bring you to the end of your self-sufficiency then He can choose you to go with Him to Jerusalem, and that will mean the fulfillment of purposes which He does not discuss with you.

We are apt to say that because a man has natural ability, therefore he will make a good Christian. It is not a question of our equipment but of our poverty, not of what we bring with us, but of what God puts into us; not a question of natural virtues of strength of character, knowledge, and experience— all that is of no avail in this matter. The only thing that avails is that we are taken up into the big compelling of God and made His comrades (cf. 1 Cor. 1:26-30). The comradeship of God is made up out of men who know their poverty. He can do nothing with the man who thinks that he is of use to God. As Christians we are not out for our own cause at all, we are out for the cause of God, which can never be our cause. We do not know what God is after, but we have to maintain our relationship with Him whatever happens. We must never allow anything to injure our relationship with God; if it does get injured we must take time and get it put right. The main thing about Christianity is not the work we do, but the relationship we maintain and the atmosphere produced by that relationship. That is all God asks us to look after, and it is the one thing that is being continually assailed.

He that hath seen me hath seen the Father. (John 14:9)

An ideal has no power over us until it becomes incarnate. The idea of beauty lies unawakened until we see a thing we call beautiful. God may be a mere mental abstraction; He may be spoken of in terms of culture or poetry or philosophy, but He has not the slightest meaning for us until He becomes incarnate. When once we know that God has 'trod this earth with naked feet, and woven with human hands the creed of creeds', then we are arrested. When once we know that the Almighty Being Who reigns and rules over His creation does not do so in calm disdain, but puts His back to the wall of the world, so to speak, and receives all the downcast, the outcast, the sin-defiled, the wrong, the wicked and the sinful into His arms, then we are arrested. An intellectual conception of God may be found in a bad vicious character. The knowledge and vision of God is dependent entirely on a pure heart. Character determines the revelation of God to the individual. 'The pure in heart see God.' Jesus Christ changes the worst into the best and gives the moral readjustment that enables a man to love and delight in the true God. Of a great almighty incomprehensible Being we know nothing, but of our Lord Jesus Christ we do know, and the New Testament reveals that the Almighty God is nothing that Jesus was not.

BE 104

THE BAFFLING CALL OF GOD

And all things that are written by the prophets concerning the
Son of Man shall be accomplished. . . . And they understood none
of these things. (Luke 18:31, 34)

God called Jesus Christ to what seemed unmitigated disaster.
Jesus Christ called His disciples to see Him put to death; He led
every one of them to the place where their hearts were broken. Jesus Christ's life was an absolute failure from every standpoint but God's. But what seemed failure from man's standpoint was a tremendous triumph from God's, because God's
purpose is never man's purpose.

There comes the baffling call of God in our lives also. The
call of God can never be stated explicitly; it is implicit. The call
of God is like the call of the sea, no one hears it but the one
who has the nature of the sea in him. It cannot be stated definitely what the call of God is to, because His call is to be in
comradeship with Himself for His own purposes, and the test
is to believe that God knows what He is after. The things that
happen do not happen by chance, they happen entirely in the
decree of God. God is working out His purposes.

If we are in communion with God and recognize that He is
taking us into His purposes, we shall no longer try to find out
what His purposes are. As we go on in the Christian life it gets
simpler, because we are less inclined to say—Now why did God
allow this and that? Behind the whole thing lies the compelling of God. "There's a divinity that shapes our ends." A Christian is one who trusts the wits and the wisdom of God, and
not his own wits. If we have a purpose of our own, it destroys
the simplicity and the leisureliness which ought to characterize
the children of God.

Thou shalt not hate thy brother in thine heart. (Leviticus 19:17)

A good way to use the 'Cursing' Psalms is in some such way as this—'Do not I hate them, O Lord, that hate Thee? . . . I hate them with perfect hatred.' Ask yourself what is it that hates God? Nothing and no one hates God half as much as the wrong disposition in you does. The carnal mind is *'emnity against God'*; what we should hate is this principle that lusts against the Spirit of God and is determined to have our bodies and minds and rule them away from God. The Spirit of God awakens in us an unmeasured hatred of that power until we are not only sick of it, but sick to death of it, and we will gladly make the moral choice of going to its funeral. The meaning of Romans 6:6 is just this put into Scriptural language—'Knowing this, that our old man is crucified with him.' The 'old man' is the thing the Spirit of God will teach us to hate, and the love of God in our hearts concentrates our soul in horror against the wrong thing. Make no excuse for it. The next time you read those Psalms, which people think are so terrible, bring this interpretation to bear on them.

BP 120

THE CROSS IN PRAYER

At that day ye shall ask in My name. (John 16:26)

We are too much given to thinking of the Cross as something we have to get through; we get *through* it only in order to get into it. The Cross stands for one thing only for us—a complete and entire and absolute identification with the Lord Jesus Christ, and there is nothing in which this identification is realized more than in prayer.

"Your Father knoweth what things ye have need of, before ye ask Him." Then why ask? The idea of prayer is not in order to get answers from God; prayer is perfect and complete oneness with God. If we pray because we want answers, we will get huffed with God. The answers come every time, but not always in the way we expect, and our spiritual huff shows a refusal to identify ourselves with Our Lord in prayer; we are here to be living monuments of God's grace.

"I say not that I will pray the Father for you: for the Father Himself loveth you." Have you reached such an intimacy with God that the Lord Jesus Christ's life of prayer is the only explanation of your life of prayer? Has Our Lord's vicarious life become your vital life? "At that day" you will be so identified with Jesus that there will be no distinction.

When prayer seems to be unanswered, beware of trying to fix the blame on someone else. That is always a snare of Satan. You will find there is a reason which is a deep instruction to you, not to anyone else.

And looking on Jesus as he walked, he saith, Behold the Lamb of God. (John 1:36)

The real life of the saint on this earth, and the life that is most glorifying to Jesus, is the life that steadfastly goes on through common days and common ways, with no mountain-top experiences. We read that John the Baptist 'looked upon Jesus *as he walked* . . . '—not at Jesus in a prayer meeting or in a revival service, or Jesus performing miracles; he did not watch Him on the Mount of Transfiguration, he did not see Him in any great moment at all, he saw Him on an ordinary day when Jesus was walking in an ordinary common way, and he said, 'Behold, the Lamb of God!' That is the test of reality. Mounting up with wings as eagles, running and not being weary, are indications that something more than usual is at work. Walking and not fainting is the life that glorifies God and satisfies the heart of Jesus to the full—the plain daylight life, unmarked, unknown, only occasionally, if ever, does the marvel of it break on other people.

PS 38

PRAYER IN THE FATHER'S HOUSE

Wist ye not that I must be in My Father's house?
(Luke 2:49, R.V.)

Our Lord's childhood was not immature manhood; our Lord's childhood is an eternal fact. Am I a holy innocent child of God by identification with my Lord and Saviour? Do I look upon life as being in my Father's house? Is the Son of God living in His Father's house in me?

The abiding Reality is God, and His order comes through the moments. Am I always in contact with Reality, or do I only pray when things have gone wrong, when there is a disturbance in the moments of my life? I have to learn to identify myself with my Lord in holy communion in ways some of us have not begun to learn as yet. "I must be about My Father's business"—live the moments in My Father's house.

Narrow it down to your individual circumstances—are you so identified with the Lord's life that you are simply a child of God, continually talking to Him and realizing that all things come from His hands? Is the Eternal Child in you living in the Father's house? Are the graces of His ministering life working out through you in your home, in your business, in your domestic circle? Have you been wondering why you are going through the things you are? It is not that you have to go through them, it is because of the relation into which the Son of God has come in His Father's providence in your particular sainthood. Let Him have His way, keep in perfect union with Him.

The vicarious life of your Lord is to become your vital simple life; the way He worked and lived among men must be the way He lives in you.

That the life also of Jesus might be made manifest in our moral flesh. (2 Corinthians 4:11)

We look for God to manifest Himself to His children: God only manifests Himself *in* His children, consequently others see the manifestation, the child of God does not. You say, 'I am not conscious of God's blessing now'—thank God! 'I am not conscious now of the touches of God'—thank God! 'I am not conscious now that God is answering my prayers'—thank God! If you are conscious of these things it means you have put yourself outside God. 'That the life also of Jesus might be made manifest in our mortal flesh'—'I am not conscious that His life is being manifested,' you say, but if you are a saint it surely is. When a little child becomes conscious of being a little child, the child-likeness is gone; and when a saint becomes conscious of being a saint, something has gone wrong. 'Oh but I'm not good enough.' You never will be good enough! that is why the Lord had to come and save you. Go to your own funeral and ever after let God be all in all, and life will become the simple life of a child in which God's order comes moment by moment.

Never live on memories. Do not remember in your testimony what you once were; let the word of God be always living and active in you, and give the best you have every time and all the time.

GH 66

PRAYER IN THE FATHER'S HONOUR

That holy thing which shall be born of thee shall be called the Son of God. (Luke 1:35)

If the Son of God is born into my mortal flesh, is His holy innocence and simplicity and oneness with the Father getting a chance to manifest itself in me? What was true of the Virgin Mary in the historic introduction of God's Son into this earth is true in every saint. The Son of God is born into me by the direct act of God; then I as a child of God have to exercise the right of a child, the right of being always face to face with my Father. Am I continually saying with amazement to my common-sense life—why do you want to turn me off here? Don't you know that I must be about my Father's business? Whatever the circumstances may be, that Holy Innocent Eternal Child must be in contact with His Father.

Am I simple enough to identify myself with my Lord in this way? Is He getting His wonderful way in me? Is God realizing that His Son is formed in me, or have I carefully put Him on one side? Oh, the clamour of these days! Everyone is clamouring—for what? For the Son of God to be put to death. There is no room here for the Son of God just now, no room for quiet holy communion with the Father.

Is the Son of God praying in me or am I dictating to Him? Is He ministering in me as He did in the days of His flesh? Is the Son of God in me going through His passion for His own purposes? The more one knows of the inner life of God's ripest saints, the more one sees what God's purpose is—"filling up that which is behind of the affliction of Christ." There is always something to be done in the sense of "filling up."

The reproaches of them that reproached thee fell upon me.
(Romans 15:3)

What reproaches fell on Jesus? Everything that was hurled in slander against God hurt our Lord. The slanders that were hurled against Himself made no impression on Him; His suffering was on account of His Father. On what account do you suffer? Do you suffer because men speak ill of you? Read Hebrews 12:3: 'For consider him that hath endured such gainsaying of sinners against himself, that ye wax not weary, fainting in your souls.' Perfect love takes no account of the evil done unto it. It was the reproaches that hit and scandalized the true centre of His life that Jesus Christ noticed in pain. What was that true centre? Absolute devotion to God the Father and to His will; and as surely as you get Christ-centred you will understand what the Apostle Paul meant when he talks about 'filling up that which is lacking of the afflictions of Christ'. Jesus Christ could not be touched on the line of self-pity. The practical emphasis here is that our service is not to be that of pity, but of personal, passionate love to God, and a longing to see many more brought to the centre where God has brought us.

BP 183

PRAYER IN THE FATHER'S HEARING

Father, I thank Thee that Thou hast heard Me. (John 11:41)

When the Son of God prays, He has only one consciousness, and that consciousness is of His Father. God always hears the prayers of His Son, and if the Son of God is formed in me the Father will always hear my prayers. I have to see that the Son of God is manifested in my mortal flesh. "Your body is the temple of the Holy Ghost," i.e., the Bethlehem of the Son of God. Is the Son of God getting His chance in me? Is the direct simplicity of the life of God's Son being worked out exactly as it was worked out in His historic life? When I come in contact with the occurrences of life as an ordinary human being, is the prayer of God's Eternal Son to His Father being prayed in me? "In that day ye shall ask in My name . . ." What day? The day when the Holy Ghost has come to me and made me effectually one with my Lord.

Is the Lord Jesus Christ being abundantly satisfied in your life or have you got a spiritual strut on? Never let common sense obtrude and push the Son of God on one side. Common sense is a gift which God gave to human nature; but common sense is not the gift of His Son. Supernatural sense is the gift of His Son; never enthrone common sense. The Son detects the Father; common sense never yet detected the Father and never will. Our ordinary wits never worship God unless they are transfigured by the indwelling Son of God. We have to see that this mortal flesh is kept in perfect subjection to Him and that He works through it moment by moment. Are we living in such human dependence upon Jesus Christ that His life is being manifested moment by moment?

One thing thou lackest: go . . . sell whatsoever thou hast, and
give to the poor : . . and come, take up the cross, and follow me.
(Mark 10:21)

These words mean a voluntary abandoning of riches and a deliberate, devoted attachment to Jesus Christ. We are so desperately wise in our own conceit that we continually make out that Jesus did not mean what He said, and we spiritualize His meaning into thin air. Jesus saw that this man depended on his riches. If He came to you or to me He might not say that, but He would say something that dealt with whatever He saw we were depending on. 'Sell that thou hast,' strip yourself of every possession, disengage yourself from all things until you are a naked soul; be a man merely and then give your manhood to God. Reduce yourself until nothing remains but your consciousness of yourself, and then cast that consciousness at the feet of Jesus Christ . . .

Am I prepared to strip myself of what I possess in property, in virtues, in the estimation of others—to count all things to be loss in order to win Christ? I can be so rich in poverty, so rich in the consciousness that I am nobody, that I shall never be a disciple; and I can be so rich in the consciousness that I am somebody that I shall never be a disciple. Am I willing to be destitute even of the sense that I am destitute? It is not a question of giving up outside things, but of making myself destitute to myself, reducing myself to a mere consciousness and giving that to Jesus Christ. I must reduce myself until I am a mere conscious man, fundamentally renounce possessions of all kinds—not to save my soul, only one thing saves a man's soul, absolute reliance on the Lord Jesus—and then give that manhood to Jesus.

SSY 58

THE SACRAMENT OF THE SAINT

Let them that suffer according to the will of God, commit the
keeping of their souls to Him in well-doing. (1 Peter 4:19)

To choose to suffer means that there is something wrong; to choose God's will even if it means suffering is a very different thing. No healthy saint ever chooses suffering; he chooses God's will, as Jesus did, whether it means suffering or not. No saint dare interfere with the discipline of suffering in another saint.

The saint who satisfies the heart of Jesus will make other saints strong and mature for God. The people who do us good are never those who sympathize with us, they always hinder, because sympathy enervates. No one understands a saint but the saint who is nearest to the Saviour. If we accept the sympathy of a saint, the reflex feeling is—Well, God is dealing hardly with me. That is why Jesus said self-pity was of the devil (see Matt. 16:23). Be merciful to God's reputation. It is easy to blacken God's character because God never answers back He never vindicates Himself. Beware of the thought that Jesus needed sympathy in His earthly life; He refused sympathy from man because He knew far too wisely that no one on earth understood what He was after. He took sympathy from His Father only, and from the angels in heaven. (Cf. Luke 15:10.)

Notice God's unutterable waste of saints, according to the judgment of the world. God plants His saints in the most useless places. We say—God intends me to be here because I am so useful. Jesus never estimated His life along the line of the greatest use. God puts His saints where they will glorify Him, and we are no judges at all of where that is.

*For thou shalt eat the labour of thine hands: happy shalt thou
be, and it shall be well with thee. (Psalm 128:2)*

This verse reveals the connection between the natural creation
and the regenerated creation. We have to be awake strenuously to the fact that our body is the temple of the Holy Ghost,
not only in the spiritual sense, but in the physical sense. When
we are born from above we are apt to despise the clay of which
we are made. The natural creation and the creation of grace
work together, and what we are apt to call the sordid things,
labouring with our hands, and eating and drinking, have to be
turned into spiritual exercises by obedience, then we shall 'eat
and drink, and do all to the glory of God'. There must be a
uniting in personal experience of the two creations. It cannot
be done all at once, there are whole tracts of life which have
to be disciplined. 'Your body is the temple of the Holy Ghost',
it is the handiwork of God, and it is in these bodies we are to
find satisfaction, and that means strenuousness. Every power
of mind and heart should go into the strenuousness of turning
the natural into the spiritual by obeying the word of God regarding it. If we do not make the natural spiritual, it will become sordid; but when we become spiritual the natural is shot
through with the glory of God.

PSB 43

THIS EXPERIENCE MUST COME

And he saw him no more. (2 Kings 2:12)

It is not wrong to depend upon Elijah as long as God gives him to you, but remember the time will come when he will have to go; when he stands no more to you as your guide and leader, because God does not intend he should. You say—"I cannot go on without Elijah." God says you must.

Alone at your Jordan. v. 14. Jordan is the type of separation where there is no fellowship with anyone else, and where no one can take the responsibility for you. You have to put to the test now what you learned when you were with your Elijah. You have been to Jordan over and over again with Elijah, but now you are up against it alone. It is no use saying you cannot go; this experience has come, and you must go. If you want to know whether God is the God you have faith to believe Him to be, then go through your Jordan alone.

Alone at your Jericho. v. 15. Jericho is the place where you have seen your Elijah do great things. When you come to your Jericho you have a strong disinclination to take the initiative and trust in God, you want someone else to take it for you. If you remain true to what you learned with Elijah, you will get the sign that God is with you.

Alone at your Bethel. v. 23. At your Bethel you will find yourself at your wits' end and at the beginning of God's wisdom. When you get to your wits' end and feel inclined to succumb to panic, don't; stand true to God and He will bring His truth out in a way that will make your life a sacrament. Put into practice what you learned with your Elijah, use his cloak and pray. Determine to trust in God and do not look for Elijah any more.

> For I say unto you, That except your righteousness shall exceed
> the righteousness of the scribes and Pharisees, ye shall in no case
> enter into the kingdom of heaven. (Matthew 5:20)

'Except your righteousness shall exceed'—not be different from but '*exceed*', that is, we have to be all they are and infinitely more! We have to be right in our external behaviour, but we have to be as right, and 'righter', in our internal behaviour. We have to be right in our words and actions, but we have to be as right in our thoughts and feelings. We have to be right according to the conventions of the society of godly people, but we have also to be right in conscience towards God. Nominal Christians are often without the ordinary moral integrity of the man who does not care a bit about Jesus Christ; not because they are hypocrites, but because we have been taught for generations to think on one aspect only of Jesus Christ's salvation, viz., the revelation that salvation is not merited by us, but is the sheer sovereign act of God's grace in Christ Jesus. A grand marvellous revelation fact, but Jesus says we have got to say 'Thank you' for our salvation, and the 'Thank you' is that our righteousness is to exceed the righteousness of the most moral man on earth.

Jesus not only demands that our external life is above censure but that we are above censure where God sees us. We see the meaning now of saying that Jesus is the most tantalizing Teacher: He demands that we be so pure that God who sees to the inmost springs of our motives, the inmost dreams of our dreams, sees nothing to censure. We may go on evolving and evolving, but we shall never produce that kind of purity. Then what is the good of teaching it? Listen: 'If we walk in the light, as he is in the light, we have fellowship with one another, *and the blood of Jesus Christ his Son cleanseth us from all sin.*' That is the Gospel.

HG 59

THE THEOLOGY OF REST

Why are ye fearful, O ye of little faith? (Matt. 8:26)

When we are in fear we can do nothing less than pray to God, but Our Lord has a right to expect that those who name His Name should have an understanding confidence in Him. God expects His children to be so confident in Him that in any crisis they are the reliable ones. Our trust is in God up to a certain point, then we go back to the elementary panic prayers of those who do not know God. We get to our wits' end, showing that we have not the slightest confidence in Him and His government of the world; He seems to be asleep, and we see nothing but breakers ahead.

"O ye of little faith!" What a pang must have shot through the disciples—"Missed it again!" And what a pang will go through us when we suddenly realize that we might have produced downright joy in the heart of Jesus by remaining absolutely confident in Him, no matter what was ahead.

There are stages in life when there is no storm, no crisis, when we do our human best; it is when a crisis arises that we instantly reveal upon whom we rely. If we have been learning to worship God and to trust Him, the crisis will reveal that we will go to the breaking point and not break in our confidence in Him.

We have been talking a great deal about sanctification—what is it all going to amount to? It should work out into rest in God which means oneness with God, a oneness which will make us not only blameless in His sight, but a deep joy to Him.

When ye pray, say, Our Father which art in heaven . . .
(Luke 11:2)

Words are full of revelation when we do not simply recall or memorize them but receive them. Receive these words from Jesus—'Father', 'heaven', 'Hallowed be thy name', 'kingdom', 'will', there is all the vocabulary of the Deity and Dominion and Disposition of Almighty God in relation to men in these words. Or take the words—'bread', 'forgiveness', 'debts', 'temptation', 'deliverance', 'evil'; in these words the primary psychological colours which portray the perplexing puzzles and problems of personal life, are all spelled out before our Father.

Or lastly, look at such words as 'power', 'glory', 'for ever', 'Amen'—in them there sounds the transcendent triumphant truth that all is well, that God reigns and rules and rejoices, and His joy is our strength. What a rapturous grammar class our Lord Jesus conducts when we go to His school of prayer and learn of Him!

DPR 26

QUENCH NOT THE SPIRIT

Quench not the Spirit. (1 Thess. 5:19)

The voice of the Spirit is as gentle as a zephyr, so gentle that unless you are living in perfect communion with God, you never hear it. The checks of the Spirit come in the most extraordinarily gentle ways, and if you are not sensitive enough to detect His voice you will quench it, and your personal spiritual life will be impaired. His checks always come as a still small voice, so small that no one but the saint notices them.

Beware if in personal testimony you have to hark back and say—"Once, so many years ago, I was saved." If you are walking in the light, there is no harking back, the past is transfused into the present wonder of communion with God. If you get out of the light you become a sentimental Christian and live on memories, your testimony has a hard, metallic note. Beware of trying to patch up a present refusal to walk in the light by recalling past experiences when you did walk in the light. Whenever the Spirit checks, call a halt and get the thing right, or you will go on grieving Him without knowing it.

Suppose God has brought you up to a crisis and you nearly go through but not quite, He will engineer the crisis again, but it will not be so keen as it was before. There will be less discernment of God and more humiliation at not having obeyed; and if you go on grieving the Spirit, there will come a time when that crisis cannot be repeated, you have grieved Him away. But if you go through the crisis, there will be the paean of praise to God. Never sympathize with the thing that is stabbing God all the time. God has to hurt the thing that must go.

We are troubled on every side, yet not distressed: we are perplexed, but not in despair. (2 Corinthians 4:8)

By Actual is meant the things we come in contact with by our senses, and by Real that which lies behind, that which we cannot get at by our senses. The fanatic sees the real only and ignores the actual; the materialist looks at the actual only and ignores the real. The only sane Being who ever trod this earth was Jesus Christ, because in Him the actual and the real were one. Jesus Christ does not stand first in the actual world, He stands first in the real world; that is why the natural man does not bother his head about him—'the natural man receiveth not the things of the Spirit of God: for they are foolishness unto him'. When we are born from above we begin to see the actual things in the light of the real. We say that prayer alters things, but prayer does not alter actual things nearly so much as it alters the man who sees the actual things. In the Sermon on the Mount our Lord brings the actual and the real together.

SSM 25–6

CHASTENING

*Despise not the chastening of the Lord, nor faint when thou art
rebuked of Him. (Heb. 7:5)*

It is very easy to quench the Spirit; we do it by despising the
chastening of the Lord, by fainting when we are rebuked by
Him. If we have only a shallow experience of sanctification,
we mistake the shadow for the reality, and when the Spirit of
God begins to check, we say—oh, that must be the devil.

Never quench the Spirit, and do not despise Him when He
says to you—"Don't be blind on this point any more; you are
not where you thought you were. Up to the present I have not
been able to reveal it to you, but I reveal it now." When the
Lord chastens you like that, let Him have His way. Let Him
relate you rightly to God.

"Nor faint when thou art rebuked of Him." We get into sulks
with God and say—"Oh, well, I can't help it; I did pray and
things did not turn out right, and I am going to give it all up."
Think what would happen if we talked like this in any other
domain of life!

Am I prepared to let God grip me by His power and do a work
in me that is worthy of Himself? Sanctification is not my idea
of what I want God to do for me; sanctification is God's idea of
what He wants to do for me, and He has to get me into the
attitude of mind and spirit where at any cost I will let Him
sanctify me wholly.

Praying always with all prayer and supplication in the Spirit.
(Ephesians 6:18)

Prayer '*in the Spirit*' is not meditation, it is not reverie; it is being filled with the Holy Ghost who brings us as we pray into perfect union before God, and this union manifests itself in '*perseverance and supplication for all saints*'. Every saint of God knows those times when in closest communion with God nothing is articulated, and yet there seems to be an absolute intimacy not so much between God's mind and their mind as between God's Spirit and their spirit.

The conscious and the subconscious life of our Lord is explained perhaps in this way. Our Lord's subconscious life was Deity, and only occasionally when He was on earth did the subconscious burst up into His conscious life. The subconscious life of the saint is the Holy Ghost, and in such moments of prayer as are alluded to in Romans 8:26—8, there is an uprush of communion with God into the consciousness of the saint, the only explanation of which is that the Holy Ghost in the saint is communicating prayers which cannot be uttered.

DPR 53

SIGNS OF THE NEW BIRTH

Ye must be born again. (John 3:7)

The answer to the question "How can a man be born when he is old?" is—When he is old enough to die—to die right out to his "rag rights," to his virtues, to his religion, to everything, and to receive into himself the life which never was there before. The new life manifests itself in conscious repentance and unconscious holiness.

"As many as received Him" (John 1:12). Is my knowledge of Jesus born of internal spiritual perception, or is it only what I have learned by listening to others? Have I something in my life that connects me with the Lord Jesus as my personal Saviour? All spiritual history must have a personal knowledge for its bedrock. To be born again means that I see Jesus.

"Except a man be born again, he cannot see the kingdom of God" (John 3:3). Do I seek for signs of the Kingdom, or do I perceive God's rule? The new birth gives a new power of vision whereby I begin to discern God's rule. His rule was there all the time, but true to His nature; now that I have received His nature I can see His rule.

"Whosoever is born of God doth not commit sin" (1 John 3:9). Do I seek to stop sinning or have I stopped sinning? To be born of God means that I have the supernatural power of God to stop sinning. In the Bible it is never—Should a Christian sin? The Bible puts it emphatically—A Christian must not sin. The effective working of the new birth in us is that we do not commit sin, not merely that we have the power not to sin, but that we have stopped sinning. First John 3:9 does not mean that we cannot sin; it means that if we obey the life of God in us, we need not sin.

Behold, God exalteth by his power: who teacheth like him?
(Job 36:22)

There is always a tendency to produce an absolute authority; we accept the authority of the Church, or of the Bible, or of a creed, and often refuse to do any more thinking on the matter; and in so doing we ignore the essential nature of Christianity which is based on a personal relationship to Jesus Christ, and works on the basis of our responsibility. On the grounds of the Redemption I am saved and God puts His Holy Spirit into me, then He expects me to react on the basis of that relationship. I can evade it by dumping my responsibility on to a Church, or a Book or a creed, forgetting what Jesus said—'Ye search the scriptures, because ye think that in them ye have eternal life; and these are they which bear witness of me; and ye will not come to me, that ye may have life.' The only way to understand the Scriptures is not to accept them blindly, but to read them in the light of a personal relationship to Jesus Christ. If we insist that a man must believe the doctrine of the Trinity and the inspiration of the Scriptures before he can be saved, we are putting the cart before the horse. All that is the effect of being a Christian, not the cause of it; and if we put the effect first we produce difficulties because we are putting thinking before life. Jesus says, 'Come unto me, and if you want to know whether my teaching is of God, do his will.' A scientist can explain the universe in which common-sense men live, but the scientific explanation is not first; life is first. The same with theology; theology is the systematizing of the intellectual expression of life from God; it is a mighty thing, but it is second, not first.

BFB 91

DOES HE KNOW ME—

He calleth . . . by name. (John 10:3)

When I have sadly misunderstood Him? (John 20:17). It is possible to know all about doctrine and yet not know Jesus. The soul is in danger when knowledge of doctrine outsteps intimate touch with Jesus. Why was Mary weeping? Doctrine was no more to Mary than the grass under her feet. Any Pharisee could have made a fool of Mary doctrinally, but one thing they could not ridicule out of her was the fact that Jesus had cast seven demons out of her; yet His blessings were nothing in comparison to Himself. Mary "saw Jesus standing and knew not that it was Jesus . . . ;" immediately she heard the voice, she knew she had a past history with the One who spoke. "Master!"

When I have stubbornly doubted? (John 20:27). Have I been doubting something about Jesus—an experience to which others testify but which I have not had? The other disciples told Thomas that they had seen Jesus, but Thomas doubted— "Except I shall see . . ., I will not believe." Thomas needed the personal touch of Jesus. When His touches come, or how they come, we do not know; but when they do come they are indescribably precious. "My Lord and my God!"

When I have selfishly denied Him? (John 21:15-17). Peter had denied Jesus Christ with oaths and curses, and yet after the Resurrection Jesus appeared to Peter alone. He restored him in private, then He restored him before the others. "Lord, Thou knowest that I love Thee."

Have I a personal history with Jesus Christ? The one sign of discipleship is intimate connection with Him, a knowledge of Jesus Christ which nothing can shake.

Even to them that believe on his name. (John 1:12)

A great thinker has said, 'The seal and end of true conscious life is joy,' not pleasure, nor happiness. Jesus Christ said to His disciples, 'These things have I spoken unto you, that my joy might remain in you, and that your joy might be full'—identity with Jesus Christ and with His joy.

What was the joy of the Lord Jesus Christ? His joy was in having completely finished the work His Father gave Him to do; and the same type of joy will be granted to every man and woman who is born of God the Holy Ghost and sanctified, when they fulfil the work God has given them to do. What is that work? To be a saint, a walking, talking, living, practical epistle of what God Almighty can do through the Atonement of the Lord Jesus Christ—one in identity with the faith of Jesus, one in identity with the love of Jesus, one in identity with the Spirit of Jesus until we are so one in Him that the high-priestly prayer not only begins to be answered, but is clearly manifest in its answering—'that they may be one, even as we are one'.

AUG 112

ARE YOU DISCOURAGED
IN DEVOTION?

Yet lackest thou one thing; sell all that thou hast . . . and come,
follow Me. (Luke 18:22)

"And when he heard this . . ." Have you ever heard the Master say a hard word? If you have not, I question whether you have heard Him say anything. Jesus Christ says a great deal that we listen to, but do not hear; when we do hear, His words are amazingly hard.

Jesus did not seem in the least solicitous that this man should do what He told him, He made no attempt to keep him with Him. He simply said—Sell all you have, and come, follow Me. Our Lord never pleaded, He never cajoled, He never entrapped; He simply spoke the sternest words mortal ears ever listened to, and then left it alone.

Have I ever heard Jesus say a hard word? Has He said something personally to me to which I have deliberately listened? Not something I can expound or say this and that about, but something I have heard Him say to me? This man did understand what Jesus said, he heard it and he sized up what it meant, and it broke his heart. He did not go away defiant; he went away sorrowful, thoroughly discouraged. He had come to Jesus full of the fire of earnest desire, and the word of Jesus simply froze him; instead of producing an enthusiastic devotion, it produced a heart-breaking discouragement. And Jesus did not go after him, He let him go. Our Lord knows perfectly that when once His word is heard, it will bear fruit sooner or later. The terrible thing is that some of us prevent it bearing fruit in actual life. I wonder what we will say when we do make up our minds to be devoted to Him on that particular point? One thing is certain, He will never cast anything up at us.

474

All things were made by him; and without him was not any-thing made. That which hath been made was life in him; and the life was the light of men. (John 1:3–4) (RV marg.)

By creation we are the children of God; we are not the sons and daughters of God by creation; Jesus Christ makes us sons and daughters of God by regeneration (John 1:12). The idea of the Fatherhood of Jesus is revealed in the Bible, though rarely mentioned. 'Everlasting Father' refers to the Being we know as the Son of God. Paul in talking to the Athenians said, 'We are the offspring of God.' But the creator-power in Jesus Christ is vested in a more marvellous way even than when God created the world through him for He has that in Himself whereby He can create His own image. God created the world and everything that was made through the Son, and 'that which hath been made was life in Him'; therefore just as God created the world through Him, the Son is able to create His own image in anyone and everyone.

OBH 25

HAVE YOU EVER BEEN
EXPRESSIONLESS WITH SORROW?

*And when he heard this, he was very sorrowful: for he was very
rich. (Luke 18:23)*

The rich young ruler went away expressionless with sorrow;
he had not a word to say. He had no doubt as to what Jesus
said, no debate as to what it meant, and it produced in him a
sorrow that had not any words. Have you ever been there? Has
God's word come to you about something you are very rich
in—temperament, personal affinity, relationships of heart and
mind? Then you have often been expressionless with sorrow.
The Lord will not go after you, He will not plead, but every
time He meets you on that point He will simply repeat—If you
mean what you say, those are the conditions.

"Sell all that thou hast," undress yourself morally before God
of everything that might be a possession until you are a mere
conscious human being, and then give God that. That is where
the battle is fought—in the domain of the will before God. Are
you more devoted to your idea of what Jesus wants than to
Himself? If so, you are likely to hear one of His hard sayings
that will produce sorrow in you. What Jesus says is hard, it is
only easy when it is heard by those who have His disposition.
Beware of allowing anything to soften a hard word of Jesus
Christ's.

I can be so rich in poverty, so rich in the consciousness that
I am nobody, that I shall never be a disciple of Jesus; and I can
be so rich in the consciousness that I am somebody that I shall
never be a disciple. Am I willing to be destitute of the sense
that I am destitute? This is where discouragement comes in.
Discouragement is disenchanted self-love, and self-love may
be love of my devotion to Jesus.

If ye love me, keep my commandments. (John 14:15)

'If you love me, you will keep my commandments,' said Jesus; that is the practical simple test. Our Lord did not say, 'If a man *obeys* me, he will keep my commandments'; but, 'If you *love* me, you will keep my commandments.' In the early stages of Christian experience we are inclined to hunt with an overplus of zeal for commands of our Lord to obey; but as we mature in the life of God conscious obedience becomes so assimilated into our make-up that we begin to obey the commands of God unconsciously, until in the maturest stage of all we are simply children of God through whom God does His will for the most part unconsciously. Many of us are on the borders of consciousness—consciously serving, consciously devoted to God; all that is immature, it is not the life yet. The first stages of spiritual life are passed in conscientious carefulness; the mature life is lived in unconscious consecration. The term 'obey' would be better expressed by the word 'use'. For instance, a scientist, strictly speaking, 'uses' the laws of nature; that is, he more than obeys them, he causes them to fulfil their destiny in his work. That is exactly what happens in the saint's life, he 'uses' the commands of the Lord and they fulfill God's destiny in his life.

MFL 53

SELF-CONSCIOUSNESS

Come unto Me. (Matt. 11:28)

God means us to live a fully-orbed life in Christ Jesus, but there are times when that life is attacked from the outside, and we tumble into a way of introspection which we thought had gone. Self-consciousness is the first thing that will upset the completeness of the life in God, and self-consciousness continually produces wrestling. Self-consciousness is not sin; it may be produced by a nervous temperament or by a sudden dumping down into new circumstances. It is never God's will that we should be anything less than absolutely complete in Him. Anything that disturbs rest in Him must be cured at once, and it is not cured by being ignored, but by coming to Jesus Christ. If we come to Him and ask Him to produce Christ-consciousness, He will always do it until we learn to abide in Him.

Never allow the dividing up of your life in Christ to remain without facing it. Beware of leakage, of the dividing up of your life by the influence of friends or of circumstances; beware of anything that is going to split up your oneness with Him and make you see yourself separately. Nothing is so important as to keep right spiritually. The great solution is the simple one— "Come unto Me." The depth of our reality, intellectually, morally and spiritually, is tested by these words. In every degree in which we are not real, we will dispute rather than come.

Worthy is the Lamb that was slain to receive power, and riches, and wisdom, and strength, and honour, and glory, and blessing. (Revelation 5:12)

The childish idea that because God is great He can do anything, good or bad, right or wrong, and we must say nothing, is erroneous. The meaning of moral worth is that certain things are impossible to it: 'it is impossible for God to lie'; it is impossible for Jesus Christ to contradict His own holiness or to become other than He is. The profound truth for us is that Jesus Christ is the Worthy One not because He was God incarnate, but because He was God Incarnate on the human plane. 'Being made in the likeness of men' He accepted our limitations and lived on this earth a life of perfect holiness. Napoleon said of Jesus Christ that He had succeeded in making of every human soul an appendage of His own—why? Because He had the genius of holiness. There have been great military geniuses, intellectual giants, geniuses of statesmen, but these only exercise influence over a limited number of men; Jesus Christ exercises unlimited sway over all men because He is the altogether worthy one.

CHI 119

COMPLETENESS

And I will give you rest. (Matt. 11:28)

Whenever anything begins to disintegrate your life with Jesus Christ, turn to Him at once and ask Him to establish rest. Never allow anything to remain which is making the dis-peace. Take every element of disintegration as something to wrestle against, and not to suffer. Say—Lord, prove Thy consciousness in me, and self-consciousness will go and He will be all in all. Beware of allowing self-consciousness to continue because by slow degrees it will awaken self-pity, and self-pity is Satanic. Well, I am not understood; this is a thing they ought to apologize for; that is a point I really must have cleared up. Leave others alone and ask the Lord to give you Christ-consciousness, and He will poise you until the completeness is absolute.

The complete life is the life of a child. When I am consciously conscious, there is something wrong. It is the sick man who knows what health is. The child of God is not conscious of the will of God because he is the will of God. When there has been the slightest deviation from the will of God, we begin to ask— What is Thy will? A child of God never prays to be conscious that God answers prayer, he is so restfully certain that God always does answer prayer.

If we try to overcome self-consciousness by any common-sense method, we will develop it tremendously. Jesus says, "Come unto Me and I will give you rest," i.e., Christ-consciousness will take the place of self-consciousness. Wherever Jesus comes He establishes rest, the rest of the perfection of activity that is never conscious of itself.

If any man come to me, and hate not his own father, and mother, and wife, and children, and brethren, and sisters, yea, and his own life also, he cannot be my disciple. (Luke 14:26)

You cannot consecrate yourself *and* your friends. If at the altar your heart imagines that loving arms are still around you, and that together, lovers as lovers, and friends as friends, can enter through this mighty gate of supreme Sanctification, it is a fond dream, doomed to disillusionment. Alone! Relinquish all! You cannot consecrate your children, your wife, your lover, your friend, your father, your mother or your own life as yours. You must abandon all and fling yourself on God as a mere conscious being, and unperplexed, seeking you'll find Him. The teaching that presents consecration as giving to God our gifts, our possessions, our comrades, is a profound error. These are all abandoned, and we give up for ever *our right to ourselves*. A sanctified soul may be an artist, or a musician; but he is not a sanctified artist or musician: he is one who expresses the message of God through a particular medium. As long as the artist or musician imagines he can consecrate his artistic gifts to God, he is deluded. Abandonment of ourselves is the kernel of consecration, not presenting our gifts, but presenting ourselves without reserve.

DL 88

THE MINISTRY OF THE UNNOTICED

Blessed are the poor in spirit. (Matt. 5:3)

The New Testament notices things which from our standards do not seem to count. "Blessed are the poor in spirit," literally—Blessed are the paupers—an exceedingly commonplace thing! The preaching of to-day is apt to emphasize strength of will, beauty of character—the things that are easily noticed. The phrase we hear so often, Decide for Christ, is an emphasis on something Our Lord never trusted. He never asks us to decide for Him, but to yield to Him—a very different thing. At the basis of Jesus Christ's Kingdom is the unaffected loveliness of the commonplace. The thing I am blessed in is my poverty. If I know I have no strength of will, no nobility of disposition, then Jesus says—Blessed are you, because it is through this poverty that I enter His Kingdom. I cannot enter His Kingdom as a good man or woman, I can only enter it as a complete pauper.

The true character of the loveliness that tells for God is always unconscious. Conscious influence is priggish and un-Christian. If I say—I wonder if I am of any use—I instantly lose the bloom of the touch of the Lord. "He that believeth in me, out of him shall flow rivers of living water." If I examine the outflow, I lose the touch of the Lord.

Which are the people who have influenced us most? Not the ones who thought they did, but those who had not the remotest notion that they were influencing us. In the Christian life the implicit is never conscious; if it is conscious it ceases to have this unaffected loveliness which is the characteristic of the touch of Jesus. We always know when Jesus is at work because He produces in the commonplace something that is inspiring.

*If any man would come after me, let him deny himself, and take
up his cross, and follow me. (Matthew 16:24)*

Is there any use in beating about the bush? We call ourselves
Christians, what does our Christianity amount to practically?
Has it made any difference to my natural individual life? It
cannot unless I deliberately give up my right to myself to Jesus,
and as His disciple begin to work out the personal salvation
He has worked in. Independence must be blasted right out of
a saint. God's providence seems to pay no attention whatever
to our individual ideas because He is after only one thing—
'that they may be one, even as we are one'. It may look like a
thorough breaking up of the life, but it will end in a manifestation of the Christian self in oneness with God. Sanctification
is the work of Christ in me, the sign that I am no longer independent, but completely dependent upon Him. Sin in its essential working is independence of God: personal dependence
upon God is the attitude of the Holy Ghost in my soul.

SHL 87

"I INDEED . . . BUT HE"

I indeed baptize you with water . . . but He . . . shall baptize you
with the Holy Ghost and fire. (Matt. 3:11)

Have I ever come to a place in my experience where I can say—
"I indeed—but He"? Until that moment does come, I will never
know what the baptism of the Holy Ghost means. *I indeed* am
at an end, I cannot do a thing *but He* begins just there—He does
the things no one else can ever do. Am I prepared for His coming? Jesus cannot come as long as there is anything in the way
either of goodness or badness. When He comes am I prepared
for Him to drag into the light every wrong thing I have done?
It is just there that He comes. Wherever I know I am unclean,
He will put His feet; wherever I think I am clean, He will withdraw them.

Repentance does not bring a sense of sin, but a sense of
unutterable unworthiness. When I repent, I realize that I am
utterly helpless; I know all through me that I am not worthy
even to bear His shoes. Have I repented like that? Or is there a
lingering suggestion of standing up for myself? The reason God
cannot come into my life is because I am not through into repentance.

"*He* shall baptize you with the Holy Ghost and fire." John
does not speak of the baptism of the Holy Ghost as an experience, but as a work performed by Jesus Christ. "He shall baptize you." The only conscious experience those who are baptized with the Holy Ghost ever have is a sense of absolute
unworthiness.

I indeed was this and that; *but He* came, and a marvelous thing
happened. Get to the margin where He does everything.

Let him deny himself. (Matthew 16:24)

The critical moment in a man or woman's life is when they realize they are individually separate from other people. When I realize I am separate from everyone else, the danger is that I think I am different from everyone else. Immediately I think that, I become a law to myself; that means I excuse everything I do, but nothing anyone else does. 'My temptations are peculiar,' I say; 'my setting is very strange; no one knows but myself the peculiar forces that are in me.' When first that big sense awakens that I am different from everyone else, it is the seed of all lawlessness and all immoralities . . .

It would serve us well if we thought a great deal more from the ethical side of our Christian work than we do. We think of it always from the spiritual side because that is the natural way for us, but when we think of it from the ethical side we get at it from a different angle. More damage is done because souls have been left alone on the moral side than Christian workers ever dream, simply because their eyes are blinded by seeing only along the spiritual line. When once the powers of a nature, young or old, begin to awaken it realizes that it is an individual; that it has a power of knowing without reasoning, and it begins to be afraid because it is alone and looks for a companion, and the devil is there always to supply the need. Remember the old proverb—'If you knock long enough at a door the devil may open it.' The Bible indicates that there is a wrong as well as a right perseverance.

PS 33

PRAYER CHOICE AND
PRAYER CONFLICT

When thou prayest, enter into thy closet, and . . . pray to thy
Father which is in secret. (Matt. 6:6)

Jesus did not say—Dream about thy Father in secret, but *pray*
to thy Father in secret. Prayer is an effort of will. After we have
entered our secret place and have shut the door, the most difficult thing to do is to pray; we cannot get our minds into
working order, and the first thing that conflicts is wandering
thoughts. The great battle in private prayer is the overcoming
of mental wool-gathering. We have to discipline our minds and
concentrate on wilful prayer.

We must have a selected place for prayer and when we get
there the plague of flies begins—This must be done, and that.
"Shut thy door." A secret silence means to shut the door deliberately on emotions and remember God. God is in secret,
and He sees us from the secret place; He does not see us as other
people see us, or as we see ourselves. When we live in the secret
place it becomes impossible for us to doubt God, we become
more sure of Him than of anything else. Your Father, Jesus says,
is in secret and nowhere else. Enter the secret place, and right
in the centre of the common round you find God there all the
time. Get into the habit of dealing with God about everything.
Unless in the first waking moment of the day you learn to fling
the door wide back and let God in, you will work on a wrong
level all day; but swing the door wide open and pray to your
Father in secret, and every public thing will be stamped with
the presence of God.

Ye are the light of the world. (Matthew 5:14)

Individuality is a smaller term than personality. Possibly the best illustration we can use is that of a lamp. A lamp unlighted will illustrate individuality; a lighted lamp will illustrate personality. The lighted lamp takes up no more room, but the light permeates far and wide; so the influence of personality goes far beyond that of individuality. 'Ye are the light of the world,' said our Lord. Individually we do not take up much room, but our influence is far beyond our calculation. When we use the term 'personality', we use the biggest mental conception we have, that is why we call God a Person, because the word 'person' has the biggest import we know. We do not call God an individual; we call God a Person. He may be a great deal more, but at least He must be that. It is necessary to remember this when the personality of God is denied and He is taken to be a tendency. If God is only a tendency, He is much less than we are. Our personality is always too big for us.

BP 150

THE SPIRITUAL INDEX

Or what man is there of you, whom if his son ask bread, will he give him a stone? (Matt. 7:9)

The illustration of prayer that Our Lord uses here is that of a good child asking for a good thing. We talk about prayer as if God heard us irrespective of the fact of our relationship to Him (cf. Matthew 5:45). Never say it is not God's will to give you what you ask, don't sit down and faint, but find out the reason, turn up the index. Are you rightly related to your wife, to your husband, to your children, to your fellow-students—are you a "good child" there? "O Lord, I have been irritable and cross, but I do want spiritual blessing." You cannot have it, you will have to do without until you come into the attitude of a good child.

We mistake defiance for devotion; arguing with God for abandonment. We will not look at the index. Have I been asking God to give me money for something I want when there is something I have not paid for? Have I been asking God for liberty while I am withholding it from someone who belongs to me? I have not forgiven someone his trespasses; I have not been kind to him; I have not been living as God's child among my relatives and friends (v. 12).

I am a child of God only by regeneration, and as a child of God I am good only as I walk in the light. Prayer with most of us is turned into pious platitude, it is a matter of emotion, mystical communion with God. Spiritually we are all good at producing fogs. If we turn up the index, we will see very clearly what is wrong—that friendship, that debt, that temper of mind. It is no use praying unless we are living as children of God. Then, Jesus says—"Everyone that asketh receiveth."

And he gave some to be apostles: and some prophets: and some, evangelists: and some, pastors and teachers; . . . till we all attain unto the unity of the faith. (Ephesians 4:11–13)

These verses do not refer to individual Christian lives but to the collective life of the saints. The individual saint cannot be perfected apart from others. 'He gave some to be apostles . . .' for what purpose? To show how clever they were, what gifts they had? No, 'for the perfecting of the saints'. In looking back over the history of the Church we find that every one of these 'gifts' has been tackled. Paul says that apostles, prophets, evangelists, pastors and teachers, are all meant for one thing by God, viz., 'for the perfecting of the saints . . . unto the building up of the body of Christ'. No saint can ever be perfected in isolation or in any other way than God has laid down. There are very few who are willing to apprehend that for which they were apprehended, they thank God for salvation and sanctification and then stagnate, consequently the perfecting of the saints is hindered.

PS 44

THE FRUITFULNESS OF FRIENDSHIP

I have called you friends. (John 15:15)

We never know the joy of self-sacrifice until we abandon in every particular. Self-surrender is the most difficult thing—I will if . . .! Oh, well, I suppose I must devote my life to God. There is none of the joy of self-sacrifice in that.

As soon as we do abandon, the Holy Ghost gives us an intimation of the joy of Jesus. The final aim of self-sacrifice is laying down our lives for our Friend. When the Holy Ghost comes in, the great desire is to lay down the life for Jesus, and the thought of sacrifice never touches us because sacrifice is the love passion of the Holy Ghost.

Our Lord is our example in the life of self-sacrifice—"I delight to do Thy will, O my God." He went on with His sacrifice with exuberant joy. Have I ever yielded in absolute submission to Jesus Christ? If Jesus Christ is not the lodestar, there is no benefit in the sacrifice; but when the sacrifice is made with the eyes on Him, slowly and surely the moulding influence begins to tell.

Beware of letting natural affinities hinder your walk in love. One of the most cruel ways of killing natural love is by disdain built on natural affinities. The affinity of the saint is the Lord Jesus. Love for God is not sentimental, for the saint to love as God loves is the most practical thing.

"I have called you friends." It is a friendship based on the new life created in us which has no affinity with our old life, but only with the life of God. It is unutterably humble, unsulliedly pure, and absolutely devoted to God.

And for their sakes I sanctify myself. (John 17:19)

How does that statement of our Lord fit in with our idea of sanctification? Sanctification must never be made synonymous with purification; Jesus Christ had no need of purification, and yet He used the word 'sanctify'. In the words, 'I sanctify myself', Jesus gives the key to the saint's life. Self is not sinful; if it were, how could Jesus say 'I sanctify myself? Jesus Christ had no sin to deny, no wrong self to deny; He had only a holy Self. It was that Self He denied all the time, and it was that Self that Satan tried to make Him obey. What could be holier than the will of the holy Son of God? and yet all through He said, 'not as I will, but as thou wilt'. It was the denying of His holy Self that made the marvellous beauty of our Lord's life.

If we have entered into the experience of sanctification, what are we doing, with our holy selves? Do we every morning we waken thank God that we have a self to give to Him, a self that He has purified and adjusted and baptized with the Holy Ghost so that we might sacrifice it to Him? Sacrifice in its essence is the exuberant, passionate love-gift of the best I have to the one I love best. The best gift the Son of God had was His Holy Manhood, and He gave that as a love-gift to God that He might use it as an Atonement for the world. He poured out His soul unto death, and that is to be the characteristic of our lives. God is at perfect liberty to waste us if He chooses. We are sanctified for one purpose only, that we might sanctify our sanctification and give it to God.

MFL 107

ARE YOU EVER DISTURBED?

Peace I leave with you, My peace I give unto you. (John 14:27)

There are times when our peace is based upon ignorance, but when we awaken to the facts of life, inner peace is impossible unless it is received from Jesus. When Our Lord speaks peace, He makes peace; His words are ever "spirit and life." Have I ever received what Jesus speaks? *"My peace I give unto you"*—it is a peace which comes from looking into His face and realizing His undisturbedness.

Are you painfully disturbed just now, distracted by the waves and billows of God's providential permission, and having, as it were, turned over the boulders of your belief, are you still finding no well of peace or joy or comfort; is all barren? Then look up and receive the undisturbedness of the Lord Jesus. Reflected peace is the proof that you are right with God because you are at liberty to turn your mind to Him. If you are not right with God, you can never turn your mind anywhere but on yourself. If you allow anything to hide the face of Jesus Christ from you, you are either disturbed or you have a false security.

Are you looking unto Jesus now, in the immediate matter that is pressing and receiving from Him peace? If so, He will be a gracious benediction of peace in and through you. But if you try to worry it out, you obliterate Him and deserve all you get. We get disturbed because we have not been considering Him. When one confers with Jesus Christ the perplexity goes, because He has no perplexity, and our only concern is to abide in Him. Lay it all out before Him, and in the face of difficulty, bereavement and sorrow, hear Him say, "Let not your heart be troubled."

> *It is enough for the disciple that he be as his master.*
> *(Matthew 10:25)*

At first sight this looks like an enormous honour: to be 'as his master' is marvellous glory—is it? Look at Jesus as He was when He was here, it was anything but glory. He was easily ignorable, saving to those who knew Him intimately; to the majority of men He was 'as a root out of a dry ground'. For thirty years He was obscure, then for three years He went through popularity, scandal, and hatred; He succeeded in gathering a handful of fishermen as disciples, one of whom betrayed Him, one denied Him, and all forsook Him; and He says, 'It is enough for you to be like that.' The idea of evangelical success, Church prosperity, civilized manifestation, does not come into it at all. When we fulfil the conditions of spiritual life we become unobtrusively real.

SHL 105

Many who knew our Lord while He was on earth saw nothing in Him; only after their disposition had been altered did they realize Who He was. Our Lord lived so ordinary a life that no one noticed Him . . . Could anything more startling be imagined than for someone to point out a Nazarene carpenter and say, 'That man is God Incarnate'? It would sound blasphemous to a Pharisee.

MU 43

THEOLOGY ALIVE

Walk while ye have the light, lest darkness come upon you.
(John 12:35)

Beware of not acting upon what you see in your moments on the mount with God. If you do not obey the light, it will turn into darkness. "If therefore the light that is in thee be darkness, how great is that darkness!" The second you waive the question of sanctification or any other thing upon which God gave you light, you begin to get dry rot in your spiritual life. Continually bring the truth out into actuality; work it out in every domain, or the very light you have will prove a curse.

The most difficult person to deal with is the one who has the smug satisfaction of an experience to which he can refer back, but who is not working it out in practical life. If you *say* you are sanctified, *show it*. The experience must be so genuine that it is shown in the life. Beware of any belief that makes you self-indulgent; it came from the pit, no matter how beautiful it sounds.

Theology must work itself out in the most practical relationships. "Except your righteousness shall *exceed* the righteousness of the scribes and Pharisees . . ." said Our Lord, i.e., you must be more moral than the most moral being you know. You may know all about the doctrine of sanctification, but are you running it out into the practical issues of your life? Every bit of your life, physical, moral and spiritual, is to be judged by the standard of the Atonement.

Casting down imaginations, and every high thing that exalteth itself against the knowledge of God, and bringing into captivity every thought to the obedience of Christ. (2 Corinthians 10:5)

Obedience to the Holy Spirit will mean that we have power to direct our ideas. It is astonishing how we sit down under the dominance of an idea, whether a right or a wrong idea, and saints have sat down under this idea more than any other, that they cannot help thoughts of evil. Thank God that's a lie, we can. If you have never realized this before, put it to the test and ask yourself why the Spirit of God through the apostle Paul should say, '. . . bringing every thought into captivity to the obedience of Christ' if we cannot do it? Never sit down under ideas that have no part or lot in God's Book; trace the idea to its foundation and see where it comes from. The Bible makes it plain that we can help thoughts of evil; it is Satan's interest to make us think we cannot. God grant the devil may be kept off the brains of the saints!

BE 71

WHAT'S THE GOOD OF PRAYER?

Lord, teach us to pray. (Luke 11:1)

It is not part of the life of a natural man to pray. We hear it said that a man will suffer in his life if he does not pray; I question it. What will suffer is the life of the Son of God in him, which is nourished not by food, but by prayer. When a man is born from above, the life of the Son of God is born in him, and he can either starve that life or nourish it. Prayer is the way the life of God is nourished. Our ordinary views of prayer are not found in the New Testament. We look upon prayer as a means of getting things for ourselves; the Bible idea of prayer is that we may get to know God Himself.

"Ask and ye shall receive." We grouse before God, we are apologetic or apathetic, but we ask very few things. Yet what a splendid audacity a childlike child has! Our Lord says—"Except ye become as little children." Ask, and God will do. Give Jesus Christ a chance, give Him elbow room, and no man will ever do this unless he is at his wits' end. When a man is at his wits' end it is not a cowardly thing to pray, it is the only way he can get into touch with Reality. Be yourself before God and present your problems, the things you know you have come to your wits' end over. As long as you are self-sufficient, you do not need to ask God for anything.

It is not so true that "prayer changes things" as that prayer changes *me* and I change things. God has so constituted things that prayer on the basis of Redemption alters the way in which a man looks at things. Prayer is not a question of altering things externally, but of working wonders in a man's disposition.

*Then the waters had overwhelmed us, the stream had gone over
our soul. (Psalm 124:4)*

One element in the alternative danger that attends the saints
of God is the agony it produces. It is strange that God should
make it that 'through the shadow of an agony cometh Redemption'; strange that God's Son should be made perfect through
suffering; strange that suffering should be one of the golden
pathways for God's children. There are times in personal life
when we are brought into an understanding of what Abraham
experienced. 'Get thee out of thy country . . . ' It is not so much
that we are misunderstood, but that suffering is brought on
others through our being loyal to God, and it produces agony
for which there is no relief on the human side, only on God's
side. When we pray 'Thy Kingdom come' we have to share in
the pain of the world being born again; it is a desperate pain.
God's servants are, as it were, the birth-throes of the new age.
'My little children, of whom I travail in birth again until Christ
be formed in you' (Galatians 4:19). Many of us receive the Holy
Ghost, but immediately the throes begin we misunderstand
God's purpose. We have to enter into the travail with Him until
the world is born again. The world must be born again just as
individuals are.

PSB 24

SUBLIME INTIMACY

*Said I not unto thee, that, if thou wouldest believe thou shouldest
see the glory of God? (John 11:40)*

Every time you venture out in the life of faith, you will find
something in your common-sense circumstances that flatly
contradicts your faith. Common sense is not faith, and faith is
not common sense; they stand in the relation of the natural
and the spiritual. Can you trust Jesus Christ where your common sense cannot trust Him? Can you venture heroically on
Jesus Christ's statements when the facts of your common-sense
life shout—"It's a lie"? On the mount it is easy to say—"Oh,
yes, I believe God can do it"; but you have to come down into
the demon-possessed valley and meet with facts that laugh
ironically at the whole of your mount-of-transfiguration belief. Every time my programme of belief is clear to my own
mind, I come across something that contradicts it. Let me say
I believe God will supply all my need, and then let me run dry,
with no outlook, and see whether I will go through the trial of
faith, or whether I will sink back to something lower.

Faith must be tested, because it can be turned into a personal possession only through conflict. What is your faith up
against just now? The test will either prove that your faith is
right, or it will kill it. "Blessed is he whosoever shall not be
offended in Me." The final thing is confidence in Jesus. Believe
steadfastly on Him and all you come up against will develop
your faith. There is continual testing in the life of faith, and
the last great test is death. May God keep us in fighting trim!
Faith is unutterable trust in God, trust which never dreams that
He will not stand by us.

They that sow in tears shall reap in joy. He that goeth forth and weepeth, bearing precious seed, shall doubtless come again with rejoicing, bringing his sheaves with him. (Psalm 126:5–6)

We make the blunder of wanting to sow and plough and reap all at the same time. We forget what our Lord said, that '—it looks as if the seed were drowned. You can see the seed when it is in the basket, but when it falls into the ground, it disappears (see John 12:24). The same thing is true with regard to Sunday school work or meetings, it looks as if everything were flung away, you cannot see anything happening; but the seed is there. 'They that sow in tears *shall reap in joy.*' 'Cast thy bread upon the waters: for thou shalt find it after many days.' The seed is the word of God, and no word of God is ever fruitless. If I know that the sowing is going to bring forth fruit, I am blessed in the drudgery. Drudgery is never blessed, but drudgery can be enlightened. The Psalmist says, 'Thou hast enlarged me in distress'; the enlargement comes through knowing that God is looking after everything. Before, when I came to a difficult bit of the way, I was staggered, but now through the affliction and suffering I can put my foot down more firmly (see Romans 8:35–9).

PSB 36

AM I CONVINCED BY CHRIST?

*Notwithstanding in this rejoice not . . ., but rather rejoice because
your names are written in heaven. (Luke 10:19, 20)*

Jesus Christ says, in effect, Don't rejoice in successful service,
but rejoice because you are rightly related to Me. The snare in
Christian work is to rejoice in successful service, to rejoice in
the fact that God has used you. You never can measure what
God will do through you if you are rightly related to Jesus
Christ. Keep your relationship right with Him, then whatever
circumstances you are in, and whoever you meet day by day,
He is pouring rivers of living water through you, and it is of
His mercy that He does not let you know it. When once you
are rightly related to God by salvation and sanctification, remember that wherever you are, you are put there by God; and
by the reaction of your life on the circumstances around you,
you will fulfil God's purpose, as long as you keep in the light
as God is in the light.

The tendency to-day is to put the emphasis on service. Beware of the people who make usefulness their ground of appeal. If you make usefulness the test, then Jesus Christ was
the greatest failure that ever lived. The lodestar of the saint is
God Himself, not estimated usefulness. It is the work that God
does through us that counts, not what we do for Him. All that
Our Lord heeds in a man's life is the relationship of worth to
His Father. Jesus is bringing many *sons* to glory.

Though our outward man perish, yet the inward man is renewed
day by day. (2 Corinthians 4:16)

The apostle Paul continually had external depression, he had
agonies and distresses, terrible persecution and tumults in his
life, but he never had the 'blues', simply because he had learned
the secret that the measure of the inner glory is the wasting of
the outward man. The outer man was being wasted, Paul knew
it and felt it, but the inner man was being renewed, every
wasting meant a corresponding winging on the inside. Some
of us are so amazingly lazy, so comfortably placed in life, that
we get no inner winging. The natural life, apart altogether from
sin, must be sacrificed to the will and the word of God, otherwise there is no spiritual glory for the individual. With some
of us the body is not wearing away, our souls are stagnant, and
the vision spiritually is not getting brighter; but once we get
into the heavenlies, live there, and work from that standpoint,
we find we have the glorious opportunity of spending all our
bodily energies in God's service, and a corresponding weight
of moral and spiritual glory remains all the time.

MIC 81

MY JOY . . . YOUR JOY

That My joy might remain in you, and that your joy might be full. (John 15:11)

What was the joy that Jesus had? It is an insult to use the word happiness in connection with Jesus Christ. The joy of Jesus was the absolute self-surrender and self-sacrifice of Himself to His Father, the joy of doing that which the Father sent Him to do. "I delight to do Thy will." Jesus prayed that our joy might go on fulfilling itself until it was the same joy as His. Have I allowed Jesus Christ to introduce His joy to me?

The full flood of my life is not in bodily health, not in external happenings, not in seeing God's work succeed, but in the perfect understanding of God, and in the communion with Him that Jesus Himself had. The first thing that will hinder this joy is the captious irritation of thinking out circumstances. The cares of this world, said Jesus, will choke God's word. Before we know where we are, we are caught up in the show of things. All that God has done for us is the mere threshold; He wants to get us to the place where we will be His witnesses and proclaim Who Jesus is.

Be rightly related to God, find your joy there, and out of you will flow rivers of living water. Be a centre for Jesus Christ to pour living water through. Stop being self-conscious, stop being a sanctified prig, and live the life hid with Christ. The life that is rightly related to God is as natural as breathing wherever it goes. The lives that have been of most blessing to you are those who were unconscious of it.

Even to them that are called according to his purpose.
(Romans 8:28)

To talk about our intercession for another soul being the means of doing what the Bible says, 'the effectual fervent prayer of a righteous man availeth much', sounds utterly ridiculous until we get the basal thinking revealed through the Atonement and the indwelling Holy Ghost, then it is an amazing revelation of the marvellous love and condescension of God—that in Christ Jesus and by the reception of the Holy Spirit, He can take us, sin-broken, sin-diseased, wrong creatures, and re-make us entirely until we are really the ones in whom the Holy Spirit intercedes as we do our part. Are we making it easy for the Holy Spirit to work out God's will in us, or are we continually putting Him on one side by the empty requests of our natural hearts. Christians though we be? Are we learning to bring ourselves into such obedience that our every thought and imagination is brought into captivity to the Lord Jesus Christ, and is the Holy Spirit having an easy way through us more and more? Remember, your intercessions can never be mine, and my intercessions can never be yours, But the Holy ghost makes intercession in our particular editions, without which inter-cession someone will be impoverished. Let us remember the depth and height and solemnity of our calling as saints.

IYA 108

SEPTEMBER

DESTINY OF HOLINESS

Ye shall be holy; for I am holy. (1 Peter 1:16, R.V.)

Continually restate to yourself what the purpose of your life is. The destined end of man is not happiness, nor health, but holiness. Nowadays we have far too many affinities, we are dissipated with them; right, good, noble affinities which will yet have their fulfillment, but in the meantime God has to atrophy them. The one thing that matters is whether a man will accept the God Who will make him holy. At all costs a man must be rightly related to God.

Do I believe I need to be holy? Do I believe God can come into me and make me holy? If by your preaching you convince me that I am unholy, I resent your preaching. The preaching of the gospel awakens an intense resentment because it must reveal that I am unholy; but it also awakens an intense craving. God has one destined end for mankind, viz., holiness. His one aim is the production of saints. God is not an eternal blessing-machine for men; He did not come to save men out of pity: He came to save men because He had created them to be holy. The Atonement means that God can put me back into perfect union with Himself, without a shadow between, through the Death of Jesus Christ.

Never tolerate through sympathy with yourself or with others any practice that is not in keeping with a holy God. Holiness means unsullied walking with the feet, unsullied talking with the tongue, unsullied thinking with the mind—every detail of the life under the scrutiny of God. Holiness is not only what God gives me, but what I manifest that God has given me.

And they heard the voice ('sound', RV marg.) of the Lord God walking in the garden in the cool of the day. (Genesis 3:8)

Until Adam fell, he was not *interested in* God, he was *one with* God in communion—a man is never interested in that which he is; when Adam fell, he became so appallingly interested in God that he was afraid of Him—'and the man and his wife hid themselves from the presence of the Lord God amongst the trees of the garden'. Sin finds us severed from God and interested only in anything we can be told about Him, consequently there is an element of fear; when we become children of God, there is no fear. As long as a child has not done wrong he enjoys perfect freedom and confidence towards his parents, but let him disobey, and the one he disobeys becomes someone in whom he is interested, with an element of fear. Conscious piety springs from being interested in God—'I want to know whether I am right with God'; if you are right with God, you are so one with Him that you are unconscious of it, the relationship is deeper than consciousness because you are being disposed by the very nature of God.

OPG 6

THE SACRAMENT OF SACRIFICE

He that believeth in Me . . . out of him shall flow . . . (John 7:38)

Jesus did not say—"he that believeth in Me shall realize the blessing of the fulness of God," but—"he that believeth in Me out of him shall escape everything he receives." Our Lord's teaching is always *anti*-self-realization. His purpose is not the development of a man; His purpose is to make a man exactly like Himself, and the characteristic of the Son of God is self-expenditure. If we believe in Jesus, it is not what we gain, but what He pours through us that counts. It is not that God makes us beautifully rounded grapes, but that He squeezes the sweetness out of us. Spiritually, we cannot measure our life by success, but only by what God pours through us, and we cannot measure that at all.

When Mary of Bethany broke the box of precious ointment and poured it on Jesus' head, it was an act for which no one else saw any occasion; the disciples said it was a waste. But Jesus commended Mary for her extravagant act of devotion, and said that wherever His gospel was preached "this also that she hath done shall be spoken of for a memorial of her." Our Lord is carried beyond Himself with joy when He sees any of us doing what Mary did, not being set on this or that economy, but being abandoned to Him. God spilt the life of His Son that the world might be saved; are we prepared to spill out our lives for Him?

"He that believeth in Me out of him shall flow rivers of living water"—hundreds of other lives will be continually refreshed. It is time now to break the life, to cease craving for satisfaction, and to spill the thing out. Our Lord is asking who of us will do it for Him?

> *As ye have therefore received Christ Jesus the Lord, so walk ye in him. (Colossians 2:6)*

Our right standing is proved by the fact that we can walk; if we are not rightly related to God in our thinking we cannot walk properly. Walk means character. If we have only our own energy and devotion and earnestness to go on we cannot walk at all; but if we are based on the revelation that if we receive Christ Jesus the Lord we are complete in Him, then we can begin to walk according to the perfection we have in Him. When God brings us up against difficult circumstances that reveal the inability of our human nature it is not that we may sink back and say, 'Oh dear, I thought I should have been all right by now'; it is that we may learn to draw on our union with Jesus Christ and claim that we have sufficient grace to do this particular thing according to God's will. If we are vitally connected with God in our thinking we shall find we can walk; but if we have not been thinking rightly we will succumb—'I can't do this'. If we are thinking along the line of God's grace, that He is able to make all grace abound unto us, we will not only stand, but walk as a son or daughter of God and prove that His grace is sufficient. To be weak in God's strength is a crime.

GW 13

THE WATERS OF SATISFACTION
SCATTERED

. . . Nevertheless he would not drink thereof, but poured it out unto the Lord. (2 Sam. 23:16)

What has been like water from the well of Bethlehem to you recently—love, friendship, spiritual blessing? Then at the peril of your soul, you take it to satisfy yourself. If you do, you cannot pour it out before the Lord. You can never sanctify to God that with which you long to satisfy yourself. If you satisfy yourself with a blessing from God, it will corrupt you; you must sacrifice it, pour it out, do with it what common sense says is an absurd waste.

How am I to pour out unto the Lord natural love or spiritual blessing? In one way only—in the determination of my mind. There are certain acts of other people which one could never accept if one did not know God, because it is not within human power to repay them. But immediately I say—This is too great and worthy for me, it is not meant for a human being at all, I must pour it out unto the Lord, then these things pour out in rivers of living water all around. Until I do pour these things out before the Lord, they endanger those I love as well as myself because they will turn to lust. We can be lustful in things which are not sordid and vile. Love has to get to its transfiguration point of being poured out unto the Lord.

If you have become bitter and sour, it is because when God gave you a blessing you clutched it for yourself; whereas if you had poured it out unto the Lord, you would have been the sweetest person out of heaven. If you are always taking blessings to yourself and never learn to pour out anything unto the Lord, other people do not get their horizon enlarged through you.

. . . so walk ye in him. (Colossians 2:6)

God has to deal with us on the death side as well as on the life side. It is all very well to know in theory that there are things we must not trust in, but another thing to know it in fact. When God deals with us on the death side He puts the sentence of death on everything we should not trust in, and we have a miserable time until we learn never any more to trust in it, never any more to look anywhere else than to God. It sometimes happens that hardly a day passes without God saying, 'Don't trust there, that is dead.'

Then He deals with us on the life side and reveals to us all that is ours in Christ Jesus, and there comes in the overflowing strength of God, the unsearchable riches in Christ Jesus. Whether God is dealing with us on the death side or the life side, it is all in order to teach us how to walk, how to try our standing in Christ Jesus. God is teaching us to try our steps in faith, and it is a very tottering business to begin with, we clutch hold of everything; God gives us any amount of encouragement, 'ribbons' of blessings, of feelings and touches that make us know His presence; then He withdraws them and slowly we get strengthened on our feet and learn how to walk in Him.

GW 13

HIS!

Thine they were, and Thou gavest them Me. (John 17:6)

The missionary is one in whom the Holy Ghost has wrought this realization—"Ye are not your own." To say, "I am not my own" is to have reached a great point in spiritual nobility. The true nature of the life in the actual whirl is the deliberate giving up of myself to another in sovereign preference, and that other is Jesus Christ. The Holy Spirit expounds the nature of Jesus Christ to me in order to make me one with my Lord, not that I might go off as a showroom exhibit. Our Lord never sent any of the disciples out on the ground of what He had done for them. It was not until after the Resurrection, when the disciples had perceived by the power of the Holy Spirit Whom He was, that Jesus said "Go."

"If any man come to me and hate not . . ., he cannot be My disciple," not, he cannot be good and upright, but, he cannot be one over whom Jesus writes the word "Mine." Any one of the relationships Our Lord mentions may be a competitive relationship. I may prefer to belong to my mother, or to my wife, or to myself; then, says Jesus, you cannot be My disciple. This does not mean I will not be saved, but it does mean that I cannot be "His."

Our Lord makes a disciple His own possession, He becomes responsible for him. "Ye shall be witnesses unto Me." The spirit that comes in is not that of *doing* anything for Jesus, but of being a perfect delight to Him. The secret of the missionary is—I am His, and He is carrying out His enterprises through me.

Be entirely His.

Ye were running well; who did hinder you . . . ? (Galatians 5:7)

An undertow is an undercurrent flowing in a different direction from the water at the surface. It is the undercurrent that drowns; a swimmer will never plunge into an undercurrent, a fool will. The spiritual undertow that switched away the Galatians was Judaism, formalism. It was not dominant, but hidden; it ran in exactly the opposite direction to the current of liberty into which they were being brought by Christ. Instead of going out to sea, out into the glorious liberty of the children of God, they were being switched away. 'Ye were running well . . . ' they had been heading straight for the ocean, but the undercurrent of ritualism bewitched them, hindered them from obeying the truth. After a big transaction with God the current of your life heads you straight out to sea, right over the harbour bar, every sail set; now be alert for the spiritual undertow that would suck you back. The undercurrent is always most dangerous just where the river merges with the sea. The undercurrent is of the same nature as the river and will take you back into its swirling current; not out into the main stream, but back to the shipwrecks on the bank. The most pitiable of all wrecks are those inside the harbour . . .

Be alert for the spiritual undertow, the current that sets in another direction. It is after the floodtide of a spiritual transaction that the undertow begins to tell, and to tell terribly. The undercurrent for each one of us is different. It is only felt at certain stages of the tide; when the tide is full there is no undercurrent.

PH 48

THE MISSIONARY WATCHING

Watch with Me. (Matt. 26:40)

"Watch with Me"—with no private point of view of your own at all, but watch entirely with Me. In the early stages we do not watch with Jesus, we watch for Him. We do not watch with Him through the revelation of the Bible, in the circumstances of our lives. Our Lord is trying to introduce us to identification with Himself in a particular Gethsemane, and we will not go; we say—"No, Lord, I cannot see the meaning of this, it is bitter." How can we possibly watch with Someone Who is inscrutable? How are we going to understand Jesus sufficiently to watch with Him in His Gethsemane, when we do not know even what His suffering is for? We do not know how to watch with Him; we are only used to the idea of Jesus watching with us.

The disciples loved Jesus Christ to the limit of their natural capacity, but they did not understand what He was after. In the Garden of Gethsemane they slept for their own sorrow, and at the end of three years of the closest intimacy they "all forsook Him and fled."

"They were all filled with the Holy Ghost"—the same "they," but something wonderful has happened in between—Our Lord's Death and Resurrection and Ascension; and the disciples have been invaded by the Holy Spirit. Our Lord had said—"Ye shall receive power after that the Holy Ghost is come upon you," and this meant that they learned to watch with Him all the rest of their lives.

And it came to pass in those days, when Moses was grown, that he went out unto his brethren, and looked on their burdens. (Exodus 2:11)

That is an indication of the vision of God's purpose for Moses, viz., the deliverance of his brethren. It is a great moment in a man's life when he realizes that he has to go a solitary way alone. Moses was 'learned in all the wisdom of the Egyptians', a man in a royal setting by the providence of God, and he saw the burden of God's people, and his whole heart and mind was ablaze with the vision that he was the man to deliver them. He *was* the man to deliver his people, but not yet, there was something in the road, and God sent him into the wilderness to feed sheep for forty years. Imagine what those years must have meant to Moses, realizing on the threshold of his manhood the vision of what he was to do; seeing, as no one else could see, the burdens of his people, and feeling in himself the certainty that he was the one to deliver them; how he would ponder over God's ways during those forty years . . .

Think of the enormous leisure of God! He never is in a hurry. We are in such a frantic hurry. We get down before God and pray, then we get up and say, 'It is all done now', and in the light of the glory of the vision we go forth to do the thing. But it is not real, and God has to take us into the valley and put us through fires and floods to batter us into shape, until we get into the condition in which He can trust us with the reality of His recognition of us.

SSY 29, 31

DIFFUSIVENESS OF LIFE

Rivers of living water. (John 7:38)

A river touches places of which its source knows nothing, and Jesus says if we have received of His fulness, however small the visible measure of our lives, out of us will flow the rivers that will bless to the uttermost parts of the earth. We have nothing to do with the outflow—"This is the work of God that ye *believe* . . ." God rarely allows a soul to see how great a blessing he is.

A river is victoriously persistent, it overcomes all barriers. For a while it goes steadily on its course, then it comes to an obstacle and for a while it is baulked, but it soon makes a pathway round the obstacle. Or a river will drop out of sight for miles, and presently emerge again broader and grander than ever. You can see God using some lives, but into your life an obstacle has come and you do not seem to be of any use. Keep paying attention to the Source, and God will either take you round the obstacle or remove it. The river of the Spirit of God overcomes all obstacles. Never get your eyes on the obstacle or on the difficulty. The obstacle is a matter of indifference to the river which will flow steadily through you if you remember to keep right at the Source. Never allow anything to come between yourself and Jesus Christ, no emotion, or experience; nothing must keep you from the one great sovereign Source.

Think of the healing and far-flung rivers nursing themselves in our souls! God has been opening up marvelous truths to our minds, and every point He has opened up is an indication of the wider power of the river He will flow through us. If you believe in Jesus, you will find that God has nourished in you mighty torrents of blessing for others.

Take heed, and beware of covetousness: for a man's life consisteth not in the abundance of the things which he possesseth. (Luke 12:15)

The thing about our Lord and His teaching which puts Him immeasurably away from us nowadays is that He is opposed to all possessions, not only of money and property, but any kind of possession. That is the thing that makes Him such a deep-rooted enemy to the modern attitude to things. The two things around which our Lord centred His most scathing teaching were money and marriage, because they are the two things that make men and women devils or saints. Covetousness is the root of all evil, whether it shows itself in money matters or in any way.

Jesus Christ nowhere stands with the anti-property league. It is an easy business for me to mentally satirize the man who owns land and money when I don't. It is easy for me to talk about what I could do with a thousand pounds if I had it; the test is what I do with the two-and-a-half pence I have got. It may be hard for a rich man to enter into the kingdom of heaven, but it is just as hard for a poor man to seek first the kingdom of God. It is not eternal perdition, it is the perdition of losing the soul for this life. Jesus thought as much of the possibility of losing the highest good through poverty as through riches. His own followers were poor, yet He said to them, 'Seek ye first'— bread and cheese? money? a new situation? clothing? food? No, 'the kingdom of God and his righteousness, and all these things shall be added unto you'. Did He know what He was talking about, this poor Carpenter who had not a pillow of His own and never enough money to pay a night's lodging and yet spoke like that, and who also said that 'the cares of this world, and the deceitfulness of riches, and the lusts of other things entering in, choke the word, and it becometh unfruitful'?

HG 67

SPRINGS OF BENIGNITY

The water that I shall give him shall be in him a well of water.
(John 4:14)

The picture Our Lord gives is not that of a channel but a fountain. "Be being filled," and the sweetness of vital relationship to Jesus will flow out of the saint as lavishly as it is imparted to him. If you find your life is not flowing out as it should, you are to blame; something has obstructed the flow. Keep right at the Source, and—you will be blessed personally? No, out of you will flow rivers of living water, irrepressible life.

We are to be centres through which Jesus can flow as rivers of living water in blessing to everyone. Some of us are like the Dead Sea, always taking in but never giving out, because we are not rightly related to the Lord Jesus. As surely as we receive from Him, He will pour out through us, and in the measure He is not pouring out, there is a defect in our relationship to Him. Is there anything between you and Jesus Christ? Is there anything that hinders your belief in Him? If not, Jesus says, out of you will flow rivers of living water. It is not a blessing passed on, not an experience stated, but a river continually flowing. Keep at the Source, guard well your belief in Jesus Christ and your relationship to Him, and there will be a steady flow for other lives, no dryness and no deadness.

Is it not too extravagant to say that out of an individual believer rivers are going to flow? "I do not see the rivers," you say. Never look at yourself from the standpoint of—Who am I? In the history of God's work you will nearly always find that it has started from the obscure, the unknown, the ignored, but the steadfastly true to Jesus Christ.

. . . be ye transformed by the renewing of your mind.
(Romans 12:2)

To renew means to transform to new life. This passage makes
it clear that we can be renewed in our mind when we choose.
We have no choice about being born into this world, but to be
born again, if we will but come to Jesus and receive His Spirit,
is within our own power. This is true all along in the Christian
life, you can be renewed in the spirit of your mind when you
choose, you can revive your mind on any line you like by sheer
force of will. Always remember that Jesus Christ's statements
force an issue of will and conscience first, and only as we obey
is there the understanding with the mind (see John 7:17). The
challenge to the will comes in the matter of study, as long as
you remain in the 'stodge' state there is no mental progress—
'I am overwhelmed by the tremendous amount there is to
know and it's no use my going on.' If you will forge through
that stage you will suddenly turn a corner where everything
that was difficult and perplexing becomes as clear as a lightning flash, but it all depends on whether you will forge ahead.
When people say, 'preach us the simple Gospel', what they
mean is, 'Preach us the thing we have always heard, the thing
that keeps us sound asleep, we don't want to see things differently'; then the sooner the Spirit of God sends a thrust through
their stagnant minds the better. Continual renewal of mind is
the only healthy state for a Christian. Beware of the ban of
finality about your present views.

BE 39

DO IT YOURSELF

Casting down imaginations and every high thing that exalteth itself against the knowledge of God. (2 Cor. 10:5)

Determinedly Demolish Some Things. Deliverance from sin is not deliverance from human nature. There are things in human nature, such as prejudices, which the saint has to destroy by neglect; and other things which have to be destroyed by violence, i.e., by the Divine strength imparted by God's Spirit. There are some things over which we are not to fight, but to stand still in and see the salvation of God; but every theory or conception which erects itself as a rampart against the knowledge of God is to be determinedly demolished by drawing on God's power, not by fleshly endeavour or compromise (v. 4).

It is only when God has altered our disposition and we have entered into the experience of sanctification that the fight begins. The warfare is not against sin; we can never fight against sin: Jesus Christ deals with sin in Redemption. The conflict is along the line of turning our natural life into a spiritual life, and this is never done easily, nor does God intend it to be done easily. It is done only by a series of moral choices. God does not make us holy in the sense of character; He makes us holy in the sense of innocence, and we have to turn that innocence into holy character by a series of moral choices. These choices are continually in antagonism to the entrenchments of our natural life, the things which erect themselves as ramparts against the knowledge of God. We can either go back and make ourselves of no account in the Kingdom of God, or we can determinedly demolish these things and let Jesus bring another son to glory.

I am crucified with Christ. (Galatians 2:20)

The evidence that I have accepted the Cross of Christ as the revelation of Redemption is that the regenerating life of God is manifested in my mortal flesh. Immediately I accept the Cross of Christ as the revelation of Redemption I am not, I must not be, the same man, I must be another man, and I must take up my cross from my Lord. The cross is the gift of Jesus to His disciples and it can only bear one aspect: 'I am not my own.' The whole attitude of the life is that I have given up my right to myself. I live like a crucified man. Unless that crisis is reached it is perilously possible for my religious life to end as a sentimental fiasco. 'I don't mind being saved from hell and receiving the Holy Spirit, but it is too much to expect me to give up my right to myself to Jesus Christ, to give up my manhood, my womanhood, all my ambitions.' Jesus said, If any man will be my disciple, those are the conditions. It is that kind of thing that offended the historic disciples, and it will offend you and me. It is a slander to the Cross of Christ to say we believe in Jesus and please ourselves all the time, choosing our own way.

TGR 99

DO IT YOURSELF

*Bringing into captivity every thought to the obedience of Christ.
(2 Cor. 10:5)*

Determinedly Discipline Other Things. This is another aspect of the strenuous nature of sainthood. Paul says, "I take every project prisoner to make it obey Christ" (MOFFAT). How much Christian work there is to-day which has never been disciplined, but has simply sprung into being by impulse! In Our Lord's life every project was disciplined to the will of His Father. There was not a movement of an impulse of His own will as distinct from His Father's—"The Son can do nothing of Himself." Then take ourselves—a vivid religious experience, and every project born of impulse put into action immediately, instead of being imprisoned and disciplined to obey Christ.

This is a day when practical work is overemphasized, and the saints who are bringing every project into captivity are criticized and told that they are not in earnest for God or for souls. True earnestness is found in obeying God, not in the inclination to serve Him that is born of undisciplined human nature. It is inconceivable, but true nevertheless, that saints are not bringing every project into captivity, but are doing work for God at the instigation of their own human nature which has not been spiritualized by determined discipline.

We are apt to forget that a man is not only committed to Jesus Christ for salvation; he is committed to Jesus Christ's view of God, of the world, of sin and of the devil, and this will mean that he must recognize the responsibility of being transformed by the renewing of his mind.

Ye are a chosen generation, a royal priesthood, an holy nation, a peculiar people. (1 Peter 2:9)

To say that the doctrine of sanctification is unnatural is not true, it is based on the way God has made us. When we are born again we become natural for the first time; as long as we are in sin we are abnormal, because sin is not normal. When we are restored by the grace of God it becomes the most natural thing to be holy, we are not forcing ourselves to be unnatural. When we are rightly related to God all our natural instincts help us to obey Him and become the greatest ally of the Holy Spirit. We disobey whenever we become independent. Independence is not strength but unrealized weakness, and is the very essence of sin. There was no independence in our Lord, the great characteristic of His life was submission to His Father.

MFL 72

Jesus Christ belonged to the order of things God originally intended for mankind; He was easily Master of the life of the sea and air and earth. If we want to know what the human race will be like on the basis of Redemption, we shall find it mirrored in Jesus Christ, a perfect oneness between God and man.

LG 25

MISSIONARY MUNITIONS

When thou wast under the fig tree, I saw thee. (John 1:48)

Worshipping as Occasion Serves. We imagine we would be all right if a big crisis arose; but the big crisis will only reveal the stuff we are made of, it will not put anything into us. "If God gives the call, of course I will rise to the occasion." You will not unless you have risen to the occasion in the workshop, unless you have been the real thing before God there. If you are not doing the thing that lies nearest, because God has engineered it; when the crisis comes instead of being revealed as fit, you will be revealed as unfit. Crises always reveal character.

The private relationship of worshipping God is the great essential of fitness. The time comes when there is no more "fig-tree" life possible, when it is out into the open, out into the glare and into the work, and you will find yourself of no value there if you have not been worshipping as occasion serves you in your home. Worship aright in your private relationships, then when God sets you free you will be ready, because in the unseen life which no one saw but God you have become perfectly fit, and when the strain comes you can be relied upon by God.

"I can't be expected to live the sanctified life in the circumstances I am in; I have no time for praying just now, no time for Bible reading, my opportunity hasn't come yet; when it does, of course I shall be all right." No, you will not. If you have not been worshipping as occasion serves, when you get into work you will not only be useless yourself, but a tremendous hindrance to those who are associated with you.

The workshop of missionary munitions is the hidden, personal, worshipping life of the saint.

Awake, thou that sleepest, and arise from the dead.
(Ephesians 5:14)

The Bible reveals that apart from the Spirit of God men have no moving emotion towards God, they are described as 'dead'; the preaching of the Gospel, the reading of the Word of God, has no answering emotion. Religious enterprise that has not learned to rely on the Holy Spirit makes everything depend on the human intellect—'God has said so-and-so, now believe it and it will be all right', but it won't. The basis of Jesus Christ's religion is the acceptance of a new Spirit, not a new creed, and the first thing the Holy Spirit does is to awaken us out of sleep. We have to learn to rely on the Holy Spirit because He alone gives the Word of God life. All our effort to pump up faith in the word of God is without quickening, without illumination. You reason to yourself and say, 'Now God says this and I am going to believe it', and you believe it, and re-believe it, and re-re-believe it, and nothing happens, simply because the vital power that makes the words living is not there. The Spirit of God always comes in surprising ways—'The wind bloweth where it listeth . . . so is everyone that is born of the Spirit.' No creed or school of thought or experience can monopolize the Spirit of God.

BE 72

MISSIONARY MUNITIONS

*If I then, your Lord and Master, have washed your feet, ye also
ought to wash one another's feet. (John 13:14)*

Ministering as Opportunity Surrounds Us. This does not
mean selecting our surroundings, it means being very selectly
God's in any haphazard surroundings which He engineers for
us. The characteristics we manifest in our immediate surroundings are indications of what we will be like in other surroundings.

The things that Jesus did were of the most menial and commonplace order, and this is an indication that it takes all God's
power in me to do the most commonplace things in His way.
Can I use a towel as He did? Towels and dishes and sandals,
all the ordinary sordid things of our lives, reveal more quickly
than anything what we are made of. It takes God Almighty
Incarnate in us to do the meanest duty as it ought to be done.

"I have given you an example that ye should do as I have
done to you." Watch the kind of people God brings around you,
and you will be humiliated to find that this is His way of revealing to you the kind of person you have been to Him. Now,
He says, exhibit to that one exactly what I have shown to you.

"Oh," you say, "I will do all that when I get out into the foreign field." To talk in this way is like trying to produce the munitions of war in the trenches—you will be killed while you
are doing it.

We have to go the "second mile" with God. Some of us get
played out in the first ten yards, because God compels us to go
where we cannot see the way, and we say—"I will wait till I
get nearer the big crisis." If we do not do the running steadily
in the little ways, we shall do nothing in the crisis.

As the Father hath sent me, even so send I you. (John 20:21)

If we are not in full conscious allegiance to our Lord, it has nothing to do with our personal salvation, but with the 'broken bread and poured out wine' aspect of life. God can never make me wine if I object to the fingers He uses to crush me with. If God would only crush me with His own fingers and say, 'Now, my son, I am going to make you broken bread and poured out wine in a particular way and everyone will know what I am doing . . . ' But when He uses someone who is not a Christian, or someone I particularly dislike, or some set of circumstances which I said I would never submit to, and begins to make *these* the crushers, I object. I must never choose the scene of my own martyrdom, nor must I choose the things God will use in order to make me broken bread and poured out wine. His own Son did not choose. God chose for His Son that He should have a devil in His company for three years. We say—I want angels, I want people better than myself, I want everything to be significantly from God, otherwise I cannot live the life, or do the thing properly; I want to be always gilt-edged. Let God do as He likes. If you are ever going to be wine to drink, you must be crushed. Grapes cannot be drunk, grapes are only wine when they have been crushed. I wonder what kind of coarse finger and thumb God has been using to squeeze you, and you have been like a marble and escaped? You are not ripe yet, and if God *had* squeezed you, the wine that came out would have been remarkably bitter. Let God go on with His crushing, because it will work His purpose in the end.

SSY 19

BY SPIRITUAL CONFUSION

Ye know not what ye ask. (Matt. 20:22)

There are times in spiritual life when there is confusion, and it is no way out to say that there ought not to be confusion. It is not a question of right and wrong, but a question of God taking you by a way which in the meantime you do not understand, and it is only by going through the confusion that you will get at what God wants.

The Shrouding of His Friendship. Luke 11:5-8. Jesus gave the illustration of the man who looked as if he did not care for his friend, and He said that that is how the Heavenly Father will appear to you at times. You will think He is an unkind friend, but remember He is not; the time will come when everything will be explained. There is a cloud on the friendship of the heart, and often even love itself has to wait in pain and tears for the blessing of fuller communion. When God looks completely shrouded, will you hang on in confidence in Him?

The Shadow on His Fatherhood. Luke 11:11-13. Jesus says there are times when your Father will appear as if He were an unnatural father, as if He were callous and indifferent, but remember He is not; I have told you—"Everyone that asketh receiveth." If there is a shadow on the face of the Father just now, hang onto it that He will ultimately give His clear revealing and justify Himself in all that He permitted.

The Strangeness of His Faithfulness. Luke 18:1-8. "When the Son of Man cometh, shall He find faith on the earth?" Will He find the faith which banks on Him in spite of the confusion? Stand off in faith believing that what Jesus said is true, though in the meantime you do not understand what God is doing. He has bigger issues at stake than the particular things you ask.

. . and he builded a city. (Genesis 4:17)

The first civilization was founded by a murderer, and the whole basis of civilized life is a vast, complicated, more or less gilded-over system of murder. We find it more conducive to human welfare not to murder men outright, we do it by a system of competition. It is ingrained in our thinking that competition and rivalry are essential to the carrying on of civilized life; that is why Jesus Christ's statements seem wild and ridiculous. They are the statements either of a madman or of God Incarnate. To carry out the Sermon on the Mount is frankly impossible to anyone but a fool, and who is the fool? The man who has been born again, and who dares to carry out in his individual life the teaching of Jesus. And what will happen? The inevitable result, not the success he would otherwise have. A hard saying, but true.

OPG 15

AFTER SURRENDER—WHAT?

I have finished the work which Thou gavest Me to do. (John 17:4)

Surrender is not the surrender of the external life, but of the will; when that is done, all is done. There are very few crises in life; the great crisis is the surrender of the will. God never crushes a man's will into surrender, He never beseeches him, He waits until the man yields up his will to Him. That battle never needs to be re-fought.

Surrender for Deliverance. "Come unto Me and I will give you rest." It is after we have begun to experience what salvation means that we surrender our wills to Jesus for rest. Whatever is perplexing heart or mind is a call to the will—"Come unto Me." It is a voluntary coming.

Surrender for Devotion. "If any man will come after Me, let him deny himself." The surrender here is of my self to Jesus, my self with His rest at the heart of it. "If you would be My disciple, give up your right to yourself to Me." Then the remainder of the life is nothing but the manifestation of this surrender. When once the surrender has taken place we never need "suppose" anything. We do not need to care what our circumstances are, Jesus is amply sufficient.

Surrender for Death. John 21:18-19. ". . . another shall gird thee." Have you learned what it means to be bound for death? Beware of a surrender which you make to God in an ecstasy; you are apt to take it back again. It is a question of being united with Jesus in His death until nothing ever appeals to you that did not appeal to Him.

After surrender—what? The whole of the life after surrender is an aspiration for unbroken communion with God.

What is man that thou art mindful of him? (Psalm 8:4)

The way we see the world outside us depends entirely upon our nervous system, and the marvel of God's construction of us is that we see things outside us as we do. For instance, the existence to us of beauty and colour and sound is due entirely to our nervous system: there is no colour to me when my eyes are shut, no sound when I am deaf, no sensation when I am asleep. If you want to know the most marvellous thing in the whole of creation, it is not the heavens, the moon and the stars, but —'What is man that thou art mindful of him? . . . Thou madest him to have dominion over the works of thy hands.' The whole of creation was designed for man, and God intended man to be master of the life upon the earth, in the air and in the sea; the reason he is not master is because of sin, but he will yet be. (See Romans 8:19–22.) Paul indicates that the problems of the grave seclusion we are in are accounted for by sin, yet it remains true that our nervous system is not a disease, but is designed by God to be the temple of the Holy Ghost.

HGM 82

IMAGINATION V. INSPIRATION

The simplicity that is in Christ. (2 Cor. 11:3)

Simplicity is the secret of seeing things clearly. A saint does not think clearly for a long while, but a saint ought to *see* clearly without any difficulty. You cannot think a spiritual muddle clear, you have to obey it clear. In intellectual matters you can think things out, but in spiritual matters you will think yourself into cotton wool. If there is something upon which God has put His pressure, obey in that matter, bring your imagination into captivity to the obedience of Christ with regard to it and everything will become as clear as daylight. The reasoning capacity comes afterwards, but we never see along that line, we see like children; when we try to be wise we see nothing (Matthew 11:25).

The tiniest thing we allow in our lives that is not under the control of the Holy Spirit is quite sufficient to account for spiritual muddle, and all the thinking we like to spend on it will never make it clear. Spiritual muddle is only made plain by obedience. Immediately we obey, we discern. This is humiliating, because when we are muddled we know the reason is in the temper of our mind. When the natural power of vision is devoted to the Holy Spirit, it becomes the power of perceiving God's will and the whole life is kept in simplicity.

I am debtor both to Greeks, and to Barbarians. (Romans 1:14)

Do I feel this sense of indebtedness to Christ that Paul felt with regard to every unsaved soul I meet, every unsaved nation? Is it a point of spiritual honour with me that I do not hoard blessings for myself? The point of spiritual honour in my life as a saint is the realization that I am a debtor to every man on the face of the earth because of the Redemption of the Lord Jesus Christ . . .

The great characteristic of Paul's life was that he realized he was not his own: he had been bought with a price, and he never forgot it . . .

'I am made all things to all men, that I might by all means save some.' Paul attracted to Jesus all the time, never to himself. He became a sacramental personality, that is, wherever he went Jesus Christ helped Himself to his life (cf. 2 Corinthians 2:14). Many of us are subtly serving our own ends, and Jesus Christ cannot help Himself to our lives; if I am abandoned to Jesus, I have no ends of my own to serve . . .

The great motive and inspiration of service is not that God has saved and sanctified me, or healed me; all that is a fact, but the great motive of service is the realization that every bit of my life that is of value I owe to the Redemption; therefore I am a bondslave of Jesus. I realize with joy that I cannot live my own life; I am a debtor to Christ, and as such I can only realize the fulfilment of His purposes in my life. To realize this sense of spiritual honour means I am spoilt for this age, for this life, spoilt from every standpoint but this one, that I can disciple men and women to the Lord Jesus.

SSY 21–3

WHAT TO RENOUNCE

But have renounced the hidden things of dishonesty. (2 Cor. 4:2)

Have you "renounced the hidden things of dishonesty"—the things that your sense of honour will not allow to come to the light? You can easily hide them. Is there a thought in your heart about anyone which you would not like to be dragged into the light? Renounce it as soon as it springs up; renounce the whole thing until there is no hidden thing of dishonesty or craftiness about you. Envy, jealousy, strife—these things arise not necessarily from the disposition of sin, but from the make-up of your body which was used for this kind of thing in days gone by (see Romans 6:19 and 1 Peter 4:1-2). Maintain a continual watchfulness so that nothing of which you would be ashamed arises in your life.

"Not walking in craftiness," that is, resorting to what will carry your point. This is a great snare. You know that God will only let you work in one way, then be careful never to catch people the other way; God's blight will be upon you if you do. Others are doing things which to you would be walking in craftiness, but it may not be so with them: God has given you another standpoint. Never blunt the sense of your Utmost for His Highest. For you to do a certain thing would mean the incoming of craftiness for an end other than the highest, and the blunting of the motive God has given you. Many have gone back because they are afraid of looking at things from God's standpoint. The great crisis comes spiritually when a man has to emerge a bit farther on than the creed he has accepted.

And as ye would that men should do to you, do ye also to them likewise. (Luke 6:31)

Over and over again we blame God for His neglect of people by our sympathy with them, we may not put it into words but by our attitude we imply that we are filling up what God has forgotten to do. Never allow that idea, never allow it to come into your mind. In all probability the Spirit of God will begin to show us that people are where they are because we have neglected to do what we ought. Today the great craze is socialism, and men are saying that Jesus Christ came as a social reformer. Nonsense! We are the social reformers; Jesus Christ came to alter us, and we try to shirk our responsibility by putting our work on Him. Jesus alters us and puts us right; then these principles of His instantly make us social reformers. They begin to work straightway where we live, in our relationship to our fathers and mothers, to our brothers and sisters, our friends, our employers, or employees. 'Consider how God has dealt with you,' says Jesus, 'and then consider that you do likewise to others.'

SSM 87

THE DIVINE REGION OF RELIGION

*But thou, when thou prayest, enter into thy closet and when thou
hast shut thy door, pray to thy Father; which is in secret.
(Matt. 6:6)*

The main idea in the legion of religion is—Your eyes upon God,
not on men. Do not have as your motive the desire to be known
as a praying man. Get an inner chamber in which to pray where
no one knows you are praying, shut the door and talk to God
in secret. Have no other motive than to know your Father in
heaven. It is impossible to conduct your life as a disciple without definite times of secret prayer.

But when ye pray use not vain repetitions . . . (v. 7). God
does not hear us because we are in earnest, but only on the
ground of Redemption. God is never impressed by our earnestness. Prayer is not simply getting things from God, that is a most
initial form of prayer; prayer is getting into perfect communion with God. If the Son of God is formed in us by regeneration, He will press forward in front of our common sense and
change our attitude to the things about which we pray.

"Everyone that *asketh* receiveth." We pray pious blether, our
will is not in it, and then we say God does not answer; we never
asked for anything. "Ye shall ask what ye *will*," said Jesus. Asking means our will is in it. Whenever Jesus talked about prayer,
He put it with the grand simplicity of a child: we bring in our
critical temper and say—Yes, but . . . Jesus said "*Ask*." But remember that we have to ask of God things that are in keeping
with the God Whom Jesus Christ revealed.

---

*We know not what we should pray for as we ought: but the Spirit
itself maketh intercession for us. (Romans 8:26)*

An abiding way of maintaining our relation to Reality is intercession. Intercession means that I strive earnestly to have my
human soul moved by the attitude of my Lord to the particular person I am praying for. That is where our work lies, and
we shirk it by becoming active workers; we do the things that
can be tabulated and scheduled, and we won't do the one thing
that has no snares. Intercession keeps the relationship to God
completely open. You cannot intercede if you do not believe
in the Reality of Redemption, you will turn intercession into
futile sympathy with human beings which only increases their
submissive content to being out of touch with God. Intercession means getting the mind of Christ about the one for whom
we pray, that is what is meant by 'filling up that which is behind of the afflictions of Christ'; and that is why there are so
few intercessors. Be careful not to enmesh yourself in more
difficulties than God has engineered for you to know; if you
know too much, more than God has engineered, you cannot
pray, the condition of the people is so crushing that you can't
get through to Reality. The true intercessor is the one who
realizes Paul's meaning when he says, 'for we know not what
we should pray for as we ought; but the Spirit itself maketh
intercession for us with groanings which cannot be uttered'.

CHI 32

WHAT'S THE GOOD OF TEMPTATION?

There hath no temptation taken you but such as is common to man. (1 Cor. 10:13)

The word "temptation" has come down in the world; we are apt to use it wrongly. Temptation is not sin, it is the thing we are bound to meet if we are men. Not to be tempted would be to be beneath contempt. Many of us, however, suffer from temptations from which we have no business to suffer, simply because we have refused to let God lift us to a higher plane where we would face temptations of another order.

A man's disposition on the inside, i.e., what he possesses in his personality, determines what he is tempted by on the outside. The temptation fits the nature of the one tempted, and reveals the possibilities of the nature. Every man has the setting of his own temptation, and the temptation will come along the line of the ruling disposition.

Temptation is a suggested short cut to the realization of the highest at which I aim—not towards what I understand as evil, but towards what I understand as good. Temptation is something that completely baffles me for a while, I do not know whether the thing is right or wrong. Temptation yielded to is lust deified, and is a proof that it was timidity that prevented the sin before.

Temptation is not something we may escape, it is essential to the full-orbed life of a man. Beware lest you think you are tempted as no one else is tempted; what you go through is the common inheritance of the race, not something no one ever went through before. God does not save us from temptations; He succours us in the midst of them (Heb. 2:18).

My soul is exceeding sorrowful, even unto death. (Matthew 26:38)

Have we for one second watched Jesus pray? Have we ever understood why the Holy Ghost and our Lord Himself were so exceptionally careful about the recording of the agony in Gethsemane? This is not the agony of a man or a martyr; this is the agony of God as Man. It is God, as Man, going through the last lap of the supreme, supernatural Redemption of the human race. We ought to give much more time than we do— a great deal more time than we do—to brooding on the fundamental truths on which the Spirit of God works the simplicity of our Christian experience . . .

Remember, what makes prayer easy is not our wits or our understanding, but the tremendous agony of God in Redemption. A thing is worth just what it costs. Prayer is not what it costs us, but what it cost God to enable us to pray. It cost God so much that a little child can pray. It cost God Almighty so much that anyone can pray. But it is time those of us who name His Name knew the secret of the cost, and the secret is here, 'My soul is exceeding sorrowful, even unto death.' These words open the door to the autobiography of our Lord's agony.

IYA 21

HIS TEMPTATION AND OURS

For we have not an high priest which cannot be touched with the feeling of our infirmities, but was in all points tempted like as we are, yet without sin. (Heb. 4:15)

Until we are born again, the only kind of temptation we understand is that mentioned by St. James—"Every man is tempted, when he is drawn away of his own lust, and enticed." But by regeneration we are lifted into another realm where there are other temptations to face, viz., the kind of temptations Our Lord faced. The temptations of Jesus do not appeal to us, they have no home at all in our human nature. Our Lord's temptations and ours move in different spheres until we are born again and become His brethren. The temptations of Jesus are not those of a man, but the temptations of God as Man. By regeneration the Son of God is formed in us, and in our physical life He has the same setting that He had on earth. Satan does not tempt us to do wrong things; he tempts us in order to make us lose what God has put into us by regeneration, viz., the possibility of being of value to God. He does not come on the line of tempting us to sin, but on the line of shifting the point of view, and only the Spirit of God can detect this as a temptation of the devil. Temptation means the test by an alien power of the possessions held by a personality. This makes the temptation of Our Lord explainable. After Jesus in His baptism had accepted the vocation of bearing away the sin of the world, He was immediately put by God's Spirit into the testing machine of the devil, but He did not tire, He went through the temptation "without sin," and He retained the possessions of His personality intact.

Strive to enter in at the strait gate. (13:24)

If you make a moral struggle and gain a moral victory, you will be a benefit to all you come across, whereas if you do not struggle, you act as a moral miasma. Gain a moral victory in chastity or in your emotional life, it may be known to no one but yourself, and you are an untold benefit to everyone else; but if you refuse to struggle everyone else is enervated. This is a recognized psychological law, although little known. Struggle to gain the mastery over selfishness, and you will be a tremendous assistance; but if you don't overcome the tendency to spiritual sluggishness and self-indulgence, you are a hindrance to all around you. These things are intangible, but they are there, and Jesus says to us, 'Strive to enter in at the strait gate.' You never get through alone. If you struggle to get through, others are the stronger and better for knowing you. The men and women who lift and inspire us are those who struggle for self, not for self-assertiveness, that is a sign of weakness, but for the development of personality. There are some people in whose company you cannot have a mean thought without being instantly rebuked.

PH 79

DO YOU CONTINUE TO GO WITH JESUS?

Ye are they which have continued with Me in My temptations.
(Luke 22:28)

It is true that Jesus Christ is with us in our temptations, but are we going with Him in His temptations? Many of us cease to go with Jesus from the moment we have an experience of what He can do. Watch when God shifts your circumstances, and see whether you are going with Jesus, or siding with the world, the flesh and the devil. We wear His badge, but are we going with Him? "From that time many of His disciples went back and walked no more with Him."

The temptations of Jesus continued throughout His earthly life, and they will continue throughout the life of the Son of God in us. Are we going with Jesus in the life we are living now?

We have the idea that we ought to shield ourselves from some of the things God brings round us. Never! God engineers circumstances and whatever they may be like we have to see that we face them while abiding continually with Him in His temptations. They are *His* temptations, not temptations to us, but temptations to the life of the Son of God in us. The honour of Jesus Christ is at stake in your bodily life. Are you remaining loyal to the Son of God in the things which beset His life in you?

Do you continue to go with Jesus? The way lies through Gethsemane, through the city gate, outside the camp; the way lies alone, and the way lies until there is no trace of a footstep left, only the voice, *"Follow Me."*

It is vain for you that ye rise up early and so late take rest, and
eat the bread of toil; for so he giveth unto his beloved sleep.
(Psalm 127:2)

I wonder if we have ever considered the Bible implications
about sleep? It is not true to say that sleep is simply meant for
physical recuperation; surely much less time than God has ordered would have served that purpose. The Revised Version
suggests a deeper, profounder ministry for sleep than mere
physical recuperation. 'For so he giveth unto his beloved *in*
sleep' (marg.). The deepest concerns of our souls whether they
be good or bad, are furthered during sleep. It is not merely a
physical fact that you go to bed perplexed and wake clear-
minded; God has been ministering to you during sleep. Sometimes God cannot get at us until we are asleep. In the Bible
there are times when in the deep slumber of the body God has
taken the souls of His servants into deeper communion with
Himself (e.g. Genesis 2:21, 15:12). Often when a problem or
perplexity harasses the mind and there seems no solution, after a night's rest you find the solution easy, and the problem
has no further perplexity. Think of the security of the saint in
sleeping or in waking. 'Thou shalt not be afraid for the terror
by night, nor for the arrow that flieth by day.' Sleep is God's
celestial nurse who croons away our consciousness, and God
deals with the unconscious life of the soul in places where only
He and His angels have charge. As you retire to rest, give your
soul and God a time together, and commit your life to God with
a conscious peace for the hours of sleep, and deep and profound developments will go on in spirit, soul and body by the
kind creating hand of our God.

PSB 38

THE DIVINE RULE OF LIFE

Be ye therefore perfect, even as your Father in heaven is perfect.
(Matt. 5:48)

Our Lord's exhortation in these verses is to be generous in our behaviour to all men. In the spiritual life beware of walking according to natural affinities. Everyone has natural affinities; some people we like and others we do not like. We must never let those likes and dislikes rule in our Christian life. "If we walk in the light as God is in the light," God will give us communion with people for whom we have no natural affinity.

The Example Our Lord gives us is not that of a good man, or even of a good Christian, but of God Himself. "Be ye therefore perfect even as your Father in heaven is perfect," show to the other man what God has shown to you; and God will give us ample opportunities in actual life to prove whether we are perfect as our Father in heaven is perfect. To be a disciple means that we deliberately identify ourselves with God's interests in other people. "That ye love one another; as I have loved you . . ."

The expression of Christian character is not good doing, but God-likeness. If the Spirit of God has transformed you within, you will exhibit Divine characteristics in your life, not good human characteristics. God's life in us expresses itself as *God's* life, not as human life trying to be godly. The secret of a Christian is that the supernatural is made natural in him by the grace of God, and the experience of this works out in the practical details of life, not in times of communion with God. When we come in contact with things that create a buzz, we find to our amazement that we have power to keep wonderfully poised in the centre of it all.

> *Therefore take no thought . . . for your heavenly Father knoweth.*
> *(Matthew 6:31–2)*

To have faith tests a man for all he is worth, he has to stand in the common-sense universe in the midst of things which conflict with his faith, and place his confidence in the God whose character is revealed in Jesus Christ. Jesus Christ's statements reveal that God is a Being of love and justice and truth; the actual happenings in our immediate circumstances seem to prove He is not; are we going to remain true to the revelation that God is good? Are we going to be true to His honour, whatever may happen in the actual domain? If we are, we shall find that God in His providence makes the two universes, the universe of revelation and the universe of common sense, work together in perfect harmony. Most of us are pagans in a crisis; we think and act like pagans, only one out of a hundred is daring enough to bank his faith in the character of God.

The golden rule for understanding in spiritual matters is not intellect, but obedience. Discernment in the spiritual world is never gained by intellect; in the common-sense world it is. If a man wants scientific knowledge, intellectual curiosity is his guide; but if he wants insight into what Jesus Christ teaches, he can only get it by obedience. If things are dark to us spiritually, it is because there is something we will not do. Intellectual darkness comes because of ignorance; spiritual darkness comes because of something I do not intend to obey.

SSM 66

MISSIONARY PREDESTINATIONS

And now, saith the Lord, that formed me from the womb to be His servant. (Isa. 49:5)

The first thing that happens after we have realized our election to God in Christ Jesus is the destruction of our prejudices and our parochial notions and our patriotisms; we are turned into servants of God's own purpose. The whole human race was created to glorify God and enjoy Him forever. Sin has switched the human race on to another track, but it has not altered God's purpose in the tiniest degree; and when we are born again we are brought into the realization of God's great purpose for the human race, viz., I am created for God, He made me. This realization of the election of God is the most joyful realization on earth, and we have to learn to rely on the tremendous creative purpose of God. The first thing God will do with us is to "force through the channels of a single heart" the interests of the whole world. The love of God, the very nature of God, is introduced into us, and the nature of Almighty God is focused in John 3:16—"*God so loved the world . . .*"

We have to maintain our soul open to the fact of God's creative purpose, and not muddle it with our own intentions. If we do, God will have to crush our intentions on one side however much it may hurt. The purpose for which the missionary is created is that he may be God's servant, one in whom God is glorified. When once we realize that through the salvation of Jesus Christ we are made perfectly fit for God, we shall understand why Jesus Christ is so ruthless in His demands. He demands absolute rectitude from His servants, because He has put into them the very nature of God.

Beware lest you forget God's purpose for your life.

Jesus, knowing that the Father had given all things into his hands, and that he came forth from God and goeth unto God . . . (John 13:3)

We might have expected the record to go on: 'He was transfigured before them'; but we read that the next thing our Lord did was of the most menial commonplace order—'he took a towel, and girdeth himself . . . and began to wash the disciples' feet'. Can we use a towel as our Lord did? Towels and basins and feet and sandals, all the ordinary sordid things of our lives, reveal more quickly than anything what we are made of. It is not the big occasions that reveal us, but the little occasions. It takes God Incarnate to do the most menial commonplace things properly.

'If I then, the Lord and the Master, have washed your feet, ye also ought to wash one another's feet.' Our Lord did not say: 'I have been the means of the salvation of thousands, I have been most successful in my service, now you go and do the same thing'—He said: '*I have washed your feet: you go and wash one another's feet.*' We try to get out of it by washing the feet of those who do not belong to our own set—we will wash the heathen's feet, or feet in the slums, but fancy washing my brother's feet, my wife's, my husband's, the feet of the minister of my church! Our Lord said—'*one another's feet*'.

Watch the humour of our Heavenly Father. It is seen in the way He brings across our path the type of person who exhibits to us what we have been like to Him. 'Now,' He says, 'show that one the same love that I have shown you.' If Jesus Christ has lifted us in love and grace, we must show that love to someone else.

SSY 83

THE MISSIONARY'S MASTER

Ye call me Master and Lord: and ye say well; for so I am.
(John 13:13)

To have a master and to be mastered is not the same thing. To have a master means that there is one who knows me better than I know myself, one who is closer than a friend, one who fathoms the remotest abyss of my heart and satisfies it, one who has brought me into the secure sense that he has met and solved every perplexity and problem of my mind. To have a master is this and nothing less—"One is your Master, even Christ."

Our Lord never enforces obedience; He does not take means to make me do what He wants. At certain times I wish God would master me and make me do the thing, but He will not; in other moods I wish He would leave me alone, but He does not.

"Ye call me Master and Lord"—but is He? Master and Lord have little place in our vocabulary, we prefer the words Saviour, Sanctifier, Healer. The only word to describe mastership in experience is love and we know very little about love as God reveals it. This is proved by the way we use the word obey. In the Bible obedience is based on the relationship of equals, that of a son with his father. Our Lord was not God's servant, He was His Son. "Though He were a Son, yet learned He obedience . . ." If our idea is that we are being mastered, it is a proof that we have no master; if that is our attitude to Jesus, we are far away from the relationship He wants. He wants us in the relationship in which He is easily Master without our conscious knowledge of it, all we know is that we are His to obey.

Know ye not that your body is the temple of the Holy Ghost?
(I Corinthians 6:19)

My body is designed to be 'a temple of the Holy Ghost', and it is up to me to stand for the honour of Jesus Christ in my bodily practices. When the Spirit of God comes in, He cleanses the temple and does not let one darling sin lurk. The one thing Jesus Christ insists on in my bodily life is chastity. As individuals we must not desecrate the temple of God by tampering with anything we ought not to tamper with; if we do, the scourge of God will come. Immediately the Spirit of God comes in we begin to realize what it means—everything that is not of God has to be turned clean out. People are surprised and say, 'I was told God would give the Holy Spirit to them that ask Him; well, I asked for the Holy Spirit and expected that He would bring me joy and peace, but I have had a terrible time ever since.' That is the sign He has come, He is turning out the 'money-changers and the cattle', i.e. the things that were making the temple into a trafficking place for self-realization. We soon find why the Gospel can never be welcome. As long as we speak winsomely about the 'meek and gentle Jesus', and the beautiful ideas the Holy Spirit produces when He comes in, people are captivated, but that is not the Gospel. The Gospel does away with any other ground to stand on than that of the Atonement. Speak about the peace of heaven and the joy of the Lord, and men will listen to you; but tell them that the Holy Spirit has to come in and turn out their claim to their right to themselves, and instantly there is resentment—'I can do what I like with my body; I can go where I choose.' The majority of people are not blackguards and criminals, living in external sin, they are clean-living and respectable, and it is to such that the scourge of God is the most terrible thing because it reveals that the natural virtues may be in idolatrous opposition to God.

SHL 71–2

THE MISSIONARY'S GOAL

Behold, we go up to Jerusalem. (Luke 18:31)

In the natural life our ambitions alter as we develop; in the Christian life the goal is given at the beginning, the beginning and the end are the same, viz., Our Lord Himself. We start with Christ and we end with Him—"until we all attain to the stature of the manhood of Christ Jesus," not to our idea of what the Christian life should be. The aim of the missionary is to do God's will, not to be useful, not to win the heathen; he *is* useful and he *does* win the heathen, but that is not his aim. His aim is to do the will of his Lord.

In Our Lord's life Jerusalem was the place where He reached the climax of His Father's will upon the Cross, and unless we go with Jesus there we will have no companionship with Him. Nothing ever discouraged Our Lord on His way to Jerusalem. He never hurried through certain villages where He was persecuted, or lingered in others where He was blessed. Neither gratitude nor ingratitude turned Our Lord one hair's breadth away from His purpose to go up to Jerusalem.

"The disciple is not above his Master." The same things will happen to us on our way to our Jerusalem. There will be the works of God manifested through us, people will get blessed, and one or two will show gratitude and the rest will show gross ingratitude, but nothing must deflect us from going up to our Jerusalem.

"There they crucified Him." That is what happened when Our Lord reached Jerusalem, and that happening is the gateway to our salvation. The saints do not end in crucifixion: by the Lord's grace they end in glory. In the meantime our watchword is—I, too, go up to Jerusalem.

Submitting yourselves one to another in the fear of God.
(Ephesians 5:21)

When the Holy Spirit first comes into us He seems to put us into a prison house; then He opens our eyes and causes us to expand in the realization that 'all things are yours', from the tiniest flower that blooms to God on His throne. When we have learnt the secret that God Himself is the Source of our life, then He can trust us with the expansion of our nature. Every expansion of our nature transforms selfhood into unselfishness. It is not peculiar to Christians, it is true of human nature apart altogether from the grace of God. Inspiration, either true or false, unites the personality, makes a man feel at one with himself and with everyone else, and he is unselfish as long as the inspiration lasts. Paul says, 'Don't be drunk with wine,' which is the counterfeit of the true transformation, 'but be filled with the Spirit', and all self-interested considerations are transformed at once, you will think only, without trying to, of the good of others and of the glory of God. Be careful what you allow to unite you and make you feel unselfish; the only power we must allow as Christians is the Holy Spirit who will so transform us that it will be easy to submit one to another in the fear of God.

BE 74

THE "GO" OF PREPARATION

Therefore if thou bring thy gift to the altar, and there thou rememberest that thy brother hath ought against thee; leave there thy gift before the altar, and go thy way, first be reconciled to thy brother, and then come and offer thy gift. (Matt. 5:23, 24)

It is easy to imagine that we will get to a place where we are complete and ready, but preparation is not suddenly accomplished, it is a process steadily maintained. It is dangerous to get into a settled state of experience. It is preparation *and* preparation.

The sense of sacrifice appeals readily to a young Christian. Humanly speaking, the one thing that attracts to Jesus Christ is our sense of the heroic, and the scrutiny of Our Lord's words suddenly brings this tide of enthusiasm to the test. "First be reconciled to thy brother." The "go" of preparation is to let the word of God scrutinize. The sense of heroic sacrifice is not good enough. The thing the Holy Spirit is detecting in you is the disposition that will never work in His service. No one but God can detect that disposition in you. Have you anything to hide from God? If you have, then let God search you with His light. If there is sin, *confess* it, not *admit* it. Are you willing to obey your Lord and Master whatever the humiliation to your right to yourself may be?

Never discard a conviction. If it is important enough for the Spirit of God to have brought it to your mind, it is that thing He is detecting. You were looking for a great thing to give up. God is telling you of some tiny thing; but at the back of it there lies the central citadel of obstinacy: I will not give up my right to myself—the thing God intends you to give up if ever you are going to be a disciple of Jesus Christ.

*Think not that I came to send peace on the earth: I came not to
send peace, but a sword. (Matthew 10:34)*

The natural pagan, a man whose word is as good as his bond,
a moral and upright man, is more delightful to meet than the
Christian who has enough of the Spirit of God to spoil his sin
but not enough to deliver him from it.

PH 168

You will never find in the Bible that things are destroyed for
the sake of destruction. Human beings destroy for the sake of
destruction, and so does the devil; God never does, He destroys
the wrong and the evil for one purpose only, the deliverance
of the good.

The purpose of the sword is to destroy everything that hinders a man being delivered. The first thing in salvation is the
element of destruction, and it is this that men object to. With
this thought in mind, recall what our Lord said about His own
mission: 'Think not that I am come to send peace on earth: I
came not to send peace, but a sword.' Our Lord reveals Himself as the destroyer of all peace and happiness, and of ignorance, wherever these are the cloak for sin (cf. Matthew 3:10).
It sounds a startling and amazing thing to say that Jesus did
not come to send peace, but He said He did not. The one thing
Jesus Christ is after is the destruction of everything that would
hinder the emancipation of men. The fact that people are happy
and peaceful and prosperous is no sign that they are free from
the sword of God. If their happiness and peace and well-being
and complacency rests on an undelivered life, they will meet
the sword before long, and all their peace and rest and joy will
be destroyed.

PS 24

THE "GO" OF RELATIONSHIP

And whosoever shall compel thee to go a mile, go with him twain.
(Matt. 5:41)

The summing up of Our Lord's teaching is that the relationship which He demands is an impossible one unless He has done a supernatural work in us. Jesus Christ demands that there be not the slightest trace of resentment even suppressed in the heart of a disciple when he meets with tyranny and injustice. No enthusiasm will ever stand the strain that Jesus Christ will put upon His worker, only one thing will, and that is a personal relationship to Himself which has gone through the mill of His spring cleaning until there is only one purpose left—I am here for God to send me where He will. Every other thing may get fogged, but this relationship to Jesus Christ must never be.

The Sermon on the Mount is not an ideal, it is a statement of what will happen in me when Jesus Christ has altered my disposition and put in a disposition like His own. Jesus Christ is the only One Who can fulfil the Sermon on the Mount.

If we are to be disciples of Jesus, we must be made disciples supernaturally; as long as we have the dead set purpose of being disciples we may be sure we are not. *"I have chosen you."* That is the way the grace of God begins. It is a constraint we cannot get away from; we can disobey it, but we cannot generate it. The drawing is done by the supernatural grace of God, and we never can trace where His work begins. Our Lord's making of a disciple is supernatural. He does not build on any natural capacity at all. God does not ask us to do the things that are easy to us naturally; He only asks us to do the things we are perfectly fitted to do by His grace, and the cross will come along that line always.

For I say unto you, that except your righteousness shall exceed the righteousness of the scribes and Pharisees, ye shall in no wise enter into the kingdom of heaven. (Matthew 5:20)

Take Saul of Tarsus as an example of Pharisaism; he says of himself in writing to the Philippians, 'as touching the law, a Pharisee; . . . touching the righteousness which is in the law, blameless . . . ' (Philippians 3:5–6): Jesus Christ says as disciples we have to exceed that. No wonder we find His statements absolutely shattering. Our righteousness has to be in excess of the righteousness of the man whose external conduct is blameless according to the law—what does that produce? despair straightaway. When we hear Jesus say 'Blessed are the pure in heart', our answer, if we are awake is, 'My God, how am I going to be pure in heart? If ever I am to be blameless down to the deepest recesses of my intentions, You must do something mighty in me.' That is exactly what Jesus Christ came to do. He did not come to *tell us* to be holy, but to *make* us holy, undeserving of censure in the sight of God. If any man or woman gets there it is by the sheer supernatural grace of God. You can't indulge in pious pretence when you come to the atmosphere of the Bible. If there is one thing the Spirit of God does it is to purge us from all sanctimonious humbug, there is no room for it.

BE 22

THE UNBLAMABLE ATTITUDE

If . . . thou rememberest that thy brother hath ought against thee . . .
(Matt. 5:23)

If when you come to the altar, there you remember that your
brother has anything against you, not—If you rake up something by a morbid sensitiveness, but—"If thou rememberest,"
that is, if it is brought to your conscious mind by the Spirit of
God: "first be reconciled to thy brother, and then come and
offer thy gift." Never object to the intense sensitiveness of the
Spirit of God in you when He is educating you down to the
scruple.

"First be reconciled to thy brother . . ." Our Lord's direction
is simple, "first be reconciled." Go back the way you came, go
the way indicated to you by the conviction given at the altar;
have an attitude of mind and a temper of soul to the one who
has something against you that makes reconciliation as natural as breathing. Jesus does not mention the other person, He
says—*you* go. There is no question of your rights. The stamp
of the saint is that he can waive his own rights and obey the
Lord Jesus.

"And then come and offer thy gift." The process is clearly
marked. First, the heroic spirit of self-sacrifice, then the sudden checking by the sensitiveness of the Holy Spirit, and the
stoppage at the point of conviction, then the way of obedience
to the word of God, constructing an unblamable attitude of
mind and temper to the one with whom you have been in the
wrong; then the glad, simple, unhindered offering of your gift
to God.

And the Lord God formed man of the dust of the ground, and breathed into his nostrils the breath of life: and man became a living soul. (Genesis 2:7)

God made man a mixture of dust and Deity. The dust of a man's body is his glory, not his shame. Jesus Christ manifested Himself in that dust, and He claims that He can presence any man with His own divinity. The New Testament teaches us how to keep the body under and make it a servant.

Drudgery is the outcome of sin, but it has no right to be the rule of life. It becomes the rule of life because we ignore the fact that the dust of the earth belongs to God, and that man's chief end is to glorify God. Unless we can maintain the presence of Divinity in our dust, life becomes a miserable drudgery. If a man lives in order to hoard up the means of living, he does not live at all, he has no time to, he is taken up with one form of drudgery or another to keep things going.

SHH 57

THE "GO" OF RENUNCIATION

Lord, I will follow Thee whithersoever Thou goest. (Luke 9:57)

Our Lord's attitude to this man is one of severe discouragement because He knew what was in man. We would have said—"Fancy losing the opportunity of winning that man!" Fancy bringing about him a north wind that froze him and "turned him away discouraged!" Never apologize for your Lord. The words of the Lord hurt and offend until there is nothing left to hurt or offend. Jesus Christ has not tenderness whatever toward anything that is ultimately going to ruin a man in the service of God. Our Lord's answers are based not on caprice, but on a knowledge of what is in man. If the Spirit of God brings to your mind a word of the Lord that hurts you, you may be sure that there is something He wants to hurt to death.

V. 58. These words knock the heart out of serving Jesus Christ because it is pleasing to me. The rigour of rejection leaves nothing but my Lord, and myself, and a forlorn hope. "Let the hundredfold come or go, your lodestar must be your relationship to Me, and I have nowhere to lay My head."

V. 59. This man did not want to disappoint Jesus, nor to hurt his father. We put sensitive loyalty to relatives in place of loyalty to Jesus Christ and Jesus has to take the last place. In a conflict of loyalty, obey Jesus Christ at all costs.

V. 61. The one who says—"Yes, Lord, but . . ." is the one who is fiercely ready, but never goes. This man had one or two reservations. The exacting call of Jesus Christ has no margin of good-byes, because good-bye, as it is often used, is pagan, not Christian. When once the call of God comes, begin to go and never stop going.

*As he came forth of his mother's womb, naked shall he return
to go as he came, and shall take nothing of his labour.
(Ecclesiastes 5:15)*

When a man dies he can take nothing he has done or made in his lifetime with him. The only thing he can take with him is what he *is*. There is no warrant in the Bible for the modern speculation of a second chance after death. There may be a second chance. There may be numbers of interesting things—but it is not taught in the Bible. The stage between birth and death is the probation stage.

SHH 65

The Sermon on the Mount produces despair in the heart of the natural man, and that is the very thing Jesus means it to do, because immediately we reach the point of despair we are willing to come to Jesus Christ as paupers and receive from Him. 'Blessed are the poor in spirit'—that is the first principle of the Kingdom. As long as we have a conceited, self-righteous idea that we can do the thing if God will help us, God has to allow us to go on until we break the neck of our ignorance over some obstacle, then we will be willing to come and receive from Him. The bed-rock of Jesus Christ's Kingdom is poverty, not possession; not decisions for Jesus Christ, but a sense of futility, 'I cannot begin to do it.' Then, says Jesus, 'Blessed are you.' That is the entrance, and it takes us a long while to believe we are poor. The knowledge of our own poverty brings us to the moral frontier where Christ works.

SSM 12

THE "GO" OF UNCONDITIONAL IDENTIFICATION

One thing thou lackest . . . come, take up the cross, and follow Me. (Mark 10:21)

The rich young ruler had the master passion to be perfect. When he saw Jesus Christ, he wanted to be like Him. Our Lord never puts personal holiness to the fore when He calls a disciple; He puts absolute annihilation of my right to myself and identification with Himself—a relationship with Himself in which there is no other relationship. Luke 14:26 has nothing to do with salvation or sanctification, but with unconditional identification with Jesus Christ. Very few of us know the absolute "go" of abandonment to Jesus.

"Then Jesus beholding him loved him." The look of Jesus will mean a heart broken for ever from allegiance to any other person or thing. Has Jesus ever looked at you? The look of Jesus transforms and transfixes. Where you are "soft" with God is where the Lord has looked at you. If you are hard and vindictive, insistent on your own way, certain that the other person is more likely to be in the wrong than you are, it is an indication that there are whole tracts of your nature that have never been transformed by His gaze.

"One thing thou lackest . . ." The only "good thing" from Jesus Christ's point of view is union with Himself and nothing in between.

"Sell whatsoever thou hast . . ." I must reduce myself until I am a mere conscious man, I must fundamentally renounce possessions of all kinds, not to save my soul (only one thing saves a man—absolute reliance upon Jesus Christ)—but in order to follow Jesus. "Come, and follow Me." And the road is the way He went.

*Wilt thou also disannul my judgment? wilt thou condemn me
that thou mayest be righteous? (Job 40:8)*

Whatever the universe is, it is not tame. A certain type of
modern science would have us believe it is, that we can harness the sea and air and earth. Quite true, you can, if you only
read scientific manuals and deal with successful experiments;
but before long you discover elements which knock all your
calculations on the head and prove that the universe is wild
and unmanageable. And yet in the beginning God intended
man to control it; the reason he cannot is because he twisted
God's order; instead of recognizing God's dominion over himself, man became his own god, and by so doing lost control of
everything else. (See Genesis 3.)

When Jesus Christ came He was easily Master of the life in
the air and earth and sky, and in Him we see the order God
originally intended for man. If you want to know what the
human race is to be like on the basis of the Redemption, you
will find it mirrored in Jesus Christ—a perfect oneness between
God and man, no gap; in the meantime there is a gap, and the
universe is wild, not tame. Every type of superstition pretends
it can rule the universe, the scientific quack proclaims he can
control the weather, that he has occult powers and can take
the untameable universe and tame it.

God says it cannot be done.

BFB 97

THE CONSCIOUSNESS OF THE CALL

For necessity is laid upon me: yea, woe is unto me, if I preach
not the gospel! (1 Cor. 9:16)

We are apt to forget the mystical, supernatural touch of God.
If you can tell where you got the call of God and all about it, I
question whether you have ever had a call. The call of God
does not come like that, it is much more supernatural. The realization of it in a man's life may come with a sudden thun-
der-clap or with a gradual dawning, but in whatever way it
comes, it comes with the undercurrent of the supernatural,
something that cannot be put into words; it is always accom-
panied with a glow. At any moment there may break the sudden consciousness of this incalculable, supernatural, surprising call that has taken hold of your life—"I have chosen you."
The call of God has nothing to do with salvation and sanctification. It is not because you are sanctified that you are therefore called to preach the gospel; the call to preach the gospel is
infinitely different. Paul describes it as a necessity laid upon
him.

If you have been obliterating the great supernatural call of
God in your life, take a review of your circumstances and see
where God has not been first, but your ideas of service, or your
temperamental abilities. Paul said—"Woe is unto me, if I preach
not the gospel!" He had realized the call of God, and there was
no competitor for his strength.

If a man or woman is called of God, it does not matter how
untoward circumstances are, every force that has been at work
will tell for God's purpose in the end. If you agree with God's
purpose He will bring not only your conscious life, but all the
deeper regions of your life which you cannot get at, into harmony.

For we wrestle not against flesh and blood, but . . . against spiritual wickedness in high places. (Ephesians 6:12)

Today spiritualism is having tremendous vogue; men and women are getting into communication with departed spirits and putting themselves in league with the unseen powers. If you have got as far as reading fortunes in tea-cups, *stop*. If you have gone as far as telling fortunes by cards, *stop*. I will tell you why—the devil uses these apparently harmless things to create a fearful curiosity in the minds of men and women, especially young men and women, and it may bring them into league with the angelic forces that hate God, into league with the principalities and the rulers of this world's darkness. Never say, 'What is the harm in it?' Push it to its logical conclusion and ask—'Where will this end?' You are absolutely safe as long as you remain under the shelter of the Atonement; but if you do not—I don't care what your experiences are—you are absolutely unsafe. At any minute dangers may beset you, terrors and darkness may take hold of you and rack your life with terrific perils.

God grant we may keep as far away from these things as we can. But if in the strange providence of God you find you are near a spiritualist meeting, pray, and keep on your praying, and you will paralyse every power of the medium if he is genuine. No spiritualistic seance can continue if there is a Christian anywhere near who knows how to lay hold of God in prayer; no spirits will communicate. I could tell you wonderful stories of how God's power has worked. Blessed be God; Jesus Christ's salvation makes us more than conqueror over the angelic forces.

SHL 29

THE COMMISSION OF THE CALL

Who now rejoice in my sufferings for you, and fill up that which is behind of the afflictions of Christ in my flesh for His body's sake. (Col. 1:24)

We make calls out of our own spiritual consecration, but when we get right with God He brushes all these aside, and rivets us with a pain that is terrific to one thing we never dreamed of, and for one radiant flashing moment we see what He is after, and we say—"Here am I, send me."

This call has nothing to do with personal sanctification, but with being made broken bread and poured-out wine. God can never make us wine if we object to the fingers He uses to crush us with. If God would only use His own fingers, and make me broken bread and poured-out wine in a special way! But when He uses someone whom we dislike, or some set of circumstances to which we said we would never submit, and makes those the crushers, we object. We must never choose the scene of our own martyrdom. If ever we are going to be made into wine, we will have to be crushed; you cannot drink grapes. Grapes become wine only when they have been squeezed.

I wonder what kind of finger and thumb God has been using to squeeze you, and you have been like a marble and escaped? You are not ripe yet, and if God *had* squeezed you, the wine would have been remarkably bitter. To be a sacramental personality means that the elements of the natural life are presented by God as they are broken providentially in His service. We have to be adjusted into God before we can be broken bread in His hands. Keep right with God and let Him do what He likes, and you will find that He is producing the kind of bread and wine that will benefit His other children.

*And he did not many mighty works there because of their un-
belief. (Matthew 13:58)*

Redemption is the great outside fact of the Christian faith; it
has to do not only with a man's experience of salvation, but
with the basis of his thinking. The revelation of Redemption
means that Jesus Christ came here in order that by means of
His Death on the Cross He might put the whole human race
on a redemptive basis, so making it possible for every man to
get back into perfect communion with God. 'I have finished
the work which thou gavest me to do.' What was finished?
The redemption of the world. Men are not *going* to be redeemed; they *are* redeemed. 'It is finished.' It was not the salvation of individual men and women like you and me that was
finished: the whole human race was put on the basis of Redemption. Do I believe it? Let me think of the worst man I
know, the man for whom I have no affinity, the man who is a
continual thorn in my flesh, who is as mean as can be; can I
imagine that man being presented 'perfect in Christ Jesus'? If
I can, I have got the beginning of Christian thinking. It ought
to be an easy thing for the Christian who thinks to conceive of
any and every kind of man being presented 'perfect in Christ
Jesus', but how seldom we do think! If I am an earnest evangelical preacher I may say to a man, 'Oh yes, I believe God can
save you', while in my heart of hearts I don't believe there is
much hope for him. Our unbelief stands as the supreme barrier to Jesus Christ's work in men's souls. 'And he did not many
mighty works there because of their unbelief.'

CHI 8

OCTOBER

THE SPHERE OF EXALTATION

Jesus leadeth them up into a high mountain apart by themselves.
(Mark 9:2)

We have all had times on the mount, when we have seen things from God's standpoint and have wanted to stay there; but God will never allow us to stay there. The test of our spiritual life is the power to descend; if we have power to rise only, something is wrong. It is a great thing to be on the mount with God, but a man only gets there in order that afterwards he may get down among the devil-possessed and lift them up. We are not built for the mountains and the dawns and aesthetic affinities, those are for moments of inspiration, that is all. We are built for the valley, for the ordinary stuff we are in, and that is where we have to prove our mettle. Spiritual selfishness always wants repeated moments on the mount. We feel we could talk like angels and live like angels, if only we could stay on the mount. The times of exaltation are exceptional, they have their meaning in our life with God, but we must beware lest our spiritual selfishness wants to make them the only time.

We are apt to think that everything that happens is to be turned into useful teaching, it is to be turned into something better than teaching, viz., into character. The mount is not meant to *teach* us anything, it is meant to *make* us something. There is a great snare in asking—What is the use of it? In spiritual matters we can never calculate on that line. The moments on the mountain tops are rare moments, and they are meant for something in God's purpose.

Not as though I had already attained, either were already perfect: but I follow after, if that I may apprehend that for which also I am apprehended of Christ Jesus. (Philippians 3:12)

We have to build up useful associations in our minds, to learn to associate things for ourselves, and it can only be done by determination. There are ideas associated in each of our minds that are not associated in the mind of anyone else, and this accounts for the difference in individuals. For instance, learn to associate the chair you sit in with nothing else but study; associate a selected secret place with nothing but prayer. We do not sufficiently realize the power we have to infect the places in which we live and work by our prevailing habits in those places.

The law of associated ideas applied spiritually means that we must drill our minds in godly connections. How many of us have learned to associate our summer holidays with God's Divine purposes? to associate the early dawn with the early dawn on the Sea of Galilee after the Resurrection? If we learn to associate ideas that are worthy of God with all that happens in Nature, our imagination will never be at the mercy of our impulses. Spiritually, it is not a different law that works, but the same law. When once we have become accustomed to connecting these things, every ordinary occurrence will serve to fructify our minds in godly thinking because we have developed our minds along the lines laid down by the Spirit of God. It is not done once for always; it is only done *always*. Never imagine that the difficulty of doing these things belongs peculiarly to you, it belongs to everyone. The character of a person is nothing more than the habitual form of his associations.

MFL 99

THE SPHERE OF HUMILIATION

If Thou canst do any thing, have compassion on us, and help us.
(Mark 9:22)

After every time of exaltation we are brought down with a sudden rush into things as they are where it is neither beautiful nor poetic nor thrilling. The height of the mountain top is measured by the drab drudgery of the valley; but it is in the valley that we have to live for the glory of God. We *see* His glory on the mount, but we never *live* for His glory there. It is in the sphere of humiliation that we find our true worth to God, that is where our faithfulness is revealed. Most of us can do things if we are always at the heroic pitch because of the natural self-ishness of our hearts, but God wants us at the drab common-place pitch, where we live in the valley according to our personal relationship to Him. Peter thought it would be a fine thing for them to remain on the mount, but Jesus Christ took the disciples down from the mount into the valley, the place where the meaning of the vision is explained.

"If Thou canst do any thing . . ." It takes the valley of humiliation to root the scepticism out of us. Look back at your own experience, and you will find that until you learned Who Jesus was, you were a cunning sceptic about His power. When you were on the mount, you could believe anything, but what about the time when you were up against facts in the valley? You may be able to give a testimony to sanctification, but what about the thing that is a humiliation to you just now? The last time you were on the mount with God, you saw that all power in heaven and in earth belonged to Jesus—will you be sceptical now in the valley of humiliation?

Jesus, the author and perfecter of our faith. (Hebrews 12:2 RV)

The business of faith is to convert Truth into reality. What do you really believe? Take time and catalogue it up; are you converting your belief into reality? You say, 'I believe God has sanctified me'—does your actual life prove He has? 'I believe God has baptized me with the Holy Ghost'—why? Because you had cold shivers and visions and marvellous times of prayer? The proof that we are baptized with the Holy Ghost is that we bear a strong family likeness to Jesus, and men take knowledge of us, as they did of the disciples after Pentecost, that we have been with Jesus, they can recognize the family likeness at once . . .

There is a great snare especially in evangelical circles of knowing the will of God as expressed in the Bible without the slightest practical working of it out in the life. The Christian religion is the most practical thing on earth. If the Holy Spirit has given you a vision in your private Bible study or during a meeting which made your heart glow, and your mind expand, and your will stir itself to grasp, you will have to pay to the last farthing in concentration along that line until all you saw in vision is made actual.

CHI 58

THE SPHERE OF MINISTRATION

This kind can come forth by nothing, but by prayer and fasting.
(Mark 9:29)

"Why could not we cast him out?" The answer lies in a personal relationship to Jesus Christ. This kind can come forth by nothing but by concentration and redoubled concentration on Him. We can ever remain powerless, as were the disciples, by trying to do God's work not in concentration on His power, but by ideas drawn from our own temperament. We slander God by our very eagerness to work for Him without knowing Him.

You are brought face to face with a difficult case and nothing happens externally, and yet you know that emancipation will be given because you are concentrated on Jesus Christ. This is your line of service—to see that there is nothing between Jesus and yourself. Is there? If there is, you must get through it, not by ignoring it in irritation, or by mounting up, but by facing it and getting through it into the presence of Jesus Christ, then that very thing, and all you have been through in connection with it, will glorify Jesus Christ in a way you will never know till you see Him face to face.

We must be able to mount up with wings as eagles; but we must also know how to come down. The power of the saint lies in the coming down and the living down. "I can do all things through Christ which strengtheneth me," said Paul, and the things he referred to were mostly humiliating things. It is in our power to refuse to be humiliated and to say—"No, thank you, I much prefer to be on the mountain top with God." Can I face things as they actually are in the light of the reality of Jesus Christ, or do things as they are efface altogether my faith in Him, and put me into a panic?

*Furnish your . . . brotherliness with Christian love. (2 Peter 1:7)
(Moffatt)*

Love, to most of us, is an indefinite thing; we do not know what we mean when we speak of love. The love Paul mentions in 1 Corinthians 13 means the sovereign preference of my person for another person, and everything depends on who the other person is. Jesus demands that the sovereign preference be for Him. We cannot love to order, and yet His word stands—'If any come to me, and *hate not* his father, and mother, and wife, and children, and brethren, and sisters, yea, and his own life also' (i.e. a hatred of every loyalty that would divide the heart from loyalty to Jesus), 'he cannot be my disciple.' Devotion to a Person is the only thing that tells; and no man on earth has the love which Jesus demands, unless it has been imparted to him. We may admire Jesus Christ, we may respect Him and reverence Him; but apart from the Holy Ghost we do not love Him.

GH 57

THE VISION AND THE VERITY

Called to be saints. (1 Cor. 1:2)

Thank God for the sight of all you have never yet been. You have had the vision, but you are not there yet by any means. It is when we are in the valley, where we prove whether we will be the choice ones, that most of us turn back. We are not quite prepared for the blows which must come if we are going to be turned into the shape of the vision. We have seen what we are not, and what God wants us to be, but are we willing to have the vision "batter'd to shape and use" by God? The batterings always come in commonplace ways and through commonplace people.

There are times when we do know what God's purpose is; whether we will let the vision be turned into actual character depends upon us, not upon God. If we prefer to loll on the mount and live in the memory of the vision, we will be of no use actually in the ordinary stuff of which human life is made up. We have to learn to live in reliance on what we saw in the vision, not in ecstasies and conscious contemplation of God, but to live in actualities in the light of the vision until we get to the veritable reality. Every bit of our training is in that direction. Learn to thank God for making known His demands.

The little "I am" always sulks when God says do. Let the little "I am" be shrivelled up in God's indignation—"I AM THAT I AM hath sent thee." He must dominate. Is it not penetrating to realize that God knows where we live, and the kennels we crawl into! He will hunt us up like a lightning flash. No human being knows human beings as God does.

*Who shall ascend into the hill of the Lord? and who shall stand
in his holy place? He that hath clean hands, and a pure heart
. . . (Psalm 24:3–4)*

Today we are in danger of being caught up in the lure of wrong
roads to the Kingdom—'Things must be worked out at once,
we cannot wait, there must be results immediately.' If to benefit mankind is the whole purpose of God, quicker results could
be produced apart from the Redemption, because the Redemption works appallingly slowly, according to our human standards. If all that is necessary is this hand-to-mouth business
there is no need for all the teaching of Jesus, no need for patience until God's purposes are fully worked out. To look on
the precepts of the Sermon on the Mount as referring to a future dispensation is to rob the Cross of its meaning. If Jesus
Christ cannot alter me now, so that the alteration shows externally in my home life, in my business life, when is He going
to alter me? What is going to transform me so that I can love
my enemies, can pray for those that persecute me, if I cannot
do it now? No suffering or discipline on my part will make me
any different; the only thing that will make me different is
being born again into the Kingdom of God. To look for death
to make me holy is to make out that death, which is 'the last
enemy', is going to do what the Atonement cannot do. The
Cross of Christ alone makes me holy, and it does so the second I am willing to let it.

  The Kingdom of God is latent in the Cross, but don't spiritualize the Kingdom into vagueness, and don't materialize it into
non-spirituality . . . To say that the Kingdom is going to be
brought in by the earth being swept clean through wars and
cataclysms is not true; you cannot introduce the Kingdom in
that way, it is impossible. Nothing can bring in the Kingdom
saving the Redemption, which works in personal lives through
the Cross and in no other way.

GW 53

THE BIAS OF DEGENERATION

Wherefore as by one man sin entered into the world, and death by sin, and so death passed upon all men, for that all have sinned. (Rom. 5:12)

The Bible does not say that God punished the human race for one man's sin; but that the disposition of sin, viz., my claim to my right to myself, entered into the human race by one man, and that another Man took on Him the sin of the human race and put it away (Heb. 9:26)—an infinitely profounder revelation. The disposition of sin is not immorality and wrong-doing but the disposition of self-realization—I am my own god. This disposition may work out in decorous morality or in indecorous immorality, but it has the one basis, my claim to my right to myself. When Our Lord faced men with all the forces of evil in them, and men who were clean living and moral and upright, He did not pay any attention to the moral degradation of the one or to the moral attainment of the other; He looked at something we do not see, viz., the disposition. Sin is a thing I am born with and I cannot touch it; God touches sin in Redemption. In the Cross of Jesus Christ God redeemed the whole human race from the possibility of damnation through the heredity of sin. God nowhere holds a man responsible for having the heredity of sin. The condemnation is not that I am born with a heredity of sin, but if when I realize Jesus Christ came to deliver me from it, I refuse to let Him do so, from that moment I begin to get the seal of damnation. "And this is the judgment" (the critical moment), "that the light is come into the world, and men loved the darkness rather than the light."

Again I say unto you. That if two of you shall agree on earth
. . . (Matthew 18:19)

Agreement in purpose on earth must not be taken to mean a predetermination to agree together to storm God's fort doggedly till He yields. It is far from right to agree beforehand over what we want, and then go to God and wait, not until He gives us His mind about the matter, but until we extort from Him permission to do what we had made up our minds to do before we prayed; we should rather agree to ask God to convey His mind and meaning to us in regard to the matter. Agreement in purpose on earth is not a public presentation of persistent begging which knows no limit, but a prayer which is conscious that it is limited through the moral nature of the Holy Ghost. It is really 'symphonizing' on earth with our Father who is in heaven.

DPR 41

Be yourself exactly before God, and present your problems, the things you know you have come to your wits' end about. Ask what you *will*, and Jesus Christ says your prayers will be answered. We can always tell whether our will is in what we ask by the way we live when we are not praying.

IYA 13

THE BENT OF REGENERATION

When it pleased God . . . to reveal His Son in me.
(Gal. 1:15, 16)

If Jesus Christ is to regenerate me, what is the problem He is up against? I have a heredity I had no say in; I am not holy, nor likely to be; and if all Jesus Christ can do is to tell me I must be holy, His teaching plants despair. But if Jesus Christ is a Regenerator, One Who can put into me His own heredity of holiness, then I begin to see what He is driving at when He says that I have to be holy. Redemption means that Jesus Christ can put into any man the hereditary disposition that was in Himself, and all the standards He gives are based on that disposition: His teaching is for the life He puts in. The moral transaction on my part is agreement with God's verdict on sin in the Cross of Jesus Christ.

The New Testament teaching about regeneration is that when a man is struck by a sense of need, God will put the Holy Spirit into his spirit, and his personal spirit will be energized by the Spirit of the Son of God, "until Christ be formed in you." The moral miracle of Redemption is that God can put into me a new disposition whereby I can live a totally new life. When I reach the frontier of need and know my limitations, Jesus says —"Blessed are you." But I have to get there. God cannot put into me, a responsible moral being, the disposition that was in Jesus Christ unless I am conscious I need it.

Just as the disposition of sin entered into the human race by one man, so the Holy Spirit entered the human race by another Man; and Redemption means that I can be delivered from the heredity of sin and through Jesus Christ can receive an unsullied heredity, viz., the Holy Spirit.

I am the way, and the truth, and the life. (John 14:6)

However far we may drift, we must always come back to these words of our Lord: 'I am the way'—not a road that we leave behind us, but the way itself. Jesus Christ is the Truth *of God*. 'No man cometh unto the Father, but by me.' We can get to God as Creator in other ways, but no man can come to God as Father in any other way than by Jesus Christ (cf. Matthew 11:27). 'I am the life.' Jesus Christ is the Life *of God* as He is the Way and the Truth of God. Eternal life is not a gift *from* God, it is the gift of *God Himself*. The life imparted to me by Jesus is the life of God. 'He that hath the Son hath the life'; 'I am come that they might have life'; 'And this is life eternal, that they should know thee the only true God'. We have to abide in the *way*; to be incorporated into the *truth*; to be infused by the *life*.

SSY 92

RECONCILIATION

For He hath made Him to be sin for us, who knew no sin, that
we might be made the righteousness of God in Him. (2 Cor. 5:21)

Sin is a fundamental relationship; it is not wrong doing, it is wrong *being*, deliberate and emphatic independence of God. The Christian religion bases everything on the positive, radical nature of sin. Other religions deal with sins; the Bible alone deals with sin. The first thing Jesus Christ faced in men was the heredity of sin, and it is because we have ignored this in our presentation of the Gospel that the message of the Gospel has lost its sting and its blasting power.

The revelation of the Bible is not that Jesus Christ took upon Himself our fleshly sins, but that He took upon Himself the heredity of sin which no man can touch. God made His own Son to be sin that He might make the sinner a saint. All through the Bible it is revealed that Our Lord bore the sin of the world by identification, not by *sympathy*. He deliberately took upon His own shoulders, and bore in His own Person, the whole massed sin of the human race—"He hath *made Him to be sin for us*, who knew no sin," and by so doing He put the whole human race on the basis of Redemption. Jesus Christ rehabilitated the human race; He put it back to where God designed it to be, and anyone can enter into union with God on the ground of what Our Lord has done on the Cross.

A man cannot redeem himself; Redemption is God's "bit," it is absolutely finished and complete; its reference to individual men is a question of their individual action. A distinction must always be made between the revelation of Redemption and the conscious experience of salvation in a man's life.

I am the way . . . (John 14:6)

Our Lord said, '*I am the way,*' not the way to any one or anything; He is not a road we leave behind us, He is the Way to the Father in which we abide (John 15:4). He *is* the Way, not He was the Way, and there is not any way of living in the Fatherhood of God except by living in Christ. 'Whoso findeth himself in Christ findeth life.' The Way to the Father is not by the law, nor by obedience, or creed, but Jesus Christ Himself, He is the Way of the Father whereby any and every soul may be in peace, in joy, and in divine courage.

DP 137

I am . . . the truth. John 14:6

Truth is not a system, not a constitution, nor even a creed; the Truth is the Lord Jesus Christ Himself, and He is the Truth about the Father just as He is the Way of the Father. Our tendency is to make truth a logical statement, to make it a principle instead of a Person. Profoundly speaking there are no Christian principles, but the saint by abiding in Christ in the way of the Fatherhood of God discerns the Truth of God in the passing moments.

DP 138

I am . . . the life. John 14:6

The superb declaration of our Lord, 'I am the life,' comes with eternal succour. He is the Life of the Father just as He is the Father's Way and the Father's Truth . . . .

Let us remember that Jesus Christ is Life, and our life, 'all our fresh springs are in Him', so that whether we eat or drink or whatsoever we do, let us do all to the glory of God.

DP 139

THE EXCLUSIVENESS OF CHRIST

Come unto Me. (Matt. 11:28)

Is it not humiliating to be told that we must come to Jesus! Think of the things we will not come to Jesus Christ about. If you want to know how real you are, test yourself by these words—"Come unto Me." In every degree in which you are not real, you will dispute rather than come, you will quibble rather than come, you will go through sorrow rather than come, you will do anything rather than come the last lap of unutterable foolishness—"Just as I am." As long as you have the tiniest bit of spiritual impertinence, it will always reveal itself in the fact that you are expecting God to tell you to do a big thing, and all He is telling you to do is to "come."

"Come unto Me." When you hear those words you will know that something must happen in you before you can come. The Holy Spirit will show you what you have to do, anything at all that will put the axe at the root of the thing which is preventing you from getting through. You will never get further until you are willing to do that one thing. The Holy Spirit will locate the one impregnable thing in you, but He cannot budge it unless you are willing to let Him.

How often have you come to God with your requests and gone away with the feeling—Oh, well, I have done it this time! And yet you go away with nothing whilst all the time God has stood with outstretched hands not only to take you, but for you to take Him. Think of the invincible, unconquerable, unwearying patience of Jesus—"*Come unto Me.*"

I am the door . . . (John 10:9)

This is a picture of the life we are to live as God's children—entering in by our Lord, who is the Door, not once for all, but every day, for everything. Is there trouble in the physical domain? enter in by the Door and be saved. Trouble in mental matters? enter in and be saved. A thousand and one things make up life as it is and in them all we have to learn to enter in by the Door. Entering in, in the Name of Jesus, is the condition of daily salvation, not salvation from sin only, but a salvation that keeps us manifestly the Lord's sheep.

Are you experiencing daily salvation, or are you shut out from Jesus Christ just now in your bodily life, in your mind, in your circumstances? is there any fog, any darkness, any weariness, any trouble? Every day there are things that seem to shut the way up, but you can always enter in by the Door and experience salvation. In the East it is the body of the shepherd himself that is the door of the fold.

We are apt to have the idea that salvation is a kind of watertight compartment and if we enter in all our liberty will be destroyed. That is not our Lord's conception; He says 'he shall go in and go out'. Are we entering in by the Door for our daily work or only at a devotional meeting? The going in and out is our Lord's picture of the freedom of a son. A servant cannot go in and out as he likes, but Jesus says, 'Henceforth I call you not servants . . . but I have called you friends.' Nothing is closed to you once you enter in by the Door.

GW 110

PULL YOURSELF TOGETHER

Yield your members servants to righteousness unto holiness.
(Rom. 6:13-22)

I cannot save and sanctify myself; I cannot atone for sin; I cannot redeem the world; I cannot make right what is wrong, pure what is impure, holy what is unholy. That is all the sovereign work of God. Have I faith in what Jesus Christ has done? He has made a perfect Atonement, am I in the habit of constantly realizing it? The great need is not to *do* things, but to *believe* things. The Redemption of Christ is not an experience, it is the great act of God which He has performed through Christ, and I have to build my faith upon it. If I construct my faith on my experience, I produce that most unscriptural type, an isolated life, my eyes fixed on my own whiteness. Beware of the piety that has no presupposition in the Atonement of the Lord. It is of no use for anything but a sequestered life; it is useless to God and a nuisance to man. Measure every type of experience by our Lord Himself. We cannot do anything pleasing to God unless we deliberately build on the presupposition of the Atonement.

The Atonement of Jesus has to work out in practical, unobtrusive ways in my life. Every time I obey, absolute Deity is on my side, so that the grace of God and natural obedience coincide. Obedience means that I have banked everything on the Atonement, and my obedience is met immediately by the delight of the supernatural grace of God.

Beware of the piety that denies the natural life, it is a fraud. Continually bring yourself to the bar of the Atonement—where is the discernment of the Atonement in this thing and in that?

*And he from within shall answer and say, Trouble me not: the
door is now shut . . . (Luke 11:7)*

There is a time in spiritual life when God does not seem to be
a friend. Everything was clear and easily marked and understood for a while, but now we find ourselves in a condition of
darkness and desolation. The parable of the importunate friend
is the illustration Jesus gives of how the Heavenly Father will
appear in times of spiritual confusion—as a man who does not
care for his friends. We are in need, or our friends or our homes
are in need, and though we go to God who has been our Friend
all through, He does nothing at all. It is as if Jesus said to His
disciples—'There are times when the Heavenly Father will look
like that, but don't give up, remember I have told you—*everyone that asks receives.'* In the meantime the friendship of God is
completely shrouded. There are things that have no explanation, but maintain your relationship to God, 'hang in' in confidence in Him, and the time will come when everything will
be explained. It is only by going through the confusion that
we shall get at what God wants us to get at.

Never say God has done what He has not done because it
sounds better to say it; never pretend to have an answer when
you have not. Jesus said 'Everyone that asketh receiveth'; we
say—'I have asked but I have not received.' It is because we
ask in spiritual confusion. Jesus said to James and John: 'Ye
know not what ye ask'; they were brought into fellowship with
Jesus Christ's cup and baptism, but not in the way they expected.

PH 95

WHEREBY SHALL I KNOW?

I thank Thee, O Father . . . because Thou hast hid these things
from the wise and prudent, and hast revealed them unto babes.
(Matt. 11:25)

In spiritual relationship we do not grow step by step; we are
either there or we are not. God does not cleanse us more and
more from sin, but when we are in the light, walking in the
light, we *are* cleansed from all sin. It is a question of obedience, and instantly the relationship is perfected. Turn away for
one second out of obedience, and darkness and death are at
work at once.

All God's revelations are sealed until they are opened to us
by obedience. You will never get them open by philosophy or
thinking. Immediately you obey, a flash of light comes. Let
God's truth work in you by soaking in it, not by worrying into
it. The only way you can get to know is to stop trying to find
out and by being born again. Obey God in the thing He shows
you, and instantly the next thing is opened up. One reads tomes
on the work of the Holy Spirit, when five minutes of drastic
obedience would make things as clear as a sunbeam. "I suppose I shall understand these things some day!" You can understand them now. It is not study that does it, but obedience.
The tiniest fragment of obedience, and heaven opens and the
profoundest truths of God are yours straight away. God will
never reveal what you know already. Beware of becoming
"wise and prudent."

Whither shall I go from thy spirit? or whither shall I flee from thy presence? (Psalm 139:7)

The Psalmist states that the presence of God is the secure accompaniment of His knowledge; not only does God know everything about him, but He is with him in the knowledge. Where is the place that God is not?—hell? No, hell is God; if there were no God, there would be no hell. 'If I make my bed in hell, behold, thou art there.' The first thing 'the fool' does is to get rid of God ('The fool hath said in his heart, There is no God,' Psalm 14:1); then he gets rid of heaven and hell; then he gets rid of all moral consequences—no such thing as right and wrong. The Psalmist is stating that wherever he may go in accordance with the indecipherable Providence of God, there the surprising presence of God will meet him. Immediately you begin to forecast and plan for yourself God will break up your programme, He delights to do it, until we learn to live like children based on the knowledge that God is ruling and reigning and rejoicing, and His joy is our strength. When we say— 'even there shall thy hand lead me, and thy right hand shall hold me', there is no foreboding anxiety, because 'His love in times past' enables us to rest confidently in Him. The only rest there is is in this abandon to the love of God. There is security from yesterday—'Thou hast beset me behind'; security for tomorrow—'and before'; and security for today, 'and laid thine hand upon me'. It was this knowledge that gave our Lord the imperturbable peace He always had. We must be like a plague of mosquitoes to the Almighty, with our fussy little worries and anxieties, and the perplexities we imagine, all because we won't get into the elemental life with God which Jesus came to give.

BE 86–7

AFTER GOD'S SILENCE—WHAT?

When He had heard therefore that he was sick, He abode two days in the same place where he was. (John 11:6)

Has God trusted you with a silence—a silence that is big with meaning? God's silences are His answers. Think of those days of absolute silence in the home at Bethany! Is there anything analogous to those days in your life? Can God trust you like that, or are you still asking for a visible answer? God will give you the blessings you ask if you will not go any further without them; but His silence is the sign that He is bringing you into a marvelous understanding of Himself. Are you mourning before God because you have not had an audible response? You will find that God has trusted you in the most intimate way possible, with an absolute silence, not of despair, but of pleasure, because He saw that you could stand a bigger revelation. If God has given you a silence, praise Him, He is bringing you into the great run of His purposes. The manifestation of the answer in time is a matter of God's sovereignty. Time is nothing to God. For a while you said—"I asked God to give me bread, and He gave me a stone." He did not, and to-day you find He gave you the bread of life.

A wonderful thing about God's silence is that the contagion of His stillness gets into you and you become perfectly confident—"I know God has heard me." His silence is the proof that He has. As long as you have the idea that God will bless you in answer to prayer, He will do it, but He will never give you the grace of silence. If Jesus Christ is bringing you into the understanding that prayer is for the glorifying of His Father, He will give you the first sign of His intimacy—silence.

*Therefore we will sing my songs to the stringed instruments all
the days of our life in the house of the Lord. (Isaiah 38:20)*

Jesus Christ taught hypocrisy to His disciples! 'But thou, when
thou fastest, anoint thy head, and wash thy face, that thou be
not seen of men to fast.' Don't say you are fasting, or that you
spent the night in prayer, wash your face; and never let your
dearest friend know what you put yourself through. Natural
stoicism was created by God, and when it is transfigured by
the indwelling Holy Ghost, people will never think of you. 'He
must increase, but I must decrease.' John is not saying that with
a quivering mouth, or out of modesty; he is expressing the
spiritual delight of his life. I am to decrease because He has
come! He says it with a manly thrill. Is Jesus Christ increasing
in my life, or am I taking everything for myself? When I get
disillusioned I see Him and Him alone, there are no illusions
left. It is a matter of indifference how I am hurt, the one thing
I am concerned about is that every man may be presented 'perfect in Christ Jesus'.

PH 57

GETTING INTO GOD'S STRIDE

Enoch walked with God. (Gen. 5:24)

The test of a man's religious life and character is not what he does in the exceptional moments of life, but what he does in the ordinary times, when there is nothing tremendous or exciting on. The worth of a man is revealed in his attitude to ordinary things when he is not before the footlights (cf. John 1:36). It is a painful business to get through into the stride of God, it means getting your second wind spiritually. In learning to walk with God there is always the difficulty of getting into His stride; but when we have got into it, the only characteristic that manifests itself is the life of God. The individual man is lost sight of in his personal union with God, and the stride and the power of God alone are manifested.

It is difficult to get into stride with God, because when we start walking with Him we find He has outstripped us before we have taken three steps. He has different ways of doing things, and we have to be trained and disciplined into His ways. It was said of Jesus—"He shall not fail nor be discouraged," because He never worked from His own individual standpoint but always from the standpoint of His Father, and we have to learn to do the same. Spiritual truth is learned by atmosphere, not by intellectual reasoning. God's Spirit alters the atmosphere of our way of looking at things, and things begin to be possible which never were possible before. Getting into the stride of God means nothing less than union with Himself. It takes a long time to get there, but keep at it. Don't give in because the pain is bad just now, get on with it, and before long you will find you have a new vision and a new purpose.

But when thou doest alms, let not thy left hand know what thy right hand doeth. (Matthew 6:3)

Do good until it is an unconscious habit of the life and you do not know you are doing it, you will be covered with confusion when Jesus Christ detects it. 'Lord, when saw we thee an hungred, and fed thee? . . . Inasmuch as ye have done it unto one of the least of these my brethren, ye have done it unto me.' That is our Lord's magnanimous interpretation of kind acts that people have never allowed themselves to think of. Get into the habit of having such a relationship to God that you do good without knowing you do it, then you will no longer trust your own impulse, or your own judgment, you will trust only the inspiration of the Spirit of God. The mainspring of your motives will be the Father's heart, not your own; the Father's understanding, not your own. When once you are rightly related To God, He will use you as a channel through which His disposition will flow.

SSM 57

Much of our modern philanthropy is based on the motive of giving to the poor man because he deserves it, or because we are distressed at seeing him poor. Jesus never taught charity from those motives: He said, 'Give to him that asketh thee, not because he deserves it, but because I tell you to.' The great motive in all giving is Jesus Christ's command. We can always find a hundred and one reasons for not obeying our Lord's commands, because we will trust our reasoning rather than His reason, and our reason does not take God into calculation. How does civilization argue? 'Does this man deserve what I am giving him?' Immediately you talk like that, the Spirit of God says, 'Who are you? Do *you* deserve more than other men the blessings you have?'

SSM 46

INDIVIDUAL DISCOURAGEMENT AND
PERSONAL ENLARGEMENT

Moses went out unto his brethren, and looked on their burdens.
(Ex. 2:11)

Moses saw the oppression of his people and felt certain that he was the one to deliver them, and in the righteous indignation of his own spirit he started to right their wrongs. After the first strike for God and for the right, God allowed Moses to be driven into blank discouragement, He sent him into the desert to feed sheep for forty years. At the end of that time, God appeared and told Moses to go and bring forth His people, and Moses said—"Who am I, that I should go?" In the beginning Moses realized that he was the man to deliver the people, but he had to be trained and disciplined by God first. He was right in the individual aspect, but he was not the man for the work until he had learned communion with God.

We may have the vision of God and a very clear understanding of what God wants, and we start to do the thing, then comes something equivalent to the forty years in the wilderness, as if God had ignored the whole thing and when we are thoroughly discouraged God comes back and revives the call, and we get the quaver in and say—"Oh, who am I?" We have to learn the first great stride of God—"I AM THAT I AM hath sent thee." We have to learn that our individual effort for God is an impertinence; our individuality is to be rendered incandescent by a personal relationship to God (see Matthew 3:17). We fix on the individual aspect of things; we have the vision—"This is what God wants me to do;" but we have not got into God's stride. If you are going through a time of discouragement, there is a big personal enlargement ahead.

The Son of man is come eating and drinking: and ye say, Behold a gluttonous man, and a winebibber. (Luke 7:34)

We are all so abominably serious, so interested in our own characters, that we refuse to behave like Christians in the shallow concerns of life. Our safeguard is the God-given shallowness. It is the attitude of a spiritual prig to go about with a countenance that is a rebuke to others because you have the idea that they are shallower than you. Live the surface common-sense life in a common-sense way, and remember that the shallow concerns of life are as much of God as the profound concerns. It is not our devotion to God or our holiness that makes us refuse to be shallow, but our wish to impress others that we are not shallow, which is a sure sign that we are prigs. We are to be of the stamp of our Lord and Master, and the prigs of His day called Him a glutton and a winebibber, they said He was not dealing with the profound things. Beware of the production of contempt for others by thinking that they are shallow. To be shallow is not a sign of being wicked: the ocean has a shore. The shallow amenities of life are appointed of God and are the things in which our Lord lived, and He lived in them as the Son of God. It is easier for personal pride not to live in them. Beware of posing as a profound person; God became a Baby.

NKW 68

THE KEY TO THE MISSIONARY

All power is given unto Me in heaven and in earth. Go ye there-
fore, and teach all nations. (Matt. 28:18-20)

The basis of missionary appeals is the authority of Jesus Christ,
not the needs of the heathen. We are apt to look upon Our
Lord as One Who assists us in our enterprises for God. Our Lord
puts Himself as the absolute sovereign supreme Lord over His
disciples. He does not say the heathen will be lost if we do not
go; He simply says—"Go ye therefore and teach all nations."
Go on the revelation of My sovereignty; teach and preach out
of a living experience of Me.

"Then the eleven disciples went . . . unto a mountain where
Jesus had appointed them." v. 16. If I want to know the universal sovereignty of Christ, I must know Him for myself, and
how to get alone with Him; I must take time to worship the
Being Whose Name I bear. "Come unto Me"—that is the place
to meet Jesus. Are you weary and heavy laden? How many
missionaries are! We banish those marvelous words of the
universal Sovereign of the world to the threshold of an after-
meeting; they are the words of Jesus to His disciples.

"Go ye therefore . . ." Go simply means live. Acts 1:8 is the
description of how to go. Jesus did not say—Go into Jerusalem and Judea and Samaria, but, "Ye shall be witnesses unto
Me" in all these places. He undertakes to establish the goings.

"If ye abide in Me, and My words abide in you . . ."—that is
the way to keep going in our personal lives. Where we are
placed is a matter of indifference; God engineers the goings.

"None of these things move me, neither count I my life dear
unto myself . . ." That is how to keep going till we're gone.

Verily I say unto you, That the publicans and the harlots go into the kingdom of God before you. (Matthew 21:31)

Read the New Testament, and you will find that Jesus Christ did not get into a moral panic over the things that rouse us. We are staggered at immorality, but Jesus faced those things in the most amazingly calm way. When He was roused to a state of passionate indignation it was by people who were never guilty of such things. What our Lord continually faced was the disposition behind either the morality or the immorality. 'If I had not come and spoken unto them, they had not had sin . . .' (John 15:22). Any man would have known without His coming that it was wrong to take life, the law is written in him; any man would have known that immorality was wrong; but no man apart from Jesus Christ would believe that 'my right to myself' is the very essence of sin. When we realize what Jesus means when He says, 'If you would be my disciple, give up your right to yourself to me', we begin to understand that 'the carnal mind is enmity against God'. 'I will not give up my right to myself; I will serve God as I choose.' Jesus Christ came to remove this disposition of self-realization.

BSG 12

THE KEY TO THE MISSIONARY MESSAGE

And He is the propitiation for our sins: and not for ours only,
but also for the sins of the whole world. (1 John 2:2)

The key to the missionary message is the propitiation of Christ
Jesus. Take any phase of Christ's work—the healing phase, the
saving and sanctifying phase; there is nothing limitless about
those. "The Lamb of God which taketh away the sin of the
world!"—that is limitless. The missionary message is the limitless significance of Jesus Christ as the propitiation for our sins,
and a missionary is one who is soaked in that revelation.

The key to the missionary message is the remissionary aspect of Christ's life, not His kindness and His goodness, and
His revealing of the Fatherhood of God; the great limitless significance is that He is the propitiation for our sins. The missionary message is not patriotic, it is irrespective of nations and
of individuals, it is for the whole world. When the Holy Ghost
comes in He does not consider my predilections, He brings me
into union with the Lord Jesus.

A missionary is one who is wedded to the charter of his Lord
and Master, he has not to proclaim his own point of view, but
to proclaim the Lamb of God. It is easier to belong to a coterie
which tells what Jesus Christ has done for me, easier to become a devotee to Divine healing, or to a special type of sanctification, or to the baptism of the Holy Ghost. Paul did not
say—"Woe is unto me, if I do not preach what Christ has done
for me," but—"Woe is unto me, if I preach not the gospel."
This is the Gospel—"The Lamb of God, which taketh away the
sin of the world!"

*But of him are ye in Christ Jesus, who was made unto us . . .
sanctification. (1 Corinthians 1:30)*

The stars do their work without fuss; God does His work without fuss, and saints do their work without fuss. The people who
are always desperately active are a nuisance; it is through the
saints who are one with Him that God is doing things all the
time. The broken and the jaded and the twisted are being ministered to by God through the saints who are not overcome by
their own panic, who because of their oneness with Him are
absolutely at rest, consequently He can work through them.
A sanctified saint remains perfectly confident in God, because
sanctification is not something the Lord gives me, sanctification is *Himself in me*. There is only one holiness, the holiness of
God, and only one sanctification, the sanctification that has its
origin in Jesus Christ. A sanctified saint is at leisure from himself and his own affairs, confident that God is bringing all things
out well.

PH 41

THE KEY TO THE MASTER'S ORDERS

Pray ye therefore the Lord of the harvest, that He will send forth labourers into His harvest. (Matt. 9:38)

The key to the missionary problem is in the hand of God, and that key is prayer not work, that is, not work as the word is popularly understood to-day because that may mean the evasion of concentration on God. The key to the missionary problem is not the key of common sense, nor the medical key, nor the key of civilization or education or even evangelization. The key is prayer. "Pray ye therefore the Lord of the harvest." Naturally, prayer is not practical, it is absurd; we have to realize that prayer is stupid from the ordinary common-sense point of view.

There are no nations in Jesus Christ's outlook, but *the world.* How many of us pray without respect of persons, and with respect to only one Person, Jesus Christ? He owns the harvest that is produced by distress and conviction of sin, and this is the harvest we have to pray that labourers may be thrust out to reap. We are taken up with active work while people all round are ripe to harvest, and we do not reap one of them, but waste our Lord's time in over-energized activities. Suppose the crisis comes in your father's life, in your brother's life, are you there as a labourer to reap the harvest for Jesus Christ? "Oh, but I have a special work to do!" No Christian has a special work to do. A Christian is called to be Jesus Christ's own, one who is not above his Master, one who does not dictate to Jesus Christ what he intends to do. Our Lord calls to no special work: He calls to Himself. "Pray ye therefore the Lord of the harvest," and He will engineer circumstances and thrust you out.

*Search me, O God, and know my heart: try me and know my
thoughts . . . (Psalm 139:23)*

We must live scrutinized by God, and if you want to know what
the scrutiny of God is like, listen to Jesus Christ: 'for from
within, out of the heart of men evil thoughts proceed . . .',
and then follows a rugged catalogue of things few of us know
anything about in conscious life, consequently we are apt to
be indignant and resent Jesus Christ's diagnosis—'I have never
felt like a murderer, or an adulterer, therefore those things
cannot be in me.' To talk in that way is proof that we are grossly
ignorant of ourselves. If we prefer to trust our ignorant innocence we pass a verdict on the only Master of the human heart
there is, we tell Him He does not know what He is talking about.
The one right thing to do is to listen to Jesus Christ and then
hand our hearts over to God to be searched and guarded, and
filled with the Holy Spirit, then the wonderful thing is that we
never need know and never shall know in actual experience
the truth of Jesus Christ's revelation about the human heart.
But if we stand on our own rights and wisdom at any second
an eruption may occur in our personal life and we shall discover to our unutterable horror that what Jesus said is
appallingly true.

SHL 47–8

GREATER WORKS

And greater works than these shall he do, because I go unto My Father. (John 14:12)

Prayer does not fit us for the greater works; prayer is the greater work. We think of prayer as a common-sense exercise of our higher powers in order to prepare us for God's work. In the teaching of Jesus Christ prayer is the working of the miracle of Redemption in me which produces the miracle of Redemption in others by the power of God. The way fruit remains is by prayer but remember it is prayer based on the agony of Redemption, not on my agony. Only a child gets prayer answered; a wise man does not.

Prayer is the battle; it is a matter of indifference where you are. Whichever way God engineers circumstances, the duty is to pray. Never allow the thought—"I am of no use where I am" because you certainly can be of no use where you are not. Wherever God has dumped you down in circumstances pray, ejaculate to Him all the time. "Whatsoever ye ask in My name, that will I do." We won't pray unless we get thrills, that is the intensest form of spiritual selfishness. We have to labour along the line of God's direction, and He says pray. "Pray ye therefore the Lord of the harvest, that He will send forth labourers into His harvest."

There is nothing thrilling about a labouring man's work, but it is the labouring man who makes the conceptions of the genius possible; and it is the labouring saint who makes the conceptions of his Master possible. You labour at prayer and results happen all the time from His standpoint. What an astonishment it will be to find, when the veil is lifted, the souls that have been reaped by you, simply because you had been in the habit of taking your orders from Jesus Christ.

Then goeth he, and taketh to him seven other spirits more wicked than himself: and they enter in, and swell there: and the last state of that man is worse than the first. (Luke 11:26)

Men say—'I can't help committing sin'; 'I can't help doing this thing'. Are they right? Perfectly right. You may talk to further orders about a weak will; there is nothing more absurd. It is not the man's weak will; he has got into league with a power stronger than he is, and when once a man gets in league with the prince of this world, I defy all his strength of will to stand before the terrific power of this world's darkness for one second. According to the New Testament, there is such a thing as obsession by unclean, malicious, wicked spirits who will damn and ruin body and soul in hell. A moral empty heart is the resort of these spirits when a man is off his guard. But if a man has been born again of the Spirit of God and is keeping in the light, he cannot help going right because he is backed by the tremendous power of Almighty God. What does the Apostle John say?—'the evil one toucheth him not'. What a marvellous certainty! God grant we may be so filled with the Holy Spirit that we listen to His checks along every line. No power can deceive a child of God who keeps in the light with God.

SHL 31

THE KEY TO MISSIONARY DEVOTION

For His name's sake they went forth. (3 John 7)

Our Lord has told us how love to Him is to manifest itself. "Lovest thou Me?" "Feed My sheep"—identify yourself with My interests in other people, not, identify *Me* with *your* interests in other people. First Corinthians 13:4-8 gives the character of this love, it is the love *of God* expressing itself. The test of my love for Jesus is the practical one, all the rest is sentimental jargon.

Loyalty to Jesus Christ is the supernatural work of Redemption wrought in me by the Holy Ghost Who sheds abroad the love of God in my heart, and that love works efficaciously through me in contact with everyone I meet. I remain loyal to His Name although every common-sense fact gives the lie to Him, and declares that He has no more power than a morning mist.

The key to missionary devotion means being attached to nothing and no one saving Our Lord Himself, not being detached from things externally. Our Lord was amazingly in and out among ordinary things; His detachment was on the inside towards God. External detachment is often an indication of a secret vital attachment to the things we keep away from externally.

The loyalty of a missionary is to keep his soul concentratedly open to the nature of the Lord Jesus Christ. The men and women Our Lord sends out on His enterprises are the ordinary human stuff, plus dominating devotion to Himself wrought by the Holy Ghost.

> *How much more shall the blood of Christ, who through the eternal Spirit offered himself without spot to God, purge your conscience from dead works to serve the living God? (Hebrews 9:14)*

Foregiveness means not merely that I am saved from sin and made right for heaven (no man would accept forgiveness on such a level); forgiveness means that I am forgiven into a recreated relationship, into identification with God in Christ.

The background of God's forgiveness is holiness. If God were not holy there would be nothing in His forgiveness. There is no such thing as God overlooking sin; therefore if God does forgive there must be a reason that justifies His doing so. If I am forgiven without being altered by the forgiveness, forgiveness is a damage to me and a sign of the unmitigated weakness of God. When a man is convicted of sin he knows God dare not forgive him; if He did it would mean that man has a bigger sense of justice than God. God, in forgiving a man, gives him the heredity of His own Son, i.e. He turns him into the standard of the Forgiver. Forgiveness is a revelation—hope for the hopeless; that is the message of the Gospel.

A man may say, 'I don't deny that God will forgive me, but what about the folks I have put wrong? Can God give me a clearinghouse for my conscience?' It is because these things are neglected in the presentation of Redemption that men are kept away from Jesus Christ. Men are kept away by honesty more than by dishonesty.

SA 18

THE UNHEEDED SECRET

My kingdom is not of this world. (John 18:36)

The great enemy to the Lord Jesus Christ in the present day is the conception of practical work that has not come from the New Testament, but from the systems of the world in which endless energy and activities are insisted upon, but no private life with God. The emphasis is put on the wrong thing. Jesus said, "The kingdom of God cometh not with observation, for lo the kingdom of God is within you," a hidden, obscure thing. An active Christian worker too often lives in the shop window. It is the innermost of the innermost that reveals the power of the life.

We have to get rid of the plague of the spirit of the religious age in which we live. In Our Lord's life there was none of the press and rush of tremendous activity that we regard so highly, and the disciple is to be as His Master. The central thing about the kingdom of Jesus Christ is a personal relationship to Himself, not public usefulness to men.

It is not its practical activities that are the strength of this Bible Training College, its whole strength lies in the fact that here you are put into soak before God. You have no idea of where God is going to engineer your circumstances, no knowledge of what strain is going to be put on you either at home or abroad, and if you waste your time in over-active energies instead of getting into soak on the great fundamental truths of God's Redemption, you will snap when the strain comes; but if this time of soaking before God is being spent in getting rooted and grounded in God on the unpractical line, you will remain true to Him whatever happens.

But he that lacketh these things is blind. (2 Peter 1:9)

When Christ is formed in us we have to see that our human nature acts in perfect obedience to all that the Son of God reveals. God does not supply us with character, He gives us the life of His Son and we can either ignore Him and refuse to obey Him, or we can so obey Him, so bring every thought and imagination into captivity, that the life of Jesus is manifested in our mortal flesh. It is not a question of being saved from hell, but of being saved in order to manifest the Son of God in our mortal flesh. Our responsibility is to keep ourselves fit to manifest Him . . .

The only way to keep yourself fit is by the discipline of the disagreeable. It is the disagreeable things which make us exhibit whether we are manifesting the life of the Son of God, or living a life which is antagonistic to Him. When disagreeable things happen, do we manifest the essential sweetness of the Son of God or the essential irritation of ourselves apart from Him? Whenever self comes into the ascendant, the life of the Son of God in us is perverted and twisted; there is irritation, and His life suffers. Growth in grace stops the moment we get huffed.

GH 74–5

IS GOD'S WILL MY WILL?

This is the will of God, even your sanctification. (1 Thess. 4:3)

It is not a question of whether God is willing to sanctify me; is it *my* will? Am I willing to let God do in me all that has been made possible by the Atonement? Am I willing to let Jesus be made sanctification to me, and to let the life of Jesus be manifested in my mortal flesh? Beware of saying—Oh, I am longing to be sanctified. You are not, stop longing and make it a matter of transaction—"Nothing in my hands I bring." Receive Jesus Christ to be made sanctification to you in implicit faith, and the great marvel of the Atonement of Jesus will be made real in you. All that Jesus made possible is made mine by the free loving gift of God on the ground of what He performed, my attitude as a saved and sanctified soul is that of profound humble holiness (there is no such thing as proud holiness), a holiness based on agonizing repentance and a sense of unspeakable shame and degradation; and also on the amazing realization that the love of God commended itself to me in that while I cared nothing about Him, He completed everything for my salvation and sanctification (see Rom. 5:8. R.V.). No wonder Paul says nothing is "able to separate us from the love of God, which is in Christ Jesus our Lord."

Sanctification makes me one with Jesus Christ, and in Him one with God, and it is done only through the superb Atonement of Christ. Never put the effect as the cause. The effect in me is obedience and service and prayer, and is the outcome of speechless thanks and adoration for the marvelous sanctification wrought out in me because of the Atonement.

Ye are a chosen generation . . . that ye should shew forth the praises of him who hath called you out of darkness into his marvellous light. (1 Peter 2:9)

Imitation is one of the first reactions of a child, it is not sinful. We come to a right knowledge of ourselves by imitating others. The instinct that makes us afraid of being odd is not a cowardly instinct, it is the only power of self-preservation we have. If you live much by yourself you become an oddity, you never see the quirks in yourself. Some people won't live with others spiritually, they live in holes and corners by themselves. The New Testament warns of those who 'separate themselves' (Jude 19). By the grace of God we are taken out of the fashion we were in and we become more or less speckled birds. Immediately you introduce a standard of imitation which the set to which you belong does not recognize, you will experience what Peter says, 'they think it strange that ye run not with them to the same excess of riot' (1 Peter 4:4).

The Spirit of God lifts the natural reaction of imitation into another domain and by God's grace we begin to imitate our Lord and shew forth His praises. It is the natural instinct of a child to imitate his mother, and when we are born again the Holy Spirit lifts this instinct into the spiritual domain and it becomes the most supernaturally natural thing for us to imitate our Lord. We grow in grace naturally, not artificially. Mimicking is the counterfeit of imitation and produces the 'pi' person, one who tries his level best to be what he is not. When you are good you never try to be. It is natural to be like the one we live with most; then if we spend most of our time with Jesus Christ, we shall begin to be like Him, by the way we are built naturally and by the Spirit God puts in.

MFL 70

DIRECTION BY IMPULSE

Building up yourselves on your most holy faith. (Jude 20)

There was nothing either of the nature of impulse or of cold-bloodedness about Our Lord, but only a calm strength that never got into panic. Most of us develop our Christianity along the line of our temperament, not along the line of God. Impulse is a trait in natural life, but Our Lord always ignores it, because it hinders the development of the life of a disciple. Watch how the Spirit of God checks impulse; His checks bring a rush of self-conscious foolishness which makes us instantly want to vindicate ourselves. Impulse is all right in a child, but it is disastrous in a man or woman; an impulsive man is always a petted man. Impulse has to be trained into intuition by discipline.

Discipleship is built entirely on the supernatural grace of God. Walking on the water is easy to impulsive pluck, but walking on dry land as a disciple of Jesus Christ is a different thing. Peter walked on the water to go to Jesus, but he followed Him afar off on the land. We do not need the grace of God to stand crises, human nature and pride are sufficient, we can face the strain magnificently; but it does require the supernatural grace of God to live twenty-four hours in every day as a saint, to go through drudgery as a disciple, to live an ordinary, unobserved, ignored existence as a disciple of Jesus. It is inbred in us that we have to do exceptional things for God; but we have not. We have to be exceptional in the ordinary things, to be holy in mean streets, among mean people, and this is not learned in five minutes.

> *. . . bringing into captivity every thought to the obedience of Christ. (2 Corinthians 10:5)*

Most of us object to giving up the energy of our minds to form the mind of Christ . . . . We construct the mind of Christ in the same way as we construct the natural mind, viz. by the way our disposition reacts when we come in contact with external things. The mind is closely affiliated with its physical machine, the brain, and we are responsible for getting that machine into rights habits. 'Glean your thinking,' says Paul (see Philippians 4:8). Never submit to the tyrannous idea that you cannot look after your mind; you can . . . . We have to rouse ourselves up to think, to bring 'every thought into captivity to the obedience of Christ'. Never pray about evil thoughts, it will fix them in the mind. 'Quit'—that is the only thing to do with anything that is wrong; to ruthlessly grip it on the threshold of your mind and allow it no more way. If you have received the Holy Spirit, you will find that you have the power to bring 'every thought into captivity to the obedience of Christ'.

MFL 49

Isaiah says that a man takes a tree and cuts it in two, uses part to cook his food, and the other part he carves into an idol to worship. 'None of us do that!' we say; but we *do*. There are other things which are wooden besides trees, viz., our heads! We use one half of our heads to earn our living, and the other half to worship God.

SA 25

THE WITNESS OF THE SPIRIT

The Spirit Himself beareth witness with our spirit . . .
(Rom. 8:16. R.V.)

We are in danger of getting the barter spirit when we come to God, we want the witness before we have done what God tells us to do. "Why does not God reveal Himself to me?" He cannot, it is not that He will not, but He cannot, because you are in the road as long as you won't abandon absolutely to Him. Immediately you do, God witnesses to Himself, He cannot witness to you, but He witnesses instantly to His own nature in you. If you had the witness before the reality, it would end in sentimental emotion. Immediately you transact on the Redemption, and stop the impertinence of debate, God gives on the witness. As soon as you abandon reasoning and argument, God witnesses to what He has done, and we are amazed at our impertinence in having kept Him waiting. If you are in debate as to whether God can deliver from sin, either let Him do it, or tell Him He cannot. Do not quote this and that person, try Matthew 11:28—"*Come* unto Me." Come, if you are weary and heavy laden; *ask*, if you know you are evil (Luke 11:13).

The Spirit of God witnesses to the Redemption of Our Lord, He does not witness to anything else; He cannot witness to our reason. The simplicity that comes from our natural common-sense decisions is apt to be mistaken for the witness of the Spirit, but the Spirit witnesses only to His own nature, and to the work of Redemption, never to our reason. If we try to make Him witness to our reason, it is no wonder we are in darkness and perplexity. Fling it all overboard, trust in Him, and He will give the witness.

Lay up for yourselves treasures in heaven. (Matthew 6:20)

If you are going to succeed in anything in this world, you must concentrate on it, practise it, and the same is true spiritually. There are many things you will find you cannot do if you are going to be concentrated on God, things that may be perfectly legitimate and right for others, but not for you if you are going to concentrate on God. Never let the narrowness of your conscience condemn the other man.

Maintain the personal relationship, see that you yourself are concentrated on God, not on your convictions or your point of view, but on God. Whenever you are in doubt about a thing, push it to its logical conclusion—'Is this the kind of thing that Jesus Christ is after or the kind of thing Satan is after?' Immediately your decision is made, act on it.

SSM 63

NOT A BIT OF IT!

If any man be in Christ, he is a new creature: old things are passed away. (2 Cor. 5:17)

Our Lord never nurses our prejudices, He mortifies them, runs clean athwart them. We imagine that God has a special interest in our particular prejudices; we are quite sure that God will never deal with us as He has to deal with other people. "God must deal with other people in a very stern way, but of course He knows that my prejudices are all right." We have to learn— "Not a bit of it!" Instead of God being on the side of our prejudices, He is deliberately wiping them out. It is part of our moral education to have our prejudices run straight across by His providence, and to watch how He does it. God pays no respect to anything we bring to Him. There is only one thing God wants of us, and that is our unconditional surrender.

When we are born again, the Holy Spirit begins to work His new creation in us, and there will come a time when there is not a bit of the old order left, the old solemnity goes, the old attitude to things goes, and "all things are of God." How are we going to get the life that has no lust, no self-interest, no sensitiveness to pokes, the love that is not provoked, that thinketh no evil, that is always kind? The only way is by allowing not a bit of the old life to be left; but only simple perfect trust in God, such trust that we no longer want God's blessings, but only want Himself. Have we come to the place where God can withdraw His blessings and it does not affect our trust in Him? When once we see God at work, we will never bother our heads about things that happen, because we are actually trusting in our Father in Heaven Whom the world cannot see.

Having their conscience seared. (1 Timothy 4:2)

The human eye may be damaged by gazing too much on intense whiteness, as in the case of snow blindness when men remain blind for months. And conscience may be damaged by tampering with the occult side of things, giving too much time to speculation; then when we turn to human life we are as blind as bats. It may be all right for angels to spend their time in visions and meditation, but if I am a Christian I find God in the ordinary occurrences of my life. The special times of prayer are of a different order. If I sequester myself and press my mind on one line of things and forget my relation to human life, when I do turn to human affairs I am morally blind. Am I trying to embrace a sensation of God spiritually for myself? When God has saved and sanctified us there is a danger that we are unwilling to let the vision fade; we refuse to take up our ordinary work, and soon we will be completely at a loss because we have hugged an experience to our souls instead of maintaining a right relationship to God who gave us the experience.

GH 70

THE VIEWPOINT

Now thanks be to God, which always causeth us to triumph in Christ. (2 Cor. 2:14)

The viewpoint of a worker for God must not be as near the highest as he can get, it must be *the* highest. Be careful to maintain strenuously God's point of view, it has to be done everyday, bit by bit; don't think on the finite. No outside power can touch the viewpoint.

The viewpoint to maintain is that we are here for one purpose only, viz., to be captives in the train of Christ's triumphs. We are not in God's showroom, we are here to exhibit one thing—the absolute captivity of our lives to Jesus Christ. How small the other points of view are —I am standing alone battling for Jesus; I have to maintain the cause of Christ and hold this fort for Him. Paul says—I am in the train of a conqueror, and it does not matter what the difficulties are, I am always led in triumph. Is this idea being worked out practically in us? Paul's secret joy was that God took him, a red-handed rebel against Jesus Christ, and made him a captive, and now that is all he is here for. Paul's joy was to be a captive of the Lord, he had no other interest in heaven or in earth. It is a shameful thing for a Christian to talk about getting the victory. The Victor ought to have got us so completely that it is His victory all the time, and we are more than conquerors through Him.

"For we are unto God a sweet savour of Christ." We are enwheeled with the odour of Jesus, and wherever we go we are a wonderful refreshment to God.

Meditate upon these things. (1 Timothy 4:15)

Meditation is not being like a pebble in a brook, allowing the waters of thought to flow over us; that is reverie. Meditation is the most intense spiritual act, it brings every part of body and mind into harness. To be spiritual by effort is a sure sign of a false relationship to God; to be obedient by effort in the initial stages is a sure sign that we are determined to obey God at all costs. Take time. Remember we have all the time there is. The majority of us waste time and want to encroach on eternity. 'Oh well, I will think about these things when I have time.' The only time you will have is the day after you are dead, and that will be eternity. An hour, or half an hour, of daily attention to, and meditation on, our own spiritual life is the secret of progress.

MFL 65

Pray without ceasing. (1 Thessalonians 5:17)

There is a quietism of devotional self-indulgence which takes the place spiritually that loafing does socially. It is easy to call it meditative prayer, but meditation is only attained in actual life by the strenuous discipline of brooding in the centre of a subject . . . . A saint is never consciously a praying one. A saint endeavours consciously and strenuously to master the technical means of expressing God's life in himself. The place of prayer in the New Testament is just this one of severe technical training in which spiritual sympathies are sustained in unsecular strength, and manifested in the vulgar details of actual life.

DPR 13

THE ETERNAL CRUSH OF THINGS

I am made all things to all men, that I might by all means save some. (1 Cor. 9:22)

A Christian worker has to learn how to be God's noble man or woman amid a crowd of ignoble things. Never make this plea— If only I were somewhere else! All God's men are ordinary men made extraordinary by the matter He has given them. Unless we have the right matter in our minds intellectually and in our hearts affectionately, we will be hustled out of usefulness to God. We are not workers for God by choice. Many people deliberately choose to be workers, but they have no matter in them of God's almighty grace, no matter of His mighty word. Paul's whole heart and mind and soul were taken up with the great matter of what Jesus Christ came to do, he never lost sight of that one thing. We have to face ourselves with the one central fact—Jesus Christ and Him crucified.

"I have chosen you." Keep that note of greatness in your creed. It is not that you have got God but that He has got you. Here, in this College, God is at work, bending, breaking, moulding, doing just as He chooses. Why He is doing it, we do not know; He is doing it for one purpose only—that He may be able to say, This is My man, My woman. We have to be in God's hand so that He can plant men on the Rock as He has planted us.

Never choose to be a worker, but when God has put His call on you, woe be to you if you turn to the right hand or to the left. He will do with you what He never did with you before the call came; He will do with you what He is not doing with other people. Let Him have His way.

And Abraham drew near, and said . . . (Genesis 18:23)

The meaning of intercession is that we see what God is doing, consequently there is an intimacy between the child and the Father which is never impertinent. We must pour into the bosom of God the cares which give us pain and anxiety in order that He may solve for us, and before us, the difficulties which we cannot solve. We injure our spiritual life when we dump the whole thing down before God and say—You do it. That spirit is blind to the real union with God. We must dump ourselves down in the midst of our problems and watch God solve them for us. 'But I have no faith'—bring your problems to God and stay with Him while He solves them, then God Himself and the solution of your problems will be for ever your own. Watch the tendency to pathetic humbug in your approach to God. If we could see the floor of God's immediate presence, we would find it strewn with the 'toys' of God's children who have said—This is broken, I can't play with it any more, please give me another present. Only one in a thousand sits down in the midst of it all and says—I will watch my Father mend this.

NKW 76

I think sometimes we will be covered with shame when we meet the Lord Jesus and think how blind and ignorant we were when He brought people around us to pray for, or gave us opportunities of warning, and instead of praying we tried to find out what was wrong. We have no business to try and find out what is wrong, our business is to pray, so that when the awakening comes Jesus Christ will be the first they meet.

PS 34

WHAT IS A MISSIONARY?

As My Father hath sent Me, even so send I you. (John 20:21)

A missionary is one sent by Jesus Christ as He was sent by God. The great dominant note is not the needs of men, but the command of Jesus. The source of our inspiration in work for God is behind, not before. The tendency to-day is to put the inspiration ahead, to sweep everything in front of us and bring it all out to our conception of success. In the New Testament the inspiration is put behind us, the Lord Jesus. The ideal is to be true to Him, to carry out *His* enterprises.

Personal attachment to the Lord Jesus and His point of view is the one thing that must not be overlooked. In missionary enterprise the great danger is that God's call is effaced by the needs of the people until human sympathy absolutely overwhelms the meaning of being sent by Jesus. The needs are so enormous, the conditions so perplexing that every power of mind falters and fails. We forget that the one great reason underneath all missionary enterprise is not first the elevation of the people, nor the education of the people, nor their needs; but first and foremost the command of Jesus Christ—"Go ye therefore, and teach all nations."

When looking back on the lives of men and women of God the tendency is to say—What wonderfully astute wisdom they had! How perfectly they understood all God wanted! The astute mind behind is the Mind of God, not human wisdom at all. We give credit to human wisdom when we should give credit to the Divine guidance of God through childlike people who were foolish enough to trust God's wisdom and the supernatural equipment of God.

> *And when thou prayest, thou shalt not be as the hypocrites are: for they love to pray standing in the synagogues and in the corners of the streets, that they may be seen of men. (Matthew 6:5)*

You perhaps have not noticed before that you always take care to tell those to whom it matters how early you rise in the morning to pray, how many all nights of prayer you spend; you have great zealousness in proclaiming your protracted meetings. This is all pious play-acting. Jesus says, 'Don't do it.' Our Lord did not say it was wrong to pray in the corners of the street, but He did say it was wrong to have the motive to be 'seen of men'. It is not wrong to pray in the early morning, but it is wrong to have the motive that it should be known . . .

Let the words come home to us personally in their New Testament setting, 'But *when* ye pray, use not vain repetitions.' Our Lord prayed the same prayer, using the same words, three times in the Garden of Gethsemane, and He gave the disciples a form of prayer which He knew would be repeated throughout the Christian centuries; so it cannot be mere repetition or the form of words that He is referring to. The latter half of the verse comes home better for personal purposes—'for they think that they shall be heard for their much speaking'—that is, Do not rely on your earnestness as the ground for being heard . . .

The phrase 'pray through' often means working ourselves up into a frenzy of earnestness in which perspiration is taken for inspiration. It is a mistake to think we are heard on the ground of our earnestness; we are heard on the ground of the evangelical basis, 'Having therefore, brethren, boldness to enter into the holiest by the blood of Jesus' (Hebrews 10:19).

DPR 18–20

THE METHOD OF MISSIONS

Go ye therefore, and teach [disciple] all nations. (Matt. 28:19)

Jesus Christ did not say—Go and save souls (the salvation of souls is the supernatural work of God), but—"Go and teach," i.e., disciple, "all nations," and you cannot make disciples unless you are a disciple yourself. When the disciples came back from their first mission they were filled with joy because the devils were subject to them, and Jesus said—Don't rejoice in successful service; the great secret of joy is that you are rightly related to Me. The great essential of the missionary is that he remains true to the call of God, and realizes that his one purpose is to disciple men and women to Jesus. There is a passion for souls that does not spring from God, but from the desire to make converts to our point of view.

The challenge to the missionary does not come on the line that people are difficult to get saved, that backsliders are difficult to reclaim, that there is a wadge of callous indifference; but along the line of his own personal relationship to Jesus Christ. "Believe ye that I am able to do this?" Our Lord puts that question steadily, it faces us in every individual case we meet. The one great challenge is—Do I know my Risen Lord? Do I know the power of His indwelling Spirit? Am I wise enough in God's sight, and foolish enough according to the world, to bank on what Jesus Christ has said, or am I abandoning the great supernatural position, which is the only call for a missionary, viz., boundless confidence in Christ Jesus? If I take up any other method I depart altogether from the methods laid down by Our Lord—"All power is given unto Me . . ., therefore go ye."

If ye abide in me, and my words abide in you, ye shall ask what ye will, and it shall be done unto you. (John 15:7)

We hear it said that a man will suffer in his life if he does not pray; I question it. Prayer is an interruption to personal ambition, and no man who is busy has time to pray. What will suffer is the life of God in him, which is nourished not by food but by prayer. If we look on prayer as a means of developing ourselves, there is nothing in it at all, nor do we find that idea of prayer in the Bible. Prayer is other than meditation; it is that which develops the life of God in us. When a man is born from above, the life of the Son of God begins in him, and he can either starve that life or nourish it. Prayer is the way the life of God is nourished. Our Lord nourished the life of God in Him by prayer; He was continually in contact with His Father. We generally look upon prayer as a means of getting things for ourselves, whereas the Bible idea of prayer is that God's holiness and God's purpose and God's wise order may be brought about, irrespective of who comes or who goes. Our ordinary views of prayer are not found in the New Testament.

IYA 9

JUSTIFICATION BY FAITH

For if, when we were enemies, we were reconciled to God by the death of His Son, much more, being reconciled, we shall be saved by His life. (Rom. 5:10)

I am not saved by believing; I realize I am saved by believing. It is not repentance that saves me, repentance is the sign that I realize what God has done in Christ Jesus. The danger is to put the emphasis on the effect instead of on the cause. It is my obedience that puts me right with God, my consecration. Never! I am put right with God because prior to all, Christ died. When I turn to God and by belief accept what God reveals I can accept, instantly the stupendous Atonement of Jesus Christ rushes me into a right relationship with God; and by the supernatural miracle of God's grace I stand justified, not because I am sorry for my sin, not because I have repented, but because of what Jesus has done. The Spirit of God brings it with a breaking, all-over light, and I know, though I do not know how, that I am saved.

The salvation of God does not stand on human logic, it stands on the sacrificial Death of Jesus. We can be born again because of the Atonement of Our Lord. Sinful men and women can be changed into new creatures, not by their repentance or their belief, but by the marvelous work of God in Christ Jesus which is prior to all experience. The impregnable safety of justification and sanctification is God Himself. We have not to work out these things ourselves; they have been worked out by the Atonement. The supernatural becomes natural by the miracle of God; there is the realization of what Jesus Christ has already done—*"It is finished."*

As thou, Father, art in me, and I in thee, that they also may be one in us. (John 17:21)

Prayer is not getting things from God, that is a most initial stage; prayer is getting into perfect communion with God; I tell Him what I know He knows in order that I may get to know it as He does. Jesus says, 'Pray because you have a Father, not because it quietens you, and give Him time to answer.'

SSM 59

God does not exist to answer our prayers, but by our prayers we come to discern the mind of God, and that is declared in John 17, 'That they may be one, even as we are one.' Am I as close to Jesus as that? God will not leave me alone until I am. God has one prayer He must answer, and that is the prayer of Jesus Christ. It does not matter how imperfect or immature a disciple may be, if he will hang in, that prayer will be answered.

IYA 55

The great thought which we do not realize sufficiently is the interchanging action of the Divine Spirit and the human spirit. This interchanging action of the Divine and human at every stage of our religious life is vividly expressed in Romans 8:26. The best example of the Divine Spirit working in a human spirit is seen in our Lord Jesus Christ in the days of His flesh. According to some expositors, we are so infirm that the Spirit of God brushes aside all our infirmities and prays irrespectively of us, but we find that our Lord recognized the difference between His own Spirit and the Spirit of God, and that His mind was always in subordination to the mind of God. 'I can of mine own self do nothing.'

IYA 99

SUBSTITUTION

*He hath made Him to be sin for us . . . that we might be made
the righteousness of God . . . (2 Cor. 5:21)*

The modern view of the death of Jesus is that He died for our
sins out of sympathy. The New Testament view is that He bore
our sin not by sympathy, but by identification. He was *made to
be sin*. Our sins are removed because of the death of Jesus, and
the explanation of His death is His obedience to His Father, not
His sympathy with us. We are acceptable with God not because
we have obeyed, or because we have promised to give up
things, but because of the death of Christ, and in no other way.
We say that Jesus Christ came to reveal the Fatherhood of God,
the lovingkindness of God; the New Testament says He came
to bear away the sin of the world. The revelation of His Father
is to those to whom He has been introduced as Saviour. Jesus
Christ never spoke of Himself to the world as one Who revealed
the Father, but as a stumbling block (see John 15-:22-24). John
14:9 was spoken to His disciples.

That Christ died for me, therefore I go scot free, is never
taught in the New Testament. What *is* taught in the New Testament is that "He died for all" (not—He died my death), and
that by identification with His death I can be freed from sin,
and have imparted to me His very righteousness. The substi-
tution taught in the New Testament is twofold: "He hath made
Him to be sin for us, who knew no sin; *that we might be made
the righteousness of God in Him.*" It is not Christ *for* me unless I
am determined to have Christ formed *in* me.

Men ought always to pray, and not to faint. (Luke 18:1)

Jesus also taught the disciples the prayer of patience. If you are right with God and God delays the manifested answer to your prayer, don't misjudge Him, don't think of Him as an unkind friend, or an unnatural father, or an unjust judge, but keep at it, your prayer will certainly be answered, for 'everyone that asketh receiveth'. 'Men ought always to pray, and not to faint,' i.e. not to cave in. 'Your heavenly Father will explain it all one day,' Jesus says, 'He cannot just now because He is developing your character.'

SSM 59

A man will get from life everything he asks for, because he does not ask for that which his will is not in. If a man asks wealth from life, he will get wealth, or he was playing the fool when he asked. 'If ye abide in me,' says Jesus, 'and my words abide in you, ye shall ask *what ye will*, and it shall be done unto you.' We pray pious blether, our will is not in it, and then we say God does not answer; we never *asked* Him for anything. Asking means that our wills are in what we ask.

You say, 'But I asked God to turn my life into a garden of the Lord, and there came the ploughshare of sorrow, and instead of a garden I have been given a wilderness.' God never gives a wrong answer. The garden of your natural life had to be turned into ploughed soil before God could turn it into a garden of the Lord. He will put the seed in now. Let God's seasons come over your soul, and before long your life will be a garden of the Lord.

SSM 85

FAITH

Without faith it is impossible to please Him. (Heb. (11:6)

Faith in antagonism to common sense is fanaticism, and common sense in antagonism to faith is rationalism. The life of faith brings the two into a right relation. Common sense is not faith, and faith is not common sense; they stand in the relation of the natural and the spiritual; of impulse and inspiration. Nothing Jesus Christ ever said is common sense, it is revelation sense, and it reaches the shores where common sense fails. Faith must be tried before the reality of faith is actual. "We know that all things work together for good," then no matter what happens, the alchemy of God's providence transfigures the ideal faith into actual reality. Faith always works on the personal line, the whole purpose of God being to see that the ideal faith is made real in His children.

For every detail of the common-sense life, there is a revelation fact of God whereby we can prove in practical experience what we believe God to be. Faith is a tremendously active principle which always puts Jesus Christ first—Lord, Thou hast said so and so (e.g., Matthew 6:33), it looks mad, but I am going to venture on Thy word. To turn head faith into a personal possession is a fight *always,* not sometimes. God brings us into circumstances in order to educate our faith, because the nature of faith is to make its object real. Until we know Jesus, God is a mere abstraction, we cannot have faith in Him; but immediately we hear Jesus say—"He that hath seen Me hath seen the Father," we have something that is real, and faith is boundless. Faith is the whole man rightly related to God by the power of the Spirit of Jesus Christ.

The holy scriptures, which are able to make thee wise unto salvation. (2 Timothy 3:15)

Am I learning how to use my Bible? The way to become complete for the master's service is to be well soaked in the Bible; some of us only exploit certain passages. Our Lord wants to give us continuous instruction out of His word; continuous instruction turns hearers into disciples. Beware of 'spooned meat' spirituality, of using the Bible for the sake of getting messages; use it to nourish your own soul. Be a continuous learner, don't stop short, and the truth will open to you on the right hand and on the left until you find there is no problem in human life with which the Bible does not deal. But remember that there are certain points of truth our Lord cannot reveal to us until our character is in a fit state to bear it. The discernment of God's truth and the development of character go together.

The life God places in the Christian worker is the life of Jesus Christ, which is continually changing spiritual innocence into glorious practical character.

AUG 34

DISCERNMENT OF FAITH

Faith as a grain of mustard seed . . . (Matt. 17:20)

We have the idea that God rewards us for our faith. It may be so in the initial stages, but we do not earn anything by faith; faith brings us into right relationship with God and gives God His opportunity. God has frequently to knock the bottom board out of your experience if you are a saint in order to get you into contact with Himself. God wants you to understand that it is a life of *faith,* not a life of sentimental enjoyment of His blessings. Your earlier life of faith was narrow and intense, settled around a little sun-spot of experience that had as much of sense as of faith in it, full of light and sweetness; then God withdrew His conscious blessings in order to teach you to walk by faith. You are worth far more to Him now than you were in your days of conscious delight and thrilling testimony.

Faith by its very nature must be tried, and the real trial of faith is not that we find it difficult to trust God, but that God's character has to be cleared in our own minds. Faith in its actual working out has to go through spells of unsyllabled isolation. Never confound the trial of faith with the ordinary discipline of life, much that we call the trial of faith is the inevitable result of being alive. Faith in the Bible is faith in God against everything that contradicts Him—I will remain true to God's character whatever He may do. "Though He slay me, yet will I trust Him"—this is the most sublime utterance of faith in the whole of the Bible.

My God, my God, why hast thou forsaken me? (Matthew 27:46)

The cry on the Cross is unfathomable to us. The only ones—and I want to say this very deliberately—the only ones who come near the threshold of understanding the cry of Jesus are not the martyrs, they knew that God had not forsaken them, His presence was so wonderful; not the lonely missionaries who are killed or forsaken, they experience exultant joy, for God is with them when men forsake them; the only ones who come near the threshold of understanding the experience of God-forsakenness are men like Cain—'My punishment is greater than I can bear', men like Esau, ' . . . an exceeding bitter cry', men like Judas. Jesus Christ knew and tasted to a fuller depth than any man could ever taste what it is to be separated from God by sin. If Jesus Christ was a martyr, our salvation is a myth. We have followed cunningly devised fables if Jesus Christ is not all that this cry represents Him to be—the Incarnate God becoming identified with sin in order to save men from hell and damnation. The depth of this cry of Jesus is deeper than any man can go because it is a cry from the heart of God. The height and depth of our salvation are only measured by God Almighty on His throne and Jesus Christ in the heart of hell.

PS 18

NOVEMBER

YE ARE NOT YOUR OWN

Know ye not that . . . ye are not your own? (1 Cor. 6:19)

There is no such thing as a private life—"a world within the world"—for a man or woman who is brought into fellowship with Jesus Christ's sufferings. God breaks up the private life of His saints, and makes it a thoroughfare for the world on the one hand and for Himself on the other. No human being can stand that unless he is identified with Jesus Christ. We are not sanctified for ourselves, we are called into the fellowship of the Gospel, and things happen which have nothing to do with us, God is getting us into fellowship with Himself. Let Him have His way; if you do not, instead of being of the slightest use to God in His Redemptive work in the world, you will be a hindrance and a clog.

The first thing God does with us is to get us based on rugged Reality until we do not care what becomes of us individually as long as He gets His way for the purpose of His Redemption. Why shouldn't we go through heartbreaks? Through those doorways God is opening up ways of fellowship with His Son. Most of us fall and collapse at the first grip of pain; we sit down on the threshold of God's purpose and die away of self-pity, and all so called Christian sympathy will aid us to our death bed. But God will not. He comes with the grip of the pierced hand of His Son, and says—"Enter into fellowship with Me; arise and shine." If through a broken heart God can bring His purposes to pass in the world, then thank Him for breaking your heart.

A Lamb as it had been slain. (Revelation 5:6)

In the days of His flesh Jesus Christ exhibited this Divine paradox of the Lion and the Lamb. He was the Lion in majesty, rebuking the winds and demons: He was the Lamb in meekness, 'who when He was reviled, reviled not again'. He was the Lion in power, raising the dead: He was the Lamb in patience—who was 'brought as a lamb to the slaughter, and as a sheep before her shearers is dumb, so He openeth not His mouth'. He was the Lion in authority, 'Ye have heard that it hath been said . . . but I say unto you . . . ': He was the Lamb in gentleness, 'Suffer the little children to come unto me . . . and he took them up in his arms, put his hand upon them and blessed them.'

In our personal lives Jesus Christ proves Himself to be all this—He is the Lamb to expiate our sins, to lift us out of condemnation and plant within us His own heredity of holiness: He is the Lion to rule over us, so that we gladly say, 'the government of this life shall be upon His shoulders'. And what is true in individual life is to be true also in the universe at large. The time is coming when the Lion of the Tribe of Judah shall reign, and when 'the kingdoms of this world shall become the kingdoms of our Lord, and of his Christ'.

One remaining paradox—In Revelation 6:16 'the wrath of the Lamb' is mentioned. We know what the wrath of a lion is like—but *the wrath of the Lamb!*—it is beyond our conception. All one can say about it is that the wrath of God is the terrible obverse side of the love of God.

CHI 121

AUTHORITY AND INDEPENDENCE

If ye love Me, ye will keep My commandments. (John 14:15. RV)

Our Lord never insists upon obedience; He tells us very emphatically what we ought to do, but He never takes means to make us do it. We have to obey Him out of a oneness of spirit. That is why whenever Our Lord talked about discipleship, He prefaced it with an IF—you do not need to unless you like. "*If* any man will be My disciple, let him deny himself," let him give up his right to himself to Me. Our Lord is not talking of eternal positions, but of being of value to Himself in this order of things; that is why He sounds so stern (cf. Luke 14:26). Never interpret these words apart from the One Who uttered them.

The Lord does not give me rules, He makes His standard very clear, and if my relationship to Him is that of love, I will do what He says without any hesitation. If I hesitate, it is because I love someone else in competition with him, viz., myself. Jesus Christ will not help me to obey Him, I must obey Him; and when I do obey Him, I fulfil my spiritual destiny. My personal life may be crowded with small petty incidents, altogether unnoticeable and mean; but if I obey Jesus Christ in the haphazard circumstances, they become pinholes through which I see the face of God, and when I stand face to face with God I will discover that through my obedience thousands were blessed. When once God's Redemption comes to the point of obedience in a human soul, it always creates. If I obey Jesus Christ, the Redemption of God will rush through me to other lives, because behind the deed of obedience is the Reality of Almighty God.

> *To every thing there is a season, and a time to every purpose under heaven. (Ecclesiastes 3:1)*

The dispensations of God are discernible only to the Spirit of God. If we mistake the dispensations of God to mean something we can see, we are off the track. Solomon is strong on the fact that God has made certain unalterable durations, but he does not say, as St Augustine and Calvin did, that therefore God is tied up by His own laws . . .

There are certain dispensational things for which God is responsible, e.g. birth and death . . . Within the limits of birth and death I can do as I like; but I cannot make myself un-born, neither can I escape death, those two limits are there. I have nothing to do with placing the limits, but within them I can produce what my disposition chooses. Whether I have a distressful time or a joyful time depends on what I do in between the limits of the durations.

SHH 22–3

No man's destiny is made for him, each man makes his own. Fatalism is the deification of moral cowardice which arises from a refusal to accept the responsibility for choosing either of the two destined ends for the human race—salvation or damnation. The power of individual choice is the secret of human responsibility. I can choose which line I will go on, but I have no power to alter the destination of that line once I have taken it—yet I always have the power to get off one line on to the other.

OPG 50

A BOND-SLAVE OF JESUS

I am crucified with Christ; nevertheless I live, yet not I, but Christ liveth in me. (Gal. 2:20)

These words mean the breaking of my independence with my own hand and surrendering to the supremacy of the Lord Jesus. No one can do this for me, I must do it myself. God may bring me up to the point three hundred and sixty-five times a year, but He cannot put me through it. It means breaking the husk of my individual independence of God, and the emancipating of my personality into oneness with Himself, not for my own ideas, but for absolute loyalty to Jesus. There is no possibility of dispute when once I am there. Very few of us know anything about loyalty to Christ—*"For My sake."* It is that which makes the iron saint

Has that break come? All the rest is pious fraud. The one point to decide is—Will I give up, will I surrender to Jesus Christ, and make no conditions whatever as to how the break comes? I must be broken from my self-realization, and immediately that point is reached, the reality of the supernatural identification takes place at once, and the witness of the Spirit of God is unmistakable—"I have been crucified with Christ."

The passion of Christianity is that I deliberately sign away my own rights and become a bond-slave of Jesus Christ. Until I do that, I do not begin to be a saint.

One student a year who hears God's call would be sufficient for God to have called this College into existence. This College as an organization is not worth anything, it is not academic; it is for nothing else but for God to help Himself to lives. Is He going to help Himself to us, or are we taken up with our conception of what we are going to be?

> *And God commanded the man, saying . . . of the tree of the knowledge of good and evil, thou shalt not eat of it: for in the day that thou eatest thereof thou shalt surely die.*
> *(Genesis 2:16–17)*

If I am going to find out a thing scientifically, I must find it out by curiosity; but if I want to find out anything on the moral line, I can only do it by obedience. God put man in a garden with the tree of knowledge of good and evil, and said, 'Ye shall not eat of it.' God did not say they were not to know good and evil, but that they were not to know good and evil by eating of the tree. They were intended to know evil in the way Jesus Christ knew it, viz, by contrast with good. They did eat of the tree, consequently the human race knows good by contrast with evil. Adam knew evil positively and good negatively, and none of us knows the order God intended. No man who has eaten of the fruit of the tree knows evil by contrast with good. The curiosity of the human heart finds out the bad things first. The fruit of the tree of the knowledge of good and evil gives the bias of insatiable curiosity on the bad line, and it is only by the readjustment through Jesus Christ that the bias on the other line enters in—a tremendous thirst after God. Jesus Christ knew evil negatively by positively knowing good; He never ate of the tree, and when a man is reborn of the Spirit of God that is the order.

SA 71

THE AUTHORITY OF REALITY

Draw nigh to God, and He will draw nigh to you. (James 4:8)

It is essential to give people a chance of acting on the truth of God. The responsibility must be left with the individual, you cannot act for him, it must be his own deliberate act, but the evangelical message ought always to lead a man to act. The paralysis of refusing to act leaves a man exactly where he was before; when once he acts, he is never the same. It is the foolishness of it that stands in the way of hundreds who have been convicted by the Spirit of God. Immediately I precipitate myself over into an act, that second I live; all the rest is existence. The moments when I truly live are the moments when I act with my whole will.

Never allow a truth of God that is brought home to your soul to pass without acting on it, not necessarily physically, but in will. Record it, with ink or with blood. The feeblest saint who transacts business with Jesus Christ is emancipated the second he acts; all the almighty power of God is on his behalf. We come up to the truth of God, we confess we are wrong, but go back again; then we come up to it again, and go back; until we learn that we have no business to go back. We have to go clean over on some word of our redeeming Lord and transact business with Him. His word "come" means "transact." "Come unto Me." The last thing we do is to come; but everyone who does come knows that that second the supernatural rush of the life of God invades him instantly. The dominating power of the world, the flesh and the devil is paralysed, not by your act, but because your act has linked you on to God and His redemptive power.

Moreover, the profit of the earth is for all: the king himself is served by the field. (Ecclesiastes 5:9)

'In the sweat of thy brow shalt thou eat thy bread, cursed is the ground for thy sake, thorns also and thistles shall it bring forth to thee.' The earth is cursed because of man's apostasy, and when that apostasy ceases in actual history, the ground will no longer bring forth the curse. The final redemption includes 'new heavens and a new earth'. 'Instead of the thorn shall come up the fir tree'; and 'the wolf shall dwell with the lamb'. Instead of the savage ferocity of the beasts, there will be the strength without the savageness—an inconceivable order of things just now.

In anything like a revolution or a war, we find what Solomon refers to here is true, that to make profit you must go back to the dust you came from. The curious thing about civilization is that it tends to take men away from the soil, and makes them develop an artificial existence away from the elemental. Civilization has become an elaborate way of doing without God, and when civilized life is hit a smashing blow by any order of tyranny, most of us have not a leg to stand on. Solomon reminds us that king and peasant alike can only gain their profit by proper tillage of the soil. The laws given in the Bible include a scheme for the treatment of the earth and they insist on proper rest being given to the land, and make it clear that that alone will bring profit in actual existence.

SHH 61

PARTAKERS OF HIS SUFFERINGS

Rejoice, inasmuch as ye are partakers of Christ's sufferings
(1 Peter 4:13)

If you are going to be used by God, He will take you through a multitude of experiences that are not meant for you at all, they are meant to make you useful in His hands, and to enable you to understand what transpires in other souls so that you will never be surprised at what you come across. Oh, I can't deal with that person. Why not? God gave you ample opportunity to soak before Him on that line, and you barged off because it seemed stupid to spend time in that way.

The sufferings of Christ are not those of ordinary men. He suffered "according to the will of God," not from the point of view we suffer from as individuals. It is only when we are related to Jesus Christ that we can understand what God is after in His dealings with us. It is part of Christian culture to know what God's aim is. In the history of the Christian Church the tendency has been to evade being identified with the sufferings of Jesus Christ; men have sought to procure the carrying out of God's order by a short cut of their own. God's way is always the way of suffering, the way of the "long, long trail."

Are we partakers of Christ's sufferings? Are we prepared for God to stamp our personal ambitions right out? Are we prepared for God to destroy by transfiguration our individual determinations? It will not mean that we know exactly why God is taking us that way, that would make us spiritual prigs. We never realize at the time what God is putting us through; we go through it more or less misunderstandingly; then we come to a luminous place, and say—"Why, God has girded me, though I did not know it!"

A man's life consisteth not in the abundance of the things which he possesseth. (Luke 12:15)

The first thing God does with us after sanctification is to 'force through the channels of a single heart' the interests of the whole world by introducing into us the nature of the Holy Ghost . . . . When we are born from above the realization dawns that we are built for God, not for ourselves. We are brought, by means of new birth, into the individual realization of God's great purpose for the human race, and all our small, miserable, parochial notions disappear.

If we have been living much in the presence of God, the first thing that strikes us is the smallness of the lives of men and women who do not recognize God. It did not occur to us before, their lives seemed to be broad and generous; but now there seems such a fuss of interests that have nothing whatever to do with God's purpose, and are altogether unrelated to the election of God. It is because people live in the things they possess instead of in their relationship to God, that God at times seems to be cruel. There are a thousand and one interests that God's providential hand has to brush aside as hopelessly irrelevant to His purpose, and if we have been living in those interests, we go with them.

SSY 103

PROGRAMME OF BELIEF

Believest thou this? (John 11:26)

Martha believed in the power at the disposal of Jesus Christ, she believed that if He had been present He could have healed her brother; she also believed that Jesus had a peculiar intimacy with God and that whatever He asked of God, God would do; but she needed a closer personal intimacy with Jesus. Martha's programme of belief had its fulfillment in the future; Jesus led her on until her belief became a personal possession, and then slowly emerged into a particular inheritance—"Yea, Lord, I believe that Thou art the Christ . . ."

Is there something like that in the Lord's dealings with you? Is Jesus educating you into a personal intimacy with Himself? Let Him press home His question to you—"Believest thou *this*?" What is your ordeal of doubt? Have you come, like Martha, to some overwhelming passage in your circumstances where your programme of belief is about to emerge into a personal belief? This can never be until a personal need arises out of a personal problem.

To believe is to commit. In the programme of mental belief I commit myself, and abandon all that is not related to that commitment. In personal belief I commit myself morally to this way of confidence and refuse to compromise with any other; and in particular belief I commit myself spiritually to Jesus Christ, and determine in that thing to be dominated by the Lord alone.

When I stand face to face with Jesus Christ and He says to me—"Believest thou this?" I find that faith is as natural as breathing, and I am staggered that I was so stupid as not to trust Him before.

For ye know the grace of our Lord Jesus Christ, that, though he was rich, yet for your sakes he became poor, that ye through his poverty might be rich. (2 Corinthians 8:9)

Our Lord Jesus Christ became poor for our sakes not as an example, but to give us the unerring secret of His religion. Professional Christianity is a religion of possessions that are devoted to God; the religion of Jesus Christ is a religion of personal relationship to God, and has nothing whatever to do with possessions. The disciple is rich not in possessions, but in personal identity. Voluntary poverty was the marked condition of Jesus (Luke 9:58), and the poverty of God's children in all ages is a significant thing. Today we are ashamed and afraid to be poor. The reason we hear so little about the inner spiritual side of external poverty is that few of us are in the place of Jesus, or of Paul. The scare of poverty will knock the spiritual backbone out of us unless we have the relationship that holds. The attitude of our Lord's life was that He was disconnected with everything to do with things that chain people down to this world, consequently He could go wherever His Father wanted Him to.

AUG 24

THE UNDETECTED SACREDNESS
OF CIRCUMSTANCES

All things work together for good to them that love God.
(Rom. 8:28)

The circumstances of a saint's life are ordained of God. In the life of a saint there is no such thing as chance. God by His providence brings you into circumstances that you cannot understand at all, but the Spirit of God understands. God is bringing you into places and among people and into conditions in order that the intercession of the Spirit in you may take a particular line. Never put your hand in front of the circumstances and say—I am going to be my own providence here, I must watch this, and guard that. All your circumstances are in the hand of God, therefore never think it strange concerning the circumstances you are in. Your part in intercessory prayer is not to enter into the agony of intercession, but to utilize the common-sense circumstances God puts you in, and the common-sense people He puts you amongst by His providence, to bring them before God's throne and give the Spirit in you a chance to intercede for them. In this way God is going to sweep the whole world with His saints.

Am I making the Holy Spirit's work difficult by being indefinite, or by trying to do His work for Him? I must do the human side of intercession, and the human side is the circumstances I am in and the people I am in contact with. I have to keep my conscious life as a shrine of the Holy Ghost, then as I bring the different ones before God, the Holy Spirit makes intercession for them.

Your intercessions can never be mine, and my intercessions can never be yours, but the Holy Ghost makes intercession in our particular lives, without which intercession someone will be impoverished.

*There is nothing better for a man than that he should eat and
drink, and that he should make his soul enjoy good in his labour.
This also I saw, that it was from the hand of God.
(Ecclesiastes 2:24)*

One great essential lesson in Christianity is that God's order
comes to us in the haphazard. We are men and women, we
have appetites, we have to live on this earth, and things do
happen by chance; what is the use of saying they do not? 'One
of the most immutable things on earth is mutability.' Your life
and mine is a bundle of chance. It is absurd to say it is fore-
ordained for you to have so many buttons on your tunic, and
if that is not fore-ordained, then nothing is. If things were fore-
ordained, there would be no sense of responsibility at all. A
false spirituality makes us look to God to perform a miracle
instead of doing our duty. We have to see that we do our duty
in faith in God. Jesus Christ undertakes to do everything a man
cannot do, but not what a man can do. Things do happen by
chance, and if we know God, we recognize that His order comes
to us in that way. We live in this haphazard order of things,
and we have to maintain the abiding order of God in it. The
doctrine of the Sacrament teaches the conveying of God's presence to us through the common elements of bread and wine.
We are not to seek success or prosperity. If we get hold of our
relationship to God in eating and drinking, we are on the right
basis of things.

SHH 17

THE UNRIVALLED POWER OF PRAYER

We know not what we should pray for as we ought: but the Spirit itself maketh intercession for us with groanings which cannot be uttered. (Rom. 8:26)

We realize that we are energized by the Holy Spirit for prayer; we know what it is to pray in the Spirit; but we do not so often realize that the Holy Spirit Himself prays in us prayers which we cannot utter. When we are born again of God and are indwelt by the Spirit of God, He expresses for us the unutterable.

"He," the Spirit in you, "maketh intercession for the saints according to the will of God," and God searches your heart not to know what your conscious prayers are, but to find out what is the prayer of the Holy Spirit.

The Spirit of God needs the nature of the believer as a shrine in which to offer His intercession. "Your body is the temple of the Holy Ghost." When Jesus Christ cleansed the temple, He "would not suffer that any man should carry any vessel through the temple." The Spirit of God will not allow you to use your body for your own convenience. Jesus ruthlessly cast out all them that sold and bought in the temple, and said—"My house shall be called the house of prayer; but ye have made it a den of thieves."

Have we recognized that our body is the temple of the Holy Ghost? If so, we must be careful to keep it undefiled for Him. We have to remember that our conscious life, though it is only a tiny bit of our personality, is to be regarded by us as a shrine of the Holy Ghost. He will look after the unconscious part that we know nothing of; but we must see that we guard the conscious part for which we are responsible.

Naked came I out of my mother's womb, and naked shall I return thither: the Lord gave, and the Lord hath taken away; blessed be the name of the Lord. (Job 1:21)

Facing facts as they are produces despair, not frenzy, but real downright despair, and God never blames a man for despair. The man who thinks must be pessimistic; thinking can never produce optimism. The wisest man that ever lived said that 'he that increaseth knowledge increaseth sorrow'. The basis of things is not reasonable, but wild and tragic, and to face things as they are brings a man to the ordeal of despair. Ibsen presents this ordeal, there is no defiance in his presentation, he knows that there is no such thing as forgiveness in Nature, and that every sin has a Nemesis following it. His summing up of life is that of quiet despair because he knows nothing of the revelation given of God by Jesus Christ.

'Blessed are they that mourn.' Our Lord always speaks from that basis, never from the basis of the 'gospel of temperament'. When a man gets to despair he knows that all his thinking will never get him out, he will only get out by the sheer creative effort of God, consequently he is in the right attitude to receive from God that which he cannot gain for himself.

BFB 11

SACRAMENTAL SERVICE

*Who now rejoice in my sufferings for you, and fill up that which
is behind of the afflictions of Christ . . . (Col. 1:24)*

The Christian worker has to be a sacramental "go-between,"
to be so identified with his Lord and the reality of His Redemption that He can continually bring His creating life through him.
It is not the strength of one man's personality being super-
imposed on another, but the real presence of Christ coming
through the elements of the worker's life. When we preach
the historic facts of the life and death of Our Lord as they are
conveyed in the New Testament, our words are made sacramental, God uses them on the ground of His Redemption to
create in those who listen that which is not created otherwise.
If we preach the effects of Redemption in human life instead
of the revelation regarding Jesus, the result in those who listen is not new birth, but refined spiritual culture, and the Spirit
of God cannot witness to it because such preaching is in another domain. We have to see that we are in such living sympathy with God that as we proclaim His truth He can create in
souls the things which He alone can do.

What a wonderful personality! What a fascinating man! Such
marvelous insight! What chance has the Gospel of God through
all that? It cannot get through, because the line of attraction is
always the line of appeal. If a man attracts by his personality,
his appeal is along that line; if he is identified with his Lord's
personality, then the appeal is along the line of what Jesus
Christ can do. The danger is to glory in men; Jesus says we are
to lift *Him* up.

And Job spoke, and said, Let the day perish wherein I was born, and the night in which it was said, There is a man child conceived. (Job 3:2–3)

Optimism is either a matter of accepted revelation or of temperament; to think unimpeded and remain optimistic is not possible. Let a man face facts as they really are, and pessimism is the only possible conclusion. If there is no tragedy at the back of human life, no gap between God and man, then the Redemption of Jesus Christ is 'much ado about nothing'. Job is seeing things exactly as they are. A healthy-minded man bases his life on actual conditions, but let him be hit by bereavement, and when he has got beyond the noisy bit and the blasphemous bit, he will find, as Job found, that despair is the basis of human life unless a man accepts a revelation from God and enters into the Kingdom of Jesus Christ . . . . It is a good thing to be careful in our judgment of other men. A man may utter apparently blasphemous things against God and we say, 'How appalling'; but if we look further we find that the man is in pain, he is maddened and hurt by something. The mood he is talking in is a passing one and out of his suffering will come a totally different relationship to things. Remember, that in the end God said that the friends had not spoken the truth about Him, whilst Job had.

BFB 16, 21

FELLOWSHIP IN THE GOSPEL

Fellow labourer in the gospel of Christ. (1 Thess. 3:2)

After sanctification it is difficult to state what your aim in life is, because God has taken you up into His purpose by the Holy Ghost; He is using you now for His purposes throughout the world as He used His Son for the purpose of our salvation. If you seek great things for yourself—God has called me for this and that; you are putting a barrier to God's use of you. As long as you have a personal interest in your own character, or any set ambition, you cannot get through into identification with God's interests. You can only get there by losing for ever any idea of yourself and by letting God take you right out into His purpose for the world, and because your goings are of the Lord, you can never understand your ways.

I have to learn that the aim in life is God's, not mine. God is using me from His great personal standpoint, and all He asks of me is that I trust Him, and never say—Lord, this gives me such heart-ache. To talk in that way makes me a clog. When I stop telling God what I want, He can catch me up for what He wants without let or hindrance. He can crumple me up or exalt me, He can do anything He chooses. He simply asks me to have implicit faith in Himself and in His goodness. Self-pity is of the devil; if I go off on that line I cannot be used by God for His purpose in the world. I have "a world within the world" in which I live, and God will never be able to get me outside it because I am afraid of being frost-bitten.

*God commendeth his love towards us, in that, while we were yet
sinners, Christ died for us. (Romans 5:8)*

If you have had no tension in your life, never been screwed
up by problems, your morality well within your own grasp,
and someone tells you that God so loved you that He gave His
Son to die for you, nothing but good manners will keep you
from being amused. The majority of people who have never
been touched by affliction see Jesus Christ's death as a thing
beside the mark. When a man gets to his wits' end and things
go hard with him, his thick hide is pierced and he is stabbed
wide awake, then for the first time he begins to see something
else—'at last I see; I thought that He was stricken, smitten *of
God* and afflicted; but now I see He was wounded for *my* transgressions.'

The great fundamental revelation regarding the human race
is that God has redeemed us; and Redemption enters into our
lives when we are upset enough to see we need it. It is an insult today to tell some men and women to cheer up. One of
the most shallow, petty things that can be said is that 'every
cloud has a silver lining'. There are some clouds that are black
all through. At the wall of the world stands God with His arms
outstretched; and when a man or woman is driven there, the
consolations of Jesus Christ are given. Through the agonies in
human life we do not make Redemption, but we see why it
was necessary for God to make it. It is not necessary for every
man to go through these agonies, but it takes a time of agony
to get the shallow scepticism knocked out of us. It is a good
thing to be reverent with what we do not understand. A moral
agony gives a man 'a second wind', and he runs better after it,
and is a good deal more likely to win.

SA 16

THE SUPREME CLIMB

Take now thy son . . . (Gen. 22:2)

God's command is—Take *now*, not presently. It is extraordinary how we debate! We know a thing is right, but we try to find excuses for not doing it at once. To climb to the height God shows can never be done presently, it must be done now. The sacrifice is gone through in will before it is performed actually.

"And Abraham rose up early in the morning . . . and went unto the place of which God had told him" (v. 3). The wonderful simplicity of Abraham! When God spoke, He did not confer with flesh and blood, i.e., your own sympathies, your own insight, anything that is not based on your personal relationship to God. These are the things that compete with and hinder obedience to God.

Abraham did not choose the sacrifice. Always guard against self-chosen service for God; self-sacrifice may be a disease. If God has made your cup sweet, drink it with grace; if He has made it bitter, drink it in communion with Him. If the providential order of God for you is a hard time of difficulty, go through with it, but never choose the scene of your martyrdom. God chose the crucible for Abraham, and Abraham made no demur; he went steadily through. If you are not living in touch with Him, it is easy to pass a crude verdict on God. You must go through the crucible before you have any right to pronounce a verdict, because in the crucible you learn to know God better. God is working for His highest ends until His purpose and man's purpose become one.

And Jesus was in the hinder part of the ship, asleep on a pillow. (Mark 4:38)

The incident recorded in Mark 4:35–41 is not an incident in the life of a man, but in the life of God as Man. This Man asleep in the boat is God Incarnate. Jesus had said to the disciples, 'Let us go over unto the other side,' but when the storm arose, instead of relying upon Him, they failed Him. The actual circumstances were so crushing that their common sense was up in alarm, their panic carried them off their feet, and in terror they awoke Him. When we are in fear, we can do nothing less than pray to God, but our Lord has the right to expect of those who name His Name and have His nature in them, an understanding confidence in Him. Instead of that, when we are at our wits' end we go back to the elementary prayers of those who do not know Him, and prove that we have not the slightest atom of confidence in Him and in His government of the world: He is asleep—the tiller is not in His hand, and we sit down in nervous dread. God expects His children to be so confident in Him that in a crisis they are the ones upon whom He can rely. A great point is reached spiritually when we stop worrying God over personal matters or over any matter. God expects of us the one thing that glorifies Him—and that is to remain absolutely confident in Him, remembering what He has said beforehand, and sure that His purposes will be fulfilled.

PH 39

THE TRANSFIGURED LIFE

If any man be in Christ, he is a new creature; old things are passed away; behold, all things are become new. (2 Cor. 5:17)

What idea have you of the salvation of your soul? The experience of salvation means that in your actual life things are really altered, you no longer look at things as you used to; your desires are new, old things have lost their power. One of the touchstones of experience is—Has God altered the thing that matters? If you still hanker after the old things, it is absurd to talk about being born from above, you are juggling with yourself. If you are born again, the Spirit of God makes the alteration manifest in your actual life and reasoning, and when the crisis comes you are the most amazed person on earth at the wonderful difference there is in you. There is no possibility of imagining that *you* did it. It is this complete and amazing alteration that is the evidence that you are a saved soul.

What difference has my salvation and sanctification made? For instance, can I stand in the light of 1 Corinthians 13, or do I have to shuffle? The salvation that is worked out in me by the Holy Ghost emancipates me entirely, and as long as I walk in the light as God is in the light, He sees nothing to censure because His life is working out in every particular, not to my consciousness, but deeper than my consciousness.

Peace I leave with you, my peace I give unto you. (John 14:27)

We talk about the peace of Jesus, but have we ever realized what that peace was like? Read the story of His life, the thirty years of quiet submission at Nazareth, the three years of service, the slander and spite, backbiting and hatred He endured, all unfathomably worse than anything we shall ever have to go through; and His peace was undisturbed, it could not be violated. It is that peace that God will exhibit in us in the heavenly places; not a peace like it, but that peace. In all the rush of life, in working for our living, in all conditions of bodily life, wherever God engineers our circumstances—'My peace'; the imperturbable, inviolable peace of Jesus imparted to us in every detail of our lives. 'Your life is hid with Christ in God.' Have we allowed the wonder of it to enwrap us round and soak us through until we begin to realize the ample room there is to grow there? 'The secret place of the Most High', absolutely secure and safe.

OBH 34

FAITH AND EXPERIENCE

The Son of God, who loved me, and gave Himself for me.
(Gal. 2:20)

We have to battle through our moods into absolute devotion to the Lord Jesus, to get out of the hole-and-corner business of our experience into abandoned devotion to Him. Think Who the New Testament says that Jesus Christ is, and then think of the despicable meanness of the miserable faith we have—I haven't had this and that experience! Think what faith in Jesus Christ claims—that He can present us faultless before the throne of God, unutterably pure, absolutely rectified and profoundly justified. Stand in implicit adoring faith in Him, *He* is made unto us "wisdom, and righteousness, and sanctification, and redemption." How can we talk of making a sacrifice for the Son of God! Our salvation is from hell and perdition, and then we talk about making sacrifices!

We have to get out into faith in Jesus Christ continually; not a prayer meeting Jesus Christ, nor a book Jesus Christ, but the New Testament Jesus Christ, Who is God Incarnate, and Who ought to strike us to His feet as dead. Our faith must be in the One from Whom our experience springs. Jesus Christ wants our absolute abandon of devotion to Himself. We never can *experience* Jesus Christ, nor ever hold Him within the compass of our own hearts, but our faith must be built in strong emphatic confidence in Him.

It is along this line that we see the rugged impatience of the Holy Ghost against unbelief. All our fears are wicked, and we fear because we will not nourish ourselves in our faith. How can anyone who is identified with Jesus Christ suffer from doubt or fear! It ought to be an absolute paean of perfectly irrepressible, triumphant belief.

It is enough for the disciple that he be as his master, and the servant as his lord. (Matthew 10:25)

In the East the women sing as they grind the corn between the millstones; and 'the sound of the millstones' is music in the ears of God. The worlding does not think it music, but the saint who is being made into bread knows that his Father knows best, and that He would never allow the suffering if He had not some purpose. Ill-tempered people, hard circumstances, poverty, wilful misunderstandings and estrangements, are all millstones. Had Jesus any of these things in His own life? He had a devil in His company for three years; He lived at home with brothers and sisters who did not believe in Him; He was continually thwarted and misunderstood by the Pharisees, and He says, 'the disciple is not above his master'. If we have the tiniest element of self-pity in us God dare not put us anywhere near the millstones. When these experiences come, remember God has His eyes on every detail.

SHL 117–18

Now we can see why our Lord lived the life He did for thirty-three years. Before He made the entrance into that life possible for any human being, He had to show us what the life of God's normal man was like. The life of Jesus is the life we have to live here, not hereafter. There is no chance to live this kind of life hereafter, we have to live it here.

PR 80

DISCOVERING DIVINE DESIGNS

I being in the way, the Lord led me . . . (Gen. 24:27)

We have to be so one with God that we do not continually need to ask for guidance. Sanctification means that we are made the children of God, and the natural life of a child is obedience—until he wishes to be disobedient, then instantly there is the intuitive jar. In the spiritual domain the intuitive jar is the monition of the Spirit of God. When He gives the check, we have to stop at once and be renewed in the spirit of our mind in order to make out what God's will is. If we are born again of the Spirit of God, it is the abortion of piety to ask God to guide us here and there. "The Lord led me," and on looking back we see the presence of an amazing design, which, if we are born of God, we will credit to God.

We can all see God in exceptional things, but it requires the culture of spiritual discipline to see God in every detail. Never allow that the haphazard is anything less than God's appointed order, and be ready to discover the Divine designs anywhere.

Beware of making a fetish of consistency to your convictions instead of being devoted to God. I shall never do that—in all probability you will have to, if you are a saint. There never was a more inconsistent Being on this earth than Our Lord, but He was never inconsistent to His Father. The one consistency of the saint is not to a principle, but to the Divine life. It is the Divine life which continually makes more and more discoveries about the Divine mind. It is easier to be a fanatic than a faithful soul, because there is something amazingly humbling particularly to our religious conceit, in being loyal to God.

Whosoever therefore shall humble himself as this little child, the same is greatest in the kingdom of heaven. (Matthew 18:4)

When the disciples were discussing who should be the greatest, Jesus took a little child in His arms and said, 'Unless you become like that, you will never see the kingdom of heaven.' He did not put up a little child as an ideal; if He had, He would have destroyed the whole principle of His teaching. If humility were put up as an ideal it would serve only to increase pride. Humility is not an ideal, it is the unconscious result of the life being rightly related to God and centred in Him. Our Lord is dealing with ambition, and had He put up a little child as a standard, it would simply have altered the manifestation of ambition. What is a little child? We all know what a child is until we are asked, and then we find we do not know. We can mention his extra goodness or his extra badness, but none of this is the child himself. We know implicitly what a child is, and we know implicitly what Jesus Christ means, but as soon as we try to put it into words it escapes. A child works from an unconscious principle within, and if we are born again and are obeying the Holy Spirit, we shall unconsciously manifest humility all along the line. We shall easily be the servant of all men, not because it is our ideal, but because we cannot help it. Our eye is not consciously on our service, but on our Saviour.

There is nothing more awful than conscious humility, it is the most Satanic type of pride.

BP 186

WHAT IS THAT TO THEE?

Lord, what shall this man do? . . . What is that to thee? Follow thou Me. (John 21:21, 22)

One of our severest lessons comes from the stubborn refusal to see that we must not interfere in other people's lives. It takes a long time to realize the danger of being an amateur providence, that is, interfering with God's order for others. You see a certain person suffering and you say—He shall not suffer, and I will see that he does not. You put your hand straight in front of God's permissive will to prevent it, and God says—"What is that to thee?" If there is stagnation spiritually, never allow it to go on, but get into God's presence and find out the reason for it. Possibly you will find it is because you have been interfering in the life of another; proposing things you had no right to propose; advising when you had no right to advise. When you do have to give advice to another, God will advise through you with the direct understanding of His Spirit; your part is to be so rightly related to God that His discernment comes through you all the time for the blessing of another soul.

Most of us live on the borders of consciousness—consciously serving, consciously devoted to God. All this is immature, it is not the real life yet. The mature stage is the life of a child which is never conscious; we become so abandoned to God that the consciousness of being used never enters in. When we are consciously being used as broken bread and poured-out wine, there is another stage to be reached, where all consciousness of ourselves and of what God is doing through us is eliminated. A saint is never consciously a saint; a saint is consciously dependent on God.

Except a grain of wheat fall into the earth and die, it abideth by itself alone; but if it die, it beareth much fruit. (John 12:24)

Death is God's delightful way of giving us life. The monks in the early ages shut themselves away from everything to prove they were dead to it all, and when they got away they found themselves more alive than ever. Jesus never shut Himself away from things, the first place He took His disciples to was a marriage feast. He did not cut Himself off from society, He was not aloof, so much was He not aloof that they called Him 'a gluttonous man, and a wine-bibber'! But there was one characteristic of Jesus—He was fundamentally dead to the whole thing, it had no appeal to Him. The 'hundredfold' which Jesus promised means that God can trust a man anywhere and with anything when he is fundamentally dead to things . . . .

We use the phrase 'drawing on the resurrection life of Jesus', but try it, you cannot draw on it when you like. You will never get one breath of that life until you are dead, that is, dead to any desire that you want a blessing for body or soul or spirit. Immediately you die to that, the life of God is in you, and you don't know where you are with the exuberance of it.

IWP 80

STILL HUMAN!

Whatsoever ye do, do all to the glory of God. (1 Cor. 10:31)

The great marvel of the Incarnation slips into ordinary childhood's life; the great marvel of the Transfiguration vanishes in the devil-possessed valley; the glory of the Resurrection descends into a breakfast on the sea-shore. This is not an anticlimax, but a great revelation of God.

The tendency is to look for the marvelous in our experience; we mistake the sense of the heroic for being heroes. It is one thing to go through a crisis grandly, but another thing to go through every day glorifying God when there is no witness, no limelight, no one paying the remotest attention to us. If we do not want medieval haloes, we want something that will make people say—What a wonderful man of prayer he is! What a pious devoted woman she is! If you are rightly devoted to the Lord Jesus, you have reached the sublime height where no one ever thinks of noticing you, all that is noticed is that the power of God comes through you all the time.

Oh, I have had a wonderful call from God! It takes Almighty God Incarnate in us to do the meanest duty to the glory of God. It takes God's Spirit in us to make us so absolutely humanly His that we are utterly unnoticeable. The test of the life of a saint is not success, but faithfulness in human life as it actually is. We will set up success in Christian work as the aim; the aim is to manifest the glory of God in human life, to live the life hid with Christ in God in human conditions. Our human relationships are the actual conditions in which the ideal life of God is to be exhibited.

And when he is come he will convict . . . of sin. (John 16:8)

We are apt to put conviction of sin in the wrong place in a man's life. The man of all men who experienced conviction of sin was the saintly apostle Paul. 'For I was alive without the law once; but when the commandment came, sin revived, and I died' (Romans 7:9). There is no mention of conviction of sin in Paul's account of his conversion, only conviction of darkness and distress and of being out of order. But after Paul had been three years in Arabia with the Holy Ghost blazing through him, he began to write the diagnoses of sin which we have in his Epistles . . . .

If you want to know what sin is, don't ask the convicted sinner, ask the saint, the one who has been awakened to the holiness of God through the Atonement; he is the one who can begin to tell you what sin is. The man writhing at the penitent form is affected because his sins have upset him, but he has very little knowledge of sin. It is only as we walk in the light as God is in the light that we begin to understand the unfathomable depths of cleansing to which the blood of Jesus Christ goes (1 John 1:7).

PS 64–5

THE ETERNAL GOAL

By Myself have I sworn, saith the Lord, for because thou hast
done this thing . . . that in blessing I will bless thee . . .
(Gen. 22:15-19)

Abraham has reached the place where he is in touch with the
very nature of God, he understands now the Reality of God.

My goal is God Himself . . .

At any cost, dear Lord, by any road.

"At any cost, by any road" means nothing self-chosen in the
way God brings us to the goal. There is no possibility of questioning when God speaks if He speaks to His own nature in
me; prompt obedience is the only result. When Jesus says—
"Come," I simply come; when He says—"Let go," I let go; when
He says—"Trust in God in this matter," I do trust. The whole
working out is the evidence that the nature of God is in me.

God's revelation of Himself to me is determined by my character, not by God's character.

'Tis because I am mean

Thy ways so oft look mean to me.

By the discipline of obedience I get to the place where
Abraham was and I see Who God is. I never have a real God
until I have come face to face with Him in Jesus Christ, then I
know that "in all the world, my God, there is none but Thee,
there is none but Thee." The promises of God are of no value
to us until by obedience we understand the nature of God. We
read some things in the Bible three hundred and sixty-five
times and they mean nothing to us, then all of a sudden we
see what God means, because in some particular we have
obeyed God, and instantly His nature is opened up. "All the
promises of God in Him are yea, and in Him Amen." The "yea"
must be born of obedience; when by the obedience of our lives
we say "Amen" to a promise, then that promise is ours.

He wakeneth mine ear to hear as the learned. (Isaiah 50:4)

Have we learned the habit of listening to what God says? Have we added this resolute hearing in our practical life? We may be able to give a testimony as to what God has done for us, but does the life we live evidence that we are not listening now, but living only in the memory of what we once heard? We have to keep our ears trained to detect God's voice, to be continually renewed in the spirit of our mind. If when a crisis comes we instinctively turn to God, we know that the habit of hearkening has been formed. At the beginning there is the noisy clamour of our own misgivings; we are so taken up with what we have heard that we cannot hear any more. We have to hearken to that which we have not listened to before, and to do it we must be insulated on the inside.

'He wakeneth mine ear to hear as the learned.' Once a week at least read the Sermon on the Mount and see how much you have hearkened to it—'Love your enemies, bless them that curse you'; we do not listen to it because we do not want to. We have to learn to hearken to Jesus in everything, to get into the habit of finding out what He says. We cannot apply the teachings of Jesus unless we are regenerated, and we cannot apply all His teachings at once. The Holy Spirit will bring back to our remembrance a certain word of our Lord's and apply it to the particular circumstances we are in, the point is—are we going to obey it? 'Whosoever . . . heareth my sayings, and *doeth* them . . . ' When Jesus Christ brings a word home, never shirk it.

GH 54

WINNING INTO FREEDOM

If the Son therefore shall make you free, ye shall be free indeed.
(John 8:36)

If there is any remnant of individual conceit left, it always says "I can't." Personality never says "I can't," but simply absorbs and absorbs. Personality always wants more and more. It is the way we are built. We are designed with a great capacity for God; and sin and our individuality are the things that keep us from getting at God. God delivers us from sin: we have to deliver ourselves from individuality, i.e., to present our natural life to God and sacrifice it until it is transformed into a spiritual life by obedience.

God does not pay any attention to our natural individuality in the development of our spiritual life. His order runs right across the natural life, and we have to see that we aid and abet God, not stand against Him and say—I can't do that. God will not discipline us, we must discipline ourselves. God will not bring every thought and imagination into captivity; we have to do it. Do not say—O Lord, I suffer from wandering thoughts. *Don't* suffer from wandering thoughts. Stop listening to the tyranny of your individuality and get emancipated out into personality.

"If the Son shall make you free . . ." Do not substitute "Saviour" for "Son." The Saviour sets us free from sin; this is the freedom of being set free *by the Son.* It is what Paul means in Gal. 2:20—"I have been crucified with Christ," his natural individuality has been broken and his personality united with his Lord, not merged but united. "Ye shall be free indeed," free in essence, free from the inside. We will insist on energy, instead of being energized into identification with Jesus.

If any man will do his will, he shall know of the doctrine,
whether it be of God, or whether I speak of myself. (John 7:17)
If ye know these things, happy are ye if you do them. (John 13:17)

If you believe in Jesus, you will not spend all your time in the smooth waters just inside the harbour, full of exhilaration and delight, but always moored; you will have to go out through the harbour bar into the great deeps of God and begin to know for yourself, begin to get spiritual discernment. If you do not cut the moorings, God will have to break them with a storm and send you out. Why not unloosen and launch all on God and go out on the great swelling tide of His purpose?

'If any man will do his will, he shall know . . . ' When you know you should do a thing and you do it, immediately you will know more. If you revise where you are stodgy spiritually, you will find it goes back to the point where there was one thing you knew you should do, but you did not do it because there seemed no immediate call to, and now you have no perception, no discernment. Instead of being spiritually self-possessed at the time of crisis, you are spiritually distracted. It is a dangerous thing to refuse to go on knowing.

AHW 118

WHEN HE IS COME

And when He is come, He will convict the world of sin . . .
(John 16:8, R.V.)

Very few of us know anything about conviction of sin; we know the experience of being disturbed because of having done wrong things; but conviction of sin by the Holy Ghost blots out every relationship on earth and leaves one relationship only—"Against Thee, Thee only, have I sinned!" When a man is convicted of sin in this way, he knows with every power of his conscience that God dare not forgive him; if God did forgive him, the man would have a stronger sense of justice than God. God does forgive, but it cost the rending of His heart in the Death of Christ to enable Him to do so. The great miracle of the grace of God is that He forgives sin, and it is the death of Jesus Christ alone that enables the Divine nature to forgive and to remain true to itself in doing so. It is shallow nonsense to say that God forgives us because He is love. When we have been convicted of sin we will never say this again. The love of God means Calvary, and nothing less; the love of God is spelt on the Cross and nowhere else. The only ground on which God can forgive me is through the Cross of my Lord. There, His conscience is satisfied.

Forgiveness means not merely that I am saved from hell and made right for heaven (no man would accept forgiveness on such a level); forgiveness means that I am forgiven into a recreated relationship, into identification with God in Christ. The miracle of Redemption is that God turns me, the unholy one, into the standard of Himself, the Holy One, by putting into me a new disposition, the disposition of Jesus Christ.

> *And the Lord turned the captivity of Job when he prayed for his friends. (Job 42:10)*

Have you come to 'when' yet? If you are in the position of Job and have shipped some trouble on board that makes you taken up with yourself, remember that when Job prayed for his friends, God emancipated him. Pray for your friends, and God will turn your captivity also. The emancipation comes as you intercede for them; it is not a mere reaction, it is the way God works. It is not a question of getting time for Bible study, but of spontaneous intercession as we go about our daily calling, and we shall see emancipation come all along, not because we understand the problems, but because we recognize that God has chosen the way of intercession to perform His moral miracles in lives. Then get to work and pray, and God will get His chance with other lives; you do not even need to speak to them. God has based the Christian life on Redemption, and as we pray on this basis God's honour is at stake to answer prayer.

BFB 109

THE FORGIVENESS OF GOD

In whom we have . . . the forgiveness of sins. (Eph. 1:7)

Beware of the pleasant view of the Fatherhood of God—God is so kind and loving that of course He will forgive us. That sentiment has no place whatever in the New Testament. The only ground on which God can forgive us is the tremendous tragedy of the Cross of Christ; to put forgiveness on any other ground is unconscious blasphemy. The only ground on which God can forgive sin and reinstate us in His favour is through the Cross of Christ, and in no other way. Forgiveness, which is so easy for us to accept, cost the agony of Calvary. It is possible to take the forgiveness of sin, the gift of the Holy Ghost, and our sanctification with the simplicity of faith, and to forget at what enormous cost to God it was all made ours.

Forgiveness is the divine miracle of grace; it cost God the Cross of Jesus Christ before He could forgive sin and remain a holy God. Never accept a view of the Fatherhood of God if it blots out the Atonement. The revelation of God is that He cannot forgive; He would contradict His nature if He did. The only way we can be forgiven is by being brought back to God by the Atonement. God's forgiveness is only natural in the supernatural domain.

Compared with the miracle of the forgiveness of sin, the experience of sanctification is slight. Sanctification is simply the marvelous expression of the forgiveness of sins in a human life, but the thing that awakens the deepest well of gratitude in a human being is that God has forgiven sin. Paul never got away from this. When once you realize all that it cost God to forgive you, you will be held as in a vice, constrained by the love of God.

Enter into thy closet, and when thou hast shut thy door, pray to thy Father which is in secret. (Matthew 6:6)

Prayer that is not an effort of the will is unrecognized by God. 'If ye abide in me, and my words abide in you, ye shall ask what ye will and it shall be done unto you,' said Jesus. That does not mean ask anything you like, but ask what you *will*. What are you actively willing? ask for that. We shall find that we *ask* very few things.

MFL 59

Think how long our Lord has waited for you; you have seen Him in your visions, now pray to Him; get a place, not a mood, but a definite material place and resort to it constantly, and pray to God as His Spirit in you will help you . . . .

Do it now, *'enter into thy closet'*; and remember, it is a place selected to pray in, not to make little addresses in, or for any other purpose than to pray in, never forget that.

DPR 31, 33

IT IS FINISHED

I have finished the work which Thou gavest Me to do.
(John 17:4)

The Death of Jesus Christ is the performance in history of the very Mind of God. There is no room for looking on Jesus Christ as a martyr; His death was not something that happened to Him which might have been prevented: His death was the very reason why He came.

Never build your preaching of forgiveness on the fact that God is our Father and He will forgive us because He loves us. It is untrue to Jesus Christ's revelation of God; it makes the Cross unnecessary, and the Redemption "much ado about nothing." If God does forgive sin, it is because of the Death of Christ. God could forgive men in no other way than by the death of His Son, and Jesus is exalted to be Saviour because of His death. "We see Jesus . . . because of the suffering of death, crowned with glory and honour." The greatest note of triumph that ever sounded in the ears of a startled universe was that sounded on the Cross of Christ—"*It is finished.*" That is the last word in the Redemption of man.

Anything that belittles or obliterates the holiness of God by a false view of the love of God, is untrue to the revelation of God given by Jesus Christ. Never allow the thought that Jesus Christ stands with us against God out of pity and compassion; that He became a curse for us out of sympathy with us. Jesus Christ became a curse for us by the Divine decree. Our portion of realizing the terrific meaning of the curse is conviction of sin, the gift of shame and penitence is given us—this is the great mercy of God. Jesus Christ hates the wrong in man, and Calvary is the estimate of His hatred.

Praying . . . for me, that utterance may be given unto me . . .
(Ephesians 6:19)

We naturally suppose it is no use praying for 'Paul', for prominent people, God will look after them all right. The prominent people for God are marked for the wiles of the devil, and we must pray for them all the time; God gives us every now and again an alarming exhibition of what happens if we don't

IYA 36

The prayers of the saints either enable or disable God in the performance of His wonders. The majority of us in praying for the will of God to be done say, 'In God's good time', meaning 'in my bad time'; consequently there is no silence in heaven produced by our prayers, no results, no performance.

HGM 79

When we pray we give God a chance to work in the unconscious realm of the lives of those for whom we pray. When we come into the secret place it is the Holy Ghost's passion for souls that is at work, not our passion, and He can work through us as He likes.

SSM 59

SHALLOW AND PROFOUND

Whether therefore ye eat, or drink, or whatsoever ye do, do all
to the glory of God. (1 Cor. 10:31)

Beware of allowing yourself to think that the shallow concerns of life are not ordained of God; they are as much of God as the profound. It is not your devotion to God that makes you refuse to be shallow, but your wish to impress other people with the fact that you are a spiritual prig. Be careful of the production of contempt in yourself, it always comes along this line, and causes you to go about as a walking rebuke to other people because they are more shallow than you are. Beware of posing as a profound person; God became a Baby.

To be shallow is not a sign of being wicked, nor is shallowness a sign that there are no deeps: the ocean has a shore. The shallow amenities of life, eating and drinking, walking and talking, are all ordained by God. These are the things in which our Lord lived. He lived in them as the Son of God, and He said that "the disciple is not above his Master."

Our safeguard is in the shallow things. We have to live the surface common-sense life in a common-sense way; when the deeper things come, God gives them to us apart from the shallow concerns. Never show the deeps to anyone but God. We are so abominably serious, so desperately interested in our own characters, that we refuse to behave like Christians in the shallow concerns of life.

Determinedly take no one seriously but God, and the first person you find you have to leave severely alone as being the greatest fraud you have ever known, is yourself.

What is that to thee? (John 21:22)

A disciple is one who minds neither his own business nor any one else's business, but looks steadfastly to Jesus and goes on following Him. We read books about the consecration of other men, but it is as so much scaffolding, it all has to go, and the time comes when there is only one thing left—following Jesus. One of the severest lessons we get comes from our stubborn refusal to see that we must not interfere in other people's lives. It takes a long time to realize the danger of being an amateur providence, i.e. interfering with God's order for others. We see a certain person suffering and we say, 'He shall not suffer; I will see that he does not,' and we put our hand straight in front of God's permissive will to prevent it, and He has to say, 'What is that to thee?' We cause delays to God by persistently doing things in our own way.

SSY 70

DISTRACTION OF ANTIPATHY

Have mercy upon us, O Lord, have mercy upon us: for we are exceedingly filled with contempt. (Psa. 123:3)

The thing of which we have to beware is not so much damage to our belief in God as damage to our Christian temper. "Therefore take heed to thy spirit, that ye deal not treacherously." The temper of mind is tremendous in its effects, it is the enemy that penetrates right into the soul and distracts the mind from God. There are certain tempers of mind in which we never dare indulge; if we do, we find they have distracted us from faith in God, and until we get back to the quiet mood before God, our faith in Him is *nil*, and our confidence in the flesh and in human ingenuity is the thing that rules.

Beware of "the cares of this world," because they are the things that produce a wrong temper of soul. It is extraordinary what an enormous power there is in simple things to distract our attention from God. Refuse to be swamped with the cares of this life.

Another thing that distracts us is the lust of vindication. St. Augustine prayed—"O Lord, deliver me from this lust of always vindicating myself." That temper of mind destroys the soul's faith in God. "I must explain myself; I must get people to understand." Our Lord never explained anything; He left mistakes to correct themselves.

When we discern that people are not going on spiritually and allow the discernment to turn to criticism, we block our way to God. God never gives us discernment in order that we may criticize, but that we may intercede.

> *Ye that have escaped the sword, go ye, stand not still: remember*
> *the Lord from afar and let Jerusalem come into your mind.*
> *(Jeremiah 51:50)*

'And let Jerusalem', the God-lit city, 'come into your mind'. Ask yourself—'What do I let come into my mind?' If a man lets his garden alone, it pretty soon ceases to be a garden; and if a saint lets his mind alone, it will soon become a garbage patch for Satan's scarecrows. Read the terrible things that Paul says will grow in the mind of a saint unless he looks after it (e.g. Colossians 3:5). The command to let Jerusalem come into our mind means we have to watch our intellect and devote it for one purpose; let only those things come in that are worthy of the God-lit city. *'Let'*. . . it is a command. See to it by the careful watching of your mind that only those thoughts come in that are worthy of God. We do not sufficiently realize the need to pray when we lie down at night, 'Deliver us from the evil one.' It puts us in the attitude of asking the Lord to watch our minds and our dreams, and He will do it.

PS 31

DIRECTION OF ASPIRATION

Behold, as the eyes of servants look unto the hand of their masters . . . so our eyes wait upon the Lord our God. (Psa. 123:2)

This verse is a description of entire reliance upon God. Just as the eyes of the servant are riveted on his master, so our eyes are up unto God and our knowledge of His countenance is gained (cf. Isaiah 53:1, R.V.). Spiritual leakage begins when we cease to lift up our eyes unto Him. The leakage comes not so much through trouble on the outside as in the imagination; when we begin to say—"I expect I have been stretching myself a bit too much, standing on tiptoe and trying to look like God instead of being an ordinary humble person." We have to realize that no effort can be too high.

For instance, you came to a crisis when you made a stand for God and had the witness of the Spirit that all was right, but the weeks have gone by, and the years maybe, and you are slowly coming to the conclusion—"Well, after all, was I not a bit too pretentious? Was I not taking a stand a bit too high?" Your rational friends come and say—Don't be a fool, we knew when you talked about this spiritual awakening, that it was a passing impulse, you can't keep up the strain, God does not expect you to. And you say—Well, I suppose I was expecting too much. It sounds humble to say it, but it means that reliance on God has gone and reliance on worldly opinion has come in. The danger is lest no longer relying on God you ignore the lifting up of your eyes to Him. Only when God brings you to a sudden halt, will you realize how you have been losing out. Whenever there is a leakage, remedy it immediately. Recognize that something has been coming between you and God, and get it readjusted at once.

*Yield yourselves unto God as those that are alive from the dead,
and your members as instruments of righteousness unto God.
(Romans 6:13)*

When I am born again my human nature is not different, it is the same as before, I am related to life in the same way, I have the same bodily organs, but the mainspring is different, and I have to see now that all my members are dominated by the new disposition (see Romans 5:13, 19). There is only one kind of human nature, and that is the human nature we have all got; and there is only one kind of holiness, the holiness of Jesus Christ. Give Him 'elbow-room', and He will manifest Himself in you, and other people will recognize Him. Human beings know human beings too well to mistake where goodness comes from; when they see certain characteristics they will know they come only from the indwelling of Jesus. It is not the manifestation of noble human traits, but of a real family likeness of Jesus. It is *His* gentleness, *His* patience, *His* purity, never mine. The whole art of spirituality is that my human nature should retire and let the new disposition have its way.

CHI 21

THE SECRET OF SPIRITUAL COHERENCE

But God forbid that I should glory, save in the cross of our Lord
Jesus Christ. (Gal. 6:14)

When a man is first born again, he becomes incoherent, there is an amount of unrelated emotion about him, unrelated phases of external things. In the apostle Paul there was a strong steady coherence underneath, consequently he could let his external life change as it liked and it did not distress him because he was rooted and grounded in God. Most of us are not spiritually coherent because we are more concerned about being coherent externally. Paul lived in the basement; the coherent critics live in the upper storey of the external statement of things, and the two do not begin to touch each other. Paul's consistency was down in the fundamentals. The great basis of his coherence was the agony of God in the Redemption of the world, viz., the Cross of Jesus Christ.

Re-state to yourself what you believe, then do away with as much of it as possible, and get back to the bedrock of the Cross of Christ. In external history the Cross is an infinitesimal thing; from the Bible point of view it is of more importance than all the empires of the world. If we get away from brooding on the tragedy of God upon the Cross in our preaching, it produces nothing. It does not convey the energy of God to man; it may be interesting but it has no power. But preach the Cross, and the energy of God is let loose. "It pleased God by the foolishness of preaching to save them that believe." "We preach Christ crucified."

Though he slay me, yet will I trust in him. (Job 13:15)

We sometimes wrongly illustrate faith in God by the faith of a business man in a cheque. Faith commercially is based on calculation, but religious faith cannot be illustrated by the kind of faith we exhibit in life. Faith in God is a terrific venture in the dark; I have to believe that God is good in spite of all that contradicts it in my experience. It is not easy to say that God is love when everything that happens actually gives the lie to it. Everyone's soul represents some kind of battlefield. The point for each one is whether we will hang in, as Job did, and say 'Though things look black, I will trust in God' . . .

The basis of a man's faith in God is that God is the Source and Support of all existence, not that He is all existence. Job recognizes this, and maintains that in the end everything will be explained and made clear. Have I this kind of faith—not faith in a principle, but faith in *God*, that He is just and true and right? Many of us have no faith in God at all, but only faith in what He has done for us, and when these things are not apparent we lose our faith and say, 'Why should this happen to me? Why should there be a war? Why should I be wounded and sick? Why should my "cobber" be killed? I am going to chuck up my faith in God.'

BFB 100

THE CONCENTRATION
OF SPIRITUAL ENERGY

. . . save in the cross of our Lord Jesus Christ. (Gal. 6:1 4)

If you want to know the energy of God (i.e., the resurrection life of Jesus) in your mortal flesh, you must brood on the tragedy of God. Cut yourself off from prying personal interest in your own spiritual symptoms and consider bare spirited the tragedy of God, and instantly the energy of God will be in you. "Look unto *Me*," pay attention to the objective Source and the subjective energy will be there. We lose power if we do not concentrate on the right thing. The effect of the Cross is salvation, sanctification, healing, etc., but we are not to preach any of these, we are to preach Jesus Christ and Him crucified. The proclaiming of Jesus will do its own work. Concentrate on God's centre in your preaching and though your crowd may apparently pay no attention, they can never be the same again. If I talk my own talk, it is of no more importance to you than your talk is to me; but if I talk the truth of God, you will meet it again and so will I. We have to concentrate on the great point of spiritual energy—the Cross, to keep in contact with that centre where all the power lies, and the energy will be let loose. In holiness movements and spiritual experience meetings the concentration is apt to be put not on the Cross of Christ, but on the effects of the Cross.

The feebleness of the churches is being criticized today, and the criticism is justified. One reason for the feebleness is that there has not been this concentration of spiritual energy; we have not brooded enough on the tragedy of Calvary or on the meaning of Redemption.

It is good that, thou shouldest take hold of this: yea, also from this withdraw not thine hand: for he that feareth God shall come forth of them all. (Ecclesiastes 7:18)

Don't be fanatically religious and don't be irreverently blatant. Remember that the two extremes have to be held in the right balance. If your religion does not make you a better man, it is a rotten religion. The test of true religion is when it touches these four things—food, money, sex and mother earth. These things are the test of a right sane life with God, and the religion that ignores them or abuses them is not right. God made man of the dust of the ground, and that dust can express either Deity or devilishness. Remember we are to be not numbskulls, but holy men, full-blooded and holy to the last degree, not anaemic creatures without enough strength to be bad. The relation to life ordained by Jesus Christ does not unsex men and women but enables them to be holy men and women. 'The love of money is a root of all kinds of evil' (1 Timothy 6:10). Money is a test, another thing which proves a man's religion; and the way a man treats the soil will also prove whether or not he is a son of God. A man needs to hold a right attitude to all these things by means of his personal relationship to God.

SHH 99

THE CONSECRATION OF SPIRITUAL ENERGY

By whom the world is crucified unto me, and I unto the world.
(Gal. 6:14)

If I brood on the Cross of Christ, I do not become a subjective
pietist, interested in my own whiteness; I become dominantly
concentrated on Jesus Christ's interests. Our Lord was not a
recluse nor an ascetic, He did not cut Himself off from society,
but He was inwardly disconnected all the time. He was not
aloof, but He lived in another world. He was so much in the
ordinary world that the religious people of His day called Him
a glutton and a wine-bibber. Our Lord never allowed anything
to interfere with His consecration of spiritual energy.

The counterfeit of consecration is the conscious cutting off
of things with the idea of storing spiritual power for use later
on, but that is a hopeless mistake. The Spirit of God has spoiled
the sin of a great many, yet there is no emancipation, no fullness in their lives. The kind of religious life we see abroad to-
day is entirely different from the robust holiness of the life of
Jesus Christ. "I pray not that Thou shouldest take them out of
the world, but that Thou shouldest keep them from the evil."
We are to be *in* the world but not *of* it; to be disconnected fundamentally, not externally.

We must never allow anything to interfere with the consecration of our spiritual energy. Consecration is our part, sanctification is God's part; and we have deliberately to determine
to be interested only in that in which God is interested. The
way to solve perplexing problems is to ask—Is this the kind of
thing in which Jesus Christ is interested, or the kind of thing
in which the spirit that is the antipode of Jesus is interested?

I must work the works of him that sent me, while it is day.
(John 9:4)

The majority of us are blind on certain lines, we see only in
the light of our prejudices. A searchlight lights up only what it
does and no more, but the daylight reveals a hundred and one
facts that the searchlight had not taken into account. An idea
acts like a searchlight and becomes tyrannous. Take a man with
an idea of evolution; as you listen to him the way seems perfectly clear, life is not difficult at all; but let the daylight of actual
experience come across his path, and there are a thousand and
one facts which the idea cannot account for, because they do
not come into the simple line laid down by the evolutionist.
When I am up against problems, I am apt to shut myself up in
my own mind and refuse to pay any attention to what anyone
says. There are many things which are neither black nor white,
but grey. There is nothing simple under heaven saving a man's
relationship to God on the ground of the Redemption of Jesus
Christ. When Jesus Christ came on the scene, His disciples
became impatient and said, 'Why don't you tell us plainly who
you are?' Jesus Christ could not, because He could only be
discerned through moral obedience. A man who talks like a
shell makes the path of a shell, that is, he makes the way
straight, but destroys a good deal in doing it. There is another
way of reaching the solution of a problem—the long, patient
way of solving things. Jesus Christ deliberately took the 'long,
long trail'. The temptation of Satan was that He should take
the 'short cut'. The temptations of Satan centre round this
point: 'You are the Son of God, then do God's work in your
own way'; and at the heart of all our Lord's answers was this:
'I came to do My Father's work in His way, not in My own
way, although I am the Son of God.'

SA 57

THE BOUNTY OF THE DESTITUTE

Being justified freely by His grace . . . (Rom. 3:24)

The Gospel of the grace of God awakens an intense longing in human souls and an equally intense resentment, because the revelation which it brings is not palatable. There is a certain pride in man that will give and give, but to come and accept is another thing. I will give myself in consecration, I will do anything, but do not humiliate me to the level of the most hell-deserving sinner and tell me that all I have to do is to accept the gift of salvation through Jesus Christ.

We have to realize that we cannot earn or win anything from God; we must either receive it as a gift or do without it. The greatest blessing spiritually is the knowledge that we are destitute; until we get there Our Lord is powerless. He can do nothing for us if we think we are sufficient of ourselves; we have to enter into His Kingdom through the door of destitution. As long as we are rich, possessed of anything in the way of pride or independence, God cannot do anything for us. It is only when we get hungry spiritually that we receive the Holy Spirit. The gift of the essential nature of God is made effectual in us by the Holy Spirit; He imparts to us the quickening life of Jesus, which puts "the beyond" within, and immediately "the beyond" has come within, it rises up to "the above," and we are lifted into the domain where Jesus lives (John 3:5).

For the word of God . . . is a discerner of the thoughts and intents of the heart. (Hebrews 4:12)

Thinking takes place in the heart, not in the brain. The real spiritual powers of a man reside in the heart, which is the centre of the physical life, of the soul life, and of the spiritual life. The expression of thinking is referred to the brain and the lips because through these organs thinking becomes articulate.

According to the Bible, thinking exists in the heart, and that is the region with which the Spirit of God deals. We may take it as a general rule that Jesus Christ never answers any questions that spring from a man's head, because the questions which spring from our brains are always borrowed from some book we have read, or from someone we have heard speak; but the questions that spring from our hearts, the real problems that vex us, Jesus Christ answers those. The questions He came to deal with are those that spring from the implicit centre. These problems may be difficult to state in words, but they are the problems Jesus Christ will solve.

BP 122

THE ABSOLUTENESS OF JESUS CHRIST

He shall glorify Me. (John 16:14)

The pietistic movements of to-day have none of the rugged reality of the New Testament about them; there is nothing about them that needs the Death of Jesus Christ; all that is required is a pious atmosphere, and prayer and devotion. This type of experience is not supernatural nor miraculous, it did not cost the passion of God, it is not dyed in the blood of the Lamb, not stamped with the hall-mark of the Holy Ghost; it has not that mark on it which makes men say, as they look with awe and wonder—"That is the work of God Almighty." That and nothing else is what the New Testament talks about.

The type of Christian experience in the New Testament is that of personal passionate devotion to the Person of Jesus Christ. Every other type of Christian experience, so called, is detached from the Person of Jesus. There is no regeneration, no being born again into the Kingdom in which Christ lives, but only the idea that He is our Pattern. In the New Testament Jesus Christ is Saviour long before He is Pattern. To-day He is being despatched as the Figurehead of a Religion, a mere Example. He is that, but He is infinitely more; He is salvation itself, He is the Gospel of God.

Jesus said, "When He the Spirit of truth is come . . . He shall glorify Me." When I commit myself to the revelation made in the New Testament, I receive from God the gift of the Holy Spirit Who begins to interpret to me what Jesus did; and does in me subjectively all that Jesus Christ did for me objectively.

*Thou shalt love the Lord thy God with all thy heart, and with
all thy soul, and with all thy mind, and with all thy strength.
(Mark 12:30)*

The outcome of Mark 12:29–31 is God four times over—God
the King of my heart, God the King of my soul, God the King
of my mind, God the King of my strength; nothing other than
God; and the working out of it is that we show the same love
to our fellow-men as God has shown us. That is the external
aspect of this internal relationship, the sovereign preference
of my person for God. The love of the heart for Jesus, the life
laid down for Jesus, the mind thinking only for Jesus, the
strength given over to Jesus, the will working only the will of
God, and the ear of the personality hearing only what God has
to say.

IWP 93

Salvation means not only a pure heart, an enlightened mind,
a spirit right with God, but that the whole man is comprehended in the manifestation of the marvellous power and grace
of God, body, soul and spirit are brought into fascinating captivity to the Lord Jesus Christ. An incandescent mantle illus-
trates the meaning. If the mantle is not rightly adjusted only
one bit of it glows, but when the mantel is adjusted exactly
and the light shines, the whole thing is comprehended in a
blaze of light, and every bit of our being is to be absorbed until
we are aglow with the comprehensive goodness of God.

SSM 88

BY THE GRACE OF GOD I AM WHAT I AM

His grace which was bestowed upon me was not in vain.
(1 Cor. 15:10)

The way we continually talk about our own inability is an insult to the Creator. The deploring of our own incompetence is a slander against God for having overlooked us. Get into the habit of examining in the sight of God the things that sound humble before men, and you will be amazed at how staggeringly impertinent they are. "Oh, I shouldn't like to say I am sanctified; I'm not a saint." Say that before God; and it means—"No, Lord, it is impossible for You to save and sanctify me; there are chances I have not had; so many imperfections in my brain and body; no, Lord, it isn't possible." That may sound wonderfully humble before men, but before God it is an attitude of defiance.

Again, the things that sound humble before God may sound the opposite before men. To say Thank God, I know I am saved and sanctified is in the sight of God the acme of humility, it means you have so completely abandoned yourself to God that you know He is true. Never bother your head as to whether what you say sounds humble before men or not, but always be humble before God, and let Him be all in all.

There is only one relationship that matters, and that is your personal relationship to a personal Redeemer and Lord. Let everything else go, but maintain that at all costs, and God will fulfil His purpose through your life. One individual life may be of priceless value to God's purposes, and yours may be that life.

*And the Pharisees and scribes murmured . . . and he spoke this
parable unto them. (Luke 15:2–3)*

In interpreting our Lord's teaching, watch carefully who He is
talking to; the parable of the prodigal son was a stinging lash
to the Pharisees. We need to be reminded of the presentation
of Jesus in the New Testament for the Being pictured to us
nowadays would not perturb anybody; but He aroused His
whole nation to rage. Read the records of His ministry and see
how much blazing indignation there is in it. For thirty years
Jesus did nothing, then for three years He stormed every time
He went down to Jerusalem. Josephus says He tore through
the Temple courts like a madman. We hear nothing about that
Jesus Christ today. The meek and mild Being pictured today
makes us lose altogether the meaning of the Cross. We have
to find out why Jesus was beside Himself with rage and indignation at the Pharisees and not with those given over to carnal
sins. Which state of society is going to stand a ripping and tear-
ing Being like Jesus Christ who drags to the ground the highest respected pillars of its civilized society, and shows that their
respectability and religiosity is built on a much more abominable pride than the harlot's or the publican's? The latter are
disgusting and coarse, but these men have the very pride of
the devil in their hearts.

Ask yourself, then, what is it that awakens indignation in your
heart? Is it the same kind of thing that awakened indignation in
Jesus Christ? The thing that awakens indignation in us is the
thing that upsets our present state of comfort and society. The
thing that made Jesus Christ blaze was pride that defied God and
prevented Him from having His right with human hearts. 'Calvary' means 'the place of a skull', and that is where our Lord is
always crucified, in the culture and intellect of men who will
not have self-knowledge given by the light of Jesus Christ.

HG 78

691

DECEMBER

THE LAW AND THE GOSPEL

*For whosoever shall keep the whole law, and yet offend in one
point, he is guilty of all. (James 2:10)*

The moral law does not consider us as weak human beings at
all, it takes no account of our heredity and infirmities, it demands that we be absolutely moral. The moral law never alters, either for the noblest or for the weakest, it is eternally
and abidingly the same. The moral law ordained by God does
not make itself weak to the weak, it does not palliate our short-
comings, it remains absolute for all time and eternity. If we do
not realize this, it is because we are less than alive; immediately we are alive, life becomes a tragedy. "I was alive without
the law once: but when the commandment came, sin revived,
and I died." When we realize this, then the Spirit of God convicts us of sin. Until a man gets there and sees that there is no
hope, the Cross of Jesus Christ is a farce to him. Conviction of
sin always brings a fearful binding sense of the law, it makes a
man hopeless—"*sold under sin.*" I, a guilty sinner, can never get
right with God, it is impossible. There is only one way in which
I can get right with God, and that is by the Death of Jesus Christ.
I must get rid of the lurking idea that I can ever be right with
God because of my obedience—which of us could ever obey
God to absolute perfection!

We only realize the power of the moral law when it comes
with an "if." God never coerces us. In one mood we wish He
would make us do the thing, and in another mood we wish
He would leave us alone. Whenever God's will is in the ascendant, all compulsion is gone. When we choose deliberately to
obey Him, then He will tax the remotest star and the last grain
of sand to assist us with all His almighty power.

> *A time to kill, and a time to heal; a time to break down, and a time to build up. (Ecclesiastes 3:3)*

Every art, every healing, and every good, can be used for an opposite purpose. Every possibility I have of producing a fine character in time, I can use to produce the opposite; I have that liberty from the Creator. God will not prevent my disobeying Him; if He did, my obedience would not be worth anything. Some of us complain that God should have made the universe and human life like a foolproof machine, so simple that there would be no possibility of going wrong. If He had, we would have been like jelly-fish. If there is no possibility of being damned, there is no need for salvation.

In the time between birth and death, most of us are in our 'shell'. There is something in us which makes us peck, and when the crack comes, instead of its being the gentle light and dawn of a new day, it is like a lightning flash. The universe we awaken to is not one of order, but a great big howling confusion, and it takes time to get adjusted. The distresses we reap in between God's decrees for us, we, together with other human beings, are personally responsible for. If we make our life a muddle, it is to a large extent because we have not discerned the great underlying relationship to God.

SHH 25

CHRISTIAN PERFECTION

Not as though I had already attained, either were already per-
fect . . . (Phil. 3:12)

It is a snare to imagine that God wants to make us perfect specimens of what He can do; God's purpose is to make us one with
Himself. The emphasis of holiness movements is apt to be that
God is producing specimens of holiness to put in His museum.
If you go off on this idea of personal holiness, the dead-set of
your life will not be for God, but for what you call the manifestation of God in your life. "It can never be God's will that I
should be sick." If it was God's will to bruise His own Son, why
should He not bruise you? The thing that tells for God is not
your relevant consistency to an idea of what a saint should be,
but your real vital relation to Jesus Christ, and your abandonment to Him whether you are well or ill.

Christian perfection is not, and never can be, human perfection. Christian perfection is the perfection of a relationship
to God which shows itself amid the irrelevancies of human life.
When you obey the call of Jesus Christ, the first thing that
strikes you is the irrelevancy of the things you have to do, and
the next thing that strikes you is the fact that other people seem
to be living perfectly consistent lives. Such lives are apt to leave
you with the idea that God is unnecessary, by human effort
and devotion we can reach the standard God wants. In a fallen
world this can never be done. I am called to live in perfect
relation to God so that my life produces a longing after God in
other lives, not admiration for myself. Thoughts about myself
hinder my usefulness to God. God is not after perfecting me to
be a specimen in His show-room; He is getting me to the place
where He can use me. Let Him do what He likes.

Then touched he their eyes, saying, According to your faith be it done unto you. (Matthew 9:29)

In human sight the thing we soon lose is what Ruskin called 'the innocence of the eye'. An artist records exactly from this 'innocence' of sight, he does not bring in his logical faculties and interfere with what he sees by telling himself what he ought to see. Most of us know what we are looking at, and instead of trusting the 'innocence' of sight, we confuse it by trying to tell ourselves what we see. If ever you have been taught by anyone to *see*, you will know what this means. Drummond says that Ruskin taught him to *see*. An artist does not tell us what he sees, he enables us to see; he communicates the unutterable identity of what he sees. It is a great thing to see *with* anyone. Jesus never tells us what to see, but when His touch is upon our eyes, we know that we see what He is seeing, He restores this pristine innocence of sight. 'Except a man be born again, he cannot *see* the kingdom of God.'

SSY 89

NOT BY MIGHT NOR BY POWER

And my speech and my preaching was not with enticing words of man's wisdom, but in demonstration of the Spirit and of power.
(1 Cor. 2:4)

If in preaching the Gospel you substitute your clear knowledge of the way of salvation for confidence in the power of the Gospel, you hinder people getting to Reality. You have to see that while you proclaim your knowledge of the way of salvation, you yourself are rooted and grounded in faith in God. Never rely on the clearness of your exposition, but as you give your exposition see that *you* are relying on the Holy Spirit. Rely on the certainty of God's redemptive power, and He will create His own life in souls.

When once you are rooted in Reality, nothing can shake you. If your faith is in experiences, anything that happens is likely to upset that faith; but nothing can ever upset God or the almighty Reality of Redemption; base your faith on that, and you are as eternally secure as God. When once you get into personal contact with Jesus Christ, you will never be moved again. That is the meaning of sanctification. God puts His disapproval on human experience when we begin to adhere to the conception that sanctification is merely an experience, and forget that sanctification itself has to be sanctified (see John 17:19). I have deliberately to give my sanctified life to God for His service, so that He can use me as His hands and His feet.

*The young man saith unto him, All these things have I kept from
my youth up: what lack I yet? (Matthew 19:20)*

No man thinks so clearly at any time or is ever so thrilled as in his 'teens'. The tragedy begins when he finds his actual life cannot be brought up to the standard of the ideal, and he closes with an agony of his own. Then he goes to preachers who talk about the ideal, or to books, thinking he will find the real thing; but too often he does not. He finds the vision there, but not working out in actual practice; and his agony deepens. The ideal presented by Jesus Christ fascinates some men right away; there is something enthralling about Him; but inevitably, sooner or later, they come to the experience of the early disciples recorded in Mark 14:50: 'They all forsook him and fled.' 'I gave all I had to the ideal presented by Jesus Christ, I honestly tried my best to serve Him, but I cannot go on; the New Testament presents ideals beyond my attainment. I won't lower my ideals, although I realize that I can never hope to make them actual.' No man is so laboured or crushed as the man who, with the religion of ideals, finds he cannot carry them out. There are many more men in that attitude than is supposed. Men are kept away from Jesus Christ by a sense of honesty as much as by dishonesty. 'I don't deny that Jesus Christ saves—but if you only knew me!— the mistakes I have made, the wrong things I have done, the blundering things—I should be a perfect disgrace to Him.' Our Lord says to such a one, 'Come unto me . . . and I will give you rest.' When a man comes, he will realize that Jesus Christ does not tell him to do his best, but—Surrender to Me, and I will put into you that which will make the ideal and the actual one, and you will be able to work out in actual life what you see by the power of vision. Without Jesus Christ there is an unbridge-able gap between the ideal and the actual.

SA 82

THE LAW OF ANTAGONISM

To him that overcometh . . . (Rev. 2:7)

Life without war is impossible either in nature or in grace. The basis of physical, mental, moral, and spiritual life is antagonism. This is the open fact of life.

Health is the balance between physical life and external nature, and it is maintained only by sufficient vitality on the inside against things on the outside. Everything outside my physical life is designed to put me to death. Things which keep me going when I am alive, disintegrate me when I am dead. If I have enough fighting power, I produce the balance of health. The same is true of the mental life. If I want to maintain a vigorous mental life, I have to fight, and in that way the mental balance called thought is produced.

Morally it is the same. Everything that does not partake of the nature of virtue is the enemy of virtue in me, and it depends on what moral calibre I have whether I overcome and produce virtue. Immediately I fight, I am moral in that particular. No man is virtuous because he cannot help it; virtue is acquired.

And spiritually it is the same. Jesus said, "In the world ye shall have tribulation," i.e., everything that is not spiritual makes for my undoing, but—"Be of good cheer, I have overcome the world." I have to learn to score off the things that come against me, and in that way produce the balance of holiness; then it becomes a delight to meet opposition.

Holiness is the balance between my disposition and the law of God as expressed in Jesus Christ.

But ye are not in the flesh, but in the spirit, if so be that the Spirit of God dwell in you. (Romans 8:9)

If we have the indwelling identification with Jesus Christ, then we are alive, and more and more alive. In the Christian life the saint is ever young; amazingly and boisterously young, certain that everything is all right. A young Christian is remarkably full of impulse and delight, because he realizes the salvation of God; but this is the real gaiety of knowing that we may cast all our cares on Him and that He careth for us. This is the greatest indication of our identification with Jesus Christ.

AUG 90

The one thing about our Lord that the Pharisees found it hard to understand was His gaiety in connection with the things over which they were appallingly solemn. And what puzzled the religious people of Paul's day was his uncrushable gaiety; he treated buoyantly everything that they treated most seriously. Paul was in earnest over one thing only, and that was his relationship to Jesus Christ. There he was in earnest, and there they were totally indifferent.

AHW 96

THE TEMPLE OF THE HOLY GHOST

Only in the throne will I be greater than thou. (Gen. 41:40)

I have to account to God for the way in which I rule my body under His domination. Paul said he did not "frustrate the grace of God"—make it of no effect. The grace of God is absolute, the salvation of Jesus is perfect, it is done for ever. I am not being saved, I am saved; salvation is as eternal as God's throne; the thing for me to do is to work out what God works in. "Work out your own salvation," I am responsible for doing it. It means that I have to manifest in this body the life of the Lord Jesus, not mystically, but really and emphatically. "I keep under my body, and bring it into subjection." Every saint can have his body under absolute control for God. God has made us to have government over all the temple of the Holy Spirit, over imaginations and affections. We are responsible for these, and we must never give way to inordinate affections. Most of us are much sterner with others than we are in regard to ourselves; we make excuses for things in ourselves whilst we condemn in others things to which we are not naturally inclined.

"I beseech you," says Paul, "present your bodies a living sacrifice." The point to decide is this—"Do I agree with my Lord and Master that my body shall be His temple?" If so, then for me the whole of the law for the body is summed up in this revelation, that my body is the temple of the Holy Ghost.

The very God of peace sanctify you wholly. (1 Thessalonians 5:23)

By the Fall man not only died from God, but he fell into disunion with himself . . . . When a man is born again of the Spirit of God he is introduced to life with God and union with himself. The one thing essential to the new life is obedience to the Spirit of God who has energized our spirits; that obedience must be complete in spirit, soul and body. We must not nourish one part of our being apart from the other parts . . . .

God never develops one part of our being at the expense of the other; spirit, soul and body are kept in harmony. Remember, our spirit does not go further than we bring our body. The spirit of God always drives us out of the visionary, out of the excitable, out of the ecstasy stages, if we are inclined that way. This blind life of the spirit, a life that delights to live in the dim regions of the spirit, refusing to bring the leadings of the Holy Spirit into the rational life, gives occasion to supernatural forces that are not of God. It is impossible to guard our spirit, the only One who can guard all its entrances is God. Never give way to spiritual ecstasy unless there is a chance of working it out rationally, check it every time. Nights and days of prayer and waiting on God may be a curse to our souls and an occasion for Satan. So always remember that the times we have in communion with God must be worked out in the soul and the body.

IWP 32, 33

THE BOW IN THE CLOUD

I do set my bow in the cloud, and it shall be for a token of a covenant between Me and the earth. (Gen. 9:13)

It is the will of God that human beings should get into moral relationship with Him, and His covenants are for this purpose. Why does not God save me? He has saved me, but I have not entered into relationship with Him. Why does not God do this and that? He has done it, the point is—Will I step into covenant relationship? All the great blessings of God are finished and complete, but they are not mine until I enter into relationship with Him on the basis of His covenant.

Waiting for God is incarnate unbelief, it means that I have no faith in Him; I wait for Him to do something in me that I may trust in that. God will not do it, because that is not the basis of the God-and-man relationship. Man has to go out of himself in his covenant with God as God goes out of Himself in His covenant with man. It is a question of faith in God—the rarest thing; we have faith only in our feelings. I do not believe God unless He will give me something in my hand whereby I may know I have it, then I say—"Now I believe." There is no faith there. "*Look unto Me*, and be ye saved."

When I have really transacted business with God on His covenant and have let go entirely, there is no sense of merit, no human ingredient in it at all, but a complete overwhelming sense of being brought into union with God, and the whole thing is transfigured with peace and joy.

For by him were all things created . . . and he is before all things,
and by him all things consist. (Colossians 1:16–17)

Our natural life is a fury of desire for the things we can see. That is the meaning of lust—I must have it at once, a fury of desire without any regard for the consequences. I have to be detached from the things I can see and be brought into a living relationship with the Creator of those things. If I am taken up with the created things and forget Jesus Christ I shall find that things disappoint and I get disillusioned. If my body is 'bossed' by personal self-realization I am defiling the temple of the Holy Ghost; I may be moral and upright but I have become ruler over my own life. 'Give up your right to yourself to me,' says Jesus, 'let me realize myself in you.' He quenches the fury of desire by detaching us from things so that we may know Him. In this way God brings us into the fulness of life. The majority of us are not in the place where God can give us 'the hundredfold more'. We say, 'A bird in the hand is worth two in the bush', while God is wanting to give us the bush with all the birds in it! It is necessary to be detached from things and then come back to them in a right relationship. A sense of property is a hindrance to spiritual growth, that is why so many of us know nothing about communion with Jesus Christ.

HGM 111

REPENTANCE

For godly sorrow worketh repentance to salvation. (2 Cor. 7:10)

Conviction of sin is best portrayed in the words:

> My sins, my sins, my Saviour,
> How sad *on Thee* they fall.

Conviction of sin is one of the rarest things that ever strikes a man. It is the threshold of an understanding of God. Jesus Christ said that when the Holy Spirit came He would convict of sin, and when the Holy Spirit rouses a man's conscience and brings him into the presence of God, it is not his relationship with men that bothers him, but his relationship with God— "against Thee, Thee only, have I sinned, and done this evil in Thy sight." The marvels of conviction of sin, forgiveness, and holiness are so interwoven that it is only the forgiven man who is the holy man, he proves he is forgiven by being the opposite to what he was, by God's grace. Repentance always brings a man to this point: I have sinned. The surest sign that God is at work is when a man says that and means it. Anything less than this is a remorse for having made blunders, the reflex action of disgust at himself.

The entrance into the Kingdom is through the panging pains of repentance crashing into a man's respectable goodness; then the Holy Ghost, Who produces these agonies, begins the formation of the Son of God in the life. The new life will manifest itself in conscious repentance and unconscious holiness, never the other way about. The bedrock of Christianity is repentance. Strictly speaking a man cannot repent when he chooses; repentance is a gift of God. The old Puritans used to pray for "the gift of tears." If ever you cease to know the virtue of repentance, you are in darkness. Examine yourself and see if you have forgotten how to be sorry.

If thou wilt be perfect . . . (Matthew 19:21)

The second 'if' is much more penetrating than the first. Entrance into life is through the recognition of who Jesus is, i.e. all we mean by being born again of the Spirit—'If you would enter into life, that is the way.' The second 'if' is much more searching—'If thou wilt be perfect . . .'—'If you want to be perfect, perfect as I am, perfect as your Father in Heaven is'—then come the conditions. Do we really want to be perfect? Beware of mental quibbling over the word 'perfect'. Perfection does not mean the full maturity and consummation of a man's powers, but perfect fitness for doing the will of God (cf. Philippians 3:12–15). Supposing Jesus Christ can perfectly adjust me to God, put me so perfectly right that I shall be on the footing where I can do the will of God, do I really want Him to do it? Do I want God at all costs to make me perfect? A great deal depends on what is the real deep desire of our hearts. Can we say with Robert Murray McCheyne—'Lord, make me as holy as Thou canst make a saved sinner'? Is that really the desire of our hearts? Our desires come to light always when we press this 'if' of Jesus—'If thou wilt be perfect . . . '

IWP 116

THE IMPARTIAL POWER OF GOD

For by one offering he hath perfected for ever them that are sanctified. (Heb. 10:14)

We trample the blood of the Son of God under foot if we think we are forgiven because we are sorry for our sins. The only explanation of the forgiveness of God and of the unfathomable depth of His forgetting is the Death of Jesus Christ. Our repentance is merely the outcome of our personal realization of the Atonement which He has worked out for us. "Christ Jesus . . . is made unto us wisdom, and righteousness, and sanctification, and redemption." When we realize that Christ is made all this to us, the boundless joy of God begins; wherever the joy of God is not present, the death sentence is at work.

It does not matter who or what we are, there is absolute reinstatement into God by the death of Jesus Christ and by no other way, not because Jesus Christ pleads, but because He died. It is not earned, but accepted. All the pleading which deliberately refuses to recognize the Cross is of no avail; it is battering at another door than the one which Jesus has opened. I don't want to come that way, it is too humiliating to be received as a sinner. "There is none other Name . . ." The apparent heartlessness of God is the expression of His real heart, there is boundless entrance in His way. "We have forgiveness through His blood." Identification with the death of Jesus Christ means identification with Him to the death of everything that never was in Him.

God is justified in saving bad men only as He makes them good. Our Lord does not pretend we are all right when we are all wrong. The Atonement is a propitiation whereby God through the death of Jesus makes an unholy man holy.

A good name is better than precious ointment; and the day of death than the day of one's birth. (Ecclesiastes 7:1)

Solomon is speaking of character, not of reputation. Reputation is what other people think of you; 'character is what you are in the dark', where no one sees but yourself. That is where the worth of a man's character lies, and Solomon says that the man who has attained a sagacious character during life is like a most refreshing, soothing, healing ointment. In the New Testament, 'name' frequently has the meaning of 'nature'. 'Where two or three are gathered together in my name', i.e. My nature (Matthew 18:20). Everyone who comes across a good nature is made better by it, unless he is determined to be bad. To say a man has a good nature does not mean he is a pious individual, always quoting texts. The test of a nature is the atmosphere it produces. When we are in contact with a good nature we are uplifted by it. We do not get anything we can state articulately, but the horizon is enlarged, the pressure is removed from the mind and heart and we see things differently.

SHH 77

THE OFFENCE OF THE NATURAL

And they that are Christ's have crucified the flesh with the affections and lusts. (Gal. 5:24)

The natural life is not sinful; we must be apostatized from sin, have nothing to do with sin in any shape or form. Sin belongs to hell and the devil; I, as a child of God, belong to heaven and God. It is not a question of giving up sin, but of giving up my right to myself, my natural independence and self-assertiveness, and this is where the battle has to be fought. It is the things that are right and noble and good from the natural standpoint that keep us back from God's best. To discern that natural virtues antagonize surrender to God, is to bring our soul into the centre of its greatest battle. Very few of us debate with the sordid and evil and wrong, but we do debate with the good. It is the good that hates the best, and the higher up you get in the scale of the natural virtues, the more intense is the opposition to Jesus Christ. "They that are Christ's have crucified the flesh"—it is going to cost the natural in you everything, not something. Jesus said—"If any man will be My disciple, let him deny *himself*," i.e., his right to himself, and a man has to realize Who Jesus Christ is before he will do it. Beware of refusing to go to the funeral of your own independence.

The natural life is not spiritual, and it can only be made spiritual by sacrifice. If we do not resolutely sacrifice the natural, the supernatural can never become natural in us. There is no royal road there; each of us has it entirely in his own hands. It is not a question of praying but of performing.

*The life which I now live in the flesh I live by the faith of the
Son of God . . . I do not frustrate the grace of God.
(Galatians 2:20–1)*

We are in danger of forgetting that we cannot do what God
does and that God will not do what we can do. We cannot save
ourselves or sanctify ourselves; God only can do that; but God
does not give us good habits. He does not give us character, He
does not make us walk aright; we must do all that. We have to
work out what God has worked in (Philippians 2:12–13). Many
of us lose out spiritually, not because the devil attacks us, but
because we are stupidly ignorant of the way God has made us.
Remember, the devil did not make the human body; he may
have tampered with it, but the human body was created by
God, and its constitution after we are saved remains the same
as before. For instance, we are not born with a ready-made
habit of dressing ourselves; we have to form that habit. Apply
it spiritually—when we are born again, God does not give us a
fully fledged series of holy habits, we have to make them; and
the forming of habits on the basis of God's supernatural work
in our souls is the education of our spiritual life.

   Many of us refuse to do it; we are lazy and we frustrate the
grace of God.

GH 52

THE OFFERING OF THE NATURAL

Abraham had two sons, the one by a bondmaid, the other by a freewoman. (Gal. 4:22)

Paul is not dealing with sin in this chapter of Galatians, but with the revelation of the natural to the spiritual. The natural must be turned into the spiritual by sacrifice, otherwise a tremendous divorce will be produced in the actual life. Why should God ordain the natural to be sacrificed? God did not. It is not God's order, but His permissive will. God's order was that the natural should be transformed into the spiritual by obedience; it is sin that made it necessary for the natural to be sacrificed.

Abraham had to offer up Ishmael before he offered up Isaac. Some of us are trying to offer up spiritual sacrifices to God before we have sacrificed the natural. The only way in which we can offer a spiritual sacrifice to God is by presenting our bodies a living sacrifice. Sanctification means more than deliverance from sin, it means the deliberate commitment of myself whom God has saved to God, and that I do not care what it costs.

If we do not sacrifice the natural to the spiritual, the natural life will mock at the life of the Son of God in us and produce a continual swither. This is always the result of an undisciplined spiritual nature. We go wrong because we stubbornly refuse to discipline ourselves, physically, morally or mentally. "I wasn't disciplined when I was a child." You must discipline yourself now. If you do not, you will ruin the whole of your personal life for God.

God is not with our natural life while we pamper it; but when we put it out in the desert and resolutely keep it under, then God will be with it; and He will open up wells and oases, and fulfil all His promises for the natural.

Therefore whosoever heareth these sayings of mine, and doeth them, I will liken him unto a wise man, which built his house upon a rock. (Matthew 7:24)

We speak of building castles in the air; that is where a castle should be—whoever heard of a castle underground! The problem is how to get the foundation under your castle in the air so that it can stand upon the earth. The way to put foundations under our castles is by paying attention to the words of Jesus Christ. We may read and listen and not make much of it at the time, but by and by we come into circumstances when the Holy Spirit will bring back to us what Jesus said—are we going to obey? Jesus says that the way to put foundations under spiritual castles is by hearing and doing 'these sayings of mine'. Pay attention to His words, and give time to doing it.

Our spiritual castles must be conspicuous, and the test of a building is not its fair beauty but its foundations. There are beautiful spiritual fabrics raised in the shape of books and of lives, full of the finest diction and activities, but when the test comes, down they go. They have not been built on the sayings of Jesus Christ, but built altogether in the air with no foundations under them.

'Build up your character bit by bit by attention to My words,' says Jesus, then when the supreme crisis comes, you will stand like a rock. The crisis does not come always, but when it does come, it is all up in about two seconds, there is no possibility of pretence, you are unearthed immediately. If a man has built himself up in private by listening to the words of Jesus and obeying them, when the crisis comes it is not his strength of will that keeps him, but the tremendous power of God—'kept by the power of God'. Go on building yourself up in the word of God when no one is watching you, and when the crisis comes you will find you will stand like a rock; but if you have not been building yourself up on the word of God, you will go down, however strong your will. All you build will end in disaster unless it is built on the sayings of Jesus Christ; but if you are doing what Jesus told you to do, nourishing your soul on His word, you need not fear the crisis whatever it is.

SSM 108–9

INDIVIDUALITY

If any man will come after Me, let him deny himself.
(Matt. 16:24)

Individuality is the husk of the personal life. Individuality is all elbows, it separates and isolates. It is the characteristic of the child and rightly so; but if we mistake individuality for the personal life, we will remain isolated. The shell of individuality is God's created natural covering for the protection of the personal life; but individuality must go in order that the personal life may come out and be brought into fellowship with God. Individuality counterfeits personality as lust counterfeits love. God designed human nature for Himself; individuality debases human nature for itself.

The characteristics of individuality are independence and self-assertiveness. It is the continual assertion of individuality that hinders our spiritual life more than anything else. If you say—"I cannot believe," it is because individuality is in the road; individuality never can believe. Personality cannot help believing. Watch yourself when the Spirit of God is at work. He pushes you to the margins of your individuality, and you have either to say—"I shan't," or to surrender, to break the husk of individuality and let the personal life emerge. The Holy Spirit narrows it down every time to one thing (cf. Matthew 5:23-24). The thing in you that will not be reconciled to your brother is your individuality. God wants to bring you into union with Himself, but unless you are willing to give up your right to yourself He cannot. "Let him deny himself"—deny his independent right to himself, then the real life has a chance to grow.

Ye search the scriptures: for in them ye think ye have eternal life: and they are they which testify of me. (John 5:39)

The Bible is the universe of revelation facts; the natural world is the universe of common-sense facts, and our means of communication with the two universes is totally different. We come in contact with the natural universe by our senses, our intellect has to be curious. Scientific knowledge, which is systematized common sense, is based on intense intellectual curiosity. Curiosity in the natural world is right, not wrong, and if we are not intellectually curious we shall never know anything, God never encourages laziness.

When we come to the universe of the Bible, the revelation facts about God, intellectual curiosity is not of the slightest use. Our senses are no good here, we cannot find out God by searching. We may have inferences from our common-sense thinking which we call God, but these are mere abstractions. We can only get at the facts that are revealed in the Bible by faith. Faith is not credulity; faith is my personal spirit obeying God. The Bible does not deal in common-sense facts; the natural universe deals in common-sense facts, and we get at these by our senses. The Bible deals with revelation facts, facts we cannot get at by our common sense, facts we may be pleased to make light of by our common sense. For instance, Jesus Christ is a revelation fact, sin is another, the devil is another, the Holy Spirit is another. Not one of these is a common-sense fact. If a man were merely a common-sense individual, he could do very well without God.

PR 20

PERSONALITY

That they may be one, even as we are one. (John 17:22)

Personality is that peculiar, incalculable thing that is meant when we speak of ourselves as distinct from everyone else. Our personality is always too big for us to grasp. An island in the sea may be but the top of a great mountain. Personality is like an island, we know nothing about the great depths underneath, consequently we cannot estimate ourselves. We begin by thinking that we can, but we come to realize that there is only one Being Who understands us, and that is our Creator.

Personality is the characteristic of the spiritual man as individuality is the characteristic of the natural man. Our Lord can never be defined in terms of individuality and independence, but only in terms of personality, "I and My Father are one." Personality merges, and you only reach your real identity when you are merged with another person. When love, or the Spirit of God strikes a man, he is transformed, he no longer insists upon his separate individuality. Our Lord never spoke in terms of individuality, of a man's "elbows" or his isolated position, but in terms of personality—"that they may be one, even as We are one." If you give up your right to yourself to God, the real true nature of your personality answers to God straight away. Jesus Christ emancipates the personality, and the individuality is transfigured; the transfiguring element is love, personal devotion to Jesus. Love is the outpouring of one personality in fellowship with another personality.

Pilate saith unto him, What is truth? (John 18:38)

The Personality of Truth is the great revelation of Christianity—'I am the Truth'. Our Lord did not say He was 'all truth' so that we could go to His statements as to a text-book and verify things; there are domains, such as science and art and history, which are distinctly man's domains and the boundaries of our knowledge must continually alter and be enlarged; God never encourages laziness. The question to be asked is not, 'Does the Bible agree with the findings of modern science?' but, 'Do the findings of modern science help us to a better understanding of the things revealed in the Bible?' . . .

The Bible is a whole library of literature giving us the final interpretation of the Truth, and to take the Bible apart from that one supreme purpose is to have a book and nothing more; and further, to take our Lord Jesus Christ away from the revelation of Him given in the Bible is to be left with one who is open to all the irreverent slanders of unbelief.

'The Truth' is our Lord Himself; 'the whole truth' is the inspired Scripture interpreting the Truth to us; and 'nothing but the truth' is the Holy Spirit, 'the Spirit of truth', efficaciously regenerating and sanctifying us, and guiding us into 'all the truth'.

GW 33, 35

WHAT TO PRAY FOR

Men ought always to pray, and not to faint. (Luke 18:1)

You cannot intercede if you do not believe in the reality of the Redemption; you will turn intercession into futile sympathy with human beings which will only increase their submissive content to being out of touch with God. In intercession you bring the person, or the circumstance that impinges on you before God until you are moved by His attitude towards that person or circumstance. Intercession means filling up "that which is behind of the afflictions of Christ," and that is why there are so few intercessors. Intercession is put on the line of—"Put yourself in his place." Never! Try to put yourself in God's place.

As a worker, be careful to keep pace with the communications of reality from God or you will be crushed. If you know too much, more than God has engineered for you to know, you cannot pray, the condition of the people is so crushing that you cannot get through to reality.

Our work lies in coming into definite contact with God about everything, and we shirk it by becoming active workers. We do the things that can be tabulated but we will not intercede. Intercession is the one thing that has no snares, because it keeps our relationship with God completely open.

The thing to watch in intercession is that no soul is patched up; a soul must get through into contact with the life of God. Think of the number of souls God has brought about our path and we have dropped them! When we pray on the ground of Redemption, God creates something He can create in no other way than through intercessory prayer.

> *. . . and that from child thou hast known the holy scriptures.*
> *(2 Timothy 3:15)*

It is not the thing on which we spend most time that moulds us, but the thing that exerts the greatest power. Five minutes with God and His word is worth more than all the rest of the day. Do we come to the Bible to be spoken to by God, to be made 'wise unto salvation', or simply to hunt for texts on which to build addresses? There are people who vagabond through the Bible, taking sufficient only out of it for the making of sermons, they never let the word of God walk out of the Bible and talk to them. Beware of living from hand to mouth in spiritual matters; do not be a spiritual mendicant.

AHW 126

> *. . . and my words abide in you . . . (John 15:7)*

Are we in the habit of listening to the words of Jesus? Do we realize that Jesus knows more about our business than we do ourselves? Do we take His word for our clothes, our money, our domestic work; or do we think we can manage these things for ourselves? The Spirit of God has the habit of taking the words of Jesus out of their scriptural setting and putting them into the setting of our personal lives.

AHW 121

THE GREAT LIFE

Peace I leave with you, My peace I give unto you: . . . Let not your heart be troubled. (John 14:27)

Whenever a thing becomes difficult in personal experience, we are in danger of blaming God, but it is we who are in the wrong, not God; there is some perversity somewhere that we will not let go. Immediately we do, everything becomes as clear as daylight. As long as we try to serve two ends, ourselves and God, there is perplexity. The attitude must be one of complete reliance on God. When once we get there, there is nothing easier than living the saintly life; difficulty comes in when we want to usurp the authority of the Holy Spirit for our own ends.

Whenever you obey God, His seal is always that of peace, the witness of an unfathomable peace, which is not natural, but the peace of Jesus. Whenever peace does not come, tarry till it does or find out the reason why it does not. If you are acting on an impulse, or from a sense of the heroic, the peace of Jesus will not witness; there is no simplicity or confidence in God, because the spirit of simplicity is born of the Holy Ghost, not of your decisions. Every decision brings a reaction of simplicity.

My questions come whenever I cease to obey. When I have obeyed God, the problems never come between me and God, they come as probes to keep the mind going on with amazement at the revelation of God. Any problem that comes between God and myself springs out of disobedience; any problem, and there are many, that is alongside me while I obey God, increases my ecstatic delight, because I know that my Father knows, and I am going to watch and see how He unravels this thing.

The natural man receiveth not the things of the Spirit of God.
(1 Corinthians 2:14)

The Bible is the Word of God only to those who are born from above and who walk in the light. Our Lord Jesus Christ, the *Word* of God, and the Bible, the *words* of God, stand or fall together, they can never be separated without fatal results. A man's attitude to our Lord determines his attitude to the Bible. The 'sayings' of God to a man not born from above are of no moment; to him the Bible is simply a remarkable compilation of literature—'that it is, and nothing more'. All the confusion arises from not recognizing this.

DDG 15

If we present the pearls of God's revelation to unspiritual people, God says they will trample the pearls under their feet; not trample us under their feet, that would not matter so much, but they will trample the truth of God under their feet. These words are not human words, but the words of Jesus Christ, and the Holy Spirit alone can teach us what they mean. There are some truths that God will not make simple. The only thing God makes plain in the Bible is the way of salvation and sanctification, after that our understanding depends entirely on our walking in the light. Over and over again men water down the word of God to suit those who are not spiritual, and consequently the word of God is trampled under the feet of 'swine'.

SSM 82

APPROVED UNTO GOD

Study to shew thyself approved unto God, a workman that
needeth not to be ashamed, rightly dividing the word of truth.
(2 Tim. 2:15)

If you cannot express yourself on any subject, struggle until
you can. If you do not, someone will be the poorer all the days
of his life. Struggle to re-express some truth of God to yourself, and God will use that expression to someone else. Go
through the winepress of God where the grapes are crushed.
You must struggle to get expression experimentally, then there
will come a time when that expression will become the very
wine of strengthening to someone else; but if you say lazily—
"I am not going to struggle to express this thing for myself, I
will borrow what I say," the expression will not only be of no
use to you, but of no use to anyone. Try to state to yourself
what you feel implicitly to be God's truth, and you give God a
chance to pass it on to someone else through you.

Always make a practice of provoking your own mind to think
out what it accepts easily. Our position is not ours until we
make it ours by suffering. The author who benefits you most
is not the one who tells you something you did not know before, but the one who gives expression to the truth that has
been dumbly struggling in you for utterance.

. . . the things of the Spirit of God. (1 Corinthians 2:14)

Everywhere the charge is made against Christian people, not only the generality of Christians, but really spiritual people, that they think in a very slovenly manner. Very few of us in this present dispensation live up to the privilege of thinking spiritually as we ought. This present dispensation is the dispensation of the Holy Ghost. The majority of us do not think according to the tremendous meaning of that; we think ante-Pentecostal thoughts, the Holy Spirit is not a living factor in our thinking; we have only a vague impression that He is here. Many Christian workers would question the statement that we should ask for the Holy Spirit (Luke 11:13). The note struck in the New Testament is not 'Believe in the Holy Spirit', but 'Receive the Holy Spirit'. That does not mean the Holy Spirit is not here; it means He *is* here in all His power, for one purpose, that men who believe in Him might receive Him. So the first thing we have to face is the reception of the Holy Spirit in a practical conscious manner.

Always distinguish between yielding to the Spirit and receiving the Spirit. When the Spirit is at work in a time of mighty revival it is very difficult not to yield to the Spirit, but it is quite another thing to receive Him. If we yield to the power of the Spirit in a time of revival we may feel amazingly blessed, but if we do not receive the Spirit we are left decidedly worse and not better. That is first a psychological fact and then a New Testament fact. So as Christians we have to ask ourselves, does our faith stand 'in demonstration of the Spirit and of power'? Have we linked ourselves up with the power of the Holy Ghost, and are we letting Him have His way in our thinking?

BE 95

WRESTLING BEFORE GOD

Wherefore take unto you the whole armour of God . . . praying always . . . (Eph. 6:13,18)

You have to wrestle against the things that prevent you from getting to God, and you wrestle in prayer for other souls; but never say that you wrestle with God in prayer, it is scripturally untrue. If you do wrestle with God, you will be crippled all the rest of your life. If, when God comes in some way you do not want, you take hold of Him as Jacob did and wrestle with Him, you compel Him to put you out of joint. Don't be a hirpler in God's ways, but be one who wrestles before God with things, becoming more than conqueror through Him. Wrestling before God tells in His Kingdom. If you ask me to pray for you and I am not complete in Christ, I may pray but it avails nothing; but if I am complete in Christ my prayer prevails all the time. Prayer is only effective when there is completeness— "Wherefore take unto you the whole armour of God."

Always distinguish between God's order and His permissive will, i.e., His providential purpose towards us. God's order is unchangeable; His permissive will is that with which we must wrestle before Him. It is our reaction to the permissive will of God that enables us to get at His order. "All things work together for good to them that love God"—to those who remain true to God's order, to His calling in Christ Jesus. God's permissive will is the means whereby His sons and daughters are to be manifested. We are not to be like jelly-fish saying, "It's the Lord's will." We are not to put up a fight with God, not to wrestle with God, but to wrestle before God *with things*. Beware of squatting lazily before God instead of putting up a glorious fight so that you may lay hold of His strength.

. . . for the Son of man cometh at an hour when ye think not.
(Luke 12:40)

The element of surprise is always the note of the life of the Holy Ghost in us. We are born again by the great surprise—'The wind bloweth where it listeth, and thou hearest the voice thereof, but knowest not whence it cometh, and whither it goeth: so is every one that is born of the Spirit' (John 3:8). Men cannot tie up the wind, it blows where it lists; neither can the work of the Holy Spirit be tied up in logical methods. Jesus never comes where we expect Him; if He did He would not have said 'Watch'. 'Be ye also ready; for in an hour when ye think not, the Son of man cometh.' Jesus appears in the most illogical connections, where we least expect Him, and the only way a Christian worker can keep true to God amidst the difficulties of work is to be ready for His surprise visits. We have not to depend on the prayers of other people, not to look for the sympathy of God's children, but to be ready for the Lord. It is this intense reality of expecting Him at every turn that gives life the attitude of child wonder that Jesus wants it to have. When we are rightly related to God, life is full of spontaneous joyful uncertainty and expectancy—we do not know what God is going to do next; and He packs our life with surprises all the time.

SSY 34

REDEMPTION CREATES THE NEED
IT SATISFIES

But the natural man receiveth not the things of the Spirit of God:
for they are foolishness unto him. (1 Cor. 2:14)

The Gospel of God creates a sense of need of the Gospel. Paul says—"If our gospel be hid, it is hid"—to those who are black-guards? No, "to them that are lost: in whom the god of this world hath blinded the minds of them which believe not." The majority of people have their morality well within their own grasp, they have no sense of need of the Gospel. It is God Who creates the need of which no human being is conscious until God manifests Himself. Jesus said—"Ask, and it shall be given you," but God cannot give until a man asks. It is not that He withholds, but that that is the way He has constituted things on the basis of Redemption. By means of our asking, God gets processes into work whereby He creates the thing that is not in existence until we do ask. The inner reality of Redemption is that it creates all the time. As the Redemption creates the life of God in us, so it creates the things belonging to that life. Nothing can satisfy the need but that which created the need. This is the meaning of Redemption—it creates and it satisfies.

"I, if I be lifted up from the earth, will draw all men unto Me." We preach our own experiences and people are inter-ested, but no sense of need is awakened by it. If once Jesus Christ is lifted up, the Spirit of God will create a conscious need of Him. Behind the preaching of the Gospel is the creative Redemption of God at work in the souls of men. It is never personal testimony that saves men. "The words that *I* speak unto you, they are spirit and they are life."

But ye shall be baptized with the Holy Ghost . . . (Acts 1:5)

Why do we want to be baptized with the Holy Ghost? All depends on that 'why'. If we want to be baptized with the Holy Ghost that we may be of use, it is all up; or because we want peace and joy and deliverance from sin, it is all up. 'He shall baptize you with the Holy Ghost', not for anything for ourselves at all, but that we may be witnesses unto Him. God will never answer the prayer to be baptized with the Holy Ghost for any other reason than to make us witnesses to Jesus. To be consciously desirous of anything but that one thing is to be off the main track. The Holy Ghost is transparent honesty. When we pray, 'Oh Lord, baptize me with the Holy Ghost whatever it means', God will give us a glimpse of our self-interest and self-seeking until we are willing for everything to go and there is nothing left but Himself. As long as there is self-interest and self-seeking, something has to go. God is amazingly patient. The perplexity is not because of the hardness of the way, but the unwilling pride of sin, the stubborn yielding bit by bit, when it might be done any second. The acceptance of the Divine nature involves in it obedience to the Divine precepts. The commands of God are enablings. God banks entirely on His own Spirit, and when we attempt, His ability is granted immediately. We have a great deal more power than we know, and as we do the overcoming we find He is there all the time until it becomes the habit of our life.

The baptism with the Holy Ghost is the great sovereign work of the personal Holy Ghost; entire sanctification is our personal experience of it.

HGM 30

THE TEST OF LOYALTY

And we know that all things work together for good to them that
love God. (Rom. 8:28)

It is only the loyal soul who believes that God engineers circumstances. We take such liberty with our circumstances, we
do not believe God engineers them, although we say we do;
we treat the things that happen as if they were engineered by
men. To be faithful in every circumstance means that we have
only one loyalty, and that is to our Lord. Suddenly God breaks
up a particular set of circumstances, and the realization comes
that we have been disloyal to Him by not recognizing that He
had ordered them; we never saw what He was after, and that
particular thing will never be repeated all the days of our life.
The test of loyalty always comes just there. If we learn to worship God in the trying circumstances, He will alter them in two
seconds when He chooses.

Loyalty to Jesus Christ is the thing that we "stick at" to-day.
We will be loyal to work, to service, to anything, but do not
ask us to be loyal to Jesus Christ. Many Christians are intensely
impatient of talking about loyalty to Jesus. Our Lord is de-
throned more emphatically by Christian workers than by the
world. God is made a machine for blessing men, and Jesus
Christ is made a Worker among workers.

The idea is not that we do work for God, but that we are so
loyal to Him that He can do His work through us—"I reckon
on you for extreme service, with no complaining on your part
and no explanation on Mine." God wants to use us as He used
His own Son.

What shall a man give in exchange for his soul? (Mark 8:37)

The modern Christian laughs at the idea of a final judgment. That shows how far we can stray away if we imbibe the idea that the modern mind is infallible and not our Lord. To His mind at least the finality of moral decision is reached in this life. There is no aspect of our Lord's mind that the modern mind detests so fundamentally as this one . . . .

The parables in the 25th chapter of St Matthew are three aspects of the Divine estimate of life. The parable of the ten virgins reveals that it is fatal from our Lord's standpoint to live this life without preparation for the life to come. That is not the exegesis, it is the obvious underlying principle.

The parable of the talents is our Lord's statement with regard to the danger of leaving undone the work of a lifetime.

And the description of the last judgment is the picture of genuine astonishment on the part of both the losers and the gainers of what they had never once thought about.

To be accustomed to our Lord's teaching is not to ask, 'What must I do to be good?' but, 'What must I do to be saved?' How long does it take us to know what the true meaning of our life is? One half second.

HG 73

WHAT TO CONCENTRATE ON

I came not to send peace, but a sword. (Matt. 10:34)

Never be sympathetic with the soul whose case makes you come to the conclusion that God is hard. God is more tender than we can conceive, and every now and again He gives us the chance of being the rugged one that He may be the tender One. If a man cannot get through to God it is because there is a secret thing he does not intend to give up—I will admit I have done wrong but I no more intend to give up that thing than fly. It is impossible to deal sympathetically with a case like that: we have to get right deep down to the root until there is antagonism and resentment against the message. People want the blessing of God, but they will not stand the thing that goes straight to the quick.

If God has had His way with you, your message as His servant is merciless insistence on the one line, cut down to the very root, otherwise there will be no healing. Drive home the message until there is no possible refuge from its application. Begin to get at people where they are until you get them to realize what they lack, and then erect the standard of Jesus Christ for their lives—"We never can be that." Then drive it home—"Jesus Christ says you must." "But how can we be?" "You cannot, unless you have a new Spirit" (Luke 11:13).

There must be a sense of need before your message is of any use. Thousands of people are happy without God in this world. If I was happy and moral till Jesus came, why did He come? Because that kind of happiness and peace is on a wrong level; Jesus Christ came to send a sword through every peace that is not based on a personal relationship to Himself.

Then will I go unto the altar of God, unto God my exceeding joy.
(Psalm 43:4)

Joy is the great note all through the Bible. We have the notion of joy that arises from good spirits or good health, but the miracle of the joy of God has nothing to do with a man's life or his circumstances or the condition he is in. Jesus does not come to a man and say 'Cheer up', He plants within a man the miracle of the joy of God's own nature. The stronghold of the Christian faith is *the joy of God*, not *my joy in God*. It is a great thing for a man to have faith in the joy of God, to know that nothing alters the fact of God's joy. God reigns and rules and rejoices, and His joy is our strength. The miracle of the Christian life is that God can give a man joy in the midst of external misery, a joy which gives him power to work until the misery is removed. Joy is different from happiness, because happiness depends on what happens. There are elements in our circumstances we cannot help, joy is independent of them all.

'That my joy might remain in you, and that your joy might be full' (John 15:11).

What was the joy of Jesus? That He did the will of His Father, and He wants that joy to be ours.

HGM 48

THE RIGHT LINES OF WORK

I, if I be lifted up, will draw all men unto Me. (John 12:32)

Very few of us have any understanding of the reason why Jesus Christ died. If sympathy is all that human beings need, then the Cross of Christ is a farce, there was no need for it. What the world needs is not "a little bit of love," but a surgical operation.

When you are face to face with a soul in difficulty spiritually, remind yourself of Jesus Christ on the Cross. If that soul can get to God on any other line, then the Cross of Jesus Christ is unnecessary. If you can help others by your sympathy or understanding, you are a traitor to Jesus Christ. You have to keep your soul rightly related to God and pour out for others on His line, not pour out on the human line and ignore God. The great note to-day is amiable religiosity.

The one thing we have to do is to exhibit Jesus Christ crucified, to lift Him up all the time. Every doctrine that is not imbedded in the Cross of Jesus will lead astray. If the worker himself believes in Jesus Christ and is banking on the Reality of Redemption, the people he talks to *must* be concerned. The thing that remains and deepens is the worker's simple relationship to Jesus Christ; his usefulness to God depends on that and that alone.

The calling of a New Testament worker is to uncover sin and to reveal Jesus Christ as Saviour, consequently he cannot be poetical, he must be sternly surgical. We are sent by God to lift up Jesus Christ, not to give wonderfully beautiful discourses. We have to probe straight down as deeply as God has probed us, to be keen in sensing the Scriptures which bring the truth straight home and to apply them fearlessly.

Jesus said, 'These things have I spoken unto you . . . that your joy may be full.' (John 15:11)

The one thing about the apostle Paul that staggered his contemporaries was his unaccountable gaiety of spirit: he would not be serious over anything other than Jesus Christ. They might stone him and imprison him, but whatever they did made no difference to his buoyancy of spirit. The external character of the life of our Lord was that of radiant sociability; so much so, that the popular scandalmongering about Him was that He was 'a gluttonous man and a winebibber, a friend of publicans and sinners!' The fundamental reason for our Lord's sociability was other than they knew; but His whole life was characterized with a radiant fulness, it was not an exhausted type of life. 'Except ye become as little children . . .' If a little child is not full of the spontaneousness of life there is something wrong. The bounding life and restlessness is a sign of health, not of naughtiness. Jesus said, 'I am come that they might have life, and that they might have it more abundantly.' Be being filled with the life Jesus came to give. Men who are radiantly healthy, physically and spiritually, cannot be crushed. They are like the cedars of Lebanon, which have such superabounding vitality in their sap that they intoxicate to death any parasites that try to live on them.

PH 198

EXPERIENCE OR REVELATION

*We have received ... the spirit which is of God that we might
know the things that are freely given to us of God. (1 Cor. 2:12)*

Reality is Redemption, not my experience of Redemption; but
Redemption has no meaning for me until it speaks the language
of my conscious life. When I am born again, the Spirit of God
takes me right out of myself and my experiences, and identifies me with Jesus Christ. If I am left with my experiences, my
experiences have not been produced by Redemption. The proof
that they are produced by Redemption is that I am led out of
myself all the time, I no longer pay any attention to my experiences as the ground of Reality, but only to the Reality which
produced the experiences. My experiences are not worth anything unless they keep me at the Source, Jesus Christ.

If you try to dam up the Holy Spirit in you to produce subjective experiences, you will find that He will burst all bounds
and take you back again to the historic Christ. Never nourish
an experience which has not God as its Source and faith in God
as its result. If you do, your experience is anti-Christian, no
matter what visions you may have had. Is Jesus Christ Lord of
your experiences, or do you try to lord it over Him? Is any
experience dearer to you than your Lord? He must be Lord over
you, and you must not pay attention to any experience over
which He is not Lord. There comes a time when God will make
you impatient with your own experience—I do not care what
I experience; I am sure of Him.

Be ruthless with yourself if you are given to talking about
the experiences you have had. Faith that is sure of itself is not
faith; faith that is sure of God is the only faith there is.

For I came not to judge the world, but to save the world.
(John 12:47)

Jesus Christ did not come to pronounce judgment. He Himself is the judgment; whenever we come across Him we are judged instantly.

One of the most remarkable things about Jesus Christ is that although He was full of love and gentleness, yet in His presence everyone not only felt benefited, but ashamed. It is His presence that judges us; we long to meet Him, yet we dread to . . .

If you look at a sheep in the summer time you would say it was white, but see it against the background of startling virgin snow and it looks like a blot on the landscape. If we judge ourselves by one another we do not feel condemned (see 2 Corinthians 10:12); but immediately Jesus Christ is in the background—His life, His language, His looks, His labours, we feel judged instantly. 'It is for judgment that I have come into the world.' The judgment that Jesus Christ's presence brings makes us pronounce judgment on ourselves, we feel a sense of shame, or of missing the mark, and we determine never to do that thing again.

HGM 42

THE DRAWING OF THE FATHER

No man can come to Me, except the Father which hath sent Me draw him. (John 6:44)

When God draws me, the issue of my will comes in at once—will I react on the revelation which God gives—will I come to Him? Discussion on spiritual matters is an impertinence. Never discuss with anyone when God speaks. Belief is not an intellectual act; belief is a moral act whereby I deliberately commit myself. Will I dump myself down absolutely on God and transact on what He says? If I will, I shall find I am based on Reality that is as sure as God's throne.

In preaching the gospel, always push an issue of will. Belief must be the *will* to believe. There must be a surrender of the will, not a surrender to persuasive power, a deliberate launching forth on God and on what He says until I am no longer confident in what I have done, I am confident only in God. The hindrance is that I will not trust God, but only my mental understanding. As far as feelings go, I must stake all blindly. I must *will* to believe, and this can never be done without a violent effort on my part to disassociate myself from my old ways of looking at things, and by putting myself right over onto Him.

Every man is made to reach out beyond his grasp. It is God who draws me, and my relationship to Him in the first place is a personal one, not an intellectual one. I am introduced into the relationship by the miracle of God and my own will to believe, then I begin to get an intelligent appreciation and understanding of the wonder of the transaction.

He was in the world, and the world was made by him, and the world knew him not. (John 1:10)

In every life there is one place where God must have 'elbow room'. We must not pass judgment on others, nor must we make a principle of judging out of our own experience. It is impossible for a man to know the views of Almighty God. Preaching from prejudice is dangerous, it makes a man dogmatic and certain that he is right. The question for each of us to ask ourselves is this: Would I recognize God if He came in a way I was not prepared for—if He came in the bustle of a marriage feast, or as a carpenter? That is how Jesus Christ appeared to the prejudices of the Pharisees, and they said He was mad. Today we are trying to work up a religious revival while God has visited the world in a moral revival, and the majority of us have not begun to recognize it. The characteristics that are manifested when God is at work are self-effacement, self-suppression, abandonment to something or someone other than myself.

BFB 22

HOW CAN I PERSONALLY PARTAKE IN THE ATONEMENT?

But God forbid that I should glory save in the cross of Our Lord Jesus Christ. (Gar. 6:14)

The Gospel of Jesus Christ always forces an issue of will. Do I accept God's verdict on sin in the Cross of Christ? Have I the slightest interest in the death of Jesus? Do I want to be identified with His death, to be killed right out to all interest in sin, in worldliness, in self—to be so identified with Jesus that I am spoilt for everything else but Him? The great privilege of discipleship is that I can sign on under His Cross, and that means death to sin. Get alone with Jesus and either tell Him that you do not want sin to die out in you; or else tell Him that at all costs you want to be identified with His death. Immediately you transact in confident faith in what Our Lord did on the Cross, a supernatural identification with His death takes place, and you will know with a knowledge that passeth knowledge that your "old man" is crucified with Christ. The proof that your old man is crucified with Christ is the amazing ease with which the life of God in you enables you to obey the voice of Jesus Christ.

Every now and again, Our Lord lets us see what we would be like if it were not for Himself; it is a justification of what He said—"Without Me ye can do nothing." That is why the bedrock of Christianity is personal, passionate devotion to the Lord Jesus. We mistake the ecstasy of our first introduction into the Kingdom for the purpose of God in getting us there; His purpose in getting us there is that we may realize all that identification with Jesus Christ means.

The Son of man came eating and drinking, and they say, Behold a man gluttonous, and a winebibber, a friend of publicans and sinners. (Matthew 11:19)

'The Son of man came eating and drinking.' One of the most staggering things in the New Testament is just this commonplace aspect. The curious difference between Jesus Christ's idea of holiness and that of other religions lies here. The one says holiness is not compatible with ordinary food and married life, but Jesus Christ represents a character lived straight down in the ordinary amalgam of human life, and His claim is that the character He manifested is possible for any man, if he will come in by the door provided for him.

SA 33

There is in our midst today a strong revival of pagan spirituality. Many are using the terms of Hinduism or Buddhism to expound Christianity, and they end not in expounding Christianity at all, but in expounding the very human experience of consecration, which is not peculiar to Christianity. The peculiar doctrine or Gospel of the Christian religion is Entire Sanctification, whereby God takes the most unpromising man and makes a saint of him.

DL 98

THE HIDDEN LIFE

Your life is hid with Christ in God. (Col. 3:3)

The Spirit of God witnesses to the simple almighty security of the life hid with Christ in God and this is continually brought out in the Epistles. We talk as if it were the most precarious thing to live the sanctified life; it is the most secure thing, because it has Almighty God in and behind it. The most precarious thing is to try and live without God. If we are born again it is the easiest thing to live in right relationship to God and the most difficult thing to go wrong, if only we will heed God's warnings and keep in the light.

When we think of being delivered from sin, of being filled with the Spirit, and of walking in the light, we picture the peak of a great mountain, very high and wonderful, and we say— "Oh, but I could never live up there!" But when we do get there by God's grace, we find it is not a mountain peak, but a plateau where there is ample room to live and to grow. "Thou hast enlarged my steps under me."

When you really see Jesus, I defy you to doubt Him. When He says—"Let not your heart be troubled," if you see Him I defy you to trouble your mind, it is a moral impossibility to doubt when He is there. Every time you get into personal contact with Jesus, His words are real. "My peace I give unto you"; it is a peace all over from the crown of the head to the sole of the feet, an irrepressible confidence. "Your life is hid with Christ in God," and the imperturbable peace of Jesus Christ is imparted to you.

Mine eyes have seen thy salvation. (Luke 2:30)

The apostle Paul speaks of 'the foolishness of God' as pitted against 'the wisdom of men', and the wisdom of men when it saw Jesus Christ said, 'That cannot be God.' When the Judaic ritualists saw Jesus Christ, they said, 'You are a blasphemer; you do not express God at all.' Anna and Simeon were the only two of the descendants of Abraham who recognized who Jesus was, hence the condemnation of the other crowd. If two who had lived a life of communion with God could detect Jehovah as the Babe of Bethlehem within the symbolism, the others who did not recognize Him are to be condemned. They did not see Him because they had become blinded on the line of absolute authority, the line of symbolism or creed, and when that which was symbolized appeared, they could not see Him.

BFB 92

HIS BIRTH AND OUR NEW BIRTH

Behold, a virgin shall bring forth a son, and they shall call His name Emanuel, which being interpreted is, God with us. (Isa. 7:14. R.V.)

His Birth in History. "Therefore also that holy thing which shall be born of thee shall be called the Son of God" (Luke 1:35). Jesus Christ was born *into* this world, not *from* it. He did not evolve out of history; He came into history from the outside. Jesus Christ is not the best human being, He is a Being Who cannot be accounted for by the human race at all. He is not man becoming God, but God Incarnate, God coming into human flesh, coming into it from outside. His life is the Highest and the Holiest entering in at the Lowliest door. Our Lord's birth was an advent.

His Birth in Me. "Of whom I travail in birth again until Christ be formed in you" (Gal. 4:19). Just as Our Lord came into human history from outside, so He must come into me from outside. Have I allowed my personal human life to become a "Bethlehem" for the Son of God? I cannot enter into the realm of the Kingdom of God unless I am born from above by a birth totally unlike natural birth. "Ye must be born again." This is not a command, it is a foundation fact. The characteristic of the new birth is that I yield myself so completely to God that Christ is formed in me. Immediately Christ is formed in me, His nature begins to work through me.

God manifest in the flesh—that is what is made profoundly possible for you and me by the Redemption.

742

> *And the angel answered and said unto her, the Holy Ghost shall come upon thee, and the power of the Highest shall overshadow thee: therefore also that holy thing which shall be born of thee shall be called the Son of God. (Luke 1:35)*

Jesus Christ was born *into* this world, not *from* it. He came into history from the outside of history; He did not evolve out of history.

Our Lord's birth was an advent; He did not come from the human race, He came into it from above. Jesus Christ is not the best human being. He is a Being who cannot be accounted for by the human race at all. He is God Incarnate, not man becoming God, but God coming into human flesh, coming into it from the outside. His Life is the Highest and the Holiest entering in at the lowliest door. Our Lord entered history by the Virgin Mary.

Just as our Lord came into human history from the outside, so He must come into us from the outside. Have we allowed our personal human lives to become a 'Bethlehem' for the Son of God? . . . The conception of new birth in the New Testament is of something that enters into us, not of something that springs out of us.

PR 29–30

PLACED IN THE LIGHT

If we walk in the light, as He is in the light . . . the blood of Jesus
Christ His Son cleanseth us from all sin. (1 John 1:7)

To mistake conscious freedom from sin for deliverance from
sin by the Atonement is a great error. No man knows what sin
is until he is born again. Sin is what Jesus Christ faced on Calvary. The evidence that I am delivered from sin is that I know
the real nature of sin in me. It takes the last reach of the Atonement of Jesus Christ, that is, the impartation of His absolute
perfection, to make a man know what sin is.

The Holy Spirit applies the Atonement to us in the unconscious realm as well as in the realm of which we are conscious,
and it is only when we get a grasp of the unrivalled power of
the Spirit in us that we understand the meaning of 1 John 1:7,
"the blood of Jesus Christ cleanseth us from all sin." This does not
refer to conscious sin only, but to the tremendously profound
understanding of sin which only the Holy Ghost in me realizes.

If I walk in the light as God is in the light, not in the light of
my conscience, but in the light of God—if I walk there, with
nothing folded up, then there comes the amazing revelation,
the blood of Jesus Christ cleanses me from all sin so that God
Almighty can see nothing to censure in me. In my consciousness it works with a keen poignant knowledge of what sin is.
The love of God at work in me makes me hate with the hatred
of the Holy Ghost all that is not in keeping with God's holiness. To walk in the light means that everything that is of the
darkness drives me closer into the centre of the light.

The Word was made flesh. (John 1:14)

In presenting Jesus Christ never present Him as a miraculous Being who came down from heaven and worked miracles and who was not related to life as we are; that is not the Gospel Christ. The Gospel Christ is the Being who came down to earth and lived our life and was possessed of a frame like ours. He became Man in order to show the relationship man was to hold to God, and by His death and resurrection He can put any man into that relationship. Jesus Christ is the last word in human nature.

AUG 44

The revelation given by Jesus Christ of God is not the revelation of Almighty God, but of the essential nature of Deity— unutterable humility and moral purity, utterly worthy in every detail of actual life. In the Incarnation God proves Himself worthy in the sphere in which we live, and this is the sphere of the revelation of the Self-giving of God.

BFB 98

WHERE THE BATTLE'S LOST AND WON

If thou wilt return, O Israel, saith the Lord . . . (Jer. 4:1)

The battle is lost or won in the secret places of the will before God, never first in the external world. The Spirit of God apprehends me and I am obliged to get alone with God and fight the battle out before Him. Until this is done, I lose every time. The battle may take one minute or a year, that will depend on me, not on God; but it must be wrestled out alone before God, and I must resolutely go through the hell of a renunciation before God. Nothing has any power over the man who has fought out the battle before God and won there.

If I say, "I will wait till I get into the circumstances and then put God to the test," I shall find I cannot. I must get the thing settled between myself and God in the secret places of my soul where no stranger intermeddles, and then I can go forth with the certainty that the battle is won. Lose it there, and calamity and disaster and upset are as sure as God's decree. The reason the battle is not won is because I try to win it in the external world first. Get alone with God, fight it out before Him, settle the matter there once and for all.

In dealing with other people, the line to take is to push them to an issue of will. That is the way abandonment begins. Every now and again, not often, but sometimes, God brings us to a point of climax. That is the Great Divide in the life; from that point we either go towards a more and more dilatory and useless type of Christian life, or we become more and more ablaze for the glory of God—My Utmost for *His* Highest.

Not many wise . . . are called. (1 Corinthians 1:26)

What is as weak as one baby? Another! And so our Lord Himself taught that we must all become babes. No wonder Paul says: 'For ye see your calling, brethren, how that not many wise men after the flesh, not many mighty, not many noble, are called.'

It is the 'baby' weakness which is so misunderstood in the New Testament teaching, and the patience of our Lord with us until we learn the absolute necessity of being born from above is only equalled by His own patience with His Father's will.

DPA 145

Jesus Christ came to make the great laws of God incarnate in human life; that is the miracle of God's grace. We are to be written epistles, 'known and read of all men'. There is no allowance whatever in the New Testament for the man who says he is saved by grace but who does not produce the graceful goods. Jesus Christ by His Redemption can make our actual life in keeping with our religious profession.

SSM 90

CONTINUOUS CONVERSION

Except ye be converted, and become as little children . . .
(Matt. 18:3)

These words of Our Lord are true of our initial conversion, but we have to be continuously converted all the days of our lives, continually to turn to God as children. If we trust to our wits instead of to God, we produce consequences for which God will hold us responsible. Immediately our bodies are brought into new conditions by the providence of God, we have to see that our natural life obeys the dictates of the Spirit of God. Because we have done it once is no proof that we shall do it again. The relation of the natural to the spiritual is one of continuous conversion, and it is the one thing we object to. In every setting in which we are put, the Spirit of God remains unchanged and His salvation unaltered, but we have to "put on the new man." God holds us responsible every time for refusing is wilful obstinacy. Our natural life must not rule, God must rule in us.

The hindrance in our spiritual life is that we will not be continually converted, there are wedges of obstinacy where our pride spits at the throne of God and says—I won't. We deify independence and wilfulness and call them by the wrong name. What God looks on as obstinate weakness, we call strength. There are whole tracts of our lives which have not yet been brought into subjection, and it can only be done by this continuous conversion. Slowly but surely we can claim the whole territory for the Spirit of God.

> *My little children, of whom I am again in travail until Christ be formed in you. (Galatians 4:19)*

What happened to Mary, the mother of our Lord, historically in the conception of the Son of God has its counterpart in what takes place in every born-again soul. Mary represents the natural individual life which must be sacrificed in order that it may be transfigured into an expression of the real life of the Son of God. The individual life is the husk of the personal life, and because of the forming of the Son of God in me, the sword must go through it. ('Yea, a sword shall pierce through thine own soul'—Luke 2:35.) It is the natural virtues that battle, not sin as we think of sin, but pride, egotism, my temperament, my affinities; all that has to have the sword run clean through it mercilessly by God, and if I stick to my natural inheritance the sword must go through me. The new creation is based on the new man in Christ (see Ephesians 4:24), not on the natural gifts of the first Adam. The natural life is not obliterated, when I come to God in the abandon of faith He creates supernaturally on the basis of His own nature, and the Spirit of God makes me see to it that my natural life is lived in accordance with the new life formed in me. Our Lord can never be spoken of in terms of the natural virtues, they don't apply to Him, and they don't apply to the new man in Christ; all that is taken knowledge of in those possessed by Christ is that they have been with Jesus, the dominating personality that tells is that of the Son of God, it is His life that is being manifested.

GW 63

DESERTER TO DISCIPLE?

From that time many of His disciples went back, and walked no more with Him. (John 6:66)

When God gives a vision by His Spirit through His word of what He wants, and your mind and soul thrill to it, if you do not walk in the light of that vision, you will sink into servitude to a point of view which Our Lord never had. Disobedience in mind to the heavenly vision will make you a slave to points of view that are alien to Jesus Christ. Do not look at someone else and say—Well, if he can have those views and prosper, why cannot I? You have to walk in the light of the vision that has been given to you and not compare yourself with others or judge them, that is between them and God. When you find that a point of view in which you have been delighting clashes with the heavenly vision and you debate, certain things will begin to develop in you—a sense of property and a sense of personal right, things of which Jesus Christ made nothing. He was always against these things as being the root of everything alien to Himself. "A man's life consisteth not in the abundance of the things that he possesseth."

We are apt to lie back and bask in the memory of the wonderful experience we have had. If there is one standard in the New Testament revealed by the light of God and you do not come up to it, and do not feel inclined to come up to it, that is the beginning of backsliding because it means your conscience does not answer to the truth. You can never be the same after the unveiling of a truth. That moment marks you for going on as a more true disciple of Jesus Christ or for going back as a deserter.

> For what the law could not do, in that it was weak through the
> flesh, God sending his own Son in the likeness of sinful flesh,
> and for sin, condemned sin in the flesh: that the righteousness
> of the law might be fulfilled in us. (Romans 8:3–4)

God does not expect us to *imitate* Jesus Christ: He expects us
to allow the life of Jesus to be manifested in our mortal flesh.
God engineers circumstances and brings us into difficult places
where no one can help us, and we can either manifest the life
of Jesus in those conditions, or else be cowards and say, 'I cannot exhibit the life of God there.' Then we deprive God of glory.
If you will let the life of God be manifested in your particular
human edition—where God cannot manifest it, that is why He
called you, you will bring glory to God.

The spiritual life of a worker is literally, 'God manifest in the
flesh'.

AUG 14

If Jesus Christ is not being manifested in my mortal flesh, I am
to blame; it is because I am not eating His flesh and drinking His
blood. Just as I take food into my body and assimilate it, so says
Jesus, I must take Him into my soul. 'He that eateth me, even
he shall live by me.' Food is not health, and truth is not holiness. Food has to be assimilated by a properly organized system
before the result is health, and truth must be assimilated by the
child of God before it can be manifested as holiness. We may be
looking at the right doctrines and yet not assimilating the truths
which the doctrines reveal. Beware of making a doctrinal statement of truth *the* truth—'*I* am . . . the Truth,' said Jesus. Doctrinal statement is our expression of that vital connection with Him.
If we divorce what Jesus says from Himself, it leads to secret self-
indulgence spiritually; the soul is swayed by a form of doctrine
that has never been assimilated and the life is twisted away from
the centre, Jesus Christ Himself.

GH 79

"AND EVERY VIRTUE WE POSSESS"

All my fresh springs shall be in Thee. (Psa 87:7, P.B.V.)

Our Lord never patches up our natural virtues, He re-makes the whole man on the inside. "Put on the new man," i.e., see that your natural human life puts on the garb that is in keeping with the new life. The life God plants in us develops its own virtues, not the virtues of Adam but of Jesus Christ. Watch how God will wither up your confidence in natural virtues after sanctification, and in any power you have, until you learn to draw your life from the reservoir of the resurrection life of Jesus. Thank God if you are going through a drying-up experience!

The sign that God is at work in us is that He corrupts confidence in the natural virtues, because they are not promises of what we are going to be, but remnants of what God created man to be. We will cling to the natural virtues, while all the time God is trying to get us into contact with the life of Jesus Christ which can never be described in terms of the natural virtues. It is the saddest thing to see people in the service of God depending on that which the grace of God never gave them, depending on what they have by the accident of heredity. God does not build up our natural virtues and transfigure them, because our natural virtues can never come anywhere near what Jesus Christ wants. No natural love, no natural patience, no natural purity can ever come up to His demands. But as we bring every bit of our bodily life into harmony with the new life which God has put in us, He will exhibit in us the virtues that were characteristic of the Lord Jesus.

And every virtue we possess
Is His alone.

Unto an inheritance incorruptible, and undefiled, and that fadeth not away, reserved in heaven for you. (1 Peter 1:4)

'. . . reserved in heaven for you.' This is a great conception of the New Testament, but it is a conception lost in modern evangelism. We are so much taken up with what God wants us to be here that we have forgotten heaven. There are one or two conceptions about heaven that have to be traced back to their home to find out whether they have their root in our faith or whether they are foreign flowers. One of these is that heaven is a state and not a place; that is only a partial truth, for there cannot be a state without a place. The great New Testament conception of heaven is 'here-after' without the sin, 'new heavens and a new earth, wherein dwelleth righteousness'— a conception beyond us. Peter is reminding every Christian that there is an undefiled inheritance awaiting us which has never yet been realized, and that it has in it all we have ever hoped or dreamed or imagined, and a good deal more. It is always *better to come* in the Christian life until the *best of all* comes.

PH 201

YESTERDAY

The God of Israel will be your reward. (Isa. 52:12)

Security from Yesterday. "God requireth that which is past." At the end of the year we turn with eagerness to all that God has for the future, and yet anxiety is apt to arise from remembering the yesterdays. Our present enjoyment of God's grace is apt to be checked by the memory of yesterday's sins and blunders. But God is the God of our yesterdays, and He allows the memory of them in order to turn the past into a ministry of spiritual culture for the future. God reminds us of the past lest we get into a shallow security in the present.

Security for To-morrow. "For the Lord will go before you." This is a gracious revelation, that God will garrison where we have failed to. He will watch lest things trip us up again into like failure, as they assuredly would do if He were not our rereward. God's hand reaches back to the past and makes a clearing-house for conscience.

Security for To-day. "For ye shall not go out with haste." As we go forth into the coming year, let it not be in the haste of impetuous, unremembering delight, nor with the flight of impulsive thoughtlessness, but with the patient power of knowing that the God of Israel will go before us. Our yesterdays present irreparable things to us; it is true that we have lost opportunities which will never return, but God can transform this destructive anxiety into a constructive thoughtfulness for the future. Let the past sleep, but let it sleep on the bosom of Christ.

Leave the Irreparable Past in His hands, and step out into the Irresistible Future with Him.

Old things are passed away. (2 Corinthians 5:17)

By 'old things' Paul does not mean sin and the 'old man' only, he means everything that was our life as natural men before we were re-created in spirit by Christ. That means a great deal more than some of us mean. The 'old things' means not only things that are wrong, any fool will give up wrong things if he can, but things that are right. Watch the life of Jesus and you will get Paul's meaning. Our Lord lived a natural life as we do, it was not a sin for Him to eat, but it would have been a sin for Him to eat during those forty days in the wilderness, because during that time His Father's will for Him was otherwise, and He sacrificed His natural life to the will of God. That is the way the 'old things' pass away.

In his Second Epistle to the Corinthians Paul uses as an illustration of this the glory which came from Moses. It was a real glory, but it was a glory that was 'to be done away' (3:7); and the writer to the Hebrews writes of a covenant which was doomed 'to vanish away' (8:13). The natural life of man is a real creation of God, but it is meant to pass away into a spiritual life in Jesus Christ's way. Watch Paul's argument in the Epistle to the Romans—'But ye are not in the flesh, but in the Spirit . . .' (8:9). Paul was talking to flesh and blood men and women, not to disembodied spirits, and he means that the old order is passed. 'You used to look at things differently from Jesus Christ,' he says, 'but now that you have turned to the Lord' (God grant you may if you have not) 'the veil is taken away', and 'where the Spirit of the Lord is, there is liberty'.

OBH 28